THE
BLACK
ANGELS

THE
BLACK
ANGELS

THE UNTOLD STORY OF
THE NURSES WHO HELPED
CURE TUBERCULOSIS

MARIA SMILIOS

virago

VIRAGO

First published in the United States by Putnam,
an imprint of Penguin Random House LLC in 2023
First published in Great Britain in 2023 by Virago Press

1 3 5 7 9 10 8 6 4 2

Copyright © 2023 by Maria Smilios

The moral right of the author has been asserted.

A CIP catalogue record for this book
is available from the British Library.

Hardback ISBN 978-0-349-00925-4
Trade paperback ISBN 978-0-349-00926-1

Book design by Elke Sigal
Printed and bound in Great Britain by Clays Ltd, Elcograf S.p.A.

Papers used by Virago are from well-managed forests
and other responsible sources.

MIX
Supporting
responsible forestry
FSC
www.fsc.org FSC® C104740

Virago Press
An imprint of
Little, Brown Book Group
Carmelite House
50 Victoria Embankment
London EC4Y 0DZ

An Hachette UK Company
www.hachette.co.uk

www.virago.co.uk

For Grace

And my mom, who taught me to love words,
and my dad, who taught me to love story

And to the Black Angels, whose courage,
dedication, and service to humanity helped cure
one of the world's greatest scourges, tuberculosis

And finally, to all the nurses
who continue to work humbly on the front lines

For the Negro Nurse there's been no easy way.
The bars have been high, the day a long day
When the hand that could tend the sick or the hurt
Must also combat Jim Crow's dirt. . . .

The bars have been high. There is no magic wand;
Only unity and faith have brought this new dawn
Where the rights of democracy to all are ceded:
Her skilled hands may serve where service is needed.
  —LANGSTON HUGHES, "WHERE SERVICE IS NEEDED"

It is the Plague of all plagues—both in age and in
power—insidious, steady, unceasing.
  —ERNEST POOLE

The Captain of all these men of death that came against
him to take him away, was the Consumption, for it was
that that brought him down to the grave.
  —JOHN BUNYAN

Contents

❖

PART I

1929–1935

PART II

1936–1939

PART III

1940–1944

PART IV

1944–1949

PART V

1949–1952

A Note to Readers

❖

In 2015, I happened upon an extraordinary story while working as a developmental editor in the biomedical sciences. It was a job where I spent my days poring over manuscripts of chilling diseases that left doctors baffled and their patients sick and living in pain. While editing a book on rare and often incurable lung diseases, I read this line:

"The cure for tuberculosis was found at Sea View Hospital in Staten Island . . ."

Curiosity, a love of science and New York history made me stop what I was doing and begin googling. And there it was, an article about Sea View, the cure, and a woman, Virginia Allen, who was part of a group of African American nurses called the Black Angels.

I contacted her, and we met at a little café inside Harlem Hospital, where she drank tea and told me snippets of this story. Our meetings at the café went on for several weeks, until one day she invited me to her home at the restored nurses' residence at Sea View, the same place she had lived sixty years earlier. As we walked through the halls and grounds outside, she pointed to the crumbling buildings and told me more details about the Black Angels, as their patients called them, who like her, she explained, had answered "the call, to work at Sea View when white nurses refused."

"Can you tell their story?" she asked.

"Are there archives?"

"No," she said.

"Any records, documents, articles, letters, diaries, journals, anything?" I asked.

"No, but I'll tell you what I know," she said, "and then give you the names of people who can tell you more."

And so I agreed, and set out to hear the story from those who had lived it, starting with Virginia, then moving to the broader Staten Island community. From there the research ballooned. Each contact led me to another name, and before long I was reaching out to—and visiting—people in Georgia, the Carolinas, Florida, Nevada, Texas, Mississippi, Arizona, and many other places. I spent hundreds of hours talking with strangers who invited me into their homes and communities to tell me the stories of their aunts, grandmothers, cousins, nieces, and friends who had come from across the American South to work at Sea View.

Many more hours were spent with Dr. Robitzek's son, who delighted in recalling stories about his father and generously shared his archives. From them, I tracked down four of the original drug trial patients, who related their experiences of being cured; there were others who worked alongside the nurses as aides or in the lab or who knew them from church or the neighborhood, including the invaluable Debbie-Ann Paige, African American genealogist, and Staten Island historian. All of them added texture, depth, and more firsthand testimony.

Soon a rich and vibrant history began to unfold, one that placed the nurses at the center of the TB story and set them against a backdrop of larger themes: Jim Crow, the Great Migration, systemic and institutional racism, front-line labor in a public health emergency, disease and the science of vaccines, and the desire to live a free and meaningful life—the impetus for so many of the nurses and the heartbeat of their narrative.

All the accounts and scenes in the book—including quotes, thoughts, and reactions—are based on oral reports, which have been corroborated by a wealth of material: newspapers, journals, letters, memoirs, marriage and death certificates, draft cards, medical records, autopsy books, nurses' logs and medicine books, hospital publications, yearbooks, previous interviews, and any other material the librarians could dig up. Time and again, I sifted through the interviews, sending my notes to family members to read and check for accuracy and authenticity in light of the bigger themes and ideas.

Eight years later, as this book emerged, I realized that it pooled together the memories and experiences of a story so vast it could fill shelves in a library. My hope is that the Black Angels will find their rightful place in history and that their story will continue to evolve as more families come forward to talk about the nurses who risked their lives when no one else would, who fought to desegregate New York City's hospital system, and whose contribution to humankind cannot be understated.

Maria Smilios
New York City, 2023

Remembrance of Things Past

Sea View Nurses' Residence

Present Day

Every morning Virginia Allen wakes and feels the weight of the hours moving. They come upon her with an urgency, hectic and nagging. She tries to push them back by keeping busy, but the passage of time is all around her. At ninety-two, she feels it when she stands up and her back seizes, when her mind mishears names, and when her lipstick bleeds into the wrinkles above her lips. Around her apartment, things once important now appear like random objects, items that belong in someone else's life. Time's passage is outside too, in the old tulip tree where the crows perch for hours, their coal-black eyes leering into her apartment. For years, their presence was welcoming, dulling the lone-liness of aging alone. But now they sit on the outstretched branches like timekeepers, reminding her of another day ending, another day of carrying the burden of a story she longs to tell.

The story, like the passing of time, is also everywhere. It dwells in the complex of abandoned hospital buildings surrounding her home, a senior residence in the restored nurses' dormitory at Sea View Hospital on Staten Island. Some five hundred yards from her doorway, in a jumble of dense forest, rise the hollowed-out remains of the children's hospital. Seeing it now carries her back seventy-six years to an autumn day in 1947 when she first arrived here.

She was sixteen and had come to work as a pediatric nurse's aide. Then, the wards were full of children, babies, and toddlers; they were in cribs and beds and wheelchairs, and they cried and coughed and winced, and she held them. The decades have erased their names and faces, leaving them as mere shadows in her mind. But if she thinks long enough, her memory unfolds and they come into focus; the nurses also appear, the Black women in white whose decades of service changed the course of medical history.

These women are never far from her mind.

There were hundreds of them. Some had worked alongside her in pediatrics, but most had worked in the adult pavilions that stood adjacent to the children's hospital. Those buildings, she says, are "in savage condition now." Originally, there were eight of them, arranged in a perfect semicircle and built exactly alike. But in 1970, workers arrived with wrecking balls and bulldozers and razed four of them. In their place, they erected the Edward R. Robitzek Building, a boxy, Z-shaped structure for people needing long-term acute rehabilitation. The city cordoned off the remaining four, and on the chain-link fences, workers tacked up bright yellow signs reading "Keep Out."

But human will could not restrain nature.

All around, trees grew wildly, their roots and branches stretching here and there, twisting through doorways and floorboards; they clawed at walls and roofs and the yellow signs. Each year, winter arrived, bringing rain and snow, darkness and icy winds that swept in from the North Atlantic; they howled and cracked, blowing out windows and plucking plaster from the ceiling. Spring yawned, awakening the vines, whose tendrils snaked along the outside walls, climbing toward the colonies of birds that gathered under the eaves. They built nests and bred and blackened out the walls and floors with their droppings. Then summer came and let loose the flies and mosquitoes and an agonizing humidity that spawned ornate patterns of mold and mildew.

Looking at the landscape now saddens Virginia.

Inside those buildings, she and the other nurses did the impossible. They came together to fight one of humanity's greatest scourges, tuberculosis, that ancient disease long known as consumption; in the first half of the twentieth century, it killed over 5.6 million people in the United States alone.

Day after day, they cared for thousands of poor and indigent New Yorkers who came to Sea View suffering from every conceivable form of tuberculosis—lung, brain, blood, bone, kidney, tongue, skin, and genital. On the wards, they followed orders from physicians who themselves were at a loss, working through trial and error and prescribing unreliable medications that often made people sicker: gamacor, sanocrysin, injections of heat-killed tubercle bacilli, chlorophyll tablets, gambine (an excellent antifreeze but of dubious tuberculostatic efficacy), sheep vaccine, and Congo red.

In the surgical rooms where her aunt Edna worked, operations turned to butchery: ribs were sawed off "in bushels," six to eight at a time; chest cavities were punctured and opened and stuffed with Ping-Pong balls, wax packs, fat, and bone to collapse the lungs. And all day on the wards, they bathed and fed and then shrouded the dead.

They did it because it was their job, because they had committed themselves to saving lives, at the risk of their own. But also because they were Black women, subjects of Jim Crow labor laws that offered them few options. For over two decades, they worked in the grip of an incurable disease, until February 20, 1952, when news of a cure broke at Sea View.

It was a glorious moment, long awaited and widely celebrated. Newspapers worldwide rang with banner headlines announcing the "wonder drug." Images from that day show the "incurables," the patients slotted to die, in the hallways laughing and dancing. Standing behind them are the Black nurses, their faces still, their eyes fixed and hesitant. They knew a more solemn story.

Now only a small handful remain, including Virginia, who lives among the ruined buildings, keeping her promise to remember them, the Black nurses, the ones "time and people tried to erase," the women who "did their jobs," and who came to be known as the Black Angels.

PART I

❖

1929–1935

Chapter 1

❖

The Call for Nurses

Spring 1929

No one knew exactly how it started or who set it in motion, but in the spring of 1929, suddenly, inexorably, the white nurses at Sea View Hospital began quitting. One by one, they hung up their uniforms and walked out.

Their reasons varied. Many of them were weary of the long commute from Manhattan to Staten Island and the successive days of twelve-hour shifts; some cited the chronic mental and physical toll their job demanded. But most were leaving to escape tuberculosis—the Great White Plague, the robber of youth, the "Captain of the Men of Death"—and its victims: the infected, incurable, indigent consumptives. That's who came to Sea View, New York's largest municipal sanatorium.

On its floors, hundreds of patients lay in iron-frame beds, languishing, their bodies swarming with millions of arrogant microbes that gnawed at their lungs, kidneys, and tongues; their spines and bones and brains. All day long, they sweated and groaned and cried out; they coughed and choked and spit up blood, each hack sending swarms of live germs onto bedpans and sheets, tables, chairs, and doorknobs. The bacteria landed on walls and nightstands and window shades; it drifted under beds and down hallways, slinking into every room and corner of the ward. It was always present, swirling, lurking, waiting to strike anyone who wasn't already sick.

And all it took was a single inhalation.

Over the years, the nurses watched their colleagues fall ill. They saw how their faces turned ashen, how their eyes burned from a fever that climbed and climbed, and how their skin exuded a sickly odor that no amount of washing could eradicate. Some recovered, at least temporarily; others died in the wards where they once worked, mouthing, "God in Heaven," or "No, no, no," or nothing at all.

These days as the city thrummed and churned and grew, working white woman had plenty of options for jobs that wouldn't kill them: salesclerks, cashiers, stenographers, secretaries, librarians, and telephone operators who worked the switchboard at the New York Telephone Company's new headquarters, a soaring art deco skyscraper, the exact opposite of the dark and sprawling Sea View. As the weeks passed, the exodus at Sea View became impossible to ignore, and soon word reached the new commissioner of health, Dr. Shirley Wynne.

A dapper gentleman who was dedicated to his job, Wynne had reorganized the city's infectious disease hospitals and was currently focused on a massive public health campaign aimed at eliminating a different disease: diphtheria, a bacterial infection responsible for killing thousands of New York's children each year.

Months before, doctors had unveiled a vaccine, but previous mishaps with antidiphtheritic drugs had left parents hesitant to vaccinate their children. Frustrated, Wynne began marketing it "in the same manner as chewing gum, a second family car, or cigarettes." Leaflets announcing its safety were slipped in with phone bills; billboards and illustrated posters went up in Times Square; and "health-mobiles," renovated snow-removal trucks retrofitted with refrigerators to store the vaccine, fanned out into the neighborhoods; inside, a nurse fluent in each area's predominant language encouraged parents to vaccinate their children.

But the staffing shortage at Sea View presented Wynne with a different crisis, one healthmobiles and vaccines couldn't fix. Tuberculosis had no cure.

❖

Since the early 1900s, tuberculosis had haunted the city, finding willing hosts in the waves of immigrants arriving from all over Europe. With their cloth sacks and boxy suitcases wrapped tight with ropes and straps, they shuffled off liners with grand names like RMS *Olympic, Adriatic,* and *Lusitania.* Some headed to Brooklyn, Queens, and New Jersey, but many walked straight from the seaport to Manhattan's Lower East Side, where they found lodging in the tenements.

Sprawling across a tangle of narrow streets and alleyways, where pigs and dogs and rats wandered beside humans, stood 80,000 five-story tenement buildings, collectively housing over two million people, then two-thirds of New York's population. These were dark places in dark times, havens of misery and despair, described by journalist Jacob Riis as "fever-breeding structures."

Inside them, narrow hallways lit by gas lamps led to tiny three-hundred-square-foot apartments where entire generations, sometimes ten to twelve people, lived shoulder to shoulder with scant fresh air and no indoor plumbing. During the day, the airless space was transformed into a workplace for punishing low-wage jobs: sewing buttons, shelling pecans, rolling cigarettes, and tying tags on clothing. At night, the people swept away the day's work and went to sleep, head to foot, four or five to a bed, or between chairs, or under tables. Some grabbed a blanket and curled up in the hallway or on the rickety stairwell, where mice and giant roaches skittered, upsetting the dust and droppings and cobwebs speckled with TB microbes.

City officials despised these tenement blocks, full of buildings with names instead of addresses—the Morgue, the Bucket, the Ink Pot—but social reformers and progressives loved them. Here they found their cause. Young rabble-rousing journalists, hoping to stop the spread of disease and raise public awareness, immersed themselves in tenement life, observing and engaging with the residents.

In "Lung Alley," a one-block stretch of buildings where over four thousand people, mainly immigrants, lived alongside dogs, cats, parrots, and a wizened old monkey, muckracking journalist Ernest Poole counted over four hundred babies scattered in the halls and courts and on the stairwells and fire escapes. He described it as "the locus of disease," a place unfit for human life. Here, Poole noted, people choked and died in the "foul air, darkness and filth" that fed "the living germs of the Great White Plague [tuberculosis]"; it did, he said, "great business."

He published his findings in a short book, *The Plague in Its Stronghold*. The slim edition, with its stories of immigrants who came hoping for a better life but instead found themselves in a neighborhood overrun by "the Plague of all plagues," drew the attention of the press and Dr. Hermann Biggs, the general medical officer for New York City's Department of Health.

An expert in bacteriology and pathology, Biggs had already prevented the spread of cholera and meningitis in the city, but it was tuberculosis he longed to conquer. After studying it under Dr. Robert Koch—the German country doctor who in 1882 discovered that the cause of TB was the pathogen *Mycobacterium tuberculosis*—Biggs knew its power and stealth and malevolence.

This was an ancient evil, one of humankind's oldest. Some believed it reached back thousands of years to the ancient Egyptians, making it "the first-born of the mother of pestilence." Since then, it had consumed tens of millions of bodies.

But whatever spawned it and wherever it came from, Biggs wasn't interested. He was concerned with the people who coughed and spit up green and yellow phlegm or clots shaped like tiny ropes, who with each heave pitched the bacteria in irreverent ways all over the city. He loathed them and the disease they harbored and vowed to eradicate both.

Society, he said, held the "power to completely wipe out pulmonary tuberculosis in a single generation." It was a lofty claim, almost absurd, about a disease whose kill rate was one in seven. But Biggs, known for his iron will, wasn't deterred.

First, he reclassified TB as an infectious and "communicable disease caused by a germ." With the new terminology, he politicized it and instituted draconian measures, starting with the Registration Law, a decree ordering doctors and nurses to report the names and addresses of every person sick with tuberculosis to the Metropolitan Board of Health. Protests erupted: doctors argued it was dictatorial, taking away their authority, and patients said it invaded their privacy. Biggs didn't care. He continued collecting the information and tallying it on a city map by marking each infected apartment with a black dot. Soon a pattern emerged: on the Lower East Side and in Harlem, areas the city considered hotbeds of disease, black dots punctuated building after building, blotting out entire floors. Biggs's emerging disease graphic proved how TB could be "counted, tracked, evaluated, and combated."

With the data from the disease maps, he secured city funding and convinced officials that social control, namely of the poor, was possible. Then he went public, embarking on a radical campaign where he declared a "war on tuberculosis." This introduced a new narrative for the disease, one that would last for decades and justify using a germ to engage in social and racial warfare.

Biggs began his "war" by recommending that hospitals cordon off entire wards for TB patients and that the city establish free clinics devoted to treating the disease. Open-air schools were commissioned, tent colonies were erected in parks and along the river, and barges were turned into day camps for TB-afflicted children. Men were directed to shave off their beards and mustaches, an appalling prospect for many, who perceived them as a sign of power and dignity. Biggs cared little for social mores. To him, those thick tufts of facial hair were prime places for bacteria to congregate, a hypothesis not rooted in science and later debunked. Nevertheless, barbershops filled, and the mustaches and beards came off.

On streetcars and billboards, big bold posters went up, their messages couched in his rhetoric of war: "The Fight Against TB," "The Crusade," "The Enemy." There were exhibits, radio broadcasts, novels, mass mailings, and pamphlets titled *Warfare Against Consumption* and *Tuberculosis* that were printed by the thousands and distributed in tenements, libraries, insurance company offices, and railroad stations. Publicity blitzes included plays written and scheduled for performance during "Tuberculosis Week," and a lawyer named A. J. Schneeman donned a clown costume and called himself Chew Chew, New York City's "health clown." In his tailcoat, polka-dot pants, and oversize shoes, Chew Chew, along with Creamo, his health-dog sidekick, sang ditties about bathing and drinking milk and opening windows to children living in the slums.

Still, the dots on the disease map kept multiplying, exasperating Biggs.

In 1903, he met with city officials and explained that to win this "war," the sick, those he regarded as "indigent consumptives" and morally bereft spreaders of disease, must be quarantined far away from Manhattan; otherwise the disease would keep spreading, becoming an epidemic. After tapping into their collective disdain for the immigrants, the Black population, and the lower classes, Biggs turned to their real concern: economics, the dollars-and-cents cost of tuberculosis.

The market price for human life "at which tubercular deaths occur," he said, "is worth to the municipality $1,500."

With ten thousand people a year dying, the annual loss of labor and productivity amounted to $15 million, and according to his TB registry, the average patient remained sick for nine months, costing the city $2.50 a day in lost revenue and care.

Biggs let them absorb the figures. Then he wrapped up his economics of human life: for the 270 days consumptives spent dying, the city lost $8 million, resulting in an annual loss of $23 million—roughly $700 million in today's dollars.

Laid out in these terms, devoid of sentimentality or humanity, the raw figures seemed staggering, an unnecessary waste of money, especially for people they perceived as "ignorant" and expendable. Biggs finished by imploring officials to build a TB hospital as a "necessary protection for those who don't have [TB] but are exposed to it by the carelessness of patients."

The city obliged, and on a brisk November day in 1913, the commissioner of charities, Michael Drummond, cut the ribbon and officially inaugurated Sea View. It was, he said, "a vast, ingenious . . . sanitary" institution, built for the sick to find warmth and comfort, rest and strength to return to their lives. But if recovery failed, Drummond hoped that God would help them "in these beautiful surroundings to prepare for the greater house of many mansions." On the first day, eight hundred people were admitted, and from there the number kept climbing. Biggs's vision was working. By 1920, the annual TB death rate in New York had dropped by almost half, from ten thousand to a little more than five thousand.

But there it stalled.

❖

Now, in 1929, at the end of what some considered a magnificent decade, the nurses were leaving the dream hospital, and Sea View's triumph had become Commissioner Wynne's nightmare: tuberculosis remained the third leading killer in the city and the fourth globally. Someone suggested transferring the patients, but that was impossible—at the moment, a powerful flu was surging through the boroughs, filling the other twenty-nine municipal hospitals to capacity. If Wynne couldn't find nurses to staff Sea View, he would need to start closing wards, and hundreds of highly contagious TB patients in various stages of illness would converge on the city: the bedbound would go home or find a shelter or street corner and eventually die; the others, who were still ambulatory, would wander through the bustling sidewalks, ride the trains and trolleys, enter bakeries and delis and taverns, their coughs flinging active bacilli into the air like pieces of confetti. Infection rates would rise and decades of progress against the longtime killer would be reversed.

Wynne wouldn't let that happen. Sea View could not close. The white nurses needed to be replaced immediately, but how and with whom were the questions.

For years, the city had grappled with a borough-wide nursing shortage caused by World War I, when droves of nurses left New York hospitals to serve on the front lines in Europe. Afterward, their ranks had never quite recovered. Wynne called emergency meetings, spending hours consulting with health officials and infectious disease experts, and gradually an idea emerged.

For the past several years, major industrial cities in the North—Chicago, Detroit, Philadelphia, and New York—had solved the problem of labor shortages by issuing hiring calls across the South. Appealing to Black sharecroppers and farmers, recruiters in fancy suits had traveled to states like Georgia, Mississippi, South Carolina, Alabama, and Tennessee with pamphlets and promises of steady work, decent pay, and housing. They made the slaughterhouses, steel mills, and factories look appealing, and millions of Black southerners, hoping to escape the strictures of Jim Crow and the agricultural curses of drought and weeds and insects, had heeded the summons. In New York City, the steady stream of newcomers had almost doubled the Black population from 152,000 in 1920 to almost 327,000 in 1929.

Nursing wasn't factory work. It required more knowledge and training, but maybe the city could accomplish something comparable. Across the country, hundreds of trained Black nurses were qualified yet un- or underemployed. The city could offer them a package: Free schooling, if necessary, at Harlem Hospital School of Nursing. On-the-job training. Housing. A salary. And above all, as they saw it, a "rare opportunity" to work at one of New York City's integrated municipal hospitals. At the time, only four of the twenty-nine city hospitals employed Black nurses—Harlem, Lincoln, Riverside, and, yes, Sea View, where most of the nursing staff was still white, although their numbers were dwindling. The solution wasn't ideal, but a shortage was a shortage, and history had proved this idea could work.

The call went out. Advertisements appeared in Black newspapers and on church bulletin boards. Recruiters from New York showed up at historically Black colleges: Tuskegee, the St. Philip School of Nursing, Hampton University, and Howard University. In the hallways, college lounges, and infirmaries, Black student nurses read about the chance for a career in New York City. News spread by word of mouth, moving down the eastern seaboard, across the Mason-Dixon Line through Virginia, Tennessee, the Carolinas, and deeper into the American South. Until one summer day it arrived in Savannah, Georgia, at the home of a preacher's daughter.

Chapter 2

The Preacher's Daughter

Summer 1929

Edna Sutton stepped out of her rented shotgun house on West Thirty-Eighth Street in Savannah, Georgia. It was barely 8 a.m., and already she felt the Georgia heat, a cloying dampness that clung to her as she walked down the block and passed the home of her childhood friend Theodosia Thurman, newly widowed with two children. At the corner, she turned onto West Broad Street and boarded the trolley.

Stepping on, she glanced at the empty seats in the whites-only section but kept moving, finding a place in the back. As the trolley rattled down the wide street strung with Black businesses, Edna stared out the window at the shops yawning to life—the Royall Undertaking Company, Charles Johnson's Barbershop, Morris Foster Dry Goods, dentists and shoemakers, and the Bessie Adams Beauty School. A mile later, before Union Station, where trains with flashy names like the *Orange Blossom Special* ferried passengers to the Northeast and farther south, she got off.

A tall woman with strong legs, she walked with an easy stride, graceful and confident. Her face was round and sculpted with high cheekbones and wide eyes, and she had a bright, immediate smile that set people at ease. She was pretty, but modesty compelled her to downplay her beauty; aside from a touch of lipstick, she wore no makeup or accessories, except for the cross around her neck, and she owned a handful of clothes, most no different from what she was wearing now: a homemade drop-waisted dress, pale in color and with an unassuming neckline. At twenty-eight, she was an independent woman, uninterested in men and marriage. What Edna wanted most was a professional nursing career, but that dream was quickly fading.

A block over, she turned and stopped and opened a door leading to a small office. Inside, the air was heavy, laden with dust and Savannah's relentless humidity, which found a way to creep into everything. She took her place behind a wooden desk, settled in, and reached for a stack of papers that needed sorting.

Her hands were slender, with long, agile fingers and immaculate nails. They were the hands of a pianist, a surgeon, a jeweler, a sculptor, made to create things, not to sort and staple and file papers in a tiny office. But times were hard, and Edna knew she should be grateful for the work. It was better than being a laundress like her mother, whose hands were chafed and calloused from hauling baskets of water and dirty clothes up and down the Savannah streets. And yet gratitude was difficult to muster in this job of drudgery, where the days passed like years, and her mind grew numb, and her beautiful hands created only small piles of papers.

Five years earlier, Edna had been on a different path, one leading toward her dream of becoming a nurse. She had enrolled in the training program at the Georgia Infirmary, a small charity hospital for "coloreds" and impoverished whites that sat on fourteen acres of desolate land. Relying on student labor and donations to stay open, the infirmary served 1,800 people a year, a burden that fell on Edna and her fellow trainees, who assisted a small staff of overworked nurses. In addition to taking vitals, learning wound care, and bathing patients, the nurses also mopped and cleaned bathrooms, changed bed linens, and laundered clothes.

Many in Savannah considered the infirmary a godforsaken place, worthy of being torn down and rebuilt. The "colored section" where

Edna mostly worked was a ramshackle add-on building, drafty and dirty with leaky ceilings and splintered floors that slanted in different directions, skewing the beds and making the prospect of falling off them very real. Local white women's organizations took an interest in the hospital by stuffing pillows and mattresses and offering up husbands and sons to paint rooms and weld broken beds and tables; benevolent farmers donated potatoes, corn, and greens to keep patients fed. But supplies were always short: lamps ran out of oil, mattresses were fitted with torn sheets, and Edna regularly found herself scrubbing blood from used bandages and assisting doctors, who tended to injuries without gloves or gowns. On occasion, there weren't enough shrouds to bury the dead.

Sometimes after her shift she was sent into the backwoods of Savannah, where scores of Black people lived in clapboard houses perched on cinder blocks with no running water or electricity. Inside, Edna found people lying on the floor or a bare mattress; they were stricken by fevers and flus and skin infections; tuberculosis, malnutrition, scabies, and dysentery. By the time she arrived, they were weary and wrecked; many prayed to die. Sometimes she could help them, administering quinine for malaria or calomel to induce vomiting and rid the body of a stomach virus; for coughs, she could give codeine. But to those too sick to treat, she suggested the Georgia Infirmary, causing most to turn away and shake their heads from side to side. No, they wouldn't go. Doctors frightened them, and many saw illness as the devil's handiwork. But Edna was committed, returning time and again to check on them, and soon they became less reticent, seeing her as an ally, an advocate, someone they could trust.

Working with this population came easy for Edna. The poverty she saw and the fear it bred had shaped the landscape of her childhood. The oldest of six, she was born in 1901, an ominous year according to the editor of *The Savannah Tribune*, who had penned a warning to the city's Black population: "The negro is passing through a crucible," he wrote, "though hard and cruel it will benefit him greatly in the end."

Edna's mother was already living the crucible. But what did it mean for her infant daughter birthed on the floor of a tar paper shack on Savannah's east side, an enclave on the fringes of a prospering city? The writer W.E.B. Du Bois had compared the coastal city to an O, "with people of color living on the outskirts of town, and whites living in the center."

On the rim of the O, tens of thousands of Black people lived in shantytowns that bordered the railroad tracks and the Savannah River. Beyond them sat empty lots and a vast countryside dotted with more squatter villages. In those narrow footpaths winding through the slums, where sewage and waste collected in stagnant streams and foul-smelling pools full of typhoid, cholera, and dysentery, Edna had learned to crawl and walk.

Her father, Richmond, a handsome, charismatic man with no formal education, was a baby when Lincoln signed the Emancipation Proclamation. But his family remained tethered by debt to their former enslaver and never managed to leave the plantation in Confederate Wilkes County, Georgia. Ambitious and determined—traits he would pass on to his daughter—Richmond wanted to "become something more" than what the South expected of him. And in 1899, after almost thirty years of tilling the earth, he put down his plow and hoe, walked off the fields, and made his way to Savannah. A year later, he met and married Amy B. V. Royal, a practical, hardworking woman almost two decades his junior.

Together they had moved to the rim of the O, where Richmond began circulating from job to job—shipbuilding, track laying, and carpentry—cobbling together enough money to make ends meet, while Amy spent her days washing clothes for wealthy white families. By the age of three, little Edna was toddling behind her mother, helping sort and fold; by eight, she was listed as a laundress in the Savannah City Directory.

Amy gave birth to four more kids, three daughters and a son, and Richmond moved his growing family a few miles north of the city to the Cuyler-Brownsville neighborhood, where the poverty was less extreme. He rented a unit in a one-story tenement building set on a dirt lot off an unpaved street. There was a single bedroom for seven people, a small kitchen, and a living room whose walls were thin, allowing the winter chill to creep through. But despite its flaws, it had proper floors and a solid ceiling, and the neighbors held more sophisticated jobs: there were postal workers, headwaiters, shop owners, teachers, and a handful of pastors and itinerant preachers.

Within a few years of moving, Richmond heard his own call to preach the gospel. He exchanged his overalls for a crisp shirt and creased pants and dropped his full name. Instead of being called Richmond V. Sutton, he became the Reverend R.V. Sutton. Under the guidance of Father Gray, a prominent pastor who'd officiated at his marriage, Reverend R.V. began preaching around Savannah.

At the pulpit, R.V. was a natural, weaving his life into the grand story of Jesus, Moses, Elijah, Isaiah, and Job. There was no prophet or person in the holy book that he couldn't stitch into America's Black experience; his sermons of redemption and hope and love soon attracted a faithful following. Sometimes even tourists came to hear him.

As his confidence grew, so did his style. He learned how to throw his voice, how to change the pitch at the right moment, to make it melodic or thunderous, as if it were tumbling from the heavens. One Sunday, a reporter from *The Savannah Tribune* came to witness the charismatic holy man, whose words, he wrote, were "a flight of eloquence that charmed" and who possessed "a magnetic influence of the Holy Spirit that gripped the audience." Word spread, and people from neighboring counties began calling on him. In 1912, he was chosen to baptize a prisoner on death row in the Chatham County jail.

Young Edna often accompanied him on these calls. Together, father and daughter went into homes where people's spirits had been siphoned off, starved by sorrow and poverty and sickness. R.V. offered last rites to dying men and women; he comforted widows, who wept and pulled at their clothing; he listened to orphaned children, who wondered why God had taken their mothers and fathers. Edna saw him, his motions, how he leaned in when people talked; how he listened, inching closer, then taking their hand and lifting it, cupping it with his palm and meeting their pain. His ability to connect, to heal, to change lives, lit a spark inside her, pulling her toward one of the most farfetched dreams a southern Black woman could imagine: becoming a surgeon.

R.V. encouraged his eldest, giving her the liberty to dream big and think radically. If he could free himself from the plantation and become a preacher, then of course she could become a surgeon. All she needed to do was finish school and go to college. But in Savannah, showing up to the Black public school was no easy feat.

Throughout elementary school, Edna elbowed her way through hallways and into classrooms jam-packed with kids who fought for the handful of desks. Regularly, *The Savannah Tribune* reported on the woeful conditions: there were "43 teachers for 2,000 students"; the rooms lacked chalk, chairs, working windows, and lights. Students shared books passed down from the white schools; they were outdated, with pages missing, information crossed out, and margins filled with messages like "you black and ugly, dumb and stupid."

Edna listened to the teachers and ignored the messages, and unlike many of her peers, she graduated elementary school with near-perfect grades, earning her a spot at the prestigious Beach Institute, a private school established in 1865 by the Colored Education Committee. Beach offered a rigorous curriculum, and the teachers were smart, dynamic local Black women who fostered a competitive environment where Edna thrived. She was studious, with a natural inclination for method and order, and solving problems came easy to her. So did math and Latin, a required language.

But it was the sciences that set her mind alight, drawing her in, especially biology. Edna fell in love with the human body and spent hours hunched over her used books, studying the black-and-white illustrations delineating muscles and tendons, organs and bones; she traced the pathways and byways with her finger, memorizing how blood flowed from one vein to another, how this nerve affected that nerve; she noted the body's intricacies and its fragility, how it could stay healthy or fall ill, how it healed or grew sicker, eventually shutting down and bringing life to a close.

In December of her senior year, a lack of funding forced Beach to close, and with few options, Edna transferred to Dorchester Academy, an esteemed boarding school several hours from Savannah. Upon graduation, her class planted a tree and chose a motto: "To Live, to Serve."

At the Georgia Infirmary, Edna had been living by the motto. And then it ended.

Sadly, these small, independent nursing schools were built on a barter system. In exchange for offering young Black women on-the-job training, the schools got good, reliable, cheap labor. After finishing, students received a certificate documenting their achievement. But the schools could not offer careers, leaving hundreds of skilled Black nurses with few opportunities. Even those who had more experience and better schooling than Edna, who held three-year degrees from accredited nursing programs at well-known universities like Tuskegee, Howard, Hampton, and Prairie View A&M, remained unemployed.

The nation that drew lines around water fountains and waiting rooms, buses, schools, museums, bathrooms, and sidewalks had also extended them to hospital wards. Black nurses could work only in Black hospitals, and in the late 1920s, America registered 210 Black hospitals, compared with 6,807 white ones.

In Savannah, only two hospitals served Black patients, the Georgia Infirmary and Charity Hospital, and both relied on cheap student labor. Newly graduated Edna quickly found herself in a catch-22, entangled in a system that kept training young Black nurses for nonexistent jobs or ones Jim Crow prevented them from touching.

Still, she looked for work in different newspapers, her eyes flitting over help wanted ads seeking nurses for private duty or for white hospitals that would rather remain short-staffed than hire a Black nurse. A few opted for a quota system and employed one or two Black women, but those were dangerous jobs.

The white supervisors delighted in publicly shaming those who were hired: Alabama's director of public health announced that Black nurses had "limited intellectual capacity," making them "incapable of abstract thinking." The superintendent of Atlanta's Grady Hospital declared they had "no morals and unless they are constantly watched, they will steal anything in sight."

Their views, however irrational, held weight, influencing seventeen nursing associations to restrict their membership to whites only, blocking job opportunities, training, networking, and equal pay. The disparity reverberated at the national level: to join the prestigious American Nurses Association (ANA), nurses needed to hold membership in their state association and pass the state board exams, a requirement for becoming a licensed registered nurse and working in an accredited hospital.

Edna's job search turned fruitless, and soon she joined the growing list of unemployed Black nurses. Some gave up, married, and became mothers; others found work as house cleaners or cooks or nursemaids, raising white babies in elegant homes with crystal chandeliers and rooms full of Lincoln Logs, rocking horses, and Raggedy Ann dolls. But Edna didn't want a life of domestic servitude like her mother's: married with babies, her days spent cleaning up the lives of white people, their dust, hair, toenails, dirty glasses, and stains. So she took a job as a clerk and lived at home and settled into a different kind of domesticity, caring for her five younger siblings, aged one to fifteen.

The years passed: 1920, 1921, 1922, and Edna began hearing about people leaving, slowly at first but then in greater and greater numbers—at one point, reports said, over five hundred people a day were fleeing the South. Some left in the early morning, others under the cloak of darkness, but however they went, most left behind their homes, their lives, and, so they thought, Jim Crow. They were heading north to join the movement, later known as the Great Migration. Up north, they said, was "freedom." The newspapers backed their claims, reporting that the migrants had new homes, well-paying jobs in factories, steel mills, and railroads; their kids had educational opportunities well beyond those in the South, and they were being treated humanely.

In 1925, as the story of Balto, the Siberian husky racing across Alaska to deliver an antitoxin for a diphtheria outbreak, broke, Edna's siblings joined the mass exodus of people and began leaving West Thirty-Eighth Street. Her nineteen-year-old brother, Samuel, took a train to Washington, DC, and her younger sister Annie, along with her husband, Lemon, found jobs in Pittsburgh. Two years later, Annie sent for her parents, Amy and R.V., who left with Edna's two teenage sisters, Mary and Ruth.

Edna watched them go. She, too, wanted to leave, but was tethered to Savannah and its nagging heat and her dead-end job by a promise. At the moment, Edna had custody of her seven-year-old sister, Americus.

Americus Sutton was Amy and R.V.'s sixth child, born when Amy was forty and R.V. fifty-seven. When the two left for Pittsburgh, they were in poor health and had asked Edna to keep Americus. She had obliged her parents, partly out of duty and partly out of adoration for her little sister, who was twenty years younger.

Besides, she had practically raised the little girl, swaddling her, rocking her to sleep, watching her take her first steps. She had showed her how to sit up tall, how to hold a spoon the right way, how to plant flowers and pick peas and can huckleberries, how to avoid gossip, and how to let things be. She had read her poetry and history, taught her math and science, and watched her become a bold and strong-willed child who roused in her a sense of wholeness, an inexplicable need, a desire to right the world. If given the chance, her sister could have a future that was different from her own.

But not in Savannah.

Recently, two of the major banks had collapsed and the *Savannah*

Tribune was begging for "colored policemen" to help stop the rampant "lawlessness." And the ongoing accounts about the state of Black schools alarmed Edna. Recent reports claimed they were "totally unfit for the purpose used," and teachers and students were working under "horrible conditions."

Edna said nothing to Americus and at night, at the kitchen table, beside the potbellied stove, began to rekindle her dream of becoming a professional nurse. There, amid the sounds of an old house—a draft passing through a door, the rattle of a windowpane, the scurry of a mouse in the wall—she looked through the newspapers for nearby jobs. Again, she found none.

Two years passed, and one day, in the summer of 1929, she ran into a former teacher from the Georgia Infirmary who told her about a tuberculosis hospital in New York City with a magical-sounding name, Sea View. It was recruiting "colored" nurses. The job included a salary, housing, on-the-job training, and free schooling—a fact that caught Edna's attention: to become a registered nurse, she needed at least another year or two of education at an accredited nursing school that accepted Black women. Her teacher encouraged her to apply. She had nothing to lose. But Edna, who had waited all her life for such a moment, for the promise of being carried away, suddenly wasn't so sure.

Chapter 3

The Wager

Late Summer–Early Fall 1929

Edna always believed in miracles, not the kind of turning water to wine, but the everyday kind, the ones that happened through faith and belief. For weeks, she recalled the information from her teacher, the words "Sea View," "New York," "salary," and "schooling." She knew that this was a once-in-a-lifetime opportunity. Many stories from Black women who had moved north told how they had traded ambition for necessity. They were the "last hired, first fired," and often ended up with the least desirable jobs: cooks, cleaners, washerwomen, or laborers in packinghouses. There were virtually no professional jobs for them as saleswomen or typists or bookkeepers. To work as a nurse and receive free schooling was a godsend. But the blessing was also a curse. Americus couldn't come.

In the years since her family left, life in Savannah had taken on a gentle rhythm for the two sisters. In the three-room house once resonant with the sounds and smells and sights of seven people, it was now just Edna and Americus. At night in the bedroom lying side by side on the worn-down mattress, the two would whisper into the darkness, tossing up their hopes and dreams:

A home

With windows—

That let in sunlight.
And at least three bedrooms.
Yes, and the bathroom—
It would be inside, not in the yard.
And a big garden—
With flowers and vegetables and chickens and rabbits and dogs.

And on they went, their words expanding—*home, garden, sunlight*—catching in crevices and splintered floorboards and cracks in the ceiling, and although Edna had no idea how any of this would happen, she always made the promise. They would have that house.

There were other promises, too, ones she had made to Amy and R.V.: schooling, manners, morals, and Sundays. Those were special days, when the two sisters woke up early, put on their good clothes, and went to church. Sitting together in a pew, they opened their Bible and prayed and sang and listened to the preacher. But Edna missed the sound of her father's voice, missed his words rising and falling, calling on his congregation to trust and believe. How sad Americus would never experience him.

After the service, they sometimes walked toward West Broad Street, passing the small markets that sold Coca-Cola and cigarettes, and the luncheonettes, where families enjoyed chicken potpies, biscuits, and fruit cobblers. As they walked, Edna told Americus all about R.V. and his sermons and how she would accompany him to bless newborns, newlyweds, and the newly dead. The little girl smiled and skipped in her good shoes beside her big sister, listening to stories of her father, a man whose face she vaguely recalled.

When they reached the Savannah pharmacy, famous for compounding medicines and for making its own ice cream, Americus dashed to the door, pulled it open, and hurried toward the soda counter. There she found two seats, and the sisters joined the other families sipping fountain drinks topped with whipped cream and cherries and eating freshly made ice cream served up in glass bowls.

In the afternoons, they sometimes walked down to the Savannah

River, where R.V. used to build ships, and watched the steamboats gliding up and down the waterway, or they caught a movie at the seven-hundred-seat Dunbar Theatre; during baseball season, they frequented the Fairview Ball Park, where they cheered the local team.

Warm evenings were their favorite. The two sat on the concrete stoop and drank iced tea with fresh spearmint and watched night fall. Then Americus and the neighborhood children would open their mason jars and chase fireflies. Watching her sister play, Edna noticed how little things had changed since her own childhood. West Thirty-Eighth Street still looked the same: narrow and unpaved, and when it rained, the red Georgia dirt still turned to mud and ran down its uneven surface in thick streams. On either side, most of her neighbors—the Gilmores, Monroes, and McTyres—were still there, and up the block, so was her longtime friend Theodosia Thurman.

Maybe she wouldn't go to New York. She could stay and wait for another job, one closer to Savannah, where she had a place to live, her community and church, her various clubs, sewing and pinochle, and close, reliable friends. There was a familiar comfort, a dull contentment, in all these things that made it bearable. But all that vanished when Edna read about the schools and saw those Jim Crow signs. This generation, she understood, would grow up with the same rules and codes and fears. In twenty years, nothing had changed.

The libraries and parks remained off-limits to Black people, and so did the white Savannah Hospital, which had killed a Black man. No one would forget that the man died because white doctors refused to treat him. Trying on clothes and shoes remained taboo, and the separate lines and waiting rooms, the neglected schools, their classrooms stocked with those schoolbooks whose pages were besieged with grotesque messages, still existed. And so did all the other tacit directives cloaked as "interracial etiquette": step off a sidewalk when a white person passed or else risk being shoved or knocked down. Regularly, on buses and trolleys, Edna saw Black people being forced out of their seats. She heard the "yes, sirs" and "yes, ma'ams," and the calls of "boy" and "girl," words that rang like tired mantras. And she felt an unease stir deep inside when she saw a crowd of white men, a feeling she taught Americus to heed.

All the rules, the endless rules keeping her trapped, demanding she submit to them or else face the indignation of white people, of men, who satiated their hate through unconscionable acts of violence—beatings, burnings, or lynchings. The last one happened in 1920, the year Americus was born.

For ten days, Savannah and the neighboring counties had been terrorized by bloodhounds and angry mobs who were in pursuit of Phillip Gathers, accused of raping and murdering a seventeen-year-old white girl thirty miles from Savannah in Effingham County. Hoping to protect Gathers, the county police called up the state guard and declared martial law. But the plan failed.

After the sheriff captured Gathers, he turned him over to the search party, who took him to the murdered girl's family for questioning. Gathers denied committing the crime, but the search party ignored him. To them, he was guilty and ready for sentencing. They shoved him in the car and drove him to the scene of the murder, where thousands of angry white men waited to mete out their revenge. When he emerged from the back seat, the mob descended on him, setting him on fire and then hanging his charred body from a tree.

Edna didn't want her little sister growing up like her and seeing the injustices of the American South, her innocence and wonder being snuffed out one story and interaction at a time. Americus deserved more. She recalled their father, R.V., who had mustered the courage to walk away from the plantation and the only life he'd known. His will had brought him out of Wilkes County, away from the greedy landlords with their bogus contracts and derelict equipment, their sick mules and dead hogs, and the pests that plagued the harvest: the boll weevils, spider mites, and aphids. And then, in Savannah, God had called him to preach the Word, to bring hope, to raise up his people, to mend their broken spirits.

The offer from Sea View was also a call, an invitation to walk away from the poverty of her youth, from the stacks of paper in her office, from West Thirty-Eighth Street, and from a place that demanded she submit. Over the years she'd heard enough success stories of Black people who had migrated north and carved out a better life.

"I make $75.00 per month . . . I don't have to mister every little white boy comes along," one migrant wrote. Another talked about the integration of schools—"my children are going to the same school with the whites"—and others talked about the freedom from Jim Crow censures. But for Edna, the price of freedom was walking away from her life and from Americus, who could not come to New York, at least not yet. It also meant breaking her promise to her parents, the one to stay with her sister.

Edna never took decisions lightly. She was a woman of few words, a listener, a reader of silences, of the pauses that came between thoughts and ideas. Living in the South, she had learned to decipher absence, fill in the gaps, read smiles and smirks and hand gestures, and then wait for clarity. She would do that now. Take her time, weigh the pros and cons of staying in Savannah and enduring its codes or following the thousands of other migrants and becoming a nurse in a TB hospital.

Growing up, Edna had seen the ruin that tuberculosis unleashed on the nearby Black communities of Yamacraw and Frogtown, how easily it spread and how indiscriminately it killed, leaving parents mourning children and children mourning parents. It was a monster illness. Unforgiving, undiscerning, and savage. If she got sick, who would care for Americus? And if she stayed, what would their future look like?

For weeks she stood at the crossroads of her life: on one side, Savannah, with its familiarity and its Jim Crowism; and on the other, New York City, with its nursing career and disease. Every night, she heard the summer droning onward; its sounds of cicadas and mosquitoes and neighbors laughing, paying her no mind as she turned her thoughts inward and prayed, asking God for a sign, something to point her in the right direction. Then one day she heard the words of Matthew 25: 14–30 "The Parable of the Talents," where Jesus tells his disciples not to squander their God-given gifts but instead to use them in the service of God.

Yes, she would wager her life, gamble it on the whims of a vicious disease in the wards of a municipal hospital. She would cast aside her fears and worries and head to New York, where, like her father, she might save people and forge a new path.

She began to make plans for Americus, assuaging her guilt with future thoughts: once settled, she would bring her to New York, the way Annie had done with R.V. and Amy and her other sisters.

Edna phoned her brother Samuel in Washington, DC, where he lived with his wife, Florence. They were a happy couple, young and outgoing, with good jobs. Their steady income had allowed them to buy a small, newly built two-bedroom brick row house in Kingman Park, an emerging middle-class Black neighborhood off the Anacostia River. Would they take Americus if needed?

Of course they would. The prospect of having a young girl to dote on thrilled them. It also thrilled Edna.

In DC, Americus would have her own room, and just down the road on over twenty-five acres of sloping land, the city was building an educational complex with four new schools—two high schools, an elementary, and a middle—specifically for Black children. Finally, Edna could put aside her worries about Americus attending school in derelict buildings. And with more than ten trains going between New York and DC daily, visiting would be easy. The solution wasn't perfect, but it was good enough for now, and it lessened her feelings about abandoning Americus to fulfill her own dreams.

After settling her sister's living situation, Edna turned her attention to collecting the required materials for Sea View: reference letters, school transcripts, and the obligatory "certificate of moral character" from her clergyman attesting that she was not a liar or a thief or sexually promiscuous. Then she filled out the application: schooling, grades, experience. At the blank space that read age, she paused. Edna was now twenty-eight, but every nurse knew that white supervisors preferred young, single Black women, believing they would be less "troublesome" or oppositional.

She wrote "23," lopping five years off her age. The decision was the first of a handful of times she would change her birthday, perhaps to alter her destiny and fight that "hard and cruel" crucible announced by *The Savannah Tribune* the year she was born. Slipping the application into an envelope, she sealed it and sent it off. The rest, she said, was "in God's hands."

Some weeks later, God delivered, and Edna and Americus walked out of their shotgun house and down the block, past the homes of their neighbors. At the corner, the two sisters turned onto West Broad Street, and for the final time in their lives—neither would ever return to Savannah—they rode the trolley to Union Station. There they walked through the terminal, under the grand rotunda, to the "colored" section, and boarded a Jim Crow car on a steam train heading north.

The segregated car was full of migrants like them, people who had made the decision to leave behind the known for the unknown. They sat packed in tight on dingy seats with bags and luggage under their feet and on their laps, as well as in slim racks above their heads and piled high in the back corner. Edna handed the porter two suitcases, Americus's and her own, stuffed only with essentials: her nurse's uniform, undergarments, some dresses, a few photographs, and her Bible. Then she slipped into the seat and placed her purse on her lap, her fingers lightly grasping the leather handle. Folded inside was her future: the letter from Sea View Tuberculosis Sanatorium inviting her to New York, her life savings, and, scrawled on a piece of paper, the address of an unknown relative in Harlem with whom she'd be staying.

As the train cut across the country, the sisters settled in for the long ride. Edna turned her head toward the window, where clouds of black smoke trailed from the engine, creating a veil that dulled the

America streaming by outside. It was at once a beautiful and devastating place: the endless small towns with their specialty shops and friendly cafés whose windows flaunted the "No Coloreds" signs besides menus and meat prices.

On the picturesque train platforms, women in tasteful coats waited alongside men in top hats and wool suits. They boarded the middle cars, away from the migrants and the smoke and soot streaming from the engine stack; the Jim Crow cars were always hitched behind the engine to bear the brunt of ash and the impact of a collision. Beyond the towns was the countryside, vast and green, with wide-open fields and endless acres of farmland. In the distance, cows grazed and plows moved and ribbons of trees extended to the horizon, where the sun dipped and stretched, casting long, languid shadows across the earth.

The hours slipped by, and on through the night the train moved, speeding through the now iron-black countryside with its sky full of constellations and galaxies and shooting stars; in the moonlight, the ash and soot from the engine swirled and danced. How magnificent it all looked to Edna. Years later, when she grew old and time had dulled her losses, leaving her with swollen legs and chronic back pain, she would recall this moment, how she was one of the few hundred professional women who fled the South to fight tuberculosis, how she had lost and saved lives, and how a chance encounter—or was it?—had steered her, a nurse from a Savannah slum, into the hands of American history. But for now, on this train, she watched the shifting darkness and tucked away the vestiges of doubt.

In Washington, Samuel and Florence were openhearted and gregarious, but Americus, always a bit shy, remained quiet and reticent. Over the next week, Edna helped her settle in. At night, over dinner, Samuel talked about many things, including the marvels of the Anacostia River in the spring and summer: all along the winding banks were fish and tadpoles and frogs, families picnicking, and kids leaping into the water to cool off. Next spring, if she liked, he would take her fishing for catfish and trout. The offer made Americus smile.

Weeks later, at Washington's Union Station, Edna pulled Americus close. She held her tight, stroking her hair and neck, and inhaled her little-girl scent, one that would fade before they'd meet again. She breathed it in and pushed back the longing, the ache that had already settled. They would write and call regularly, Edna promised, and then she loosened her hold and boarded the train bound for New York City.

In her seat, she waited for the train to depart, for the red-capped porters pushing heaping baggage carts around people standing on the platform, waving goodbye, to finish loading in the luggage. And there, amid the commotion, was her family, Florence and Samuel, with Americus beside him. Edna saw her, and her body winced, overcome by a maternal pull that seemed to whisper, *Go to her, to the piece that makes you whole.* But she stayed in her seat and blew kisses at the little girl with the giant tears streaming down her face.

Then came the hiss of steam and the grind of wheels, and the darkness of the terminal gave way to sunlight, and the platform with her sister grew smaller and smaller, until she disappeared, leaving Edna hurtling toward her historic future alone.

Chapter 4

Harlem

January 1930–February 1932

The address scrawled on the piece of paper brought Edna to a four-story walk-up on West 122nd Street, just off Seventh Avenue, a major thoroughfare better known as "Black Broadway." Night and day, traffic moved in streams up and down this great wide avenue split by a median of flowers and trees. On both sides rose a multitude of famous theaters and ritzy hotels. There were churches too, historic and grand with giant spires that stretched up toward the heavens. Every Sunday thousands of parishioners in suits and splendid hats walked through their doors to worship beneath high ceilings and stained-glass windows.

Tucked between the landmarks were hundreds of Black-owned businesses: barbershops and funeral homes, jewelry stores, pawnshops, restaurants, real estate agencies, laundries, beauty salons, and cabarets. The sidewalks were always busy with a constant drift of people. Numbers runners scooted around the flow of pedestrians. There were newsboys and children playing and soapbox speakers and quack healers who stood by park benches selling phony cures. Men and women, young and old, paused in doorways and storefronts, on stoops and in shops, to talk about the weather or the news or each other.

This was Harlem, the place Reverend Adam Clayton Powell Jr.

declared "the symbol of liberty and the Promised Land to Negroes everywhere." Here there were no mobs or lynchings or "colored" signs; no stepping off sidewalks or sitting in separate parks. Here Edna could walk through the front door of any shop, she could eat at any counter, and she could sit wherever she wanted. Here Black artists conjured a life of ingenuity, one where words and ideas and music spilled outside the salons and smoky clubs and mixed with the sounds of sidewalk preachers and corner buskers. From basements, theater groups like the fabled Krigwa Players staged plays rooted in the Black experience and drew audiences in the hundreds.

Here writers Nella Larsen and Claude McKay and poets Richard Wright and Countee Cullen built paragraphs and verses trying to capture Harlem's ever-shifting essence. And for the philosopher Alain Locke, Harlem became the capital of "the New Negro," a place where Black Americans could finally emerge from their painful history and redefine themselves, "no longer as vehicles for backbreaking labor," he said, "but as creators of joy and culture."

Here, too, were the agitators and civil rights activists: investigative journalist Ida B. Wells; scholar W.E.B. Du Bois; an army of intellectuals, reformers, and anti-lynching crusaders; and the founders of the National Association for the Advancement of Colored People, known as the NAACP. Its official magazine, *The Crisis*, edited by Du Bois, focused on investigative news and politics about current issues of racism in the military, the financial struggles of Black universities, and the discrimination by white union leaders. Between the news stories, Du Bois published poetry and literature by Langston Hughes, Zora Neale Hurston, and Gwendolyn Bennett, turning them into household names.

Harlem readers loved *The Crisis*, but for more immediate news they turned to *The New York Amsterdam News*, one of the oldest Black papers in the country, or *The New York Age*, which, at a mere ten pages an issue, was considered one of the most influential publications in America for its bold condemnations of racial injustice.

Both were located on Seventh Avenue, along Edna's route home. While walking, she noted how the people and cars bustled against a landscape of grayness and concrete and buildings that often hindered the sunlight. She tried to find the beauty in the harsh, cold, and urban setting. For all of its ills, Savannah was a pretty place, lush and green and warm, and with her cheeks rubbed red from a northeast wind, she found herself missing Georgia's heat and its languid pace. Now she pulled her coat tight and focused on keeping stride with the crowds of people, who lowered their heads and hurried down the sidewalk, weaving and bumping into each other, leaving newcomers like her stunned.

Daily, Harlem welcomed more and more people. They came from the South and the Caribbean and streamed into its three square miles, swelling the population and making it one of the most densely occupied Black areas in New York City. In 1925, white neighborhoods averaged 223 people per acre, but Harlem averaged 336. By 1930, the figure had doubled to 671 people per acre; according to one historian, the block of 140th to 141st Street was "reputed to be the most crowded dwelling area in the world."

With the crowds came the noise, a clamor so endless it was almost shocking. Day and night, the sounds of horns, trolley bells, police whistles, jackhammers, and snippets of music from Seventh Avenue came crashing through Edna's windows; so did the noise of the traffic accidents. Newspaper reports claimed these averaged ten a day. On the streets, Edna felt the press of the masses: while walking or boarding the bus or subway, she was often jostled and pushed, her body touched in awkward and uncomfortable ways. Manners seemed to elude people, and so did patience.

But beyond the crowds and noise and traffic lurked grander problems. Unhappy with the ongoing influx of Black people, white residents fled, opening the door for landlords of both races to begin charging exorbitant rents to thousands of Black residents. Unable to pay and facing evictions, families were forced to subdivide rooms and take in boarders, who paid for floor space or single beds. Many also offered "hotbeds"—beds rented to day workers at night and to night workers during the day. Some rented out their bathtubs and fire escapes and closets; no place was off-limits to people and, unfortunately, germs. Others became creative and threw rent parties, tacking up invitations on lampposts and hallways and churches. The cost for entry was a quarter.

But despite their best efforts, tenants still came up short, and those in power, the bankers and landlords, white businesses owners and city officials, refused to lower rents or hire Black workers. Their indifference turned swaths of Harlem slum-like. Newspapers reported that whole areas, particularly up along Lenox Avenue, famous for its glitzy nightclubs, began rivaling the tenements on the Lower East Side.

In the shadows cast from the brightly lit marquees lurked the once elegant, currently neglected, buildings; bottles and cups, wrappers and papers swirled along their curbs and sidewalks and entranceways. Inside the buildings, adorned with crown molding, ornate mirrors, cornices, and high-end wood floors, paint now peeled and pipes leaked; brown water often poured from the taps, and sometimes the toilets didn't flush. Writer Wallace Thurman declared the area was "Harlem's Bowery."

Edna took it in, all of it, and although she was awed by Harlem's intensity, one so palpable it seemed to shake the air, the poverty and constant hustle also overwhelmed her. At night in her room with the noise slinking in, she pulled the blanket around her and wondered whether she could stay here, make this city, this place with its towering buildings, freezing winds, lack of trees, and crush of people who all seemed to want something, her home. She didn't know. But for the foreseeable future she had no choice. This, Harlem, was part of the bargain she had struck to leave Savannah.

To begin working at Sea View, Edna needed another year plus of schooling. Along with a handful of other new hires, the city sent her to Harlem Hospital School of Nursing, one of only two Black nursing schools in the metropolitan area and the go-to training hospital for restaffing the ailing Sea View. In an arrangement closely mirroring that at the Georgia Infirmary, Edna would attend Harlem's nursing school tuition-free and, in exchange, work on the wards of the hospital. After, she would graduate with an accredited nursing degree and then transfer to Sea View. It was a small sacrifice for a professional degree, or so she thought.

In late February 1930, days before starting her Harlem tenure, Edna moved from the cramped apartment on West 122nd Street to the nurses' residence, an old brick building that abutted the backside of the hospital. Her room was a tiny space, furnished with an old twin bed, a desk, and a dresser; and the sole window, torso-sized, faced a busy side street. When open, it brought in the world outside, for good or ill.

At night, while she was reading about blood transfusions, enemas, burns, how to lay out treatment trays and use restraints or how tuberculosis ruined the brain, Edna's window would fill with throngs of people promenading down the block. If she looked up from her studies, she could see the streetlamps illuminating the silhouettes of women in long silk dresses draped on the arms of sharp-looking men in long chesterfield coats and fancy shoes.

They walked with an air of elegance, as if the street and all its surroundings belonged to them, and then carried that air into the speakeasies and gambling joints and famous Harlem clubs: Connie's Inn, Club Hot-Cha, and Small's Paradise, celebrated for its ads bragging about "café au lait girls and dancing waiters." There they watched shows and danced and drank illegal booze, imported whiskey, and bathtub gin until the wee hours of the morning, when they stumbled out and disappeared, and the street filled with Harlem's working class. For these wage earners, the energy and excitement and glitter of the Harlem Renaissance was a nuisance, an illusion.

"The ordinary Negroes hadn't heard of the Negro Renaissance," Langston Hughes declared, "and if they had, it hadn't raised their wages any." It also hadn't paid their rent or kept them healthy, a fact Edna learned within weeks of starting at Harlem Hospital, an arresting five-story brick building on Lenox Avenue that spanned the entire block between 137th and 138th Streets.

Built in 1873, it had originally functioned as an emergency branch, a "catchment" center for New York's prestigious Bellevue Hospital. For decades, despite its location in the heart of Harlem, it had been a mostly white space: administrators, board members, doctors, and student nurses were all white and it served a mostly white patient population. But over the years as Black nurses and doctors were hired and white residents left, it had changed.

Although the administration remained white, the nursing school was mainly attended by Black women, and most patients were Harlem's Black residents. In a never-ending stream, they came through its doors, men and women, old and young, complaining to Edna about headaches, breathing issues, chest tightness, and stomach pains. They had rashes and unexplained fevers, fatigue and muscle loss, and many were malnourished. They talked about bugs and rats in their walls, cold air that gusted through cracked windows, and the uncollected garbage in the air shafts of their buildings that produced unbearable smells. Some believed the stench itself was making them sick.

Edna triaged them, writing down their symptoms, and then took her place behind the doctor and watched as he examined them. Soon she learned which diseases ran rampant in the community: pneumonia and heart disease, caused by poverty that led to poor nutrition; and venereal disease, such as syphilis and gonorrhea, which struck Harlemites at twice the rate they struck white people. Tuberculosis was everywhere in all its forms: TB deaths rates were the highest in the city, killing Black residents at almost triple the rate of whites. The proliferation of disease offered a breeding ground for quacks and "root workers," who promised their oils, potions, and powders "could cure everything from a broken heart and overly curly hair to the most lethal ailments." The remedies didn't cure, but they allowed the sick to stave off seeking legitimate medical care, at least for a while.

Residents told Edna their fears about hospitals, worries she'd heard before in Savannah. Hospitals were "dens of death," they said, and Harlem Hospital, dubbed "the Morgue" or "the butcher shop," had a staggering mortality rate. Despite their resistance to come, most people had no choice. Almost all New York City hospitals, except four, were notorious for turning away Black patients. The few that accepted them also segregated them. And so they came here and prayed not to die.

But prayers couldn't fix a hospital that was short-staffed and in disarray.

The hospital had 325 beds to accommodate as many as 450 people at a time, so nurses were forced to play a game of human Tetris. Every day they moved the less ill onto chairs or couches or cots rolled into rooms or hallways that were already packed tight with stretchers four lanes deep. At night the nurses on duty reshifted the patients who had been moved in the morning and now slept slumped in chairs or hanging off couches. Supplies ran out and the patients' elevators rarely worked, leaving doctors and nurses to transport the sick in elevators meant for trash. And up on the wards, especially maternity, one of the busiest units, things got worse.

There nurses and midwives raced to save Black mothers who were dying in childbirth at twice the rate of white mothers. "You should have come sooner" was a standard refrain among the nurses. Many *had* come before, but unless they were fully dilated and ready to push, interns, hoping to prevent a backlog, sent them away. Stories of mothers leaving the hospital and then giving birth in vestibules or alleyways or in their bathrooms appeared regularly in the Black papers.

For years, the NAACP had been lobbying the mayor, imploring him to address the situation and the discriminatory hiring practices in twenty-five of twenty-nine municipal hospitals. Only four—Harlem, Lincoln, Metropolitan, and Sea View—employed Black nurses, doctors, and interns. Having a diverse staff in every hospital, they reasoned, one that represented all the citizens of New York, not just the white population, would create more equitable care, improve treatment outcomes, and save lives. The mayor listened and nodded, but conditions worsened.

Hoping to help the NAACP's fight for integration, the National Association of Colored Graduate Nurses (NACGN) stepped in.

Founded in 1908, the organization was the brainchild of Martha Minerva Franklin, a young, tenacious nurse from Connecticut. As the profession began to establish itself, Franklin had grown frustrated with the lack of advancement for Black nurses and decided they needed a professional association of their own. Over the course of two years, she had handwritten hundreds of letters to fellow nurses, superintendents of nursing schools, and nursing organizations, surveying them on the issue. Her efforts caught the attention of Ada Thomas, the acting director of the Lincoln School for Nurses in the Bronx, New York. After being denied a promotion to director of nursing, Thomas shared Franklin's exasperation over the status of Black nurses.

Using her position, Thomas organized a meeting, and on August 25, 1908, fifty-two nurses from across the country converged on the historic St. Mark's Methodist Church in midtown Manhattan. For three days, the women talked about the need for a national organization to ensure equality in health care; on the last day, they elected Franklin as president of their new organization, the NACGN, and then set three goals: to achieve higher professional standards; to uproot the system of inequality in nursing schools, jobs, and associations; and to develop strong leadership among Black nurses. They also came up with a motto: "Not for ourselves, but for humanity."

Since its inception, the organization had made some good progress. It had established a local headquarters at the YWCA in Harlem and created a national jobs registry for Black nurses. Franklin had also built up membership and recognition: in 1921 President Warren G.

Harding and his wife acknowledged her efforts to integrate and seek equality by presenting her with a basket of American Beauty roses at the White House. She thanked them and asked to have the NACGN placed on record as an "organization of . . . trained nurses ready for service when needed." They obliged the request, but World War II would expose it as a perfunctory indulgence.

Smaller victories followed the White House visit: The NACGN pressured the city to move a handful of Black medical professionals into positions of power. Lincoln Hospital saw a Black nurse promoted to supervisor and another to head nurse. And to help combat the wild spread of tuberculosis in Harlem, they named Mabel Keaton Staupers, a fast-talking, intrepid Black nurse—who would later dissolve the NACGN—as executive secretary for the Harlem Committee of the New York Tuberculosis Health Association. Staupers's appointment was considered a big win; years earlier, she had helped establish the Booker T. Washington Sanatorium in the city, the first inpatient center for Black residents with tuberculosis.

But now in 1930, the NACGN was no longer thriving: over the last year membership had dropped and the drive to keep pushing for change had slowed. The organization lacked funds, a salaried director, and friends among the city's political and social leadership, a must-have for any Black association to succeed. To mount a sustained fight against unfair hiring and the mistreatment of Black nurses in the New York City hospital system, run and managed by white men and women, the NACGN needed new energy, and needed it quick. Until then, Black nurses would remain trapped, subjected to the biases of white nurses who said terrible things: "One-sixth of the black nursing students couldn't be compared to even the most mediocre white student," declared one nurse educator. Another said that they "created problems because of their marked tendency to organize against authority."

Their words became the impetus for white nurses to walk off wards and quit en masse after being assigned to work beside or take direction from a Black woman. "Discipline" on the wards, wrote one supervisor, could not be maintained "unless there is firm and competent white direction."

Mrs. Sadie O'Brien, Edna's new boss and Harlem Hospital's superintendent of nurses, hewed to this way of thinking. A Bellevue graduate with twenty years of experience in nursing and management, Mrs. O'Brien was an overbearing woman, small in stature with a haughty sneer, who believed in responsibility and accountability, and she prided herself on having improved conditions at the hospital. But the recent increase in patients and decrease in staff began eroding her achievements. The prior year, 11 of her 391 student nurses, almost all young Black women, had fallen sick from tuberculosis, with one dying and another being told to "remain on duty" and keep working through her illness. Later, when questioned, the forty-eight-year-old O'Brien claimed that the "demanding social routines of the nurses," not their work with a highly contagious disease, made them susceptible to TB.

And she added, "They also wanted to remain thin, and their cigarette smoking had increased."

While she mentioned the heavy patient loads, she omitted the pressure the nurses were under to obey her rules: how they were forced to attend chapel each morning, how they had to wear a girdle, and how their hair, nails, faces, hats, and uniforms were inspected every day for cleanliness. The nurses knew, "one misstep and you were grounded."

Pressure also came from the working conditions: twelve-hour days with no pay and being shuffled from ward to ward. One day Edna might be working in the emergency room, the next in pediatrics, and the following mopping the hallway. Owing to Mrs. O'Brien's lack of oversight, Edna and her fellow nurses encountered orderlies who ignored their requests for help, leaving them to search for empty gurneys, clean linens, and supplies. As the nurses struggled, the orderlies stood by heckling and antagonizing them.

With Mrs. O'Brien ignoring their grievances, the trainee nurses found solace—and later, power—in one another. Often they congregated in their dorm rooms, sitting on the bed, the floor, and even the desk, to share stories about Mrs. O'Brien and her indifference toward Black nurses, now and in the past. There was the dispute between Nurse Potts and Nurse Cassidy, and the Agnes Boozer incident.

The latter had happened one night two years earlier when Nurse Boozer was trying to put through a call and dialed the white switchboard operator Mr. Legassi for help. After a brief back-and-forth, Legassi grew frustrated and began bullying and deriding her over the wire. Initially, Boozer ignored him, but he persisted, his insults growing more cutting and acute. When she verbally retaliated, he became enraged, left his post, and raced up the stairs to "give Miss Boozer a call-down."

Bursting onto the ward, his face twisted into a scowl, he found Nurse Boozer and screamed, "Nigger!" With that, Boozer raised her hand and "slapped his sassy face." A stunned Legassi closed his fists and lifted them from his sides, ready to strike. But the other nurses gathered around their colleague, daring him to lay a hand on her.

Legassi skulked away.

Minutes later, the superintendent, Rudolph Rapp, summoned both Legassi and Boozer to his office. Without a single question, he blamed Boozer for the entire incident. Smugness draped itself over Legassi, and Boozer, standing beside him, could sense it. That and hearing Rapp talking, each word spinning a grander narrative, a lie that faulted only her, inflamed her sense of injustice. She tried to block out his voice, ignore his words, but he spoke louder, his words cutting into the air, filling it with more and more acrimony, until she broke.

No, she was not solely to blame.

No, she did not leave the floor to confront him.

How could Legassi be innocent, absolved of any responsibility? How?

Rapp had little interest in hearing Boozer. He wanted her voice silenced, gone; every second she kept talking amplified his anger and hatred. Enough. He shouted, raising his voice louder—so loud, witnesses said, that "it distressed the patients." He didn't care. Overcome by a primal fury, Rapp glared at Boozer, picked up the phone, and called the white policeman on duty.

"Arrest Miss Boozer," he shouted.

"No," the officer said. Rapp hung up and called the local precinct.

"Arrest Miss Boozer," he fumed into the phone. No, they would not. The following night, Miss Boozer was dismissed from Harlem Hospital. Predictably, Mrs. O'Brien did nothing. She blamed Nurse Boozer, who, in her eyes, was unprofessional, rowdy, and hapless, like, she believed, so many other Black nurses. Not a single "negro nurse in Harlem is capable of holding the position of supervisor," she said. Her statement stung, but it was also absurd. With the hospital's acute staffing shortages and patient overload, most of the time the Black nurses were running the wards.

For Edna, the dorm meetings were eye-opening. They introduced her to the long-standing issues of bias in New York's hospital system and the problems Black nurses faced with white supervisors, problems she'd encounter again and again at Sea View. They also were the start of organized social activism and where she met radical young women. One of them, Salaria Kea, an iron-willed nursing student from Ohio, inspired her classmates by telling them things could be different, that "there was nothing inviolable about the old prejudices." They could be, she said, "changed and justice established."

As the school year wound down, many of the student nurses were wearied by Mrs. O'Brien and the patients who yelled and cursed and threw things after waiting too many hours for care. Kea had emboldened them, and they approached Mrs. O'Brien to ask for changes. She nearly laughed before waving them off and reminding them how 25 percent of Harlem was unemployed, and they were among the most privileged. Their nursing jobs came with meals and a clean room, an education, and a meager stipend. If they couldn't do the job, they were free to leave. But walking out wasn't easy. Transferring between hospitals required them to quit and reapply and lose any seniority and wage increases.

Edna knew her fellow nurses were right, and although she wanted to support them, she stayed quiet. It wasn't the time or the moment for her to speak. Harlem Hospital, she believed, was a stop on the pathway God had laid out for her, not the place to mount a fight against inequity. And given Mrs. O'Brien's temper and penchant for reproaching Black nurses, Edna knew how a confrontation could end with her dismissal. And then what? Where would she go? What would she do? She would have her moment later.

For now, to cope with all the bias and enmity, she leaned back into the years of sitting in pews and listening to her father preach his sermons. So many had come from the book of Isaiah. R.V. loved the great prophet, who spoke of judgment, restoration for the righteous, and God's plan for the world. In her room, with its torso-sized window and the world of Harlem and its people spinning outside, she, too, sought the prophet's words to carry her to the end: "Do not fear, for I have redeemed you . . . Remember not the events of the past."

In February 1932, Edna entered her final month of training. Hopes for the time to pass uneventfully ended one day in the dining room. Similar to all hospital dining rooms at the time, Harlem's had a formal setup: tables outfitted with cloths and plates and silverware and waitresses taking orders and serving food. Seating for the staff and nurses was by rank and race, but usually only a few tables were reserved for Black nurses, leaving many with nowhere to sit. Older Black nurses had "cautioned that this had always been so and nothing could be done about it."

On that day, as cooks prepared plates of food, Salaria Kea, the petite Ohioan, entered the dining room with five nurses and sat at the only vacant table. As they picked up their napkins and waved them open, a waitress came forward: "This table," she said, "was reserved for white social workers."

Kea looked at her.

She knew how the Black press had spilled vats of ink reporting on the troubles and confrontations of the segregated dining; how all the articles fleshing out the incidents also implored those in power to abolish the practice. But time and again, officials read them, talked, and then silence.

Kea turned away from the waitress and swept the room with her eyes, taking in the tables of white nurses, their bodies relaxed and easy in the chairs. In one area, the white supervisors and Mrs. O'Brien laughed and drank their morning coffee as if there were no separation, and then, Kea saw, far away from everyone, the Black nurses sitting crammed into their designated space. In that moment, the inventory of indignities, past and present, the antics of Mrs. O'Brien, the sneers and whispers from white colleagues, the "reserved tables," and the frustration and efforts of the last decade to unify a dining room reared in her mind. She wanted change, and knew that setting it in motion rested on them, the Black nurses.

She tossed her napkin on the table, pushed back her chair, and stood up. Looking at the other five nurses around the table, she turned her palms up, in a motion that said "rise."

As they stood, the voices and dining room sounds of silverware clinking and chairs scraping lulled, and dozens of eyes turned to Kea and the five nurses clutching the tablecloth. On Kea's cue, they lifted it and pitched it upward, and in a shutter-snap moment, the room watched as plates and glasses and coffee cups collided with forks and spoons before crashing to the floor. Their shatter silenced the room.

Later that day, Kea was reprimanded but not deterred. She planned to catch the attention of Mayor Jimmy Walker, known as the "nightclub mayor." Walker had spent five years in office, but his carousing and nepotism had resulted in charges of corruption. Kea knew he might be running for reelection and would need the Black vote to boost his standing and increase his chance of winning.

She crafted a petition demanding three things: an end to the dining room segregation, the hiring of a Black dietitian, and more authority for the hospital's Black head nurses, who, she said, had been reduced to "straw bosses" and "petty foremen." The petition garnered ninety-plus signatures from the nursing staff, and when it landed on Walker's desk, he called for an immediate investigation. Within days, the hospital's system of whites-only tables had ended.

The Black nurses celebrated Kea and her victories, and at the end of February 1932, Edna finished her tenure at Harlem Hospital. As she packed up her dorm room, with its tiny window overlooking the heart of Harlem, her time here, now falling into hindsight, began to crystallize.

She had endured the crowds and noise, the frantic pace of the city, Mrs. O'Brien and her staff of white supervisors. She had struggled to stay the course, to become a professional nurse and forge a greater distance between herself and the tar paper shack of her youth, over eight hundred miles away, where the ominous crucible warning was handed down the year of her birth. And she had prevailed. Along the way, she'd also met courageous women who encouraged her to join the NACGN in their fight for equality; they had taught her how to organize and enact change. But despite all this, nothing could prepare her for what lay across the river on Staten Island.

Chapter 5

❖

Contagion on the Island

Early March 1932

The ferry cost a nickel. Edna bought a ticket and followed a crowd of neatly dressed ladies into the women's cabin on the lower deck. There she found a seat in the middle of the boat, facing the big glass windows. She smoothed the skirt of her nurse's uniform, crossed her legs, and settled in for the quick trip across New York Harbor. As the boat cut through the murky waters, Edna watched the passing landscape, dotted with landmarks symbolizing so much of America's history: Lady Liberty, Ellis Island, and the Robbins Reef Lighthouse, known for employing the first female lighthouse keeper. Twenty-five minutes later, the boat pulled into its slip at St. George Terminal, and Edna stepped onto New York City's most remote borough, Staten Island.

The air was misty and damp, and the wind blew in wild bursts, tossing up skirts and tipping off hats. Edna glanced at her wristwatch. It was pretty, with a petite oyster-colored face and miniature black hands, a gift to herself for finishing her training at Harlem Hospital. Some thought it was too delicate for nursing, but the tiny hands kept perfect time, and for a nurse, time was essential. It was now almost 8 a.m.

She pulled her coat tighter and began the short walk to Bay Street, where she would catch the R111 bus to Sea View. The bus was a new addition to Staten Island, having recently replaced the old electric-powered trackless trolleys. It was small and outfitted with two rows of narrow double seats barely big enough for two people, and in keeping with all New York buses, it had no "colored section." Edna stepped on, slipped into a front seat, something she could never do in Savannah, and gathered her blue nurse's cape to make room for another passenger. But no one sat down. Instead, people walked by quickly, casting side glances or covering their mouths; some stopped and turned their heads. The bus pulled away with the seat beside her empty and the passengers glaring at her, daring her to look at them.

She turned away and looked out the window, her mind cataloging the beats and moods of this new place. Later she would recall them in letters and phone calls to Americus. She would tell how the bus rattled down Victory Boulevard, a long, winding cobblestone road flanked by side streets with names reminiscent of English love poems: Silver Beech, Seven Gables, Pleasant Valley, Grymes Hill. Here, unlike Manhattan, there were no sweatshops, shantytowns, or children sleeping on back-alley gratings—just blocks and blocks of quaint houses with bookcases and cozy couches and kitchen tables set for breakfast.

Across from the charming homes stretched Clove Lakes Park, home to acres of park, the oldest living tulip tree, and a lake teeming with crayfish and trout and tree frogs that lingered in alder bushes and cedar trees. There was also an old cemetery full of worn stones and retold stories: a woman murdered by her husband, a grandfather who mysteriously died in the fields, a stillborn baby. Rumors of buried treasure on Staten Island also swirled, and sometimes at night a man with a lantern would come and dig in the graveyard.

But in this place of isolation, where 158,000 people enjoyed fifty-eight square miles—practically empty, compared with Manhattan's twenty-three square miles crowded with 1.9 million people—there was also fear: of the past and the present. Edna felt it emanating from the people riding the R111 bus. Their unease went beyond a disdain for her skin color; they feared where she was going in her nurse's whites.

To the islanders, Sea View was a "pest house," and nurses like Edna were contagion, walking vessels of disease. Tuberculosis, they believed, lived on their uniforms, in their hair, on their bags. They sat and rubbed it on the seats and windows; every gesture they made sent the microbes into the air for others to breathe. Given their long history with infectious disease, the residents felt justified in their scorn.

For two hundred years, New York City had exploited its uninhabited harbor islands—Blackwell's Island, Wards Island, and North Brother Island—to protect residents from the sick, the criminally insane, the destitute, and others perceived as social misfits. On these small plots of land, surrounded by the swift-moving currents of the East River, politicians approved places like the Blind Asylum, the New York City Lunatic Asylum, the Idiot Asylum, the Hospital for Incurables, the Smallpox Hospital, and the House of Refuge for juvenile delinquents. Tens of thousands of New Yorkers were ferried over to these places and lived in conditions Charles Dickens once described as "naked ugliness and horror."

Although Staten Island was inhabited, it failed to escape the eyes of the city or its philanthropists. Much to the chagrin of its residents, throughout the nineteenth and early twentieth centuries, buildings, orphanages, asylums, and institutions for disease rose on its lush hillsides. There was the Bethlehem Orphan and Half Orphan Asylum for children whose parents had died from influenza; the Mount Loretto orphanage, staffed with heavy-handed nuns skilled in corporal punishment; and, the most unwelcome, the Quarantine Station.

Seventy years before Edna arrived at the ferry port, twenty buildings spread over thirty acres were used to house thousands of sick people who were pulled off merchant and immigrant ships entering New York Harbor. Every day, the islanders watched as the afflicted, suffering from yellow fever, cholera, typhus, smallpox, and other diseases, were stripped naked and laid in wagons that boatsmen pushed from the piers up the Quarantine pathways. The sick immigrants passing in wagons were an affront to residents and their neighborhood. They were "annoying," many islanders said, "from their indecency and filthiness." So was the hospital.

Surrounded by a six-foot brick wall, it had become "a pest and a nuisance of the most odious character," its presence a harbinger of what lurked in the air: disease, carried in the bodies of yellow-fever-bearing mosquitoes and staff, especially the nurses.

"Some of them," one store owner said, "pass my door every day going to and from their work," leaving a trail of germs, and they also disrupted the pious order of the community by "frequently coming out to procure spiritous liquors." If the Quarantine Station was gone, Staten Islanders believed they would be free from the pestilences devaluing their property and giving the island a bad reputation.

Years passed, the animosity mounted, and by the summer of 1858, tensions between the locals and the Quarantine staff had reached a breaking point. Residents demanded a meeting with the local board of health. In the heat of an August night, the board noted all the islanders' grievances: how their peaceful towns, swaddled by morning mists and sounds of gleeful birds, were now infiltrated by drinkers and thieves, sick foreigners and irreverent nurses; how dead bodies were wheeled through the streets and buried on their land; and how the outbreaks of disease kept shutting down their businesses.

Hours later, the board of health reached a conclusion: the Quarantine had indeed brought "death and desolation to the very doors of the people." They resolved that "the citizens of this country protect themselves by abating this abominable nuisance without delay."

They pasted their resolution on the station walls.

Two weeks later a mob, led by prominent landowners, swarmed

the Quarantine. They came armed with matches and hay and hatchets, and all the ire and hate of years, and lit its buildings on fire. As the flames danced about, igniting bigger flames, residents watched doctors and nurses carry out patients, who screamed and shouted in different languages. The people were unmoved and continued staring at the yellow fever hospital, the smallpox hospital, the outhouses, power-houses, and staff residence burning bright, the yellow and red and blue flames setting the night sky ablaze.

Three fire companies were called, but all took their time arriving. Witnesses said that when the firemen appeared, they approached the burning shanties but then stopped and did "nothing more than look at the fire," claiming "that someone had cut their hoses." Eventually they put out the fire, and while, surprisingly, no one was killed, all the buildings, save for the female hospital that housed sixty patients, were burned. The next morning headlines read, "The Quarantine War."

Wanting to finish the job, the arsonists returned the following night and burned down the women's facility. Two local residents were arrested and prosecuted for starting the fires, but the judge acquitted them. "The citizens of Staten Island," the judge said, "had endured fifty years of abuse from taking in the sick." To him, their actions were warranted. Staten Island was now free from the tyranny of the Quarantine Station.

But the Station's burial ground never went away. In the decades after the fire, relics from the graves would surface. While walking along the shore or fishing, islanders might stumble upon a skull, ribs, part of a pelvis, tibias, fibulas, a jaw, or teeth, reminders of the disease imposed on their community.

Now, in 1932, the bones were replaced by the Black nurses, whose presence provoked the residents into reliving the Quarantine War of seventy years earlier. "On the bus, they moved away, like I had the plague," one nurse said. "Like the germs were going to jump out at them."

The small bus carrying Edna turned onto Brielle Avenue, and suddenly the quiet streets with comely houses and the open land vanished into a thin gray mist that draped itself over a narrow, curving road flanked by tall trees. The bus lurched, its engine grinding, straining to climb the changing grade.

Up it went, deeper into a neighborhood of nowhere, of vacancy, where any hope for anything seemed to die. But something drew Edna to this remote stretch of land, this place where the city sent its poor suffering from the plague-like disease, tuberculosis. It was rugged and harsh and lonely, a wilderness that recalled places in the holy book where God showed Himself and revealed His power.

On the single-lane entryway into Sea View, Edna's viewed shifted again. In front of her stood a lone smokestack, exhaling plumes of black smoke. This was the powerhouse, where men shoveled heaps of coal into blasting furnaces to keep Sea View running. Just beyond it, the patient pavilions came into view, their red rooftops shimmering in the morning light. The bus slowed and pulled into the courtyard.

"Last stop," shouted the driver.

Chapter 6

The Most Magnificent Institution

March–May 1932

Edna stepped off the bus and immediately felt the sting of wind that, at four hundred feet above sea level, drove itself with more force against the vast complex of buildings that rushed around her. There were dozens of them, corralled together in an area the shape of a half-moon.

Directly in front of her stood the administration building, the hospital's second-most important building after the powerhouse. It was built to record all the daily activities, to store patient files, to sign in visitors, to triage incoming patients, and to house the patient registry, a nearly two-foot ledger with the name, address, birth date, occupation, race, ethnicity, citizenship, and discharge or death date of every person admitted to Sea View.

To the left and right there were other buildings, the surgical ward, nurses' residence, staff house, and dining room. And behind sprawled an octagonal-shaped structure, the kitchen, where vents puffed out steam and smoke from the ovens and cauldrons bubbling and boiling and churning out thousands of meals a day.

Except for the nurses' residence, all the buildings were capped at two or three stories and were finished in bland colors that were brushed onto flat walls. Some of them flaunted enticing flourishes, gables of varying heights, cornices, eaves, columns, and dormers, turning their exteriors into a grab bag of architectural styles: Colonial, Tudor, and Spanish Mission. But the eye didn't register the assortment of architecture; instead it followed the symmetry of an enclosed corridor that wound itself along the entire perimeter of the half-moon, joining all the buildings.

Behind the winding corridor and the complex of lower buildings were the grande dames of Sea View, the eight pavilions constructed to be "commensurate with the magnitude of the evil" tuberculosis. In the morning light, the pavilions seemed to come alive, to stretch and rear against the sky. Edna studied them, shifting her eyes left to right, up and down, her mind taking in how they sat in a perfect arc formation and insinuated themselves onto the pastoral setting, interrupting the serenity with their sense of urgency and insistence.

Unlike the lower buildings with their hodgepodge of architecture, giving each a bit of charm, these eight buildings had none. They were unnervingly compact, narrow and rectangular, and fashioned with curt and angular lines that pierced the air and demanded the onlooker stop and marvel at their symmetry, at how every builder had nailed and screwed and plastered every floor, stairwell, window, and wall in the exact same way to create eight identical structures. But inside, each harbored its own hell, its own remarkable catalog of tragedies: suicides, stabbings, chokings; people suffocating or starving or dying any other way tuberculosis was moved to kill.

Edna lowered her eyes and they settled on the open-air balconies flanking both sides of every floor.

Each one was filled from end to end with beds and people who were taking the "rest cure"—the gold-standard treatment at the time. Some were tucked under heaps of blankets, asleep, their bodies pressed into old mattresses; others were propped on pillows, their heads wrapped in scarves and their eyes vacant, drained of promise. They stared into the bareness of the forest, where winter crows darted and dove and cawed and branches splayed into strange and menacing shapes that swayed in the wind, reaching and bending toward the buildings.

Beneath the shadow of this monumental vision called Sea View, the one that animated the dream of New York's social reformers and power-hungry officials like Hermann Biggs, Edna glimpsed the first human attempt to contain the disease, to overcome this "evil," this sickness that swallowed all hope.

She dropped her gaze and began walking left down a pathway toward the surgical building, a two-story structure with a smooth white façade and a roof with seven small gables. After being shuffled through different wards at Harlem Hospital, Edna had been chosen to work as a surgical nurse. It was a demanding job, assisting in surgery and pre- and postoperative care, but she welcomed the challenge, and the post fulfilled her lifelong dream to understand the workings and failings of the human body and to help heal it. And it brought a salary of $720 a year, not quite the $1,100 salary of a white nurse, but a decent one nonetheless.

"Movement" is how one nurse described the surgical ward—"nonstop movement." Spanning the entire second floor, it was split by a narrow corridor running down the center that led to the main operating room. A series of small recovery rooms outfitted with six beds lined either side. There were other rooms as well: a nurses' changing room, a surgeons' dressing room, rooms for bandage manufacturing and sterilizing and x-raying. On the ceiling, enormous skylights brought in sunlight and sky, giving the floor a feeling of airiness and vitality, an unexpected sensation, considering most patients who came through could barely breathe.

Under the ever-shifting light, nurses hustled up and down the long hallway with thoroughness and speed. Doors opened and closed, and women in crisp white uniforms and starched hats entered and exited the different rooms. Some carried bedpans or X-rays or trays of sutures and newly made, neatly stacked bandages. Others wheeled large oxygen tanks into recovery rooms or pushed metal carts full of surgical equipment: scalpels, glass syringes, mercury thermometers, steel needles, knives, and glass bottles filled with powders and pills and elixirs that clanked together. One or two pushed patients in wheelchairs, heavy wooden chairs with high wicker backs and giant wheels.

In those first weeks, Edna met her coworkers, a small group of young women who had also been carefully selected to work in surgery and who, over the years, would become essential in ushering in new surgical techniques and saving patients' lives. Overseeing and training them was Miss R., their supervisor, a vibrant and gracious woman who managed the ward with a precise set of rules. But unlike many of her white counterparts, nurses said, Miss R. focused her authority on "success, not suspicion." The change of pace from the overbearing Mrs. O'Brien was refreshing but not long-lasting. Sea View had its own version of Harlem's supervisor, Miss Lorna Doone Mitchell, a Teutonic woman who, nurses said, "lurked in the hallways and spied on them," making sure they followed her rules.

"You don't want to get caught not washing your hands," one nurse warned.

"Or be late," said another.

"Always look busy."

"And," added one more, "know her gaze could freeze the devil himself."

Edna heard the talk about Miss Mitchell, whose presence, even when she was absent, seemed to dominate. She took in their words and, in her usual manner, watched the pauses and breaks and things left unsaid. But she wouldn't let the shadow of Sea View's supervisor unnerve her or make her lose focus. She pushed aside thoughts of Miss Mitchell and turned her attention to Miss R. and all the particulars of being a surgical nurse.

Taking in each word, Edna became a gatherer of information, assessing and filing away each new thing she learned: how to prepare patients for different surgeries; how to set up an oxygen tent and surgical tray; how to lift emaciated bodies without breaking bones; and how to explain Gaffky counts, the numeric rating used to classify the number of TB bacilli present in sputum—she would soon learn how much this number, ranging between one and nine, mattered to patients, how they pinned all their hopes on it.

Aurally, her ears adapted quickly to the nuances of the different coughs—the hack, the wheeze, the gurgle, the choke, the bark—relaying and pinging through the wards endlessly. And her eyes began to distinguish between the assortment of bandages, catheters, syringes, and surgical equipment, which tools were used for cutting, which for grasping and clamping and retracting. Often she came in early and stood in front of the shelves in the medicine room, committing to memory the bottles of elixirs: sodium chloride for dehydration, resorcinol for eczema, rose geranium oil for diarrhea, Caroid for an upset stomach, iron, quinine, and so many others.

While preparing the surgical trays, she studied the shapes and sizes of forceps and clamps, scalpels and syringes, and scissors whose steel blades curved and dipped in unnatural ways; there were so many: bone, tonsillar, nasal, rectal, uterine, and ones for skin grafts. She lifted them, feeling their weight in her hand, and catalogued them in her mind like she had the declensions of Latin.

When Miss R. talked about showing deference to the surgeons, Edna made it clear that she understood. In this age of patriarchal medicine, nurses were handmaidens to doctors, and their jobs were to "understand and anticipate the physicians' needs and decisions." When nurses walked through the double doors of the main operating room at the far end of the ward, their thoughts and opinions didn't matter.

That room belonged to the surgeons.

Within months, Edna settled into her new role of assisting Sea View's rotating staff of surgeons, including Dr. Goldberg, Dr. Fishberg, and the renowned Dr. Pol N. Coryllos. She was poised, with impeccable timing, knowing exactly when to pass the doctor a particular clamp or syringe or knife. Unlike some nurses, she remained unruffled when surgeons sliced open chest cavities, revealing lungs whose surfaces resembled the moon, full of craters and rims, or when their fingers slipped inside their broad incisions and pared off chunks of rotted tissue and then dropped them into small kidney-shaped metal basins. Not even the stench of an infected body, one that rose from the flesh like an invisible dark matter, seemed to shake her resolve while she worked.

Sometimes the operations took hours, and other times they went by quickly, but when the surgeons were finished, they pulled off their gloves and walked out. If Edna wasn't on pre-op duty, she often cleaned, rolling up the sheets and heaps of bloody towels and placing them into linen bags to be laundered. She collected and wrapped the used equipment and marked it for sterilization; then she scrubbed the operating table and the surrounding tiles with bleach. Afterward, in the waning light of day, she paused and looked at the room. Its sterility appealed to her sense of order, but all that whiteness belied its reality.

The job was dangerous and so was Sea View.

Doctors performed surgery and then breezed through the recovery rooms on their rounds, leaving the nurses bedside to contend with the clumps of phlegm, the blood and vomit, and all the bodily fluids that tossed the microbe into the world. A single sneeze blasted forty thousand infected droplets twenty-seven feet into the air at a hundred miles an hour, and a cough sent out three thousand of them. But disease wasn't the only hazard. Patients, too, could be dangerous.

Many had been there for months and years. Edna read charts showing three, four, or five consecutive years, over a thousand days of being cooped up at Sea View, all of them filled with the same protocols, turning tuberculosis into a dreadful job, a grotesque career. She read in the charts how patients were depressed and angry and saw them lash out at the staff about things big and small. During mealtimes, they barraged the nurses with complaints. The food was "filthy and decayed," they said, showing her bread with roaches baked into it, or worms crawling around their side dishes.

Patients also shouted about cracked plates and torn blankets and droned on about being "stuck in Sea View," a grim place full of terrible stories: the eighty-three-year-old man who jumped from a second-story window; the 117 immigrants who had illegally entered the country and were arrested for working as hospital attendants and porters; orderlies who stole cars; and gangs that met in the woods behind the kitchen. One, the Rattlesnake gang, was accused of killing the eight-year-old son of a cop. On they talked, telling more stories about broken things, other suicides, and mean doctors, their anger mounting, and soon a scuffle turned to a shove and a shove to a blow.

In those early days, during her two-and-a-half-hour morning commute, beginning at the Sixth Avenue elevated subway, Edna wrote letters to Americus. As the train snaked down the avenue, its wheels clicking and clanking along the track, passing billboards advertising Old Drum tobacco, Barbasol shaving cream, Yuban coffee, and Watkins Mulsified beauty shampoo, she described sidewalks crowded with people; they entered and exited shops and markets and luncheonettes that streamed by like a series of moving stills.

But everywhere life was interrupted by the Depression.

From above, she could see the breadlines stretching farther down the blocks, curling around corners, past men in crumpled suits selling apples and oranges from wooden wheelbarrows. And the empty lots weren't so empty anymore. More people arrived every day with their boxy baby carriages or metal pull wagons piled high with their belongings to set up camp.

She also wrote to Americus about her new job.

Currently, there was a staff shortage, about 150 mostly Black nurses were working under white supervisors, a trifling number for a hospital with almost a thousand patients needing constant care. And the shifts were long, twelve to fourteen hours with a quick break. And yet, with all the problems that punctuated her day—lack of staff, long shifts, a nearly five-hour round-trip commute, the high patient load, and the disease—she was happy, determined to stay, to follow this course and honor the Florence Nightingale Pledge, which every nurse recited upon graduation: "I solemnly pledge myself before God . . . to devote myself to the welfare of those committed to my care."

The patients at Sea View came from other hospitals in the five boroughs but originated from around the globe. In the oversize registry in the administration building, they wrote their names and birthplaces—Italy, Spain, Poland, Germany, Russia, Ireland, and Greece. Many, the registry book showed, used to hold jobs as plumbers, cigar rollers, electricians, hatters, seamstresses, stenographers, waiters, cooks, chauffeurs, housewives, or meat cutters. Some were prostitutes and petty thieves, drunks and Bowery bums. Public health officials and the press routinely called them "vicious consumptives," "incorrigible," "unteachable," "deplorable," and "morally bereft." Those terms angered Edna, who saw only people, sick, anxious, and afraid.

In the pre-op room while she unraveled their bandages, tied off a vein, or felt their surging pulse and fever-wet skin, they told her the moment they knew something was very wrong: one woman was ironing and coughed up blood; another woke up and couldn't move; another was haggling with a street peddler and began to sweat; and another was just sitting at home.

Doctors eventually confirmed their suspicions, saying the word, the one that occupied such a powerful place in everyone's fears, "tuberculosis."

And in that instant, their lives were fractured, split in two: before TB and after.

They had lost friends and family and jobs; they were stigmatized and vilified by their communities; their lives were now at the mercy of doctors who commanded them to lie still for hours each day in the freezing cold or mosquito-ridden heat on Sea View's open-air balconies taking the rest cure. When that failed, they were sent to surgery and carved up. They told her these things and more; while talking, some remained stone-faced and stoic; others turned their heads and wept, asking about the surgeries with terrifying names: plombage, lung re-section, thoracoplasty, lobectomy, and phrenic nerve crush.

Edna listened, and while they spoke, she held their hand, curling her fingers over their knuckles to explain the procedures. But sometimes words failed to quell the panic stirring within, that simmering dread of being cut open, of imagining a surgery gone awry: nerves accidently being sliced apart, muscles torn, uncontrolled bleeding, or, worse, the grim thought of waking mid-operation, groggy but alert, and seeing the surgeon bringing down the knife, or feeling the cautery burning some tissue, or hearing your organs being shifted.

Some pulled her close and whispered, the stench of sickness trailing from their words, telling her about the shadows they saw each night moving about the floor.

"Like wisps of white smoke," one man said.

"But sometimes they just appeared and stood beside you," another told her, their ghostly shape swaying, making unintelligible mur-muring sounds. Others told her about the Bone Man, another version of the Grim Reaper. He prowled the wards collecting the souls of the dead.

Many talked about dying, about leaving behind family, friends, and their lives, about things left undone. They agonized about the process taking weeks, their body writhing, recoiling into itself, shutting down slowly, organ by organ, struggling just to die. Many feared dying too quickly, and not atoning and being cast into hell.

"Does God forgive the sick?" she was often asked.

Edna never answered these questions. She wasn't allowed to give her thoughts on God and death, a regular event at Sea View. And besides, what could she say? That death at Sea View was not peaceful or gentle or easy, that it tended toward violence, that what happened here, in this hospital, eluded much of human reason.

Time and again, Edna saw how tuberculosis annihilated the body in fantastic ways. Indifferent to gender or age, it dug deep, devouring the spines of the children and mashing up the brains of aspiring singers. In the immigrant stonemason, it had pulverized his lungs, nearly liquefying them. As he lay dying from sepsis, coughing up blood and clumps of mucus, Edna had stayed with him all night, placing ice chips on his lips while telling him things were all right, even though they weren't. In the morning when the sun rose and the sky above Staten Island glowed red, his heart finally shut down, ending his torment.

Days and nights like these rendered Edna speechless. She didn't share these stories with Americus but kept them to herself, and on her nightly commute back to Harlem, she sat on the ferry staring at the city with its twinkling lights, and prayed like R.V. had taught her. Many nights she repeated Isaiah, finding comfort in his words. "Then your light will shine out from the darkness," he had written, "and the darkness around you will be as bright as noon."

For Edna, few places were darker than Sea View, and until there was a better treatment for tuberculosis, this was where she was called. To this island, this hospital, these people that the city had damned.

"Sea View is the great clearinghouse for tuberculosis patients," officials had declared. "No one ever recovers at Sea View."

Chapter 7

The Scourge

Spring–Fall 1932

Miss Mitchell burst onto the surgical ward soon after Edna arrived. She stormed down the hallway straight into Miss R.'s office, shutting the glass-paned door with force. Through the glass, she could be seen saying something and holding up a pair of rubber gloves. While she talked, she pulled at the pointer finger of the glove, stretching it to twice its size. Miss R. stood across from her, listening and nodding in a manner that said *I understand* and, *Yes, of course something will be done*—a promise she would keep at the next staff meeting, when she would recap proper sterilization techniques, the issue Miss Mitchell wanted addressed.

The way she moved and held the gloves, she was everything Edna's colleagues had described. Tall, with a striking appearance, one of contrasts: a pale face edged by short jet-black hair, worn pinned up, and her lipstick was a bold shade of red. Over her uniform, she wore a long woolen cape of the deepest navy that fell from her shoulders in generous folds, gathering around her legs. Watching her, the way she kept her back straight, as if pulled up by an invisible thread, Edna understood why people feared her: Miss Mitchell, the superintendent of nurses, and the second most powerful official at Sea View, was a woman who took up space.

In 1929, the year the white nurses began quitting, the city had recruited her to Sea View with high expectations. Officials loved her credentials, her administrative skills and knowledge about infectious diseases, and they believed that she could rebuild the hospital's ranks and fix the problem of staff turnaround by training a reliable team of nurses who abided by proper protocols, previously not taught or enforced. In tandem with the recently hired medical director, Dr. George Ornstein, the hospital board had grand ideas: they hoped to transform Sea View's reputation from a "pest house" into "a magnificent hospital" built specifically "for New York's deserving poor," as it was originally envisioned in 1913. Miss Mitchell was happy to oblige.

She brought years of expertise, reaching back to her childhood when she had watched her father practice medicine. He was the only physician in a rural Virginia town, nestled in the Blue Ridge Mountains, and during the Civil War he had served the Confederacy as a surgeon. Of his four daughters, only Lorna Doone followed his path.

In the early 1920s, after her husband left with their young daughter, Miss Mitchell quit her job as a housekeeper and traded in the rustic farmhouses, orchards, and mountain views of Virginia for the skyscrapers of New York, where she enrolled in Bellevue Hospital's School of Nursing, the same program Mrs. O'Brien had attended. Upon graduation, she took a job at Willard Parker Hospital, one of New York's oldest and earliest hospitals to specialize in communicable diseases, scarlet fever, diphtheria, and tuberculosis. With a bed capacity of 424 but a daily patient load of 494, it had the heaviest traffic in the country.

Her drive and penchant for detail allowed her to quickly rise through the ranks at Willard Parker, becoming superintendent of nurses and managing a full-time staff of white nurses in addition to the white student nurses. As a leader, she had a stellar reputation for maintaining order and training top-notch nurses. The only blight on her impressive résumé were claims that the hospital had been engaging in "discriminatory practices." But it wasn't enough to stop Sea View from hiring her to oversee its growing staff of mostly Black nurses.

Now at forty, Miss Mitchell was eager to establish herself in this new role by committing to Sea View and its nurses. For her, this wasn't a job but a career move. She knew those high-ranking men who lorded over the world of medicine would be hawking her, thinking that she, a woman, wasn't as capable as them. Determined to prove them wrong, and knowing all the reasons her colleagues disliked working with Black nurses, she readjusted her ways and adopted a more rigorous method of supervising, laying down rules like a series of commandments.

At staff meetings, with the nurses sitting together in neat rows, she was reminded of her opportunity to achieve great success, for her and them, if they followed her rules. And so she always arranged herself, pulling her shoulders back, lifting her chin, and in a deliberate tone repeated her moral codes: gossiping, lying, stealing, laziness, lateness, and disrespecting authority and patients' needs were all off-limits. And she would not, she explained, hesitate to "let them go."

Often to prove her point, she asked them to stand. As they rose, she walked around them, her heels striking, then echoing off the floor, and the folds of her cape swishing around her legs. She eyed them like a general, checking that their uniforms were clean and starched, their shoes polished, their hair tied back, and their nails clean and filed. Unkempt hands and hair and wrinkled uniforms unnerved her. So did crooked or limp caps, her pet peeve. Miss Mitchell's cap, one nurse said, "sat on her head like a porcelain sculpture."

There were other rules, too, ones about techniques: doffing and donning gowns and sterilization, especially regarding gloves—her outrage the day she burst into Miss R.'s office was over a nurse's failure to properly clean the gloves and check them for holes. She was also a stickler for sanitation and the proper disposal of all things soiled and bloodied: sheets, pillows, pajamas, and bandages; toothbrushes, combs, tissues, masks, and, of course, sputum cups.

Collect them with rubber gloves, then "burn them," she said.

If possible, she would've also burned the mattress of the dead. But she couldn't. Instead, she ordered nurses to "wash them down until they seemed new." It was an odd request, considering many were decades old and no amount of washing or rubbing could ever give them a different appearance. But of all the rules, handwashing was her obsession. She believed that most, if not all, diseases were preventable through handwashing, not an uncommon perception in the 1930s.

Regularly, she held handwashing meetings, calling the nurses around a square metal sink built into the wall to reinforce the proper technique. Standing beside it, she lifted her own hands and held them palms facing out toward the nurses. Hands, she would say, needed to be scrubbed "for two minutes *before* and *after* caring for the patient." Usually, she called on one or two nurses to demonstrate how to cup the soap and lather the hands, how to scrub starting from the inner part of the wrist, moving over the palm toward the fingers and into their spaces, and ending at the nails.

Rumor had it that she secretly timed nurses washing their hands. No one knew for sure, but one nurse said, "We washed for two minutes and then some."

To keep nurses from becoming lax, Miss Mitchell made daily unannounced visits to the wards, but fear of becoming sick kept her from spending long periods inside them. At any time, nurses might look up to see her figure, crowned with the rigid cap, moving down the hallway toward the open ward to inspect it and ensure that nurses were following her protocols for keeping the spaces germ-free.

Wary of stepping in too far, she remained by the swinging double doors and cast her eyes upward, moving them from window to window and door to door, checking that they were open no matter the weather. It was imperative, she believed, for the cross breeze to come through and cleanse the room of the unrelenting spray of dead tissue and living microbes the sick unleashed into the air.

On some days she lingered, walking to the pea-green walls and running her fingers down their surface, feeling for anything other than peeling paint, anything that might interrupt their smoothness: food, blood, feces, vomit, dirt, or whatever else patients might fling onto them. She did this until her hand reached hip level; then she paused, cocking her head to the side to examine the floor and baseboards for similar kinds of dirt. All this scrutiny was to ensure that both were being scrubbed hard with amounts of bleach so copious that, as one nurse said, "we felt the smell in our noses."

To comply, nurses scrubbed until, they said, "the walls breathed bleach."

Before leaving the ward, she collected the nurses' logbook and returned to her office to check their work. Alone, she flipped through the pages, glancing at the handwritten notes that she required her nurses to write. The book was one of sadness, a chronicle of lives spent in agony, of men and women who passed their days banging on metal bed frames, who stood by the big open windows barefoot and weeping, and whose bodies were being eaten up by a tiny rod-shaped microbe, barely two microns long—the period at the end of this sentence can fit about four hundred microns.

The first two years had gone well for Miss Mitchell. The nurses were learning her ways, and the partnership with Harlem Hospital enabled her to keep filling the thinned-out ranks, although they were still short-staffed. But she had marked a few nurses, ones she believed pushed back or were uninvested or careless at their jobs. She kept their names private and warned them again how she could "let them go." She didn't want sick nurses who would exacerbate the shortage and jeopardize her career. She was hired to keep her staff physically and mentally fit, able to contend with Sea View's often unpredictable population.

All the nurses knew how the disease tested their patience, how they needed to remain calm, read body language and facial expressions, and step into the consciousness of the sick all day, every day. Along with their clinical duties, they were tasked with lifting depressions, silencing anxiety, and, as Edna knew, allaying fears of dying when dying was all around. They also had to offer words and gestures of compassion, to keep up the pretense of living, as if this sickness were curable, a mere moment in time, a blip in their patients' lives, and would soon end. But the nurses knew it was a lie. Nothing at Sea View resembled ordinary life.

Here, time as people knew it fell away, transforming into sick time, disordered and messy. Nurses tried to reorganize it through the sanatorium's routine, its regimented, near monastic set of cues demarcating the day and reducing the sick to children by stealing their independence.

Edna's colleagues on the main wards told patients when to wake; when, what, and how much to eat—pre-breakfast, patients had to drink a half pint of milk and eat toast, chewing slowly until it turned to mush. They were told when to bathe, sleep, and read and, if possible, when to stand and sit and exercise.

The time cues led to the rituals, the hallmarks of sanatorium life— the weekly weigh-ins, daily temperature charts, sputum counts—and to the maxims, proverbs pounded into the psyche of the patients, who repeated them like broken mantras:

"The labor which best repays a sick man is to get well."

"Your most important duty is to get well. Let all other duties be secondary."

"Desire but one thing [to get well], and that with all thy heart."

And one of Miss Mitchell's favorites: "Whatever is worth doing is worth doing well."

This was the motto that had guided her life, shaped her as a person and a professional, making her conscientious and excellent at her job. In all these years working at Willard Parker among a whirling constellation of bacteria, she had stayed healthy and disease-free by aspiring to "do well," and that meant assiduously following procedures.

Now as Sea View's superintendent of nurses, she was determined to pass on this principle of labor and worth to the Black nurses, to make them adept, accomplished professionals, first-rate caregivers attentive to every detail surrounding tuberculosis, that beautifully rendered bacteria designed for longevity and torment.

She would teach them everything about it, how its cell wall had a waxy coating that made it impervious to antibiotics, weak disinfectants, and desiccation, allowing it to hibernate in cool, dark places for months or sometimes years. She would remind them how it could hang in the air for hours, wandering here and there, waiting for someone to inhale it. And once inside the body, how the microbe meant business.

Miss Mitchell knew its trajectory well, how it slid down the windpipe and into the bronchi, tumbling deeper through the curving air passages into the bronchioles, and deeper still to the farthest edges of lungs, the alveoli, those tiny air sacs, where it burrowed and began feeding on the warm, oxygen-laden blood. This was a deadly disease but different from so many others: the plague, smallpox, yellow fever, typhoid, and influenza. Those came on swift and strong, raging wildly; in days, they caused pustules and rashes, boils, fevers, and peeling skin that maimed and dehumanized. They killed rapidly. But not tuberculosis; its microbes were patient and pervasive. They grabbed on to a lung, a vocal cord, a lymph node, a vertebra, the brain, or whatever organ they chose, and began reproducing slowly, once every twenty-four hours, a process that took twenty times longer than that of most other bacteria. This pace kept the developing disease hidden, letting its symptoms emerge over weeks or months instead of hours.

As the microbe continued cloning itself, producing more and more wriggling wormlike creatures that crawled over one another, pressing down on muscles and veins and boring into tissues and blood vessels, the body's immune system began to wear thin. With nothing to stop them, the microbes grew insatiable, unstoppable, invincible.

And at Sea View there was no escaping them.

They flowed from everything, the cups full of sputum coughed up and collected every day; the clots and thick and gooey expectorations hacked up by patients; the urine and vomit and open wounds; and the screams and sneezes and simple sighs. The average time to clean and care for a bedridden patient was three hours; that meant 180 minutes of continuous exposure every day. There was no room for error. If the nurses weren't vigilant, always on guard, the bacteria would happily consume them.

"Never let familiarity breed a lack of respect for the Tubercule Bacilli," Miss Mitchell would say, her face stern and her mouth enunciating the words, making certain the nurses registered them, understood them, wove them into the fabric of their being.

Despite their diligence, most of the nurses had tested positive for TB, but only a small fraction (5 to 12 percent) fell ill. For the rest, the bacteria remained dormant, held in check by the immune system. Although sometimes, for reasons unknown, the microbe escaped and began insinuating itself into a lung, a liver, a kidney, or a bone. To stave off illness, Miss Mitchell advocated building a robust immune system through her "systematic pattern of living," which included "wholesome food, at least a pint of milk a day," and "sufficient sleep." Most important was not becoming overly fatigued—a strange suggestion for nurses working double shifts. But a series of recent studies were challenging her ideas. Keeping nurses healthy required more stringent on-the-job protections.

Some hospitals began administering periodic TB tests, known as Mantoux tests, or biyearly lung X-rays. For J. Arthur Myers, a leading physician and staunch advocate for nurses, the tests and X-rays were progress, but still not enough. The best protection was isolating highly contagious patients and requiring them to wear masks when receiving care. During daily rounds, he advised all staff to wear gowns, gloves, and masks. But many hospitals, including those in New York, scoffed at his recommendations.

Bellevue's superintendent swore that frequent handwashing was enough to fend off tuberculosis, rendering gloves and face masks unnecessary. Miss Mitchell agreed, adding that except for very "specific instances like surgery," her training didn't include wearing masks. Daily mask use, she said, gave nurses a "false sense of security against the disease," making them complacent and relaxed around the bacteria.

The nurses found this reasoning egregious, an easy excuse used to perhaps disguise deeper, more sinister thoughts. Some suspected that Miss Mitchell and other city officials supported the old antebellum lies, fictions, put forth by now-dead doctors such as Samuel Cartwright.

A prominent Southern surgeon, physician, and scientist, Cartwright argued against germ theory but was best known for his die-hard pro-slavery ideas and invention of "Drapetomania," or "Runaway Slave Syndrome," a "disorder," he said, of enslaved Black people who desired freedom. He penned articles with wild claims: Science, he said, proved that Black people "had smaller brains, more sensitive skin, and over-developed nervous systems," and that they were less likely to catch tuberculosis, or "phthisis."

"Negroes are sometimes, though rarely afflicted with . . . phthisis," Cartwright declared, adding, "Phthisis is, par excellence, a disease of the sanguineous temperament, fair complexion, red or flaxen hair, blue eyes, large blood vessels. It is a disease of the master race and not of the slave race—it is the bane of the master race of men."

Although many saw Cartwright's theory as offensive, full of pseudoscience, it still held a surprising amount of traction in the medical community, then and now. At Sea View, Dr. Ornstein, the new director, had embarked on a long-term study using the Black nurses to ascertain whether Cartwright and others who supported him were correct.

His results would determine the fate of their safety.

Chapter 8

Elke

Early to Mid-1933

By 1933, Edna's train rides had turned bleak. Daily, people boarded, shuffling onto crowded cars, holding newspapers announcing how the Depression had wound itself tight around every state in America, leaving over 24 percent of the country unemployed and tens of thousands homeless. Leaning into each other, eyes wide, hands in gestures of disbelief, passengers talked about the headlines and articles, sometimes adding their own opinions.

Their voices rose, mingling with the noises of the train, the rumble and crack of wheels on the track and the grinding screech of brakes: Suicide rates were at an all-time high, schools were closing, and babies were starving. In the Midwest, dust storms were blotting out the sun, turning day to night, and in some places, people were killing snakes and hanging them, belly up, hoping the ancient folklore would work and bring rain. Others snubbed the snakes and hired rainmakers, charlatans who sent rockets of dynamite and nitroglycerine into the sky, believing the explosions would blast apart clouds and send down rain. But many turned to God; they went to church, fell on their knees, and prayed for rain and their souls in case it was the end-times.

Outside the train window, New York's passing landscape mirrored the talk inside. Neighborhoods once bustling with life now reeled from businesses gone dark and people out of work. Edna saw them: a woman holding the hand of a smudge-faced toddler, her face a portrait of worry; a group of hard-pressed men with heads down, shoulders slouched, milling about begging for work or food or anything at all. At the corners, more men gathered, sitting on wooden crates, cigarettes pinched between their lips, selling junk they'd found in alleys and shaftways. And along the riverbanks, under the bridges, and in parks, improvised neighborhoods sprang up.

Uptown, Central Park became home to a conglomerate of shacks known as "Depression Alley" or "Hoover Valley," named to mock former president Herbert Hoover, whose response to combating the Depression had been to replace government action with a good old-fashioned bootstrap mentality. These shanties, fashioned from cardboard, tin, old metal, newspapers, and whatever materials one found, stood beneath some of New York's most expensive buildings: the San Remo, the Majestic, and the Dakota.

The stately buildings with cantilevered terraces, high gables, spires, and gargoyles rose over the park. They were manned by white-gloved doormen who ushered people into open-air courtyards and lobbies with arched ceilings and marble floors. Inside their expansive apartments lived movie stars, art dealers, business tycoons, filmmakers, theater directors, and financiers who cringed at the view beyond their lavish drapes. "From their windows," wrote one journalist, "the 'Haves' may look on the humble houses of the 'Have Nots,'" and with a sweep of the curtain blot them out. But the "Haves" could not eliminate the miasma of sickness, the flus, pneumonia, dysentery, and tuberculosis that simmered and churned in the air, moving across the city and sickening thousands.

At Sea View, Edna felt the impact of the daily headlines and train talk as people of all races and creeds were delivered to the hospital. They arrived from the shantytowns, Harlem, lower Manhattan, and the surrounding neighborhoods, forcing her and her team to work around the clock.

Nurses moved through the crowded hallways, around the ambulatory patients, men and women strong enough to get dressed and walk unassisted. They usually came to Edna's ward for minor procedures that didn't take too long: wound drainage, post-op checkups, or getting stitches snipped out. When the procedures were over, they were taken back to their wards, and nurses updated charts while doctors readied themselves for the more complex patients, the ones in big wooden wheelchairs or gurneys lined up in the hallway.

They looked gaunt and sickly, and their bodies harbored burst appendixes, infected tonsils, broken bones, and bulging hernias. Barring any complications, they could leave the ward within a day or two. Edna enjoyed working with the patients who felt better quickly. They brought a much-needed feeling of hope, a sense that medicine could work, that it could fix people. But most who entered the second-floor surgical ward came with microbes dividing out of control. This was Elke, a young German girl whose chart read "critical."

Some years earlier, at twenty-two, Elke, following many Germans, had bought a one-way ticket to New York City. Fleeing economic woes, unemployment, poverty, and the rising power of Adolf Hitler, the failed art student from Austria, she hoped to carve out a better life for herself.

Before her face turned thin and sallow and her fingers arched into fists by her chest, Elke had worked in a millinery shop. Every day she stood behind the counter, her hands full of vigor plucking hats from stands and shelves for customers to try. As she handed them the hats, she told them about the designers who'd created the styles, many full of whimsy and femininity, to cheer people during the Depression.

All day long, the shop door opened and closed, and women came in asking to try on bonnets, berets, and tams. Some pointed at the stands showcasing gold turbans, perfect to wear with shimmering evening gowns; others asked for less flashy headwear, like shallow-crowned hats with small drooping brims finished off with veils and ribbons. A few opted for Marlene Dietrich's bold signature look, the French beret, a style that eventually got bigger, with jauntier angles. "Hats are more hilarious than ever this year," one designer declared. "If they don't vanquish the Depression, nothing will."

For Elke, nothing could vanquish the Depression. It had made her sick.

No one knew how it happened. Maybe the bacteria came from someone in the shantytowns or one of the thousands who rode the trains or loitered on the corners; maybe it slipped into her body from a customer who was asymptomatic or from someone in her boarding-house or the bakery—the possibilities were endless. But it didn't matter anymore. At some point, she had inhaled someone's exhalation, and the one microbe had settled on her lungs and birthed millions.

Edna took Elke's hand and pushed down on her inner wrist and detected a pulse so slight it felt like a tiny vibrating cord. She counted the beats, then placed Elke's hand back down across her stomach, and reached for her chart to record the number and the quality, clearly poor. Holding the chart, Edna began noting the texture of Elke's skin, chalky, then her scalp, dry; she looked at her eyes, ears, facial expression, and mental state, which appeared apathetic and depressed.

Over the last few years, Edna had treated Elke several times, hoping each one would be the last, but the disease always prevailed, grinding its way deeper into her already mangled lungs and returning her to Sea View. This time, if doctors couldn't stop the spread, she might never leave. Now, with her days of hats long gone, flicked to a faraway place in her memory, Elke waited for Edna to begin prepping her for a last-ditch surgery that might save her life.

In 1822, Dr. James Carson introduced using surgery to treat pulmonary tuberculosis. Knowing that TB thrived on oxygen, Carson suggested surgically collapsing the infected lung to cut off its oxygen supply. Without oxygen, Carson speculated, the "diseased part would be placed in a quiescent state"; in time, the germ would suffocate, and the patient would heal. After collapsing the lungs of animals, Carson, who viewed tuberculosis as a disease that "crops the flower of the human race," moved to a human trial, consisting of two men suffering grievously from the disease. Carson convinced a colleague to attempt a forced pneumothorax, a deliberate lung collapse.

Standing beside his surgeon friend, Mr. Henry Bickersteth, Carson watched as he cut between ribs six and seven, and made an "incision calculated to admit air freely into the chest." But instead of hearing the telltale hiss signaling the air passing into the chest and an imminent lung collapse, there came only silence and blood.

The first patient died a month after surgery; the second man hemorrhaged on the table and died two days later. After this, Carson gave up his work with tuberculosis, and his name fell into the annals of history for decades.

Sixty years later, in 1882, the year Koch discovered the TB bacilli, Dr. Carlo Forlanini, an Italian surgeon, believed that Carson was onto something but that his approach had been haphazard. Rather than puncture the chest wall with a knife, Forlanini began constructing a safer device, one that would pierce the lung but not injure it. The result was a simple apparatus relying on inserting a needle into the pleural cavity, the thin space between the membranes that line and surround the lungs. Once the needle entered the cavity, the device would send nitrogen through a tube, filling it with air and collapsing the lung. With no oxygen, the TB bacilli would starve and die, halting the spread of disease. It worked, and soon Forlanini's patients began to improve, bringing him success and leading to a new procedure, properly called "artificial pneumothorax."

As the procedure, done with a local anesthetic, became routine, nurses contended with the assortment of side effects. The pumped air often gathered under the armpits, causing agonizing gas, bloating, and severe arm pain lasting for seven to ten days. Then it began seeping out of the puncture hole. While patients walked or slept, smoked or talked or played cards, their bodies leaked air and made strange whistling, tooting, or hissing noises. Once it was gone, patients returned for a "pneumo-refill." Some were "refilled with air" over a hundred times. But while many celebrated the procedure for its quick and excellent results, there were enough opponents, skeptics who believed doctors inserted the needle too quickly, tearing membranes, lacerating lungs, and puncturing the heart. Fully conscious patients suffered seizures, shock, loss of consciousness, and sometimes death.

There were also secondary complications, including hemorrhages from the chest wall, fluid buildup, air underneath the skin, neuralgia, skin infections, and pleurisy, an inflammation of the membranes surrounding the lungs.

Arguments arose that Forlanini's device was "the most dangerous weapon ever placed in the hands of a physician." But criticisms failed to stop its rise. By 1930, Sea View doctors had performed three thousand pneumothorax procedures a year; by 1935, the annual number would reach over 30,000.

If artificial pneumothorax therapy failed, doctors resorted to other surgeries that punctured and pierced and sliced the flesh in a more intrusive manner: cutting into nerves, paralyzing diaphragms, and stuffing wax packs into chest cavities. All those paled beside the thoracoplasty.

In this two- or sometimes three-part operation, surgeons aimed to permanently collapse one lung by altering the rib cage, the main structure of the chest protecting the diaphragm, liver, heart, and lungs. After making a long incision, starting at the base of the neck, continuing downward along the border of the shoulder blade, and ending under the armpit, surgeons reached inside the body and clipped out rows of ribs, sometimes eight or nine.

Without ribs, the pleural cavity, housing the fluid needed to keep the lungs lubricated and functioning optimally, becomes disrupted and subsequently causes the lung to collapse. Now with the lung flat and empty of oxygen, the microbes would begin to starve and die away.

Elke's doctors hoped for this outcome. Edna wasn't so sure.

Although thoracoplasty worked, it often brought a cascade of complications; cardiorespiratory issues, sepsis, hemorrhage, tears in the pleura, postoperative shock, surgical-wound infections, and anoxemia, low oxygen that could lead to death; many of these were common in patients too sick and too weak to recover from such a severe operation. And Elke was very sick and frail. The surgery was a bad idea. There would be an infection or a hemorrhage or heart issues or some other complication, perhaps deadly.

If Edna could speak her mind, she might ask them to stop and wait until Elke was a little stronger. Although she understood Elke might never get stronger. It was an ethical dilemma, one she faced all the time, having to prep patients for surgeries that might kill them.

Chapter 9

Vows

Summer 1933–Spring 1934

Every two weeks was payday, and Edna and her friends traded out their uniforms for colorful dresses with cinched waists and easy-flowing skirts. They cast aside their thick white tights in favor of silk stockings and swapped their nurse's shoes for round-toed oxfords. Some put on blush and eyeshadow in deep violet or gold and used a pencil to line their eyebrows, making them more dramatic; almost all wore a touch of lipstick. After picking up their checks from the administration building, they walked outside to catch the R111.

On the bus, they squeezed into the tiny seats, angling their heads toward one another to better hear the conversations about boyfriends, or hopes to find one, parents and siblings, their "tired feet," patients who called, "Nurse, Nurse," all day long, Miss Mitchell, upcoming teas, and sports, especially baseball. Many were avid fans of either the Yankees, Edna's team, or the Brooklyn Dodgers, and as the bus rattled along the uneven street picking up passengers who sneered at them, they compared and debated starting lineups and previous seasons and made predictions about the postseason.

"The Yankees were the best team," Edna would say with a slight grin, never failing to mention their stars, Lefty Gomez and Lou Gehrig, who made history in June 1932 by hitting four home runs in one game.

And Babe Ruth, the "Sultan of Swat," who during Game 3 of the 1932 World Series at Chicago's Wrigley Field stood at home plate and, amid a frenzied crowd, held up two fingers, pointed toward the center field bleachers, then stepped into the batter's box, lifted his bat, and—*crack*—sent Charlie Root's curveball soaring four hundred feet into the air, passing the flagpole and landing in the precise spot he'd gestured. Who could ever forget that?

A mile from Sea View, at Meiers Corner, the nurses stepped off and walked to Reiman's Hardware Store, a neighborhood staple. All day people opened and closed the pockmarked screen door, coming in to buy tools, paint, pots, cleaning products, utensils, sponges, and keys from Mr. Max J. Reiman, a short, brown-eyed man who loved his pipe. Standing in front of a wall lined with hundreds of tiny drawers full of screws, nails, drill bits, and more, he rang the register, checking out customers and cashing paychecks for the nurses, many of whom were wary of using banks.

Mr. Reiman held a soft spot for the nurses, and although at forty he wasn't much older than many of them, he saw himself as a protector, a father figure. A child of German Jewish immigrants, he had grown up in Harlem in the late nineteenth and early twentieth centuries, when it was mostly an Italian, German, and Jewish neighborhood. Entrenched in the Jewish community, he was raised with the old-world values of charity, good deeds, and fighting against injustice and discrimination. And here, with Jim Crowism scattered all over the island, he was in a position to put those values to work.

From behind the counter, he kept watch on the locals, people he'd known for years: neighbors, churchgoers, do-gooders, teachers, and grandmothers who volunteered their time knitting blankets for orphans but didn't hesitate to cast derisive glances at or step away from the Black nurses when they entered. From the aisles where they shopped, he heard their chatter, drifting above toilet plungers and fans, brooms and irons and axes, about barring the nurses from moving to the island:

"Not on my street."

"We won't let them."

"Can you think of what will happen?"

He didn't tell the nurses about these things, although he imagined they heard them. Instead, he treated them to cold Coca-Colas, and while they drank, he talked baseball stats or regaled them with stories of his earlier life in Harlem, where he had lived on 129th Street, blocks from Edna. The nurses were grateful for his support, and when they finished their Cokes, they thanked him. As they made their way out, holding his pipe in one hand, he leaned over the counter and hollered after them "to call if they needed anything."

Some nurses got back on the R111 bus and went to the St. George Theatre to watch Shirley Temple tap her way across the big screen, or to the pier by the ferry port to see the majestic views of lower Manhattan and watch the sunset and the city lights flicker to life. Others liked to go out. They boarded the ferry and headed to Harlem to eat and dance. Sometimes Edna rode with them but split off in Harlem, going home to her boarding room, where the elevated train passed so close to her window that she could see the passengers. On rare occasions, she joined the nurses, who glimpsed her more playful side.

They all loved the Savoy Ballroom on Lenox Avenue between 140th and 141st Streets. The club spanned the entire block, and its flashing marquee and strings of small globe lights, hundreds of them illuminating the roof, were visible for blocks and blocks. The poet Langston Hughes called it the "heartbeat of Harlem" because the pulse and thrum went on all night. And unlike some of the other glitzy clubs, it welcomed Black people.

Inside the grand lobby, with its pink walls and cut-glass chandeliers, the nurses nudged their way through the crowds, grabbing hands and weaving their way up the marble staircase to the second floor, where they ducked into the ladies' room. Amid a flurry of women, they peered close into the mirror and touched up their lipstick and hair and then entered the ballroom.

Stepping onto the ten-thousand-square-foot dance floor, known as "the Track," they joined thousands of people—the club's capacity was four thousand—lindy-hopping to the raw, swinging rhythm of the flamboyant Fess Williams and His Royal Flush Orchestra or Chick Webb, who loved competing in band contests. The nurses spent hours dancing under the colored lights, holding hands, tucking and twirling, their skirts swinging and whirling, with the tragedies of Sea View—its smells and blood, the indignation of patients, their pain and end-of-life wishes—fading away.

On one of those nights in 1933, Edna's life changed. A mutual friend introduced her to Forest Ballard, a debonair, smooth-talking longshoreman who worked intermittently on the Brooklyn docks. Lean, standing about five feet six, with dark brown eyes and a slight scar on his lower left cheek, he had impeccable style, wearing double-breasted suits and spit-shined shoes from Stacy Adams, a popular brand for men looking "to set trends, not chase them." He finished every outfit with a Stetson hat, a felt fedora in black or brown that he wore proudly, snapped tight over his right eye. The night he met Edna, he took his hat off and leaned forward, a gesture that left the often-restrained nurse smitten.

Originally from Virginia, Forest had come north for work some years before Edna. "He brought a suitcase full of hopes and grand dreams," she said. But they slowly fizzled as the Depression grew. Now every day Forest hauled the remnants of those dreams to the Brooklyn piers, where he hoped to find work.

With almost two thousand piers spread across seven hundred miles of shoreline, New York Harbor cleared about ten thousand oceangoing ships a year. Handling the 150 tons of cargo entering the city required over thirty-five thousand longshoremen. The job was grueling and dangerous, especially for men with slighter builds like Forest.

Cargo, no matter how rough or burdensome, was loaded and un-loaded by hand, using the most elementary inclines, pulleys, and winches. The job required cooperation between teams of men who pushed and pulled together. But in twentieth-century New York, working collaboratively was a fraught proposition.

The Italians hated the Irish, the Irish disliked the Germans, the Germans detested the Poles, and almost all shunned Black people. Often there was little cooperation, resulting in vulgar, verbal fights and, worse, accidents. While unloading bales of textiles or sacks of coffee or barrels of liquor, longshoremen regularly lost fingers, toes, legs, and arms, and sometimes their lives. Slipping off the catwalks was a genuine risk; so was being crushed by falling cargo. Back injuries and pulled muscles were par for the course. Forest, so far, had remained unscathed. But finding work was tough.

The New York docks were a world unto themselves, ruled by mob bosses from the different ethnic groups. The Irish and Italians reigned, controlling several docks and reserving the best jobs for their own. Mob bosses like "Socks" Lanza and Louis "Lepke" Buchalter, along with "syndicate killers" Albert "Mad Hatter" Anastasia and his brother Anthony "Tough Tony," had infiltrated dock unions, governing them with impunity. Those men hoping to penetrate their stronghold arrived in their news caps and worn sweaters at sunrise.

In the soft shadows of morning, the bosses gathered the scores of men for "shape-up" and began choosing their workers. Most overlooked Black men, and for Forest and his fellow Black longshoremen, the "shape-up" process recalled another version of the slave market, leaving him without work and feeling degraded.

Although Black men were represented in Local 968, the International Longshoremen's Association, there was no Black union rep at the New York district level. Without advocates, they weren't guaranteed work, and those who were chosen by the bosses got "every lousy job that had to be filled because white workers wouldn't do it," said I. Philip Sipser, a lawyer representing Local 968. Boats with banana shipments, Sipser said, were considered "Black cargo," because "there were rats as big as cats down there [and the] the stink was terrible." Forest had unloaded more than his fair share of bananas.

The pay was awful as well. Depending on the cargo, pier work in New York City paid between $1 and $1.95 an hour, unless you were a Black man. Then you banked about 95 cents an hour, and after paying the required kickback, or "contribution," to mob bosses for future work that rarely happened, the total was less. A Black longshoreman summed up the experience: "You know what it is to be a Negro on these docks?" he said. "It's to be a nigger again. To the boss, you're a nigger. To the guy next to you, you're a nigger. And to yourself, you're a nigger. That's the worst part of being a Negro on the docks."

Forest and his fellow longshoremen sought refuge from the daily degradation in the underground pool halls, where they commiserated, hoping to make a quick buck playing "sociable." He wasn't a shark, but he was good at fast-moving games that involved slight hustles for fast winnings—nine balls, one-pocket, bank pool, and rotation.

Edna didn't like the pool halls or his unsteady work, and his eighth-grade education was no match for her professional degree, but she enjoyed his laid-back temperament and his love for life. And he was funny. In many ways, he balanced her, and she recognized the hustle in him, a rush that called up shades of her preacher father, who'd spent his life scrambling to get ahead.

The two also shared a love of jazz music, dancing, card games, and baseball. On her days off, they took the elevated train to 161st Street to watch the Yankees. At the game, Forest treated her to a hot dog and a soda, and they passed the afternoon sitting in the bleachers, cheering the world champs.

Sometimes they joined her friends and went to the Savoy. But as their relationship grew more serious, Edna preferred the smaller, cozier jazz clubs where three-piece bands played. The intimacy allowed her and Forest to sit at a small cocktail table and lean into each other, their voices mixing with the darkness of a note. Afterward they often stopped at one of the many storefront restaurants on Lenox Avenue that served late-night food to go. Sometimes if it was warm, they sat on a stoop and ate and huddled together watching the avenue buzzing with cars and limousines and cabs, ferrying white partygoers back and forth. For Edna, those late-fall nights in 1933 when their hands were greasy with food and they sat together among the reverie, as if no one else existed, were magical.

So were Sunday afternoons.

Edna loved taking long strolls in the park and around the streets of Harlem, but they took on a fresh feeling with Forest. Holding her hand, he would lead her through the crowds and deepening cold with ease, and his nonchalance about everything—the pace, all the people, the weather—soothed her. They window-shopped and stopped for lunch, but Edna's favorite thing was seeing all the churches.

There were over 140 scattered across 140 square miles, and two-thirds were in storefronts or the ground floor or back room of private homes. On Sundays, they sprang to life, and the sounds of worship spilled onto the streets. The shouts, foot stomps, and handclaps re-called the days Edna's father stood at the altar, rousing people to lift their arms and praise the Lord with alleluias and amens.

But Forest would never meet Edna's parents, Amy or Richmond. Both had recently died, leaving Edna with a gnawing grief that would allow some years to pass quietly and others to torment her with memories, reminding her that her mother and father were dead.

Almost overnight, she went from having two parents to none. One morning after the New Year in 1934, Edna learned that her father had gone to sleep and had never woken up. Unable to take time off, Edna was forced to mourn the father she adored from afar. It was hard to fathom that he was gone, that she would not see the priest blessing his body and pray as it was lowered into the dark, damp earth. She shared with Forest how strange it was that R.V.'s voice was now silent.

To hear his words reading from the holy book, she thought of saying to Forest, was transcendent. But she didn't. Forest had little interest in religion, and stories of jealous brothers and naked people in a garden, who were eventually smitten by the God who'd created them, made little sense to him. But in the years to come, while she walked to church and Forest stayed home, she would always wonder whether R.V. could have changed Forest's perception about God and faith.

Less than two months after R.V. died, on March 1, a blustery 27-degree day, Edna's sister called. Their mother had died. This time, Edna was able to take a few days off and travel to Pittsburgh for the funeral.

On the almost four-hundred-mile ride through Pennsylvania, Edna thought of her mother. Amy as a domestic, carrying buckets of water, scouring and scrubbing and washing, the scent of lye and lavender and rosemary emanating from her skin. Amy as a nurturer, nursing babies and stoking the flames of the potbellied stove to keep them warm. Amy as a healer, standing in the kitchen and tossing blossoms and roots and herbs from the garden into the mortar and grinding, her wrist twisting and turning like it did on the washboard, then giving the blends to her children to heal stomachaches, head-aches, bruised bones, and wounded skin. Amy as a wife, dutiful, loving, ironing trousers and shirts and sublimating her desires so R.V. could fulfill his. Amy, who had learned how vows could break a woman and conveyed to her daughters to become educated and independent, to follow their dreams and then marry.

In Pittsburgh, Edna walked up the steep and narrow street of the Hill District to her sister Annie's house, where she joined the rest of her family, her siblings, aunts and uncles, nephews, and three-year-old niece, Virginia Allen. A precocious and delightful child, Virginia wanted to be a nurse and barraged her aunt with questions about sickness and uniforms. Americus had come too, traveling from DC, with Samuel and Florence.

Over the course of the grief-filled days between making funeral arrangements and doing all the things one needed to bury the dead, the sisters talked. Americus was almost fourteen, practically a young woman. Her presence, her youth, her promise epitomized how quickly time passed, how separation and missed memories were the cost of this movement, this Great Migration.

Looking at Americus, Edna noticed how nothing of the little girl remained. Soon to be a freshman at Dunbar High School, one of the best Black high schools in the country, Americus now had definitive thoughts and ideas and dreams of her own. She loved the sciences and was considering studying nursing, and she also loved fishing.

Samuel was an angler and belonged to a fishing club. Three times a week, he went out on the Anacostia River and fished for blue catfish and bass, and he often took Americus. On the dock or in the boat, waiting for the fish to bite, Samuel talked about hooks and hanging bait and their family. When they returned home with their catch, Florence showed Americus how to clean and freeze the fish. Eventually Americus would become a master at catching and cooking fish, inspiring Edna to start a fishing club on Staten Island.

The talk shifted, as talk does at family gatherings, and someone asked Edna about her job and if she was afraid of getting sick. She didn't tell them she already had tuberculosis; that months after arriving, she had tested positive and that the disease was sitting latent in her lungs, waiting for the moment to become active.

The hours passed and night fell, and inside, dust swirled in the lamplight illuminating the room where the sisters sat talking, crying, and then laughing, sharing memories of Amy and R.V. and of Savannah.

Remember the bedroom?

The kitchen?

And the smell of Amy's cookies? We all loved her cookies.

And what about Edna performing The Merchant of Venice *for the school play?*

And West Thirty-Eighth Street and the neighbors—the Gilmores and McTyres.

Were they still there?

And what about Theodosia?

Did she remarry?

Weren't her children all grown now?

The night wore on, and they kept talking, recalling school choirs, Sunday picnics, their father, and Amy. She had buried two children and worked all day to support R.V.'s dream.

She didn't mind the sacrifice.

Really?

She had given up so much.

Had she?

Remember how she crossed her ankles when she sewed R.V.'s clothes?

Or the glint of light catching on the clothes she hung with precision in the backyard?

How the years had slipped away.

Sitting with her sisters and recalling their past brought Edna joy, a comfort that blunted the pain of their collective loss, but she disliked such memories. Too often, moments were taken out of context, out of the larger whole; the fear was forgotten, sentimentalized, and the moment became worthy of a joyous recollection, like the play.

Yes, Edna remembered it, but that was the year World War I started and Savannah sent its Black men to fight, young boys she knew who returned home without a hero's welcome. Of course she recalled Amy crossing her ankles; it also happened when she sewed for the white people. And in the early part of the century, before her sisters were born, she couldn't forget how the KKK had paraded through Savannah in full regalia carrying burning crosses.

Days later, Edna stood graveside, surrounded by her sisters, and buried her face in her hands and wept. She cried for the mother whose service went unheeded; for the woman whose dreams remained looped inside her and who, in her quiet way, had influenced her daughter as much as R.V. had.

For Edna, the firstborn, who had witnessed all her siblings come into the world, being together was bittersweet. The years had aged and changed them. Annie's cooking job had worn her down, her sister Mary also looked exhausted, and Americus was different. She no longer needed Edna in the same way. These were the truths Edna would take back with her, realities she would reckon with for a long time on Staten Island.

❖

On a freezing Saturday, three weeks after Amy's funeral, Edna and Forest boarded a downtown train to city hall, where a justice of the peace married them. It was a simple affair, no fancy dress or band or cake, just two witnesses, her friend from Sea View and Forest's sister. Edna was happy, even though she believed that Forest "lacked a lot of common sense and money slipped out of his hands." But at heart, she said, "he was a good man," and he had no qualms about Americus living with them one day.

For now, the newlyweds would live in Edna's small boarding room to save money for the house she had promised her sister. After returning from Pennsylvania, where time seemed to have swallowed years, the hands of the clock spinning into a blur, Edna became more determined to make owning a home a reality. How it would happen, she still didn't know, and now that she was living with Forest, new realities emerged. She noticed how little he worked and how much time he spent shooting pool with his friends Mump Fudge and Dirty Johnson—men who had a nickname for her new husband: "Snake."

Chapter 10

❖

The Thoracoplasty

March 1934

At Sea View in the nurses' dressing room, Edna and her team began prepping for surgery. In the small space, the women moved around silently, each focusing on the task at hand. One flipped her wrists and unfurled a gown; another in a cap and mask counted gauze pads, which she passed to her colleague, who stacked them in neat piles.

Edna stood at the sink holding a soapy scrub brush and began moving it over the creases of her palms, in between her fingers, and under her nails, counting the minutes as if Miss Mitchell were standing behind her. While scrubbing, she considered the instruments she would handle in the operating room and pushed aside any pre-op doubts, those "what if . . . ?" and "did I . . . ?" moments that wormed their way into the psyche of many nurses prior to surgery.

All of them always checked and rechecked their work, but certain pieces of equipment nagged at them, especially the bone-cutting tools and the cannulas, long tubes used for irrigating and draining a surgical site. These were difficult to clean; they accrued micro-remains of human tissue, pieces of bone, hair, or fecal matter, all fodder for pathogens to fester and potentially infect a patient. If that happened, many surgeons immediately blamed the nurses, scolding them and calling them "saboteurs" and "slovens."

Edna rinsed her hands, and one worry replaced the others: Miss Mitchell.

After five years, the men running Sea View and the Department of Hospitals had finally recognized her dedication to make the hospital top-notch at whatever cost. Their approval brought her peace of mind, job security, and an enhanced confidence to exert her power, sometimes indiscriminately.

Recently, she had embarked on a firing spree, purging the ranks of nurses. It was "distinctly an advantage to have the turnover in personnel," she wrote in the annual report to Sea View's medical superintendent. Some nurses had left of their own accord, but many, she explained, had lost interest in Sea View and "were requested to leave." Those who were fired, she continued, "were unwilling to cooperate with the new regime," one focused on training outstanding nurses, experts in tuberculosis, who would have long careers here at Sea View.

Edna could not afford a single misstep.

She dried her hands, pulled on her gloves, and pushed open the double doors leading to the operating room. It was bright, submerged in sunlight that gushed through the immense window, whose glass curved upward toward the ceiling and melded with the skylight. Her eyes took a moment to adjust to the rays gleaming off the white tiles, the metal basins and bowls, and the young woman who was lying anesthetized on the narrow steel slab with an endotracheal tube protruding from her mouth. It was Elke.

She was turned on her left side and held in place by four-inch adhesive strips that passed over her buttocks and attached to the table. Earlier nurses had draped her body in sheets, leaving only a large patch of exposed skin on the upper right side, where the surgeon would operate. It was bound by towels, clamped to the bare skin that a nurse was cleaning with different topical antiseptics: benzoin, followed by ether, then alcohol, and finally two coats of picric acid, a pale yellow antiseptic.

As the nurse stepped away from Elke, holding the used gauze pads soaked in antiseptics, the surgeon moved forward, a cue for Edna to take her place beside him. Standing there, she gave a final glance at the instruments lying on the different trays: scissors, trocars, and elevators, used for scraping and dissecting bones; retractors, heavy L-shaped instruments for holding back organs and tissues; rongeurs, for gnawing holes in bones; mouth gags and bone cutters and rib cutters, whose tips were molded into shapes that resembled steel beaks.

Seeing them lined up, their handles and blades and tips glistening in the light, excited and unsettled her. Each one was symbolic of medicine's progress but also of its stagnation, a reminder that tuberculosis still lacked drugs, that opening the body and whittling out the illness remained the only option.

The surgeon leaned his head toward Elke and Edna blotted out the world, focusing all her energy on his hands. "Scalpel," he said.

Edna had already picked it off the tray; now she placed it in his hand, which was covered by a thick black rubber glove. It had a sinister look, otherworldly, inhuman, and appeared a strange contrast to the life-preserving effort it was undertaking and to its curious history of romance and love.

Some forty-four years earlier, in 1890, Dr. William Halsted, chief of surgery at Johns Hopkins and a proponent of aseptic techniques, hired a scrub nurse, Miss Caroline Hampton. Halsted had stringent rules for working in the operating room, including that hands be disinfected with mercuric chloride, now known to have toxic effects and cause corrosive injury, gastrointestinal issues, renal failure, and death. Fortunately, Hampton, who followed her boss's request, developed only a severe case of dermatitis on her arms and hands, but the rash and peeling skin were enough to render the junior nurse unable to work. The news devastated Halsted, who'd fallen in love with his talented young nurse. In an effort to solve the problem, he asked the Goodyear Tire & Rubber Company to make thin rubber gloves with gauntlets.

The gloves arrived, and Halsted proposed and then gifted them to Hampton, who tested them out. Again and again, her hands remained rash-free following surgery. The two were overjoyed, celebrating not only their love but also what it had brought: the invention of rubber gloves. In the words of Halstead's assistant, "Venus came to the aid of Aesculapius." Soon after, rubber gloves became the standard for doctors and nurses, but unlike modern latex surgical gloves, these gloves were not disposable, and in between uses, nurses were given the arduous task of cleaning them.

Days ago, before Elke's surgery, Edna had sterilized the gloves and then checked for holes and minute tears by blowing into them. Slowly, she watched as her breath inflated each glove, the palm and fingers growing bigger, stretching and swelling, expanding like a bloated hand. When she was done, she had listened for leaky air. Nothing. The glove had remained full. But as she watched the surgeon's hands moving closer to the bare skin, preparing to slice into Elke, the usual fear arose: What if there were a tiny hole, one invisible to the naked eye, that would allow bacteria to pass through and enter the girl's body? Germ transmission through gloves happened all the time.

It was too late now—the knife came down some centimeters from Elke's neck, and in a swift motion continued moving along the perimeter of her shoulder blade, curving just under the armpit and then stopping. The skin sprang apart. Blood. There was always so much blood. It spilled forth from the capillaries and arterioles, and multiple nurses rushed over, holding forceps with gauze pads soaked in 110-degree saline solution. They stuffed the pads into the incision and clamped off blood vessels to stop the bleeding.

After separating the skin, the surgeon cut through the connective tissue and arrived at the rib cage.

"Bone clamp," he said, and then inserted it into the incision and seized a rib.

"Rib cutter." He clasped it without looking and deftly maneuvered the tool with its beaklike tip deep inside, past the wall of muscles being held back by a retractor, toward the base of rib 4. Once there, he opened the tip and with force pressed the handle.

The snap of bone echoed into the sterile, white-walled room; he repeated the procedure for ribs 3, 2, and 1. As each one slipped away from its juncture, leaving behind a knob of bone, he placed it on a tray, where the growing pile resembled a sequence of shrinking crescent moons. After snipping out the final one, he cut out the stumps of remaining bone and removed any clots and tissue fragments from the incision. Nurses doused the wound with ether to prevent infection, and he inserted a drainage tube.

Edna checked the time. Almost twenty-five minutes had passed; it was astonishing how a rib cage that took years to reach adult form could be dismantled that quickly. Imagine what might happen in an hour or two or three.

"Sutures," said the surgeon.

Edna handed him the sutures from a glass tube stamped "Catgut with Needle"—a misnomer, as they really came from sheep or cow intestines. Taking the needle, he reached back into the incision and began stitching the muscles. When he finished, Edna handed him a thinner strand of sutures, "Catgut 1," and watched as he hooked the needle into the skin and pulled the string through the flesh. He repeated the motion over and over, moving the needle down the long gash and leaving behind a trail of brownish stitching.

It was a sloppy job; the stitches were too wide apart. Sewing like that on a garment would have split the seams. Edna's mother had taught her the importance of alignment, of making small, evenly placed stitches on fabric to create a clean and balanced effect. If Edna had become a surgeon, she would not have sewn so recklessly.

With the top half of her ribs gone and gauze bandages covering a shoddily stitched-together wound, Elke was wheeled to the recovery room, where Edna would stay with her for the next twelve hours, refilling her IV drip and making sure her pulse and respiration and oxygen counts were stable.

Every half hour she took Elke's blood pressure and roused her to try to cough and spit so that her body wouldn't fill with mucus and blood. Elke tried, and with every breath, her face crumpled from a searing pain. Edna wished she could give her a painkiller, but their effect on the body caused the respiratory tract to narrow, and so patients were forced to endure hours and hours of postoperative pain without any drugs.

In the days following surgery, Edna tended to her. Every afternoon, in the light of the setting sun, Elke appeared almost healthy. But up close, her face had the color and texture of finely ground chalk, and when Edna lifted the sheet, her body looked old and ravaged and broken. Bones jutted in sharp geometric angles, and her skin was thin and mottled, like aged butterfly wings.

One afternoon, while preparing to change her bandage, Edna noticed Elke's chest heaving, wheezing, laboring to breathe, and the gauze was saturated in a grayish-yellow liquid, purulent drainage. She took scissors from her cart, slipped her finger between the top of the gauze and the skin, and began snipping it down the middle, each cut letting loose the stench of infection.

Pulling apart the bandage, she saw the long, swooping wound snaking across Elke's right side. It was swollen and bright red, and the crooked, sloppy stitches had grown taut, inuring themselves into the skin. Long red streaks trailed from the edges of the incision; they moved across her belly toward the lymph nodes in her groin. Heat emanated from the infected skin. Edna knew it was strep.

Underneath a microscope, *Streptococcus pyogenes* was beautiful, appearing like a strand of broken pearls. But uncontained, it was deadly. The bacteria lurked almost everywhere—in dirt, skin, nasal passages, and unsterilized instruments—and was easily passed on from the hands, nasal secretions, and contaminated food sources. Most strains were harmless, but a handful weren't. Those baffled doctors.

Unlike tuberculosis, strep replicated with lightning fastness. Scratches easily became skin infections or, worse, cellulitis, an infection of the subcutaneous tissue. In the blood, the germ caused sepsis, which often led to multi-organ failure. In the 1920s, Europe and North America saw over 1.5 million yearly deaths from strep-related illnesses. If Elke's infection spread, it could set off a bacterial brushfire, sickening the entire ward; inevitably, the surgeon and Miss Mitchell would cast the blame on some nurses, including Edna.

She called a doctor, who removed the stitches, and then Edna began cleaning the wound with gauze soaked in Dakin's solution, a diluted bleach used to kill bacteria and viruses, and azochloramide, a powerful germicide. Her hands moved gently across the raised line running down Elke's upper right side, but every touch caused a milky-colored pus mixed with blood to ooze out. The young woman flinched and shuddered and squeezed her eyes tight, as if the gesture could magically erase the pain.

Edna saw her reaction, but kept going, sliding the gauze around Elke's navel, her concave stomach, and the indented area where her ribs once sat. When she was done, she repeated the process with picric acid, the yellow antiseptic, swabbing the area until Elke's right side was the color of a brilliant sunset. Then she covered it with alcohol-soaked towels. The work was a formality, a token gesture. Aside from an antibacterial drug that didn't exist in America, nothing could stop the catastrophe unraveling inside Elke's body.

Edna pulled up the sheet, readjusted the pillows, and sat down. At this point, Edna would have called Elke's parents, telling them to come, to bring a holy man or just themselves. They could have stayed long into the night saying goodbye to their daughter. But they were in Europe. No one would come for Elke, whose mind was reeling, her years of life distorting and falling away at dizzying speeds.

The dying girl looked at Edna. She wanted water, but the words wouldn't form. They flitted around her tongue. A jumble of syllables and consonants, nouns and verbs and adjectives, crashed together. She tried to talk, but the words melted into a low gurgling sound.

Edna took hold of Elke's hand, feeling the fingers that were once agile, that held books and pens and all those pretty hats. She clutched it tight, fastening the young girl to her, to this place, this life. If she could have, with this simple gesture and her will, saved her, kept her in this world, magically made her heal, she would have, but Elke was called to die. Within hours, her body would fall into septic shock, and her organs would begin closing down: kidneys, liver, lungs, and heart. And the crooked stitches and deformed right side wouldn't matter anymore.

That night, Edna stayed beside Elke as she fell further away from the living. Soon her mother would find out and feel that unimaginable sorrow of loss, of infinite mourning, of waking and remembering that her baby, her daughter, was no longer there, that she would never come back.

And here at Sea View, word of her death would trickle down to the administration building, and the clerk would turn the pages of the oversize registry, find Elke's name, and then, beside it, end her story by penning a single word: *deceased.*

Chapter 11

❖

The Movement

April–October 1934

The trees were already blooming around New York City in April 1934, but in Harlem, few took note. Many, including Edna, were hard-pressed to celebrate the coming season. All around her, things seemed bleak. Landlords tacked eviction notices onto doors with impunity, and utility companies worked round the clock shutting off gas and electricity, plunging thousands of residents into darkness.

In the papers, and everywhere Edna went, people with anxious eyes and furrowed brows talked about the churches running out of money and shutting down their soup kitchens, the social workers who arrived from the Department of Child Welfare to take children away from parents who couldn't care for them, and the skyrocketing unemployment: over fifty thousand Harlem residents, more than half the Black population, were out of work, including Forest.

Jobs once known as male "Negro jobs"—elevator operators, barbers, bellboys, waiters, janitors—now went to white men. The utilities and transportation companies also announced they were hiring only white men. Now, people said, "any job was a white man's job."

Black women were also struggling, as white women snatched up their domestic jobs. Desperate for work, groups of Black women gathered on the corners of Walton and Jerome Avenues in the Bronx for the daily "slave market." They arrived between 8:00 a.m. and 1:00 p.m., in rain or snow or boiling heat, and waited by the Woolworth's and Jack Fines Men's Clothing store to "barter for 'slave wages'" with the wealthy white housewives, the "madams."

Wearing chic dresses and high-heeled shoes, the madams walked in front of the Black women, appraising them like they would "a pig or a cow."

"Let me see your hands. Now your knees," the housewives would command, looking closely for rough hands and knees, an indication that the women had experience with washboards and scrubbing floors. Then, "How much?"

It was a rhetorical question, meant to mock the Black women. They all knew the madam set the price, usually about ten or fifteen cents an hour. And sometimes, after a day's work, the madam refused to pay the women and sent them home home empty-handed. The city knew about the slave market, but no one cared enough to stop it.

The medical field was also in flux.

White nurses were leaving private-duty careers in increasing numbers to work on hospital staffs, and in turn, preventing Black nurses from advancing. Edna saw it firsthand. Three years into her tenure at Sea View, almost none of her colleagues had received promotions, and working conditions had become unsustainable.

To start, Miss Mitchell was having problems finding nurses to replace those she had fired, casting the burden of keeping the wards running onto Edna and her colleagues, who were working consecutive double shifts in a place that compromised the health and well-being of their patients: springs snapped from beds, roofs leaked onto pillows, mice ran freely around the wards, food trays and linens were in short supply, and many handwashing basins needing replacing. How much longer could this go on? many started asking. And where could they go? All these problems extended beyond Sea View.

Across the harbor at Harlem Hospital, things were no better. The

NAACP had launched an investigation into Edna's old boss, Mrs. O'Brien, for discriminatory practices, endangering patients' lives, and failing to improve the working conditions of Black nurses. To support the NAACP, Harlem doctors, churchgoers, and activists reached out to Reverend Adam Clayton Powell Jr., who called for a mass demonstration.

Weeks later, almost five thousand Harlemites marched eight miles from the Abyssinian Baptist Church to city hall with a petition for Mayor John O'Brien (unrelated to Mrs. O'Brien), demanding Harlem Hospital remove its leaders and hire more Black staff. Their petition failed to sway the mayor, but the investigation into Mrs. O'Brien was successful.

She had lied about her nursing credentials, the NAACP learned. The white-haired superintendent had completed only two years of high school, rather than the four required to enter nursing school. She should be removed, the NAACP recommended, and if the city wanted to replace her, "there were far more qualified [Black] nurses who held MAs from Columbia" that could run the hospital.

City officials noted the complaint and notified Mrs. O'Brien. Silence. Until some months later when the dining room at Harlem Hospital, the one Salaria Kea had fought to desegregate years earlier, once again became segregated. Although Black nurses and Harlemites were incensed, they found a new hope in the recently inaugurated mayor, Fiorello H. La Guardia.

A charismatic Italian American lawyer, La Guardia had recently represented Harlem in the New York House of Representatives. Devoted to immigrant causes and labor rights, he became known as "the people's attorney." As mayor, he wanted to expand social welfare programs, including a minimum wage, worker's compensation, pensions, and rent control. When a reporter asked how the Democratic Party would achieve this, the take-charge mayor snapped: "There is no Democratic or Republican way of cleaning the streets."

For La Guardia, turning social welfare into a political game that pitted one party against another was preposterous. He vowed that his administration would create a "vital, new type of government . . . for the benefit of all the people." But for the moment, his concern was the Department of Hospitals, an organization awash in immorality and racial discrimination. To revamp it, he appointed a new commissioner, Dr. Sigismund Goldwater.

Leaders from the National Association of Colored Graduate Nurses had celebrated La Guardia's appointment of Goldwater. For them, it was an opportunity to reestablish relations and create lasting change. Eager for Goldwater to hear their demands firsthand, they scheduled their first regional conference in New York, at Lincoln Hospital, and extended invitations to him, La Guardia, the heads of Black nursing schools, the NAACP, and two white executives from the American Nurses Association (ANA); the guest list also included representatives from the Frances Payne Bolton Foundation, the Julius Rosenwald Fund, and the General Education Board.

Hundreds had attended the meeting held two months earlier, where speaker after speaker pointed out how Black nurses were *always* underpaid, bypassed for promotions, and denied entry to postgraduate courses at Bellevue and Kings County Hospitals. Most agreed that for any change to happen, the NACGN needed to be revitalized.

Presently, the organization was floundering, struggling with low membership, funding, and support, particularly from wealthy white donors, and it needed a closer working relationship with the ANA. Their cause struck a chord with philanthropist Frances Payne Bolton, heiress to the Standard Oil Company, who was revolted by the bigotry of city officials and the ANA.

She pledged her support to the NACGN and its quest to end exclusion by matching donations dollar for dollar. No one knew her motives for helping, but they inspired others. M. O. Bousfield, a Black physician and the associate director of the Julius Rosenwald Fund, joined Bolton and donated tens of thousands of dollars. The new funds allowed the NACGN to open a much-needed national headquarters at Rockefeller Center and hire a paid executive director, Estelle Massey Riddle, to spearhead the change.

Riddle, with her flawless sense of style and penchant for exquisite jewelry and hats, loved a challenge. She saw racial barriers as obstacles, hurdles to overcome, and in her brief career, her determination to conquer them was apparent in a résumé saturated by firsts. She was the first Black nurse to receive an MA in nursing education, the first Black instructor at Harlem Hospital, and the first director of nursing at Freedmen's Hospital in DC. By hiring her, the NACGN was banking on her patience, quiet tenacity, and impeccable negotiating skills to convince the ANA to admit Black nurses.

But she couldn't do it alone.

Mabel Keaton Staupers was well known in Harlem as a quick-thinking, bold woman with boundless energy that she poured into her work. Lillian Harvey, the former dean of nursing at Tuskegee, said that Staupers "wasn't afraid of anything or anyone." Years earlier, she had organized the Booker T. Washington Sanitarium and worked with the Harlem TB Association and forged hundreds of connections with politicians, doctors, and administrators; it was the kind of network the NACGN needed.

Riddle hired her, and together the two women formed a powerful team. Self-confident and politically savvy, they moved seamlessly between different Black and white organizations and were seen as "shrewd agents for social change within the profession of nursing." Their immediate priority was creating an alliance with the ANA. But the organization was reluctant to help them.

While some in the ANA supported integration, many members felt a partnership would jeopardize the organization's all-white autonomy. Alma Haupt, associate director of the National Organization for Public Health Nursing, expressed her concerns about racial integration to the ANA's board: "They have still such a long way to go,"

Haupt said of Black nurses. "Few of them ever sat on a committee and only a few know how to preside at a meeting."

The irrationality of the comment was overlooked, and Haupt continued, posing questions, some rhetorical and others designed to pull members into an ethical quagmire.

"Is our final objective to bring them in with us?" she asked, then responded with her own sentiments: "I think they would like to be included and be considered as professional equals—not social but professional—but they realize that is a long time in the future."

❖

Everyone was tired of waiting—NACGN members, Edna, and her colleagues. At Sea View and in Harlem, conversations moved from less pressing issues to the mounting fight for Black workers' equality happening in cities across America.

In late spring 1934, news from Chicago trickled into Harlem's papers. A new grassroots jobs campaign called "Don't Buy Where You Can't Work" was gaining traction. Black citizens, wanting to win back jobs during the Depression, began refusing to shop in white-owned businesses until they employed more Black workers. Through boycotts, picket lines, and community meetings, the movement had swayed some white business owners to hire Black workers.

Harlem leaders were inspired by the success in Chicago and launched their own "Don't Buy Where You Can't Work" movement with similar goals of persuading white businesses to hire Black workers for more prominent jobs such as cashiers, clerks, and salespeople. Almost overnight, thousands of leaflets were printed and slipped under doors and affixed to walls, bulletin boards, storefronts, and lampposts; people handed them out at subway stations and bus stops and on street corners.

Every day Edna and Forest and anyone else who walked through Harlem was handed another flyer, telling them where to shop and where to picket. On the boycott list were small drugstores, markets, and Woolworth's, whose manager swore that no Black person would ever serve at his counter. But the campaign's biggest focus was Blumstein's department store, a five-story art deco building on 125th Street, Harlem's most important thoroughfare.

In June 1934, *The New York Age* backed the movement to boycott Blumstein's, hoping to convince the manager to hire Black workers for clerical and sales positions. In scathing editorials, it targeted Mrs. L. M. Blumstein: "As a Jew," the paper said, "she is much concerned with Hitler's oppression of her people but . . . she oppresses the hell out of the Negroes."

Readers reacted, and soon Edna, on her way to work, saw the sidewalk in front of Blumstein's swell with hundreds of angry picketers holding signs and pleading with would-be shoppers to take their business elsewhere. New flyers begged "all self-respecting people in Harlem to REFUSE TO TRADE WITH L. M. BLUMSTEIN."

Twelve days later, facing a revenue loss exacerbated by the Depression, Mr. Blumstein agreed to hire fifteen Black women as clerks immediately and twenty more in the fall. Woolworth's, despite the manager's racist comments, followed suit, agreeing to hire thirty-five Black clerks. Harlemites celebrated the news with a parade. Over 1,500 people gathered in front of the Abyssinian Church and, despite the downpour, made their way triumphantly through Harlem.

Against this backdrop, where equal opportunity seemed possible, a twenty-four-year-old Black nurse from Atlanta, Miss Alyce Eugenia Greene, applied for postgraduate training at the prestigious Bellevue Hospital. Nurses clamored for admission to the highly competitive program, hoping to be accepted and broaden their qualifications, making them eligible for supervisory positions that offered higher pay, more power, and greater respect. Greene was a stellar student with all the right qualifications. There was no reason she should've been denied.

Weeks later, she opened the letter from the director: "At present there are no post-graduate courses in New York City for negro nurses.

I would advise you to make inquiries concerning such a course at St. Philip's Hospital, Richmond, Virginia."

Greene read the letter and refused to accept the decision. She wasted no time contacting the head of the NAACP, Walter White, a fellow Atlantean and fervent activist. White referred the matter to his secretary, Roy Wilkins, who wrote to Goldwater. Was there "any rule, custom, or tradition in the City of New York which excludes applicants for postgraduate nurse training on account of color?" Wilkins asked.

Goldwater, a sixty-one-year-old with a testy temperament and autocratic style of leadership, had a long history of serving in administrative positions in New York City. In the early part of the twentieth century, he headed Mount Sinai Hospital and in 1914 had been appointed commissioner of health. Now, with the Depression pushing municipal hospitals to an occupancy rate of 97 percent, Goldwater had a singular focus: to keep hospitals running. Although his more personal goal was to eventually shift the city's health priorities from epidemics such as tuberculosis and infant mortality toward chronic disease and elder care. Hospital integration was nowhere on his agenda.

Wanting to silence Wilkins's agitating and address the question of postgraduate nursing segregation, the Department of Hospitals organized a citywide meeting. They invited representatives from the ANA, all twenty-nine municipal hospitals, and the NACGN. In a New York City ballroom, Black and white nurses joined Goldwater and the representatives to hear the president of hospitals speak.

At the podium in front of a crowded room, the president justified why Black nurses were relegated to four hospitals. Integration would cause white nurses to quit, he explained, but there was another reason why Black nurses were sent to Sea View: "In twenty years," he said, "we won't have a colored problem in the United States of America because they'll all be dead of tuberculosis."

The words spun and fell and silenced the room.

From somewhere came a noise, a scrape of a chair that echoed, the sound causing people to crane their necks and look around. Eyes settled on twenty-one-year-old Salaria Kea, who during Edna's last month at Harlem Hospital had petitioned former mayor Jimmy Walker to desegregate the hospital dining room. She was at Sea View now, working as the head nurse in what she called the "no-return unit." With the same fierce tone she'd used to address Mayor Walker, Kea shouted at the smug man standing behind the podium.

"And *you* are trying to make the dead lie!"

Whatever Kea meant by the phrase is unclear, but the room erupted, applauding the courageous nurse, while the president stood motionless, saying nothing. The next day, Kea reported to work on Sea View's "no-return unit." Sometime midday, as she later recalled, her supervisor walked in and demoted her from head nurse to a desk job in the employee clinic. But her efforts to call out the racist comments of the president didn't go unnoticed. Thanks to Kea, Goldwater's bigotry and his refusal to address the president's remarks about hiring Black nurses to solve America's "colored" problem were splashed across the Black papers, prompting the NAACP to try to open an investigation into Goldwater and the Department of Hospitals; the effort failed.

Undeterred and wary of the same old story of bias from hospital officials, they vowed to keep Goldwater on their radar and wait for the right moment to strike.

Meanwhile, city leaders, responding to pressure from white business owners, passed a law in October 1934 making picketing illegal—effectively suppressing Black protesters.

All throughout Harlem, a collective frustration began churning. Edna sensed it, and it frightened her. It was in the air, moving through the streets like a gathering storm, one so powerful it threatened the whole of New York City.

Chapter 12

The Breakthrough

Some forty miles from Harlem, at Rutgers's College of Agriculture in New Brunswick, New Jersey, Dr. Selman Waksman, a forty-six-year-old tenured professor, made his way down a long hallway. Notorious for wearing wrinkled clothing and wool vests picked at by moths, the bespectacled, dark-haired Waksman was headed to see his graduate student Chester Rhines in the microbiology lab, where Rhines had been working on a clandestine and strange experiment.

The lab was old and cramped, a mere eighteen square feet, and truncated streaks of light crept in from two half windows. Tables dotted with Bunsen burners and test tubes spanned the wall; above them were shelves stacked with beakers, funnels, flasks, and graduated cylinders. In a corner by the sink, an ancient hand-cranked autoclave puttered away, sterilizing the glassware and needles. But the shoddy surroundings didn't bother Rhines, who was committed to his work. To some, his current research was macabre. He wanted to know whether decomposing bodies full of TB released the bacteria into the soil; if so, did the bacteria survive? If not, what microorganism was doing the killing?

To find out, Rhines grew the bacteria that caused Avian 531 tuberculosis, a low-risk strain for humans, on a culture medium in petri dishes. Once the TB colonies appeared, he dropped tiny beads of distilled soil containing different bacteria and fungi over them. Then he waited. Again and again, Rhines noted the TB bacteria continued to live in the soil; this wasn't surprising, as many believed that the TB microbe had originated in the soil and was comfortable in that environment.

Recently, however, he had added fresh manure to one batch of soil, then distilled it, and dropped it onto the medium in the petri dishes brushed with Avian 531 TB. Over a period of weeks, Rhines had checked the dishes and tallied the number of surviving TB microbes. Now he wanted to show Waksman the results.

Inside the lab, the professor, who harbored a pathological fear of tuberculosis, draped a tattered apron over his clothes and moved closer to Rhines, where the smell of rich, dark, dung-laden soil rose from the table. To most, the smell was sickening, but for Waksman, it evoked fantastic memories of home.

An immigrant from Novaia-Priluka, in western Ukraine, a place he described as a "mere dot in the boundless steppes," he'd grown up surrounded by chernozem, a fertile, black, potent-smelling soil that, he recalled, "so filled my lungs that I was never able to forget it." He was happy there until the anti-Semitism sweeping his country forced him to flee. He arrived in the United States and won a scholarship to Rutgers University, where he fell in love with soil and its underground world.

Just beneath his feet, billions of organisms teemed with life. They were all connected through a network of fungi, protozoa, nematodes, mites, algae, and parasites that lived and fed off one another. But alongside the molds, worms, bugs, and plants lived the pathogens that caused deadly diseases: typhoid fever, streptococcus, influenza, polio, plague, scarlet fever, diphtheria, smallpox, and tuberculosis.

At first, Waksman believed these microscopic organisms lived in anarchy. But in time, he discovered their differences, their nuances, the mystery of how they existed. Peering down his microscope lens, he witnessed a dynamic show of miniature forces that could nourish seeds, turning the tiniest kernels into towering redwoods and delicate sunflowers. A slight movement and the same forces could also kill them. He watched how the fungi and mites and pathogens lived harmoniously together, not "alone . . . but as *mixed populations . . .* side by side," he said. And they did it "without destroying one another completely and without one kind becoming predominant in suppressing all the others."

He kept studying them, learning how the pathogens lived and also how they died.

No different from other living things, the microbes in the soil relied on food to survive; if they lost their food supply, they died, but their death, Waksman noted, was a curious event. They didn't just shrivel up and die; rather, when the microbes were starved, they vanished as if the air were a black hole consuming them into a void of nothingness. He learned more. Microbes needed personal space. If placed too close to each other, they grew agitated and territorial, and fighting ensued. The duel unfolded like a scene pulled from a sci-fi movie: the two microbes fought each other, not with physical force, but by releasing chemicals, until one vaporized the other.

All this enthralled Waksman, leading him to wonder whether soil microbes could ever become antibiotics, effective drugs used to fend off and cure diseases. He was about to see.

Rhines pulled out the petri dishes with Avian 531 TB and the non-manured soil from the incubator. Both he and Waksman looked at it, and there, rising in vast numbers, were tiny sand-colored mounds of TB bacteria. He pushed the first dish aside and reached for the second dish, the one containing the Avian 531 TB and manured soil. Again, the men looked down at the dish, but in this one, the TB colonies were far smaller, leading both scientists to conclude that "certain fungi are able to repress [TB's] development, especially in manured soil."

Their findings were striking, stunning, a cause for celebration.

Something in the soil was killing the TB bacteria. Could this be the start of a cure, and the end to eons of agony? To the medically un-qualified Waksman, who had no research funds and knew nothing about the pathology of disease, "this was all very interesting," he said, "but it was leading . . . nowhere."

Perhaps if Waksman had seen the enduring devastation that TB had cast upon humankind, or gone to Sea View and walked through the wards, or stood beside Edna as surgeons gouged out ribs and batches of lung tissue, he would have rethought his comment and con-tinued investigating his discovery. But he shelved it and moved on, believing that "the results didn't suggest any practical applications for the treatment of tuberculosis." So he thought.

Chapter 13

The Riot

Spring–Fall 1935

The storm hit Harlem on March 19, 1935, when Lino Rivera, a sixteen-year-old Black Puerto Rican boy, stole a ten-cent penknife from a Kress's five-and-dime store on 125th Street. Caught by the store's manager, the frightened Rivera bit the older man's hand, prompting someone to call an ambulance. As it arrived outside, a police officer inside the store was taking Rivera downstairs, claiming that he wanted to let him out through the back entrance, away from the emerging crowd. The scene alarmed a Black woman who'd been shopping. Believing that the officer was going to kill Rivera, she began shouting: "Just like down South where they lynch us."

Outside, the parked ambulance seemed to support her claim that the officer had injured Rivera. The ruckus might have ended there, except there was a hearse parked nearby. Seeing the hearse and the ambulance, the crowd became suspicious: "What happened to the boy?" people asked the police.

"None of your business," the officers replied, shoving and arresting anyone who tried to address the crowd, now getting bigger. But the people insisted, asking them again, and soon, without any answers, the rumor began. It was emblazoned on a leaflet: "CHILD BRUTALLY

BEATEN!" Beneath was a summary of the event and instructions to "protest against this Lynch Attack of Innocent Negro People."

Kress's closed, but the crowd didn't disperse. Instead, it grew. Soon it numbered in the thousands. One protester threw a rock and broke a window and, with that singular gesture, unleashed years of pent-up anger over police brutality and skyrocketing unemployment.

The crowd moved east and west of 125th Street, looking for white-owned businesses that had denied Black citizens jobs. They passed Blumstein's and tossed rocks and bottles through its front windows, sending mannequins dressed in floral-print dresses tumbling onto the sidewalk. On Lenox Avenue, protesters shattered the windows of the Manhattan Renting Agency, Savoy Food Market, Krasdale's Grocery, and the Natural Blooming Cigars.

Across Harlem, white store owners pulled down their gates and posted signs: "Colored Help Employed Here." It didn't work. The people knew the truth. Mounted police and those on foot circulated photos of Rivera to prove he wasn't dead; the image only sparked more anger and more rumors: the photo was fake. The rioting continued into the night, and finally, the following morning, the tumult died down, but its aftermath had only begun.

Throughout the day, white visitors thronged to Harlem's sidewalks, hoping to experience firsthand what had transpired the night before. They stood around, leaning against buildings and lampposts, and watched residents sweep the sidewalks, the sound of broken glass grating against the concrete.

❖

For Mayor La Guardia, who prided himself on his public image, the rioting was a public relations nightmare. With America watching and Harlem volatile, he needed to act fast. Almost immediately, La Guardia heeded the NAACP's demand to appoint a biracial commission made up of Black lawyers, heads of organizations, labor leaders, ministers, social reformers, and cultural figures to investigate the riots.

While the committee worked, La Guardia continued trying to regain the trust of his Black constituents by publicly urging Goldwater to dismantle the prevailing racist hiring practices at city hospitals. Goldwater responded publicly, claiming his hands were tied. Each hospital "had control over its own program," he said, preventing him from intervening. Besides, he noted, 18 percent of the city's nursing staff were Black women. Then he added the go-to sentiment so often repeated by white administrators: hiring Black nurses caused white nurses to flee, leading to high turnover.

Tired of Goldwater's foot-dragging, La Guardia took matters into his own hands and announced that the new Queensboro-Hillcrest Hospital in Flushing, Queens, slotted to open in the fall, was hiring Black nurses. In addition, any Black nurse looking to transfer from Sea View or Harlem or Lincoln could do so without needing to resign and reapply as a new hire. That mandate was officially gone. Now Black nurses could keep their seniority, their rights, and their pay. *The New York Age* praised the ruling, calling it a "golden opportunity for colored women to rise to greater heights in a profession in which too few opportunities have been afforded them."

The NACGN was excited by the news and hoped it would inspire the ANA to finally open its membership to Black nurses. Word reached Sea View. Nurses were elated. The offer, for some, meant they could work without fearing for their lives—by 1935 most of the nurses had tested positive for TB; over 2 percent had active TB, and several had died. Others longed for more excitement—tuberculosis nursing was repetitive and "boring," some said—but many wanted greater opportunities.

In June, twelve nurses put in applications to transfer.

Then the applications crossed Miss Mitchell's desk.

No. No. No. She would not let her nurses go. She had trained them, given them her time, her energy, and her expertise. And after last year's housecleaning, when she'd fired scores of nurses, granting transfers to the remaining staff would further the shortage. She would look incompetent, as if she had failed at her job of retaining staff. Finding nurses to work on TB wards was near impossible. She could not afford to lose any more bodies, and well-trained ones, no less. She snatched the applications and called a meeting with the entire staff.

Taking her usual stance, back straight, head high, and cape cascading from her shoulders, she announced the transfer was not applicable to Sea View's nurses. There was a "rule," she said, forbidding them from leaving and switching hospitals. These were hard times, and if any of them tried to transfer, well, she said, "it will get back to me."

That was enough. Years of seeing Black nurses like Kea and Riddle and Staupers and now Alyce Greene, who was still fighting Bellevue's discriminatory policies, rushed together, and someone picked up the phone and called the Seventh Street headquarters of *The New York Age*. Within days, a searing editorial appeared in the paper for all New York to read.

Miss Mitchell was a "prejudiced white person" who would do anything to prevent Black nurses from succeeding, and her rules for them, the editorial said, were sterner, harsher, more severe; preventing them from transferring was another way of brandishing her power. The editorial concluded by suggesting that Miss Mitchell should stop and listen to the Black nurses she despised; from them, she might learn "how to truly be a nurse."

Emboldened, the Sea View nurses took the matter further, reporting their boss to the Committee for Equal Opportunity, a city organization designed to ensure equality in the workplace. The committee agreed to investigate her actions; in the meantime, nurses were encouraged to apply to Queensboro-Hillcrest. Two of the original twelve reapplied, and in October, the city approved their transfer requests.

Edna, too, celebrated a victory.

In the fall of 1935, weary of the long commute and the ongoing tensions in Harlem, she moved into the nurses' residence. Living on campus meant she could pick up extra shifts and put the additional money toward her hoped-for house, and she could also spend more time with friends.

Unfortunately, the dorms prohibited spouses, so for now, Forest would stay in Harlem. Edna found the separation less than ideal; it left her feeling uneasy and stirred her fears that Forest would never come home at night, that he would squander whatever money he made playing pool with Mump Fudge and Dirty Johnson and the other men who hung around the boozy, smoke-filled pool halls.

Sometimes her mind filled with more sinister thoughts. Forest being beaten or stabbed over one of those games, his lithe body tossed in an alley, his nose and eyes bloodied, his ribs broken, and no one stopping to help. But she pushed them aside, sublimating them, casting them to the place where all her other worries lay, the ones about Americus and houses and TB and sick patients and time passing too quickly. If she didn't move now, there would be no progress. She would spend her life working and paying rent and continuing to line someone else's pocket with her hard-earned money.

At the time, the nurses' residence, built in 1913, was being expanded and renovated: drafty old windows were being replaced, floors refinished, and the small, outdated kitchen and dining room updated. But despite the residence's imperfections, nurses loved its old-world charm.

Four stories high, with dormer windows and a grand entrance flanked by Greek columns, the residence, in many ways, evoked places that barred Black women from entering, except through the back door—plantation estates and stately mansions, like the ones Edna's mother used to clean.

Of all the places inside, nurses loved the rumpus room, a magnificent common space on the ground floor. With vaulted ceilings and a fireplace that on winter days filled the room with warmth and amber light, it was their haven away from the wards and Miss Mitchell, from the sickness and demands of patients who were dying to keep living.

Floor-to-ceiling mahogany bookcases lined its walls, filled with books curated by a staff librarian and the nurses themselves. Novels by William Faulkner, Langston Hughes, Pearl S. Buck, Stella Gibbons, and Nella Larsen shared space with the poetry of James Weldon Johnson, Jean Toomer, and Claude McKay and mysteries by Agatha Christie and David Frome, a pen name of Zenith Jones Brown. There were also shelves of magazines, medical books, and journals. Across from the bookshelves stood a baby grand piano, available for anyone to play. And scattered throughout the room were couches and big, comfy lounge chairs and tables where nurses could read, write, talk, listen to the radio, or play cards.

Throughout the day, nurses filtered in and out. Anyone peeking in would always see a few sitting on the chairs or couches, legs crossed, and a magazine, maybe *Vogue* or *Good Housekeeping*, open on their laps. In between flipping the pages, they talked:

"There's a new doctor . . ."

"This skin cream promises to erase wrinkles, and this bra is . . ."

"Anyone going to the St. George this weekend?"

"Or the Yankee game?"

"Did you hear about the woman in Pavilion Two?"

And then . . . Miss Mitchell. Someone always brought up Miss Mitchell. "It wasn't a conversation," one nurse said, "without mentioning Miss Mitchell and something she had done."

Sometimes they tossed aside the magazines, turned up the radio, and danced to Benny Goodman, Fred Astaire, or Louis Armstrong. Edna loved spending time in the rumpus room, but she also relished her time alone.

Her room on the fourth floor recalled the one at Harlem Hospital, small, furnished with a bed, a dresser, and a desk. But this window, the only one, looked out toward the forest and bay, not a busy, noisy street. When she opened it, the breeze rushed in, lifting the curtain and filling the room with an earthy freshness from the surrounding woods. In letters to Americus, Edna wrote about the window and how she wanted an entire house full of them; windows that brought in light and fresh air, right on Staten Island.

In the last four years, Edna had become enamored of the island's rough beauty, its rural feel, and its neighborhoods full of graceful homes, sweet-smelling gardens, and children playing on paved streets. She loved all the open spaces, the parks and the lakes, where herons flitted over the water and the pulsing, high-pitched chirps of tree frogs resounded through the air; she loved the birdsong and swaying leaves that replaced the car horns and sirens blaring through the city streets.

At night, when she left the surgical building, she often meandered down one of Sea View's pathways, following it to a garden or a pergola. Sometimes she sat on a bench under the canopy of stars pinpricking the sky, with the moon darting in and out of the clouds, and let her mind drift.

Around her was the forest. Looking at it, she saw nothing but an impenetrable darkness, the kind her father must have encountered when he left the Wilkes County plantation and made his way to Savannah. When her patients looked at the trees, Edna knew they endured a different kind of darkness, one that came from living every day in limbo, of straddling this world and the next, of having their wants and needs reduced to whispers and gurgles and moans. There was never any stillness or silence; instead, peace for Sea View's patients came in the spoonfuls of codeine that suppressed their coughing, and in the pills or injections to induce sleep. Then they fell into fevered dreams that dragged them through the archives of their life or took them into strange worlds of tunnels and murky caverns or cliffs that sent them tumbling to the ground.

Seeing the wards at night from the outside, their lights low and everyone in bed, brought Edna a solace, a feeling of being near her patients. That closeness also pulled her deeper into the world of tuberculosis, into the violent cyclone of human need.

Sea View was a chasm of need, especially Pavilion 1, which stood directly across from the nurses' residence. It housed the children, four floors of them, babies, toddlers, little kids, and young teens who wanted something all the time. There were so many of them: Anne, Georgie, Robert, Camille, Michael, Joey, and Hilda Ali, the petite little girl with the giant brown eyes made bigger by the scrawniness of her face.

Most remembered the first time she was admitted, over a year ago; at barely two, she had stayed for eighteen months. When her parents came to take her home in August 1935, months before Edna moved to the dorms, they thanked God and the nurses, who celebrated her release with a small party and cards and hugs goodbye. They would miss the little girl who had learned her ABC's on the ward and had charmed them with her openness.

Everyone believed, or wanted to believe, that Hilda would be one of the lucky ones, one of the few who would beat the disease. But two months after her discharge, on Halloween night, with a stuffed animal in tow, she returned to the children's ward, which was decorated with paper pumpkins and witches and ghosts.

Hilda's diagnosis made her family anxious, their unease moving beyond her illness. Immigrants from Bengali, India, they worried about being ostracized from their community, where people still believed Biggs's antiquated narrative that tuberculosis was a disease of the dirty, the poor, and the morally bankrupt. They also feared for Mr. Ali, her father and the breadwinner. If he became infected, there would be no one to work. And now, they were told, she was very, very sick, sicker than before.

Every day, her mother traveled from upper Manhattan—Spanish Harlem—taking trains and ferries and buses to Sea View; it was a long, tiresome trip, one Edna knew well. Sitting beside her daughter, Mrs. Ali took out coloring books, toys, pajamas, and jars of homemade food, much to the chagrin of other children who stared, longing for their own parents, many of whom held jobs that made visiting impossible, and many more who had admitted their children and never returned, for whatever reason. The children ached and cried for daddy

or mama or home—words that flitted about the halls, lodging themselves into the nurses' psyches.

Living here, Edna realized, would require a new courage, as there
was no escape from the agony of sickness. No horns or whistles or
sounds of worship coming from churches; no jazz clubs or strolls on
Seventh Avenue; no corner buskers or preachers or newsboys to distract
her from the long days and nights of seeing the internal markings of
this pestilence.

Here there was only the Great White Plague and its victims, old
and young, too young, like Hilda, and of course the Black nurses, who
worked and worked, trying to fight a disease that had not one effective
drug and continued killing too many of them.

PART II

❖

1936–1939

Chapter 14

Ward 64

September 1936

Early morning broke over Staten Island, and the light outside slipped from black to blue to a fiery orange. It blanketed the sky above the city and the harbor and rolled up the hill, falling through the windows of Sea View in slats, and extending itself onto the nightstands and beds of Ward 64.

Newcomer Missouria Louvinia Meadows-Walker stood beside her nurse's cart, her hands busy dipping a cloth into a basin of warm water positioned next to a straight razor and a cup of fresh shaving lather. She wrung out the cloth, set it aside, and turned to her patient, Albert K., a forty-four-year-old former subway worker from Brooklyn.

"Good morning," she said and drew him forward, slipping a pillow behind his neck and another behind his head in preparation for his morning shave.

He muttered a word strung together with only consonants. Years of being sick had wasted his muscles and turned his arms and legs into mere appendages that served little purpose. Mr. Albert, as he was called, could no longer stand or walk or even lift a spoon. Now he spent his days in bed with his lips pursed in an expression of reproach, as if to say, "It's all your fault that I'm here."

Before starting, Missouria reached into her pocket, pulled out a mint, and placed it in her mouth. It was a habit she had acquired many years before, along with wearing a copper bracelet on her wrist "to ward off illness," she said.

Sliding the mint between her cheek and upper gum, she lifted the warm, wet cloth from her cart and moved close to the bony face with its tight lips. She began patting it with the towel, softening the gray and white stubble that poked out like tiny thorns. Dropping the cloth onto the tray, she lifted the shaving brush from the cup of lather. In gentle swirling motions, she coated Mr. Albert's chin. He winced and clenched his teeth and let out a long, muffled snarl. Missouria regarded the gesture and moved the brush slower until his face was covered in soft white foam. Then she took the straight razor and placed it beneath his ear; the blade sank into the cream, and she pulled downward, gently scraping his skin and slicing off the coarse nubs of stubble.

"Damn it, damn it," Mr. Albert cried out, launching into his daily ritual of cursing, directed at Sea View, at the disease, at his ward mates, and at the nurses who shaved and changed and bathed him. Missouria kept working, focusing on keeping her hand steady. It was a task that needed to be done, even though he loathed it.

Shaving and bathing and using the bathroom were once intimate, private acts, routines done to start the day. But here at Sea View, these had become public spectacles, performed by a nurse as part of her everyday duties. Although Missouria took her time, it provided little comfort to formerly self-sufficient men like Mr. Albert. To them, a nurse wielding a razor or washcloth or bedpan was a humiliating reminder of how much their life had devolved, of their helplessness, and of the disease that had no cure.

Sure, the baths and haircuts and manicures felt good. But many men saw them as formalities, done to keep up the appearance of normalcy, to pretend sickness could be conquered with clean nails, neat hair, or a smooth face. For Mr. Albert, all they did was drive home his isolation, the reality that if Missouria didn't clean him, no one would. In the three months since she'd started working on the ward, not a single person had visited him; on his nightstand, beside the sputum cup and enamel water pitcher, there were no photographs.

During her rounds, Missouria, with her deep-set eyes that people said could "track a fly," often looked at the snapshots posed on the small nightstands separating the beds. Some showed families gathered at a picnic or around a table set with food; some were of a single woman, a mother, a sister, perhaps a girlfriend. Others had professional photos of their wedding day.

In those crisp and sharp images, the men looked like different people. Dressed in pressed suits, they stood beside their new brides, smiling and happy; a few were caught in a kiss. These days, when the former brides visited, they, too, looked different. Their dewy freshness was replaced by exhaustion and worry over how they would pay the butcher or the iceman or the landlord or anyone else who came knocking on the door to collect money. How would they care for the kids? Would they become widowed?

One or two of the men had photographs with curling edges and a fading image. They were sepia-toned, and in them, women in homemade dresses, their hair braided or tied back in a kerchief, stood beside men with thick hands and loose-fitting pants. Sometimes there were children, sitting down or poking their heads from behind someone's waist or standing smack in the front. Often the people were expressionless, posed in front of stone walls, gardens, and groves in rural villages in faraway countries: Italy, Greece, Spain, Russia, Poland, and France, places the men on the ward had left behind. They had packed up their lives, taken clothes, heirlooms, trade tools, and toiletries, and traveled to America, hoping for a better life.

Instead, they found Ward 64.

Missouria lifted Mr. Albert's chin, and again he scowled and cursed, but this time, his words flew with more rage. She felt the hotness of his breath and the spittle that settled on her hands and neck. But she didn't stop, she kept doing her job, and so did the nurses across from her struggling to feed a patient, and the two several beds down straining to reposition a man with his leg in traction. He, too, yelled in pain, catching the attention of his ward mates.

Some men stopped what they were doing and looked at the nurses fussing with the traction man, but most were unfazed. They continued rolling their cigarettes—a habit that was not discouraged despite their disease—or fussing with their blankets or shouting from across the ward, the words soaring over beds. They asked about lunch or the girl in Ward 32 or the German Adolf Hitler, a name they saw more frequently in the papers. A handful enjoyed playing a macabre game by speculating who would die next. They took bets.

Would it be the new guy who rarely sat up?

Robert?

Or Mr. Albert?

Some of the talk shocked the twenty-four-year-old Missouria, but most of it didn't. She was from Clinton, South Carolina, a hard-line Jim Crow town deep in the southern part of the state. There, the actions of men far surpassed the glum humor and pent-up wrath of sick TB patients on Staten Island.

Clinton was a place of gossip and rumor and stifling southern heat, run by a mean white sheriff who bought moonshine from Missouria's uncle. The eighth of twelve children, Missouria was born on March 12, 1912. Most remembered that year for the sinking of the *Titanic*, not for the milestones of Harriet Quimby becoming the first woman to fly across the English Channel or Robert Scott reaching the South Pole.

From a young age, Missouria loved books and music and anything daring. She was a tough part-Cherokee tomboy who climbed thirty-foot trees and could outrun any boy. "Nothing scared her," her niece said. Her boldness allowed her to dream, to imagine revolutionary shifts on a global scale.

"I want to change the world," Missouria would say.

Her family was loud, close-knit, and headed by her single mother,

Mama Amy, a laundress who washed clothes for Clinton's white elite. She was a proud woman who loved all her children but harbored a weakness for Missouria, who shared her passion for history, justice, and family lore.

Mama Amy taught her growing daughter many things: the art of wringing a chicken's neck; the right way to grow herbs and mix them together to make remedies; how to bake and cook and read the stars. At night, she would take her outside and point at the sky, and all those random points of light would rearrange themselves into meaningful shapes of animals, people, and mythic beings who had stories.

Mama Amy loved telling stories. After dinner, she would sit in her high-backed mahogany chair, the legs carved like lion paws, and weave together the threads of family history: the Newberry Plantation, where she was born; her mother dying; her father "hiring her out" as a domestic at age eight; and her marriage, at thirteen, to William "Will" Meadows, Missouria's father.

Will was a gambling man twenty-eight years older than Mama Amy who, she said, "loved his cards more than his kids." After two decades of washing and ironing his trousers and shirts, while he disappeared for days, squandering her money, Mama Amy found her justice.

One late-summer afternoon in 1920, Missouria, then eight, was up in the pecan tree shaking down nuts when two well-dressed white men crossed the tracks and continued down Carolina Avenue to her gate, the dust from the road kicking up behind them. They walked up to the porch, where Mama Amy was slouched over her washbasin, and without removing their hats, they stood in front of her. She raised her eyes but said nothing.

"We're here to collect the cow that Will owes us," the white men said.

"You're not taking that damn cow. I got children to feed," Mama Amy replied, continuing to scrub a shirt against the washboard.

"It's ours. He lost it in a hand."

"You're not taking my cow," she said, dropping the shirt into the soapy water. "Wait here."

Drying her hands on her apron, she walked inside and left them standing on the porch, with the chickens clucking and pecking around the yard.

One of Mama Amy's hobbies was guns; she loved having them and shooting them. "She was a good shot," her nephew said.

In the corner of the living room, leaning against the wall, stood a two-barrel shotgun; three more were placed throughout the house. Upstairs in her dresser, Mama Amy kept her handgun, a pearl-handled derringer that she sometimes took with her when shopping in town. There was also a machete behind the icebox. She thought for a moment—the machete? the handgun?—then walked to the living room, grabbed the two-barrel shotgun, and returned to the porch, where the men were waiting.

"You're not leaving with the cow," she told them.

They looked at her, standing there, unwavering, holding the gun across her chest.

"It's ours," they repeated.

"Open your hands," she said.

The men hesitated.

Mama Amy raised the gun and turned it toward their feet. Up in the tree, Missouria watched her mother.

"Open your hands," she repeated louder.

The men stepped back. Mama Amy moved the gun. One threw open his palm.

With the gun still pointed at their feet, she lifted it, cracked open the chamber, and tilted the barrels upward. Two shotgun shells slid into her hand. The men didn't move. Neither did Mama Amy, who stared them in the eye with a look people said "could make the devil dance."

She snapped the chamber closed, stepped forward, and dropped both shells into the man's open palm.

"Tell Will." She paused, then continued. "This here is from the cow."

No one ever saw Will again. Some said the two white men killed him with Mama Amy's shells; others said he fled from Clinton and remarried. Mama Amy really didn't care what happened to him.

"He was gone, and I was free," she said.

These moments and stories, and there were hundreds, shaped Missouria's sense of self.

Throughout her life, she often recalled them to her family: "There was a story for everything," her niece said. While Mama Amy believed in the power of oral history, she knew the importance of a traditional education.

"It's the only way out," she used to tell Missouria.

In 1931, Missouria received her ticket out of Clinton.

Along with a handful of women, she was accepted into the prestigious nursing program at Freedmen's Hospital School of Nursing at Howard University, the same school that NACGN executives Riddle and Staupers had attended. Set in the center of a segregated DC on a sprawling campus, the nursing school offered a rigorous three-year curriculum that included lectures and hospital experience in different areas: obstetrics, psychology, surgery, and pediatrics, a field that excited Missouria. Equally exciting was the faculty, full of leading scholars, one being Riddle, who before joining the NACGN had served as the educational director of Freedmen's.

Missouria was captivated by her teachers, by their passion, precision, and dedication to integrating the profession. They inspired her, nurturing her childhood dream to study nursing and change the world. And so when Missouria noticed the Sea View flyer calling for "negro nurses" tacked up in the student lounge, she didn't hesitate to apply.

The calling was a blessing, offering her everything she wanted, a steady job and good pay, and being closer to Riddle and her vibrant colleague Staupers. In recent years, their work for the NACGN and its strides, however small, toward abolishing segregation in the nursing field, enticed Missouria, and she wanted to join them, to stand behind her fellow nurses as they fought for equality. The other lure was Harlem, with its jazz and contemporary Black writers, many of whom inspired Missouria, setting off a longing to experience the place that Alain Locke, himself a Howard professor, said brought rebirth and renewal to Black America.

"The day of 'aunties,' 'uncles' and 'mammies' is equally gone. Uncle Tom and Sambo have passed on," Locke wrote. It was time to "scrap the fictions" and emerge, transformed. His words shook Missouria down to her soul. She, too, was ready for change.

After she finished shaving Mr. Albert, she dropped the razor into the basin of dirty water, where tiny pieces of stubble floated on the surface. His face was clean and smooth, and she emptied some aftershave oil into her palms and patted it over his cheeks while he muttered and glowered, tossing bits of saliva onto her hands and neck. But she was finished, her task complete. Turning away, she picked up a towel and wiped his spit off her body, then held up a small mirror and showed him her work.

When she'd started at Sea View, one nurse had told her, "You don't want to work on the men's ward," adding, "Ask for transfer before it's too late."

Chapter 15

❖

A President's Son

November 1936

The saga began in November 1936, two weeks before Thanksgiving, when FDR Jr., newly engaged to heiress Ethel du Pont, developed a sore throat. Within days, the pain grew worse, and doctors admitted him to Boston's Massachusetts General Hospital. Accounts of his sickness, reported as a sinus infection, filtered out to the press, and soon the nation began following his story. Every day, Americans waited to hear about the twenty-two-year-old's condition.

Was it really a sinus infection?

Had he improved?

Was he still in the hospital?

Brief updates came in small articles, some fewer than fifty words, and they were vague. He was still feeling sick, or he was a little better, or he might go home—but nothing more. Truth was, the president's son was becoming sicker, prompting his mother, the First Lady, to call in Dr. George Loring Tobey Jr., the best eye, ear, nose, and throat doctor in the Northeast.

Tobey examined him and found an abscess on his cheek. Suspecting it might be strep, he operated and drained it. Initially, the young man seemed better. But soon his fever soared, his throat closed, and he began hemorrhaging and coughing up blood. Blood tests confirmed Tobey's worst fears: the president's son had strep, and the bleeding from his throat suggested the bacteria was already in his bloodstream, threatening sepsis.

Twelve years earlier, sepsis from a strep infection had killed President Calvin Coolidge's son. Tobey didn't know if this was the same strain, but if it was, he had no drugs to treat it and FDR Jr. would die. Only one drug might work: Prontosil, a sulfa-based antibiotic. But it was available only in Europe.

Sulfanilamide, or sulfa, was first discovered by an Austrian chemist in 1908 and was patented a year later. An everyday molecule prized by textile companies as a binding agent for their dyes, it was cheap and easy to manipulate. But no one had considered using it for medicinal purposes until 1932.

In those pre-antibiotic days when dying from strep was commonplace, Dr. Gerhard Domagk, a German scientist employed at Bayer Pharmaceuticals in Elberfeld, Germany, was on a mission. He wanted to create a drug that would kill common bacterial infections such as strep, staph, and tuberculosis without harming the surrounding organs or tissues. In other words, he was searching for a magic bullet, a pill that would target the affected area but leave everything else intact.

After years of failed research with drugs that proved too toxic for humans, one day Domagk combined sulfa with a synthetic red dye that had no germicidal properties. The result was Prontosil, a radiant red powder. The drug proved effective against a handful of bacterial infections, and soon it emerged as the world's first-ever manufactured antimicrobial drug.

Almost immediately after Prontosil entered the European market, physicians began calling it a "wonder drug" and tweaking it, hoping to improve its efficacy and fight more illnesses. French doctors at the Pasteur Institute took matters further. They broke it apart and discovered that sulfa, not the red dye, was the active ingredient. With this information, they began manipulating the sulfa base, creating different compounds and administering them to patients sick with strep and staph and childbed fever, a deadly postpartum infection. The new variations were stronger and proved more effective, and soon the excitement reawakened the race for a TB cure, which had waned after the world had pinned its hopes on the only anti-TB vaccine, bacillus Calmette-Guérin (BCG).

In 1900, after farm animal serums and fantastic pills of chlorophyll and garlic failed to cure tuberculosis, two French chemists, Albert Calmette and Camille Guérin, introduced a vaccine. The men had invested thirteen years developing it from an attenuated version of the TB bacteria and seven more testing it. In 1921, they orally gave the vaccine to a newborn whose mother had died of TB. The baby survived. Within three years, over two hundred children had safely received it, and the League of Nations deemed it safe. Mass production began, and the world rejoiced: TB was cured.

Then came 1930, when a tainted batch killed seventy-two babies in Lübeck, Germany. The medical community reeled, and doctors grew wary of the vaccine. They feared a repeat of Lübeck; no one wanted the blood of babies on their hands, and soon enthusiasm for the drug faded. And the hope for a cure came to a standstill.

Now, the sulfa-based Prontosil was ushering in a new era of optimism.

Scientists began hypothesizing: if this combination of sulfa killed the *Streptococcus* bacteria, maybe another variation of it could kill the TB microbe.

European chemists flocked to their labs and concocted endless combinations of sulfa-based drugs, testing them on TB-infected mice, bunnies, and guinea pigs. Animals died by the thousands, but their autopsies showed encouraging results. Soon medical journals in Germany, France, and England abounded with articles about the efficacy of Prontosil and other sulfa drugs.

But in the United States, sulfa was nowhere to be found. No one was testing it, and America's premier medical journal, *The Journal of the American Medical Association* (*JAMA*), had intentionally omitted mentioning its discovery or current success. Its delay was in part because of "insufficient drug importation"; according to one prominent physician, another reason was that "America had become unimpressed with the scientific contributions coming out of Hitler's Germany." The US medical establishment wanted nothing to do with an alleged "Nazi wonder drug."

Many professionals cringed at the phrase "wonder drug," which conjured images of hucksters on street corners and patent medicine makers, those men in hats and wool coats who took out full-page advertisements in newspapers. Reputable companies made drugs; charlatans made "wonder drugs." And America was awash in charlatans. There was Swaim, whose Panacea purported to cure ulcers and boils and tuberculosis; Hamlin, whose Wizard Oil promised relief from backaches and venomous insect bites; and William J. Bailey, whose Radithor, radioactive radium water, claimed to do wonders for impotency. If Americans wanted another "wonder drug," one doctor said, it certainly wouldn't be from Hitler's Germany.

The country would have remained sulfa-free if a late-December update hadn't brought dismal news: FDR Jr. was dying. Tobey explained his predicament to Mrs. Roosevelt: Prontosil might save her son, but he had none. She could solve that problem.

From her White House office, Mrs. Roosevelt dialed Johns Hopkins, where she had learned that two junior researchers were in the middle of testing Prontosil, known in the United States under the trade name Prontylin and administered in a tablet form.

Could she have some for her son?

Tobey warned her that he knew nothing about dosing or side effects or how long to administer it. But Mrs. Roosevelt insisted, agreeing to use her son "as a Guinea pig," she said.

FDR Jr. received a first dose, then a second and a third, and soon his fever broke. On December 15, 1936, he opened his eyes and asked to eat.

Two days later, a nation awoke to the headline "Young Roosevelt

Chapter 16

❖

What They Carried

By 1937, Edna was almost thirty-six years old and ready to leave the nurses' residence. For all its joy and sisterhood, it had become a place of longing and loss, played out daily in the scramble for the mail.

After their shifts, the nurses dashed to the residence to collect their letters. Many headed to the rumpus room, sat down on the couches and chairs or stood against the bookcases, and tore open the envelopes. The postmarks came from places across the South—Georgia, Tennessee, the Carolinas, Mississippi—and from northern cities like Detroit, Pittsburgh, and Chicago. Edna's arrived from Washington, DC, and brought the latest news about Americus, now well into her high school years. It was hard to grasp that they'd left Savannah eight years earlier.

So much had happened in that time: births, deaths, marriages, new opportunities, and the growing weight of time passing. Americus had matured into a confident young girl and serious student who earned high grades. She was an avid angler, a reader, and a baker of pies, and was hoping to follow in Edna's footsteps and become a nurse. All this delighted Edna, but still she couldn't reconcile herself to having missed years of her sister's childhood; all the endings and beginnings that each one brought had been reduced to sentences on a page. The adult years, they arrived, and once here continued until death, but not childhood. Those years danced and flitted like they would burn forever but really vanished in a blink. If it were possible, Edna would have stopped time and spooled it back up like thread.

For weeks after she'd left Americus on that platform with her brother, her absence felt like someone had cleaved off an essential part of her. And then time began its forward march, and Edna began counting days. Soon the days turned to months, then years, and the world moved on with its Depression, and dust storms, new presidents, discoveries of radio waves from space, and now rumbles of another war. And here she was at Sea View, still counting days and thinking about all the years lost to what-ifs and what-could-have-beens.

When she finished reading the letter, she folded it and slipped it back into the envelope and stayed in the quiet of the room, where her friends continued reading pages telling about different things: parents falling ill or needing money or losing jobs, siblings graduating, homes that needed fixing, boyfriends who missed them or no longer thought of them, and more people leaving.

Almost every nurse at Sea View had walked away from someone, had made the decision to leave and board those segregated trains and pursue a better future. Most had come alone, taking only what they could carry. One nurse brought a book of poetry; another, her grandmother's recipes; and another, from North Carolina, carried a clove of garlic to ward off "the devil and tuberculosis." Missouria, whose letters came from Mama Amy, had carried seeds from her garden in Clinton, but only after America incinerated parts of Japan with the atomic bomb, ending the war, would everyone see Mama Amy's seeds in full bloom; for now, Missouria had tucked them away. Many also carried secrets, stories of their past that emerged over their weekly card games.

Early on, Edna had joined a table of nurses playing pinochle, a fast-moving trick-taking game. With each shuffle and deal, pass and bet, the nurses at Edna's table—Missouria, Janie B. Shirley, and Edna's old friend Clemmie Philips—revealed more of their lives, their worries and hopes, their visions and purposes for coming to Sea View.

Clemmie and Janie were also from Georgia, and both had come in the last year. They were young and eager and assigned to the evening shift on the men's ward, alongside Missouria. All were hardworking, but Clemmie, who was tall and slender with an expansive, sometimes bawdy sense of humor, took Sea View by storm.

Her bedside manner, stern and efficient but still compassionate, impressed the nearly unimpressible Miss Mitchell, and she was now on track to become a supervisor. After the 1935 incident when Miss Mitchell tried to block nurses from transferring and the press shamed her, she was working toward refashioning her public image and had recently given a promotion to Nurse Eula Phillip, making her the first Black supervisor at Sea View.

Janie was the opposite of Clemmie, Edna, and Missouria. Vivacious and outgoing, she flaunted a big, animated personality and loved shopping and parties. She also had a penchant for talking about everything and anything, especially her father.

In between shuffles, she talked about his days of being enslaved by a white doctor. For reasons unknown, Janie's father's enslaver liked him and taught him the art of medicine. Once emancipated, her father settled in the rural town of Royston, Georgia, home to baseball legend Ty Cobb. There he became known as the "medicine man."

From an early age, he took Janie to wild patches of land, the forest and the hillside, and revealed his secrets. He showed her how to find and forage for bark, berries, leaves, herbs, and roots, like sassafras, jimsonweed, valerian, ginger, and comfrey. In their kitchen, she stood beside her father as he brewed the herbs and made infusions, creating poultices for boils, toothaches, bunions, menstrual cramps, digestive problems, broken bones, and tuberculosis. Janie, whose mother had died from the Spanish flu, soaked up the mysteries of natural healing, which inspired her to study nursing.

But the industrious man had also impressed upon her a far more radical knowledge: the principle of owning property. He owned four hundred acres of farmland, Janie told them, and grew corn, soybeans, sugarcane, peanuts, legumes, and cotton.

"Land," he told her, "was the key to economic security and not being held hostage by the white man."

They all loved Janie's stories about her father, how he managed to buy all those acres and two farmhouses, and how, instead of working for a boss, he *was* the boss, employing dozens of people. Edna marveled. Her own father had lost years of his life working on the plantation in Wilkes County, and no matter how hard he toiled, he owned nothing, except endless debt to a farmer who worked him until his knees twisted and his hands knotted from clutching hoes and spades and shovels. Even in Savannah, when God called him and he answered, devoting his later life to spreading the Word, he died owing. One evening in the rumpus room, Edna confessed her dream: she, too, wanted to own a home, here on Staten Island.

Some nurses sitting around raised their brows. Owning a home was a lofty aspiration for any Black person, but for a Black woman, well, that seemed downright audacious. No one would give her a mortgage or a loan, especially with Forest working in fits and starts, and it would take years to save the cash for a down payment. Edna knew all this, heard them, and nodded.

❖

On payday, Edna often skipped the rumpus room. After cashing her check at Mr. Reiman's store, she returned to her room and closed the door. Opening her dresser drawer, she took out a well-worn envelope marked "My House" and sat at her desk. Despite knowing all the impediments, all the reasons she couldn't or shouldn't, she still counted out the cash from her paycheck, slipping most of it into the envelope.

Sometimes she paused and looked at the growing stack. It seemed disproportionately small compared with her years of hard work. Recently, she had begun feeling the mental strain of long hours and back-to-back shifts. At night, lying in her twin bed, she closed her eyes and the sounds from the forest—the flutter of wings, the chittering of bats, and the snapping of twigs—merged with images of her job: a woman pulling out her own catheter; another trying to eat but missing her mouth; the operating room that reached 107 degrees in the summer months; the surgical tools with their sharp steel tips that carved apart men and women; and the people, the never-ending drift of people, all the Elkes and Hildas, who came through her ward with mutilated lungs and prognoses full of gloom.

More and more, the mental pressure of the job leaked into Edna's body, which nagged at her, impatient for a break: her back ached and her legs swelled, often forcing her to wrap them in Ace bandages. She wasn't young anymore—in fact, at thirty-six, she was the oldest in the residence and, as a married woman, desired the comfort and touch of her husband.

She missed Forest, his jokes and ability to make her laugh, and his easygoing approach to things, which calmed her. Despite their talking regularly and seeing each other on her days off, she worried about him. His irregular work and his pool habit consumed her thoughts, keeping her on edge and rousing that gut feeling of something happening to him. "Don't worry about me," he'd say when she told him. His response made her worry more.

She began house hunting in earnest, and quickly realized that despite the absence of those overt "Whites Only" signs, the discriminatory practices thwarting Black people from owning homes on the island were just as rampant as in the South. Of the approximately four hundred thousand Black people living in New York City in 1937, only about four thousand owned homes, and a mere handful lived on Staten Island. Edna quickly realized why.

Behind closed doors, white real estate agents, overseeing the sale of most homes, struck deals with residents. To preserve the homogeneity of many neighborhoods, they refused to show homes to Black people, spinning shameless lies: the home's been sold, they'd say, or taken off the market; or they would increase the price when a potential Black buyer appeared. If a house was available and affordable, Edna experienced the insurmountable odds of trying to buy it.

After seeing her skin color and only one steady income, bankers instantly ruled out the possibility of a mortgage. Either Edna would need to pay cash or "contract buy," an arrangement where investors sold homes to Black purchasers but denied them full ownership, often withholding deeds until all payments were complete. A spurious, illegal practice, it preyed on hardworking Black people looking for a piece of the American dream.

Sellers openly flouted housing regulations by charging sky-high interest rates and demanding large down payments. They took monthly installments, meant for paying the balance, and put them toward the interest, leaving buyers with no equity and no proof of owning their home. Sellers looking to be more vicious created bald-faced lies, claiming buyers missed payments, which gave them a reason to re-possess the house and then resell it.

Edna knew all this but refused to give up.

She bought the local paper and, at night or before work, spent hours combing through the listings, circling potential homes. More hours were spent walking through the different neighborhoods around Sea View, getting a sense of each place—noting what drew her in and what created unease.

Todt Hill, on the south side of the island, with its multifloored homes abounding with windows and wrought-iron balconies facing New York Harbor, was gorgeous but out of reach. Besides the homes being too big, residents and real estate agents would never let Edna buy there. On the north side, the neighborhood of Castleton Corners was close to Sea View, but those houses were above her price range; it was also an all-white neighborhood with rumors of a KKK presence—which Missouria would later bring to light.

At the urging of her friend, Edna looked at Staten Island's Black neighborhoods: Stapleton, Tompkinsville, and New Brighton. All were down by the piers, where the ferry brought a constant flow of delivery trucks and people. This was the din Edna wanted to escape. And soon observers would denounce New Brighton as "a shantytown settlement of half-hearted frame houses," with "a bad element of boisterous and unruly individuals." To refine the area, the city was contemplating razing many of the houses and replacing them with new developments.

Edna didn't want commotion or a house that might be bulldozed, so she pressed on, ignoring the statistics and pessimism. And maybe because she was determined to rise from the crucible that *The Savannah Tribune* had portended the year she was born, or because the idea was so fantastic, almost as wild as her father leaving the plantation, Edna believed it could happen.

Chapter 17

❖

The Elixir

After the FDR Jr. story, sulfa loomed large in the minds of American doctors and chemist and quacks, who deluged US patent offices with applications for "sulfa pills, capsules, injectable solutions, and powders." Every day, these applications arrived by the bagful, thousands of them, all promising relief from minor headaches to major illnesses. Without careful consideration and based mostly on demand, the patents were approved. Sales soared, money flowed, and, in 1937, the moment found a name in the United States: the great American sulfa boom.

But for all its strengths, the novel drug had one great weakness: its inability to dissolve. For years, European chemists had tinkered with it, trying to liquefy the white powder and turn it into a syrup. They mixed it with a litany of liquids, but the results were always the same: flasks full of white lumps. The repeated failure to dissolve the drug caused many to quit trying. But a handful persisted.

Dr. Samuel Evans Massengill, a Tennessee-based doctor—although he never practiced—and president of the S. E. Massengill Company, was spurred by visions of Nobel Prizes and bank accounts overflowing with money. Obstinate and rapacious, and overly proud of his ancestors, who were among the first white settlers in the area, Massengill, no matter the cost, was determined to convert pure sulfa powder into a sweet syrup, a flavored red medicinal elixir he intended to distribute to doctors and pharmacies in the rural South. His sales rep scouted the areas and reported to Massengill that there was demand for a "sweetened liquid form" of the antibiotic sulfa. Some down south actually believed that if you couldn't "give colored people or children a red liquid medicine, then you aren't any kind of doctor at all."

Massengill considered himself a superior doctor. He would make this elixir.

As Massengill's chemist, Harold Cole Watkins, worked round the clock to produce the elixir, sulfa variations continued to fill pharmacy shelves, and soon the stories began emerging. Patent medicine makers were repackaging pure sulfa instead of compounding it with another ingredient to vary its effects. The American Medical Association (AMA) grew alarmed and, fearing the sulfa boom was turning into a medical free-for-all, issued a warning to physicians.

With all the sulfa being produced, some forms could be poisonous; doctors should purchase it only from reputable distributors. Prestigious medical journals backed the AMA, warning that the drug was being used "widely and indiscriminately in private practice" and that dosing was still uncertain. Prescribe with caution, they said.

The warning was taken lightly. All summer long, the sulfa craze raged on.

In early August, Watkins presented Massengill with a beautiful deep-red liquid that smelled and tasted like raspberry. Wasting no time, Massengill prepared seven hundred gallons for distribution. In September, Elixir Sulfanilamide became part of Massengill's ever-growing catalog of tablets, elixirs, and ointments that were distributed to over forty thousand doctors, pharmacies, and hospitals in the United States. The stock brought him a revenue of $1.6 million a year. This new elixir came in brown glass bottles of two sizes: one gallon and one pint. Around the bottle's cork stopper, Massengill wrapped a company sticker printed with the words "Quality Pharmaceuticals."

And like that, with no testing, medical review, or government oversight, the elixir went out to over six hundred commercial recipients in thirty-one states. Pharmacies, hospitals, clinics, and local physicians received it. A heavy concentration went to states with large rural Black communities—Texas, Georgia, Alabama, and Mississippi.

Fall arrived, bringing an economic downturn, more drought in the Midwest, and a sudden spate of children dying. In a two-week period in Tulsa, Oklahoma, half a dozen children died. Pathologists confirmed the children had ingested Massengill's Elixir Sulfanilamide. Then, a more terrifying revelation: thousands of children were still being prescribed the liquid poison.

News of the ongoing tragedy blazed throughout the country. At Sea View, the nurses worried. Was the elixir at the hospital?

Had anyone seen it?

Every day more people died: a twenty-nine-year-old in Kansas, an eighteen-year-old in Texas, a two-year-old in Oklahoma. The list kept growing. The public became outraged. Once more, the poor and Black populations had become victims of America's failure to pass federal regulations protecting its citizens from greedy drug makers like Massengill.

Lawmakers, doctors, and nurses had spent years calling for a complete overhaul of the Pure Food and Drug Act. Passed in 1906 as part of a progressive-era package, it was the first attempt to clean up unsanitary practices in packinghouses by inspecting meat and to protect people from quacks by regulating drugs. But thirty years later, as pharmaceutical companies began producing more drugs at quicker rates, the drug portion of the law remained unchanged. To most, it was outdated and unsafe and didn't reflect current times. In it, there was no mention of using clinical trials, human or animal, to test drugs for safety and efficacy, and listing dosages, side effects, or ingredients on labels also wasn't required; unless a drug was a narcotic, it could be sold without a prescription.

The few stated regulations were vague and focused specifically on advertising and misbranding. Among the violations were mislabeling and nondisclosure of potentially harmful active ingredients like alcohol, morphine, cocaine, and heroin. But these guidelines meant little: if the chemist was caught, most times the FDA gave a slap on the wrist.

Now in 1937 legislators were still urging Congress to revise the law and require drug testing and label transparency. They also wanted consumer protection from hucksters and patent medicine makers, whose ads for pills and salves claiming to cure gout, canker sores, and sad bowel movements littered the pages of newspapers and magazines. To prove that unregulated drugs were dangerous, the chief of the FDA educational department, Ruth deForest Lamb, created "American Chamber of Horrors," a traveling exhibit of different posters showing the catastrophes of patent drugs. The poster for Lash Lure, an eyelash and eyebrow dye containing a hazardous chemical, featured a young woman whose eyeballs ulcerated, leading to blindness. Another featured a woman who was paralyzed and lost her teeth and eyesight after using Koremlu, a depilatory whose main ingredient was a rodenticide.

Government officials knew these claims on drugs and beauty products were bogus, but patent medicine was big business; in the early 1930s, some estimated it was the fourth-largest industry in the nation. But no one, including the FDA, was powerful enough to fight the lobbyists in the patent industry. Consequently, nothing had changed, leaving the American public to trust men like Massengill, whom the FDA hoped would be honest.

In mid-October, with the death toll mounting, the AMA received a list of the ingredients in Massengill's elixir. One stood out: diethylene glycol (DEG), a noxious solvent used in varnishes and paint thinners and as a moistening agent in the production of resins and explosives. In one of its rare advisories, the FDA had discouraged the use of DEG in consumer products. The solvent, it warned, was lethal in animals. But despite the warning, Massengill's chemist had added it, and no one knew. As written, the current law allowed him to either list the ingredient or not. He chose the latter. To list it meant that he couldn't call his medicine an "elixir"—the FDA loosely defined elixirs as those using alcohol as a solvent. Those that didn't use alcohol were considered "solutions." Massengill's had diethylene glycol, making it a solution.

Fearing mass casualties and unable to lawfully prosecute him or force a recall, the FDA dispatched hundreds of agents to recover the bottles and large industrial drums sitting in hospitals and storerooms. They crisscrossed the country, rifling through prescriptions, some with only a name or a street; they interviewed doctors and pharmacists, many of whom remained aloof, unwilling to reveal information for fear the authorities would charge them with murder and they would lose their business. Still, the agents pressed on, in what one paper called a "nationwide race with death."

Every day the newswires hummed with updates, their reports swinging between elation—they found more bottles—and devastation: more people had died. But as the weeks passed, some papers began ignoring facts and the nuances of science, writing that sulfa was the poison, not the DEG.

A *New York Times* headline read, "Sulfanilamide Is Subjected to Attention Following Cures and Some Fatalities."

"Warn Surgeons to Be Cautious with New Drug," announced the *Chicago Tribune.*

But other papers praised sulfa: "Ill Babies Helped by 'Sulfa' Drug."

Still others focused on saving Massengill's reputation, claiming he was a doctor of integrity. The *Bristol Herald Courier* blasted a headline condemning the treatment of Massengill: "'Time' Article Is Unfair to Massengill Company, One of Leading Drug Manufacturers."

The public was confused.

Almost a month into the tragedy, the search turned painstaking, burdensome, exacerbated by Watkins, who was arrogant and glib, blaming sulfa and not DEG. He admitted that no "meaningful laboratory or animal tests were conducted," but after the first Tulsa deaths he said that "a few guinea pigs were injected," adding, "I also drank half a cup of diethylene glycol" and "took teaspoon doses of the elixir itself."

The FDA investigator asked him if he experienced anuria, the inability to urinate, the most common side effect of DEG.

Watkins responded that his had increased.

If he was lying, no one would ever know, and Massengill didn't care. He stood by his employee and issued a public statement:

"My chemists and I deeply regret the fatal results but there was no error in the manufacture of the product . . . I do not feel that there was any responsibility on our part."

By late October, most of the bottles had been recovered; fortunately, none were at Sea View. The death toll surpassed one hundred and the victims were primarily those Massengill had targeted with his sweet-flavored elixir: mostly children, and more than half were Black people. But under the current drug law, the one from 1906, Massengill was protected, and his charge for omitting DEG on the label and calling his sweet-tasting syrup an "elixir" and not a "solution" was "misbranding," not murder.

Eventually, he pleaded guilty to "174 federal counts of adulterating or misbranding the elixir." In years to come, he would receive twelve more citations from the FDA for misbranding, including one for his company's longest-lasting and most popular product: Massengill Powder, a "cleansing douche for hygienic purposes after menstruation and coitus." Made up of boric acid, alum, and carbolic acid, a highly toxic chemical, the douche was advertised as having therapeutic effects; "many medical authorities," Massengill said, "agree that such a cleansing, two or three times a week, serves a useful purpose." The FDA found these claims scientifically unsustainable. And yet, despite the citations, the company prevailed, eventually making millions from feminine hygiene products.

But Harold Watkins, his chemist, the man responsible for turning the elixir into a stunning liquid, met a different fate: after the trial, police found him lying facedown, his spectacles lodged beneath his body, with a single self-inflicted gunshot wound to his heart.

The tragedy shook the nation. Americans were angry. Most of the deaths had taken place in the South and along the border, rural places stricken with poverty and havens for patent medicine makers. Fed-up residents raised their voices, and soon Congress could no longer ignore the collective clamor. Legislators began rethinking their positions: Did they want more deaths on their hands? How long before the next incident? Their waffling had a ripple effect. The vice president of Bristol-Myers, one of the largest drug manufacturers, began urging government action to "prevent such calamities as had been caused by Massengill's concoction."

The AMA followed, and soon more and more groups, including the League of Women and the American Association of Public Health, joined the chorus of dissenting voices demanding that Congress pass a new Food and Drug Act, one that regulated drugs, ensuring their safety, and put the consumer before the corporation. It would take a year for the new law to pass and clear the shelves of junk remedies, making room for a new era of drugs. What they might be, no one was quite sure.

Chapter 18

❖

"Reserved for Whites"

November 1937

That November day in 1937 broke clear and crisp and began with a celebration of the renovated nurses' residence. Finally, after two years of enduring the noise of jackhammers, cement trucks, and bulldozers, of breathing dust and dirt, and of dealing with men trudging through the residence with muddy boots and wandering eyes, it was done. The new building, the nurses agreed, was gorgeous.

But by midmorning, the mood shifted, and word began to spread throughout the hospital.

It started with a group of disconcerted nurses who were standing at the entrance of the new dining room.

From there, it slipped through the renovated dormer windows and out the main entrance, making its way across the lawn to the new children's hospital. Inside, it passed the cribs and cots and the bed of Hilda Ali, who had returned, until it reached the pediatric nurses, who heard it: "reserved for whites." Then they passed it on.

The phrase snaked down the tunnels and fanned out into the administration building and pavilions, making its way up to the adult wards.

"Reserved for whites," heard Missouria, then Clemmie, then Janie, and the other nurses working that shift.

The three words drifted out to the balconies; they floated over those taking the rest cure and down toward the surgical ward.

"Reserved for whites," Edna heard.

On the phrase moved through Sea View, passing the kitchen, where the cooks prepared dinner, and the medical director's office, and Miss Mitchell's door, until by early evening, it seemed everybody knew.

If it was true, no one should enter the new dining room. Instead, everyone should come together to support the nurses, who continued standing outside its entrance, wondering about the signs inside and who was responsible.

❖

This wasn't supposed to happen again. Mayor La Guardia had promised the Black community that these incidents would end.

A year after the Harlem riot of 1935, the committee had presented La Guardia with a 126-page report detailing the reasons for the riot. They had written about the terrible housing conditions, underfunded schools, and widespread racial discrimination that contributed to the shocking rates of unemployment. And tuberculosis, which was running rampant in Harlem. Investigators believed it came from poor living conditions and the influx of "migrations from the south." The report ended with the committee's recommendations for enforcing housing codes, improving schools, and soliciting the cooperation of labor unions. It also demanded that "colored doctors and nurses be admitted to all municipal hospitals."

La Guardia agreed with the committee's findings, but after reading the report, instead of making it public, he slipped it into a drawer and kept quiet. Later on, some speculated the findings had painted a grim picture of Harlem and would have been too politically tricky for him to tackle. Whatever the reason, he had ignored them, and now reports were trickling in about hospitals continuing their racist practices.

At Bellevue, the white superintendent who had turned away Alyce

Greene continued rejecting the applications of qualified Black applicants to its postgraduate program; at Lincoln Hospital, the superintendent, on a whim, decided to require meal tickets for its Black student nurses, allowing them to eat only during designated times; otherwise, they had to pay, which they couldn't afford.

But the most chilling account belonged to Harlem Hospital.

Salaria Kea, after being fired from Harlem Hospital, had been rehired to work on the maternity ward. Her return sent an important message to Black nurses that protesting inequity and racism didn't have long-term, career-ending consequences. But the message was premature.

Not long after arriving, Kea found conditions on the ward alarming. And despite being warned about agitating, she began talking. Without mincing words, she penned detailed reports to the administration on how the unit was overcrowded and short-staffed; how expectant mothers were going into labor without a nurse or doctor; and how there was one nurse in charge of the entire ward and fifty babies, many with communicable diseases. Sometimes, Kea observed, infectious mothers were wandering off into the area designated for healthy babies.

Then babies started dying, and Kea involved the Black press, which printed the story. It reinforced to Harlemites that the hospital was a "Death House," a perception that incensed the administrators.

Kea should "mind her own business," they said.

She refused and kept talking and writing reports, and they kept warning until they were "fed up" and again fired her for being outspoken. The administrators may have silenced her, but the problems on the maternity ward didn't end. Following her dismissal, nineteen babies died from infantile diarrhea.

Her report also exposed La Guardia's indifference toward solving any of Harlem's problems, and turned the spotlight on the National Association of Colored Graduate Nurses and their work toward ending racial discrimination. Then the message became clear: if the city officials wouldn't do anything to fix the problem, then Black nurses would.

Taking matters into their own hands, Riddle and Staupers spent months traversing America on Jim Crow trains and buses, stopping at universities and hospitals and holding conferences to let Black nurses know their power and how collectively they could make a change. Their words struck a chord with hundreds of nurses who joined the NACGN's fight for equality, including most of Sea View's Black nursing staff currently grappling with the "Reserved for Whites" placards.

Now, on the wards, the nurses wanted to know if the whispers of "reserved for whites" were true or just a rumor. Word spread again. Yes, "reserved for whites" was true.

Everywhere, more talk ensued.

Who had put them on the tables? Was it Miss Mitchell? Or another white supervisor? A nurse? An aide?

No one knew. And at this moment, it didn't matter to the nurses still standing in front of the dining room. They wanted them removed. Immediately. But how?

A sit-in wouldn't work—it would cost them pay. And a protest might frighten the patients. Letters to the administration would take too long, and so would a boycott. But calling the press would yield immediate results. For years, Riddle and Staupers and Kea, currently serving in the Spanish Civil War as the only Black nurse from America, had reached out to New York's Black press to publicize their fight against discrimination. In response, *The New York Age*, *The Crisis*, and *Opportunity* regularly covered the nurses' plight, publishing stories and feature-length articles on their struggles and contributions.

The nurses made the call to *The New York Amsterdam News*, which broke the story the following day. "Nurses Stage Walkout for Discrimination," read the headline.

And below it:

"The entire group of 350 Negro staff nurses at Sea View staged a 24-hour walkout from the new dining room in protest of what they charge was an attempt to segregate them."

For La Guardia, the situation was another public relations disaster, and making matters worse, someone had discovered the riot report that he'd squirreled away and sent it to the *Amsterdam News*. Hoping to make him squirm and finally act, the paper published the findings in increments, as a serial story. La Guardia had been skewered. In Harlem, he could not afford any more bad press.

When the dining room incident reached his desk, he called Goldwater, and they caught the next ferry to Sea View for a damage-control meeting with Miss Mitchell and other hospital officials. That afternoon, the three—La Guardia, Goldwater, and Mitchell—addressed the press: "Such segregation would not be tolerated," they said, and the "Reserved for Whites" signs were removed. Before the meeting ended, they promised further action would follow "after a suitable investigation."

Everyone seemed satisfied, and the following day, the nurses entered the dining room, their mood subdued and skeptical. Many feared retaliation from Miss Mitchell or Goldwater. But concerns about Goldwater quickly dissipated.

According to the NAACP investigation, Bellevue's superintendent had no legal right to deny Alyce Greene admission. There were no laws or written policies prohibiting Black nurses from attending the school; that was a bogus, made-up rule to keep the school white, and Goldwater should have overridden the rejection and ended the discriminatory practices. Instead, he had supported them, claiming that "integration would introduce a deleterious influence" in the hospital system and make white nurses flee. He also continued echoing the thoughts of many white supervisors: "A great number of Negro nurses," he said, "do not function as efficiently as many of the other group."

Fed up with Goldwater's rebuttals justifying Jim Crowism, the investigating committee informed him that his city agency was the only one practicing "overt and widespread discrimination." In their eyes, he was guilty, and "deliberate segregation was a widespread practice in city nursing programs."

To avoid more negative press, Goldwater announced that New York's nursing schools and hospitals would now accept Black nurses. But he added that none of the institutions had found any qualified ones. The NAACP fixed his problem by sending him two exceptional nurses, both previously rejected by Bellevue. They became the first Black nurses to work at the storied all-white hospital.

The victory brought renewed optimism for the NACGN and Black nurses, who hoped for more progress. Maybe now Goldwater would intercede and work toward integration and, in doing so, inspire the American Nurses Association to open its membership to Black nurses.

But hopes that these successes might lead to ANA membership and full integration were short-lived. When top administrators at the ANA heard the news, they began assembling to discuss how to pause the momentum and keep Black nurses out.

Saved by New Drug." And overnight, the Herculean effort by the AMA to keep Germany's drug at bay collapsed. Sulfa had officially landed on American soil.

The news spread through the medical world, and as predicted, people began asking if a TB cure was imminent. At Sea View, on December 29, two weeks after sulfa appeared, brown-eyed Hilda Ali went home from the hospital, completing another eighteen-month stay. Once again, the nurses threw a party for the little girl, now four and learning to write. After saying goodbye, the nurses prayed she would never return, but if she did, this time, there just might be a drug to save her.

Chapter 19

❖

The Fight

January 1938

Missouria didn't heed the nurses' warning to transfer from the men's ward. Instead, she gradually got used to it. Situated on the third floor of Pavilion 4, the ward housed about thirty-five to forty men, racially and ethnically diverse and ranging in age from sixteen to seventy. All of them, save for the critically ill, lived together on a ward whose layout was repeated on every floor of every pavilion.

The elevator opened onto a long corridor dotted with a series of wooden doors leading to a patients' bathroom, a staff room, a floor kitchen, a storeroom, and a nurse's station. Partway down the hall, the doors on either side stopped and gave way to a six-bed glass-enclosed unit.

Inside, patients lay pinned to their beds, their mouths opening and closing, gasping for air, and their chests heaving and caving, emitting sounds that resembled broken flutes. They were the "incurables," the people who caused passersby to avert their eyes and feel their most potent fears begin to stir.

A little beyond the "incurables" was a set of double doors that opened into a great room, a loftlike space. On either side, against the wall of windows—the ones Miss Mitchell demanded remain open—rows of metal-frame beds were arranged end-to-end. Each one was separated by only a nightstand. Here lived dozens of men, their lives on display for all to see.

"The wards were the great equalizers," one man said. "If you wanted privacy, this wasn't the place."

Half the men were ambulatory patients. The rest were a mix of those who could sit up unaided, those who were bedridden but not critical, and the "lungers," long-term patients whose time at Sea View spanned three or four years or who, similar to Hilda Ali, were on an endless cycle of discharge and admittance. At the moment, Missouria's ward hosted two lungers: Philip Thompson and Mr. Albert.

Seven years earlier, Thompson had contracted TB from working twelve hours a day in an unventilated laundry room, pulling mounds of clothes from washers and dryers in heat that soared above 120 degrees. Unlike his ward mate, Mr. Albert, Thompson was a gregarious man with a rasping laugh, well known across Sea View for his humor about being sick longer than most on the floor.

"I'm an old hand at TB," he repeated over and over.

While doing her rounds, Missouria often caught snippets of conversation that drifted between the ambulatory men, who enjoyed congregating in different groups. From one side of the ward, she heard about politics: FDR and his New Deal were always hot topics. But now so was Hitler and the growing wave of fanaticism sweeping through Germany.

Another group sent up opinions about the stock market. They hunched together over the newspaper and reviewed corporations and commodities, talking with conviction as if they weren't penniless and the outcomes of General Motors opening three new factories or the rise in steel and rail had an effect on their lives.

Then came the ones who bypassed politics and stocks and opted for more dramatic news. They relayed stories of robberies and murders and disasters. Recently the Honeymoon Bridge at Niagara Falls had collapsed. One hundred feet of ice twisted its steel frame, sending it plunging into the frozen gorge. Maybe, some speculated, FDR's New

Deal would fix the bridge, but who knew, as so much of America was broken.

Most of their conversations bored her, their words grazing her ears, then slipping by, becoming background noise, but sometimes they piqued her interest, and she was drawn in, her mind composing responses. That's what happened one day in January.

There was nothing unusual when she entered the ward with her cart that afternoon and continued rolling it toward the far end, where the winter light was shining as it always did, in streaks. It fell across the bed of a man squirreled under his covers and reached farther, touching the pieces on a precariously placed checkerboard between two men who played all day. But it stopped short at the feet of a man who sat with his legs dangling over the side of his bed, spitting phlegm into a tissue. Next to him Missouria's colleague Nurse Janie Shirley was pulling out a bedpan. The two women exchanged hellos, and then Missouria continued toward the end of the ward, where the sports fanatics liked to gather.

Their recent conversations were about boxing, a sport Missouria loved. One man, whose lungs were a mishmash of cavities and frayed nerves, was ranting about the German underdog who, on a hazy June night at Yankee Stadium two summers earlier, in 1936, fought twenty-two-year-old Joe Louis.

The German was a Nazi, a fascist, he said, his voice expanding and contracting, the excitement causing his chest to make peculiar jangling sounds, as if his lungs were wound in metal chains.

Back in 1936, the press had hyped the fight between the German and the American, turning it into a geopolitical battle. Louis was a natural talent. Powerful and quick, the young Black man from Detroit possessed a calm and easygoing demeanor in the ring, and a remarkable ability to take a punch. Ernest Hemingway said Louis was the "most beautiful fighting machine" he'd ever seen, and Louis's becoming heavyweight champion of the world was inevitable.

His opponent, the former world heavyweight champion Max "Maxie" Schmeling, was the opposite of Louis. A cautious and more patient fighter, the hulking German possessed a mastery of timing and counterpunching and had a bestial right punch that was perfect for exploiting Louis's weakness of dropping his guard for a split second between jabs.

Under the bright floodlights of the stadium that fateful night in 1936, forty-five thousand fans watched as the twelfth round started. Schmeling wasted no time pouncing on his opponent, his right hooks continuing to maul young Louis's face, causing him to stagger along the ropes. Schmeling was relentless tracking him, and then two minutes and twenty-nine seconds into the round, his right fist flew. It hit the "Brown Bomber," who fell, crumbling to the ground in a heap. The referee hovered above him and then called the fight. But instead of turning to the victor, Schmeling, he helped lift Louis up.

Schmeling didn't care.

He ran out into the ring in front of the thunderstruck crowd and waited until the referee officially declared him the winner. That night, Hitler sent Schmeling a cable congratulating him, and Joseph Goebbels, his propaganda minister, wrote in his journal: "The white man defeats the black man, and the white man was German!" Then he sent Schmeling a message: "That was a German victory," he wrote. "Heil Hitler!" Exalted, Schmeling returned to Germany, where the Führer declared him a national hero.

Here in America, Louis became a villain.

"He was," wrote Margaret Garrahan of *The Birmingham News*, "a tan-skinned throw-back to the creature of primitive swamps who gloried in battles and blood."

"His invincibility as a fighter is a shattered myth," penned another.

"He blinked stupidly and with patient resignation, but thousands of Uncle Toms have done it better and with more moving effect . . . up there . . . was the white master, Max Schmeling." The Black community was also angry, but their disappointment came from a different place. Louis's defeat struck a more delicate chord with them: the young boxer had emerged as a symbol of pride, a victor in a sport dominated by whites.

"The negro race has been betrayed," wrote one journalist.

And worse, his loss happened on June 19, known as Juneteenth, the anniversary celebrating the arrival of federal messengers in Texas in 1865, heralding the news of President Lincoln's Emancipation Proclamation that ordered "all persons held as slaves henceforward shall be free."

"The events of that fatal Friday [were] like a nightmare," Harlem residents told news reporters.

Windows were smashed, and fights broke out. People who had lost bets brawled; there was a stabbing, and someone was shot in the leg. Several attempted suicides were thwarted, including that of a young girl who tried to drink poison. Reverend Henry Swan never gave his opinion of the fight. When the referee declared Schmeling the winner, Swan fell to the ground, water in hand, and died of a heart attack.

"I walked down Seventh Avenue," Langston Hughes wrote, "and saw grown men weeping like children, and women sitting in the curbs with their head in their hands."

Now, on the ward, the man with the rattling chest was still ranting. The German Max Schmeling was returning to New York City for a rematch.

Would Louis give up his womanizing and train properly this time?

Would he focus and beat Schmeling, who liked to carouse with the Nazis?

More men joined in; some from across the room. And soon the talk became a hot-tempered debate infused with racial slurs. Missouria heard the discussion shift. She kept her head down, but cast her eyes up, glancing at her colleagues busy collecting sputum cups and changing patients. Her jaw tightened and her body tensed, a visceral reaction to moments like this.

Many such incidents had internally marked her, lodging themselves in her muscle memory. The "Hat Story" was one.

❖

Clinton, no different from other southern towns, had hemmed its Black population into an area bordered by two sets of railroad tracks. Getting to and from church, school, stores, and the cotton fields required a circuitous alternative route, one that would avoid Mill Town, where the white workers employed by the Lydia Cotton Mill lived. In their spare time, they heckled Black people, standing on their porches and tossing rocks and garbage and yelling terrible things.

To avoid the abuse, the Black community had carved out a path that ran through the woods. Although the route was longer, and in the summer there were snakes, gnats, and giant mosquitoes, most of the time, it was safer. But sometimes, to stave off boredom, white men went into the woods. They hid behind trees, hoping, they said, "to have fun with the Black girls."

That summer day under the searing South Carolina sun, eleven-year-old Missouria, dressed in her Sunday best, wasn't expecting any trouble. She was hot and her thoughts were on staying cool, on arriving home and having a glass of Mama Amy's spearmint iced tea, the leaves pulled right from the garden, when the white boy jumped out from behind a tree, startling her. He stood in front of her, blocking her way. Thoughts of tea and heat fell away and were replaced by a surge of adrenaline.

She stared at him, then tried to go around him like Mama Amy once told her: "Look at them," she had said, "then get out of the way. Find a path around them. Just don't try to make sense of them."

But she couldn't go around him. When she went left, he went left. When she went right, he went right. The two stood at an impasse. He smiled, watching her eyes narrow.

"Nigger!" he yelled, reaching for her head and grabbing her hat.

Missouria tried to grab it back, but he pulled it away.

"Nig-ger. Nig-ger," he repeated, and laughed, then threw her hat into the air, where it caught on a tree branch.

Missouria looked at him, regarded his face, then raised her hand high. They were big hands, her family said, "like baseball mitts." They weren't good for picking—her fingers snagged on the points of the cotton boll, leaving the tips and cuticles scratched and bleeding—but they were perfect for slapping. Down it came, open palm landing hard on his cheek, flesh meeting flesh and leaving a big red mark.

The boy cursed and spit, then skulked away.

Missouria, in her dress, climbed the tree and got her hat and walked home, feeling her power. But her older brother Roy raged over the story.

"Let it go," Mama Amy told him. But he couldn't forget, couldn't let it go. He took his fury to the streets of Clinton to search out the white boy. When he found him, Roy unleashed all his pent-up ire with tight fists that landed on the boy's eye and jaw and chin.

The following evening, just after dinner, the Clinton sheriff called Mama Amy to the fence. He got his moonshine, "the best around," from Mama Amy's brother, and believed she deserved a warning for booze that good. By the time the mob of white boys came chanting down Carolina Avenue, kicking up the dirt, Roy was miles away. Mama Amy heard them from her living room, where she sat behind drawn curtains with the shotgun resting on her thighs and wept into cupped hands.

"My boy," she kept saying, over and over for hours. "My boy, my boy."

Now, as the men continued their argument, Missouria pushed her cart just enough so the glass bottles of alcohol, iodine, elixirs, and codeine clanked against one another. The men quieted.

She slowed and looked at them, wanting to ask why they talked like that. Did they believe what they were saying? Did they see her when they said it? But she couldn't ask them.

She felt sorry for them, even when they were at their worst. Inside one, a clot was forming, the blood was gathering, pooling together, and soon it would burst in a flash; another knew his days were numbered, death was imminent; and another had just surpassed 1,266 days at Sea View.

They were all so wrecked, living in bodies that hated them. No amount of cod-liver oil or vitamins could fight back the disease that mashed up their organs and lives. Showers, baths, and cologne couldn't mask the stench of illness lingering on their skin. She knew their minds were foggy, a muddle of thoughts that turned time into a heap of hours, one minute rolling into the next without form or meaning. They bantered all day like vaudeville characters about boxing matches and the New Deal, unemployment and the "coppers and commies," and the "vamps" in Ward 33 being the perfect cure; about Tom's latest flame, Harry picking meat from the garbage, the "sourpuss" nurses, and B.G., who could "swear like a sailor's parrot." Hour after hour, they talked. Nothing could change these realities.

But sometimes their banter turned to begging, and they grabbed her hand and pleaded for "something, anything," they said, "for the pain." And sometimes she could help them, and that brought her comfort.

She looked at them a moment longer, deliberating, then lowered her head and moved her cart. For now, she had work to do.

Chapter 20

❖

The Offer

Late Spring 1938

Edna's house hunting was going slow. A year into her search, there were still few houses available to her. Many were too far away, in unfamiliar areas, or in neighborhoods that she disliked or that wouldn't let her buy. But she liked Bradley Avenue, a mile from Sea View in the neighborhood officially known as Willowbrook, and unofficially as "Dogpatch" because of all the roaming dogs.

She was familiar with the steep, roughly paved road and its assortment of sparse homes and vacant lots from her friend Miss Leola Demby, who worked in Sea View's women's ward and owned a shotgun house at the end of the avenue beside a small creek. During the summer, Miss Demby enjoyed throwing grand parties in her backyard with music and platters of food. An invitation was highly sought after by the nurses, who arrived in bunches and stayed late into the night.

At one of these parties, Edna had met Miss Marion Evans, and the two became fast friends. Miss Evans was also a nurse at Sea View and also lived on Bradley Avenue with her husband, Arthur, a window washer prone to gambling, like Forest. Their home was five doors up from Miss Demby's. It was a small two-story, wood-frame house with a sad picket fence hedging in a yard of dead grass and shrubs. But there was something about it, a feeling that drew Edna to the house and to

Bradley Avenue. It wasn't a pretty street—it never would be—but she
believed it held possibility. Apart from Miss Demby and Miss Evans,
the few other families who lived on Bradley Avenue were Italian immigrants.

In the early 1900s, Bradley Avenue was a popular destination
for many Italian immigrants, who purchased land and built small
wood-framed cottages as summer homes. They came from Brooklyn
to escape the heat and crowds and stayed for days or weeks or sometimes
the entire summer. But over the years, as they prospered, they stopped
coming, and the homes became abandoned and worn down. Some
collapsed, others were collapsing, and still others had become refuges
for the abundance of stray animals that prowled the area—goats and
packs of emaciated dogs and cats, yowling and howling and sifting
through trash cans.

Recently, an appraiser from the Home Owners' Loan Corporation
(HOLC), created in 1933 by the US government to slow down housing
foreclosures, had denounced the neighborhood. According to the assessor, a portion of it was rife with noxious fumes from a nearby oil plant.
The odors, he claimed, lingered in the air and wafted into the surrounding areas. Another set of chemical plants, he explained, emitted
gases that drifted outward, killing vegetation. The streets, including
Bradley Avenue, lacked sewers, and the Farm Colony poorhouse, with
over thousands of indigent workers, abutted its southern part.

But the smells and Farm Colony were minor issues. Two miles
away, the city was building a sprawling five-thousand-bed "asylum for
mentally defective children," prompting the assessor to determine that
Edna's hoped-for side of Bradley Avenue was undesirable, with many
"detrimental influences."

The report ended with a warning: "If this area should be taken
over by the colored employees of Seaview Hospital and the Asylum for
Mental Defectives," he wrote, "some decreases in values will be inevitable. It appears at present that the area is headed in just that direction."

If he was right, the neighborhood would be starved for resources and investors, allowing it to decline further. But Edna wasn't interested in the assessor's perception of this neighborhood. To her, Willowbrook/Dogpatch was fine, maybe not for white homeowners, but definitely for the "colored employees of Seaview," who saw its potential. She told Miss Evans and Miss Demby she wanted to live there.

In June, Miss Evans invited Edna and Forest to listen to the long-awaited rematch between Joe Louis and Max Schmeling. She also wanted to make them an offer.

That night, the two couples sat in the Evanses' living room and, with food and drinks on the table, gathered around the radio, a scene that was repeated across the country—in Plains, Georgia, a teenager named Jimmy Carter, the future US president, was listening under a mulberry tree. In New York, however, there was no such languidness. Here, the air was electric, bristling with nervous energy, especially up in Harlem. There people gathered on street corners and packed into bars, clubs, shops, and living rooms. Everywhere seemed to be a hot spot to tune in. At Sea View, nurses brought radios into staff rooms and dining rooms and the wards, where patients sat clustered together on the beds.

Minutes before 10 p.m., the fast-talking voice of a radio announcer, live from Yankee Stadium, came rushing through the radio's front speaker: "Besides the unseen audience that is listening to this," he stammered above cheers, "is this great enthusiastic crowd that have come out here and expect to see one of the greatest fights they ever witnessed."

For many, this fight transcended the sport. They saw it through the same lens as the previous one, a political battle between two superpowers, the democratic United States and the autocratic Nazi Germany. Since the first match two years earlier, Louis had fought his way to becoming the heavyweight champion of the world, a title held by Schmeling from 1930 to 1932. But for the Brown Bomber, it wasn't enough.

"I ain't no champion till I beat Schmeling," he had said.

Schmeling, meanwhile, had become a national hero, with his home-turf bouts turning into Nazi pageants. In his free time, he went hunting with Nazi military leader Hermann Göring, and Anny, Schmeling's movie-star wife, would watch him fight while sitting alongside Joseph Goebbels and his family. Despite mingling with the Nazi Party, Schmeling never joined it; however, with his manager being a Jewish American, in the eyes of the world, including those of President Roosevelt, Germany's prizefighter was a Nazi. When Louis visited the White House, Roosevelt told him, "Joe, we need muscles like yours to beat Germany."

At 10 p.m., the men on Ward 64, Edna and Miss Evans, the seventy thousand fans at Yankee Stadium, and the hundred million other listeners heard the ring announcer declare: "This is the feature attraction, fifteen rounds for the world's heavyweight championship."

Then he introduced Schmeling. Wearing purple shorts, the German made his way into the stadium. The crowd booed and pelted him with banana peels, cigarette packs, soda cups, napkins, and spit.

"Never in my life did 100 meters seem this long," Schmeling later recalled.

Then the long-awaited moment: "Weighing one ninety-eight and three-quarters, wearing black trunks," the announcer shouted, "the famous Detroit Brown Bomber, world heavyweight champion, Joe Louis!"

People sprang to their feet when Louis walked into the stadium, the air exploding with cheers and chants: *Louis, Louis, Louis.* He lifted his fists high, and the cheers became roars. Louis reveled—but also trembled: he was a boxer, a world champion, but on this night he was "a black man . . . representing all of America," he said. "They were depending on me to K.O. Germany."

The two fighters dropped their satin robes and, fists cocked, moved to the center of the ring. They began dancing around each other, trading jabs. In minutes, Louis landed an explosive right to Schmeling's jaw, stunning the German. The crowd erupted.

Louis followed with a series of cleaving punches to the head.

"Louis with the old one-two. First a left and then the right," said the radio announcer, and then another blow square in the jaw.

The men on Ward 64 bent in closer to the radio and clenched their fists so hard their bony knuckles turned white. Missouria, still listening, looked over at her patients. Louis had to win—a thought shared by everyone in Harlem and Miss Evans's living room. Schmeling spun, went down, and then stood up again. But after that, Louis owned him. The Black American heaped on more punches.

The announcer called the shots, his voice rising and falling: "Right and left hooks snapping back and forth at Schmeling's face."

At two minutes and four seconds into the match, Louis hurled one final explosive left that sent Schmeling tumbling to the mat. Some ringsiders said they heard Schmeling "let out a scream—half human, half animal." The crowd watched as Hitler's national hero crawled on his knees, dazed, until he collapsed.

"The count is five. Five, six, seven, eight," the announcer declared. "The men are in the ring. The fight is over—on a technical knockout."

At Sea View, the men on Ward 64 clapped and shouted; the American had won. In Miss Evans's living room, they hugged and cheered and hoped that his victory would change things for Black Americans, that finally they would be seen as equals. For the moment, as the Brown Bomber's victory was celebrated across America with wild abandon, it really seemed that way.

In Louis's hometown of Detroit, a ten-piece orchestra played swing music while people came running from their homes and clubs to dance in the street; in Chicago, drivers tied old tubs and tin cans to their car bumpers and paraded through the streets; and in Pittsburgh's Hill District, there was singing and fireworks and an anti-Nazi demonstration. But the largest celebration was in Harlem.

On his way to the hospital, Schmeling saw the dancing crowds and bands along the avenues and streets, punctuated by the calling of Joe Louis's name. Clubs were jam-packed with revelers, both ordinary and famous. At the celebrated Smalls Paradise, the mayor of Detroit, fresh off a plane, joined New York's politicians and socialites to toast and cheer and drink champagne. Down the block among the smashing bottles and confetti, Black and Jewish New Yorkers paraded past the *Amsterdam News* offices carrying signs: "Aryan Supremacy Taboo," "Joe Louis Wins—Hitler Weeps." In the street, little children screamed, "Joe Louis knocked him out . . . that's too much!"

During his press conference, Louis, normally reserved, gave a rare smug grin. "Now," he said, "I feel like a champ."

Sometime after the fight, Miss Evans told Edna that she and Arthur co-owned their home with an Italian family from Rome, the Pedalinos, who lived downstairs. Recently, the Pedalinos had defaulted on their mortgage, causing them to also default. Now, the Home Owners' Loan Corporation was threatening to foreclose, and if that happened, she and Arthur would be homeless.

Would Edna want to remortgage the house?

Chapter 21

Homecoming

Summer 1938–Winter 1939

Edna sat in the nurses' station, writing her daily notes in the logbook: patient updates, who to watch and who to transfer, medications to dispense, tray setups, and the usual note about the linens—almost weekly, Miss Mitchell reminded them about linen overuse. Once she finished, she changed out of her uniform and into a day dress, removed her cap, fixed her hair, put on some lipstick, and wished her colleagues a good afternoon.

Outside, the day was bright and the sun still warm. Edna stopped a moment to look at the wildflowers that danced and swayed in the summer breeze. Then she began walking, but instead of her usual routine of turning left and heading to the nurses' residence, she turned right and took the path leading to the administration building.

It was a short walk on a busy path, full of commotion: people entering and exiting the building and taxis and ambulances dropping off new patients whose names, by evening, would be added to the oversized registry. And then just beyond the R111 bus stop, where visitors and staff waited for the rickety old bus, she saw Forest with his summer fedora coming toward her. They hugged, and he took her hand, and together they set off for the main exit of Sea View.

It was a pretty walk, especially in the summer, when everything was lush and green and in bloom. If one ignored the nurses who sat on benches reading to patients slumped in wheelchairs and the pavilions with their porches full of sick people lying in beds gazing into a sky the color of indigo, it was easy to believe this place was a park or the gardens of someone very wealthy. But the power station puffing out black smoke and staining that indigo sky, and the hearses rambling up the road, whizzing by Edna and Forest toward the morgue, always gave it away. This was no park.

On they walked, the complex falling farther behind them. Occasionally Forest would glance away from the surroundings, setting his eyes on his wife. He was proud of her, knew her worth, respected her independence and her drive to have a professional career, and unlike many men of his time, he didn't expect her to stay home and cook and clean for him. And for that, she was grateful. She knew few men in the 1930s who would grant a woman that kind of freedom, and in turn, she didn't try to change him or his pool habit, regardless of how much worry it caused her.

Exiting Sea View, they stepped onto winding Brielle Avenue, which led to Bradley Avenue, where they turned and headed down the hill toward the culmination of Edna's long-held dream, a home, on this street. They moved quicker now, ignoring the empty lots and odd assortment of houses until they reached 358, the house with two small steps that led to a crooked front door. Edna slipped the key into the lock, pushed open the door, and stepped into the first-floor apartment.

The past few days had been a blur. Earlier in the week, she'd reached into the contents of the envelope marked "My House" and remortgaged the house from HOLC, and in the process, saved the Evanses from becoming homeless. For now, they would continue to live upstairs and pay Edna rent. To celebrate, the nurses threw her a goodbye party in the rumpus room. "Congratulations," they said. "Come back and visit." "God bless you, Miss Sutton."

All of them knew it was a remarkable achievement: in America, only about 21 percent of Black people owned a home, and Edna Sutton, the daughter of an enslaved man, who'd grown up in a tar paper shack in Savannah's slums, was now one of them.

❖

Edna's house brought her joy. She reveled in coming home from her late-night shifts and stretching out on her couch and not worrying about Forest dying in a pool hall brawl. And Americus, newly graduated from high school, was coming to live with them soon. But the Sunday post-church luncheons that she hosted for her nursing friends brought her the greatest joy.

The get-togethers were social, with food and cards and friendly conversation that eventually turned political, recalling the rumpus room and dorm meetings at Harlem Hospital—those days when the hours slipped by while they talked about the injustices of dining rooms, superintendents, and colleagues like Mr. Legassi, who refused to put through phone calls. Not much had changed since then, except Edna, who was ready to fight against inequality by opening her home and making it a place for nurses to come together and make change for the next generation.

Recently, the nurses were preoccupied with the crushing health crisis created by the Depression that left millions of New Yorkers sick and poor and desperate for help. With no insurance, they flocked to city hospitals, clogging the hallways and begging to be seen. But all the hospitals were operating over capacity, with dwindling funds and only half the staff. They couldn't accommodate the masses and began turning people away, sending them back into the streets, where they spread more sickness. Black New Yorkers, as always, faced a more dismal situation: only four hospitals were open to them, and the rest either refused to treat them or did it with contempt. The fault was La Guardia's. His failure, driven by Commissioner Goldwater's indifference to helping the Black community by integrating hospitals, had now created this dire, life-threatening scenario.

In November, *The New York Amsterdam News* reported a chilling story. A pregnant Black woman was admitted to the segregated maternity ward at St. John's Hospital, notorious for its shameless discrimination. In a room alone, she began having contractions and screamed for a doctor, but no one came. Her contractions grew worse, coming with more force and fury. Unable to hold back, she pushed, and in those nanoseconds between pushing, she kept yelling, "Nurse! Nurse! My baby is coming."

Still, no one came.

Realizing she would deliver alone, she clutched the edges of the mattress and tried to sit up, to catch the baby tumbling out of her, but she couldn't lift herself up. Suddenly, the baby lurched itself from her body, coming to rest on the bloody sheets with the cord around its neck, making what the mother described as "strangling noises."

A white nurse eventually came in, saw the child, and ran out. Seconds later, she returned with a second nurse, who cut the cord and whisked away the newborn, leaving the mother dazed and bleeding.

"Where's my baby?" she asked them. "Where's my baby?"

Finally, a nurse told her that "it was sick, with pneumonia," and the hospital had transferred it to Kings County Hospital in Brooklyn. Weeks later, the parents, who had never laid eyes on their baby, received a telegram telling them it was dead. The mother filed a police report, and after finding the staff's behavior suspicious, authorities were now treating it as a murder.

The story had enraged the NAACP. Such tragedies were preventable, its leaders believed. If only Goldwater had listened to their grievances and allowed Black doctors and nurses to staff the understaffed wards of city hospitals. And yet, despite the bad press, the pressure from the NAACP and NACGN, the mayor, and the Harlem community, Goldwater had refused to budge,

preferring to remain mired in his belief that Black medical professionals didn't belong in the city's hospitals and publicly questioning
"the competence and ability of the Negro nurses." The comments were
the last straw for the Black community. They demanded that La
Guardia remove him. But before the mayor had a chance, Goldwater
resigned.

When thinking about his resignation, some believed it could be
traced back to a singular person: Alyce Eugenia Greene, one of their
own. Her patience and tenacity in fighting her rejection from
Bellevue's postgraduate program led directly to the four-year
investigation into Goldwater's prejudice and to his great public un-
masking as the man who, the National Council of Negro Women said,
"practiced Hitlerism on Negro doctors and nurses." Change was
coming, they thought. But following Goldwater's resignation, La
Guardia stalled in appointing his replacement, leaving the aging commissioner still legally in power. The situation didn't bode well for
anyone, especially for nurses. Recently, newspapers were reporting a
dire nursing shortage, a problem Goldwater had helped to create by
refusing to end discriminatory hiring practices. For the Sea View
nurses, the news struck hard: the recent addition of 157 more beds had
made their shortage more acute and their work conditions more dangerous.

And now, Dr. Ornstein, the hospital's director of medicine, had
completed his long-term study exploring whether "the Negro race" was
more "racial susceptible" to tuberculosis. After following one thousand
of Sea View's nurses and aides for over four years, he found that Black
people weren't predisposed to the disease; rather, environmental conditions affected infection rates, leading him to conclude that Sea
View's nurses were "subjected to a definite occupational hazard resulting from their occupation."

There it was. Finally, someone admitted what the nurses knew all
along: that working at Sea View was dangerous. Ornstein's report was

seminal and inspired much discussion on protecting nurses. Dr. Myers, who first observed the high rates of tuberculosis among student nurses in 1930, agreed with Ornstein and suggested the staggering infection rates were avoidable with masks and gowns. In recent years, some hospitals were beginning to soften in their resistance to the idea. Not at Sea View.

By 1939, Miss Mitchell was considered an authority on nursing and tuberculosis and was invited by the National Conference for Tuberculosis to speak alongside other prominent TB experts. Her talk, titled "Tuberculosis as an Occupational and Compensable Disease from the Standpoint of the Employee," focused on keeping her nurses safe, but she ignored Ornstein's findings and the emerging studies advising nurses to wear protection.

To Miss Mitchell, many of these studies were inaccurate, compiled by men who didn't see the nurses' daily activities, how a nurse would put on a gauze mask and, as she explained, "wear it for hours, and then dampened and warmed by her breathing on the inside, grossly contaminated by her close contact with a highly positive patient . . . roll it in a neat little ball and tuck it away in her pocket for later use." According to her, these behaviors were disgusting and unprofessional and the real reason for high infection rates among nurses.

"I am of the opinion that the development of tuberculosis in nurses could be radically reduced, if each nurse would practice a more careful technic and guard her health more carefully." By putting the onus on the nurses to stay healthy, she absolved herself of any responsibility when they fell ill: "Nursing in a tuberculosis institution is not as dangerous as we are led to believe," she said, and "those who are careless usually pay the price." They die.

As the decade came to a close, Black nurses had little to celebrate. Every step forward seemed marked by two steps back. Miss Mitchell refused to safeguard their health, and the ANA was still denying them membership, and they remained underpaid, with few opportunities for advancement. If Black nurses wanted to change their status, they knew it would take something much bigger than calling a newspaper or Goldwater's resignation or wearing a mask. They needed something huge, something cataclysmic, something that would be felt on a global scale, something like a war.

Part III

❖

1940–1944

Chapter 22

Dr. Edward Robitzek

November 1940

Dr. Edward Robitzek opened the door and stepped into the low-lit, musty morgue at Sea View, leaving behind the bluster of a freezing winter day. Inside, he blew into his hands before unbuttoning his woolen coat and hanging it on a hook. Still feeling the chill from outside, a nip that would continue all afternoon, as the morgue itself always leaned cold, he pulled out a clean surgical gown and unfurled it.

As he dressed, his mind sometimes wandered to different things: his career, his new wife, a book he was reading, tuberculosis, and the war. It was November 1940, more than a year since Hitler had invaded Poland, and things were deteriorating. Tanks and bombers now annihilated Europe, and nation after nation—Denmark, Norway, the Netherlands, Belgium, and France—fell to the Nazis. He pushed this thought aside, knowing it could easily consume all others, slipped a pair of rubber gloves over his hands, and moved the tray table with his equipment to the center of the room, toward the body on the table.

It was small and frail, and in the dim light, the waxen face looked peaceful, almost pretty. The lashes were long, and the hair fell in long strands, hiding the wooden block that supported the neck.

As the hospital's newest doctor, the tall and lanky twenty-seven-year-old, with movie-star good looks, was putting in twelve-hour shifts, and even those weren't enough to manage the bodies arriving on gurneys at all hours. He was tired, and before starting, he paused and took off his glasses, revealing sky-blue eyes shadowed by dark circles. The left one felt especially fatigued; it always did, as it compensated for his right one, left blind by a childhood injury. He closed them and with his index finger and thumb squeezed the bridge of his nose to relieve some of the strain.

According to the case report, the body on the table belonged to M.L., a sixteen-year-old Puerto Rican female. Admitted two years earlier with pulmonary tuberculosis, M.L. had undergone a series of operations. The most recent was a phrenic nerve crush, a procedure where doctors cut the phrenic nerve on one side of the neck to temporarily paralyze half the diaphragm, the primary muscle responsible for inhaling and exhaling. When cut, the diaphragm ceased contracting, leaving the lung static, or at rest. Doctors hoped that in this immobile state, the lung might heal. But M.L. had spiked a fever, and two nights ago she had died. Her family consented to an autopsy, hoping their daughter's lungs could add to Sea View's growing research on tuberculosis.

Robitzek had always been drawn to pathology, to the interior of the human body; to him, each set of lungs, a part of the brain, a fragment from the spine, or a cord from the larynx provided another clue in the seemingly never-ending mystery that was tuberculosis. "The human body never lies," he always said, and maybe through all these pieces of livers, kidneys, brains, lungs, and intestines, he could uncover new truths about this disease, understand how it manifested in and through the body, and why it spread. Only then could a cure happen.

Born in the Bronx in 1912, Robitzek was the only child of Kate and Arthur Robitzek. He was a quiet kid, smart and curious, who enjoyed spending time with his parents, especially his father, a generous gentleman, who co-owned a prosperous coal company with his two brothers. Their profits enabled all the brothers to buy homes with lawns and servants, vast kitchens, guest bedrooms, and stunning views. Life was good for the brothers Robitzek, until 1922, when the dread disease arrived in Arthur's home.

The diagnosis shocked the family. Tuberculosis wasn't supposed to breach the lungs of a healthy and wealthy forty-five-year-old man like Arthur. He lived in a large, clean house, ate good food, and exercised, and his job kept him mostly outdoors. According to the thinking of the time, Arthur Robitzek had nothing in common with the typical victims of tuberculosis, but the bacteria had found him anyway.

His doctor suggested going to a sanatorium to rest and hopefully heal. Sea View was twenty-three miles from the family's home, allowing for easy visits from his wife and son, but his doctor refused to admit him. Men of Arthur's status went to the Trudeau Sanatorium in Saranac Lake, a small, private, boutique-like sanatorium founded by Dr. Edward Livingston Trudeau in 1885. Stricken by tuberculosis, Trudeau had originally gone to this remote lake, tucked hundreds of miles away in the Adirondack Mountains, hoping to die amid crystal brooks and tall, swaying trees, but instead of dying, he was healed. Fifty-five years later, his place, with its quaint cottages and philosophy that the cure was "not a hospital stay, but a way of life . . . a conversion to a nearly religious regimen of health," had become world renowned. Over the years, it had attracted the likes of novelist Robert Louis Stevenson, New York Giants pitcher Christy Mathewson, a litany of vaudeville stars, and now Arthur Robitzek.

He arrived in autumn 1923, tired and weak and much too thin. His cottage room was small and rustic, with a dresser and a twin bed covered with a patchwork quilt, and his shared wooden porch faced the forest, where trees blazed with fall colors. Upon admittance, he received the standard booklet, *Getting the Most out of Your Cure*, outlining his role in getting well and the sanatorium rules. The entire place, all of it, was a radical departure from his stately home, with its large, well-furnished rooms, but he was grateful and eager to get well.

Arthur was a good patient, diligently following Trudeau's regimen:

rest and long periods of time sitting outside in a 'Rondack Reclining Chair, a combination bed and chair specially designed to make the prescribed bed rest more comfortable. As he improved, Arthur spent his "chair time" writing long letters to his son, telling him about foxes and deer and how he was "feeling better." Finally, he wrote about "coming home cured." Later in life, Robitzek would recall his father's letters and realize how naïve the word "cure" sounded, how it was a relative term, almost absurd.

Six months later, Arthur was discharged, with orders to live a healthy lifestyle and follow the rest-cure regimen at home. Two years passed, Arthur was feeling healthy, his strength had returned, and tuberculosis began receding from the Robitzek family. Then one day, he spiked a fever, followed by a cough and lethargy and loss of appetite. The second diagnosis fell hard: laryngeal tuberculosis. This, he learned was more contagious than the original diagnosis of pulmonary tuberculosis. It was also far more cunning and difficult to treat.

Arthur weighed his options. He didn't want to return to Saranac Lake and spend his days lounging in 'rondack recliners and sleeping under patchwork quilts; nor did he want to try any invasive surgical procedures at Sea View. Rather, he wanted to live his remaining time at home, surrounded by his family. But death was cruel to Arthur. It came slowly in a drawn-out process that tormented him and his wife and his sixteen-year-old son.

Recalling those days watching his father's demise, Robitzek remembered how the disease transformed him from a robust middle-aged gentleman into a wheezing old man with unresponsive eyes and indented cheeks. For weeks, young Robitzek sat beside his father, watching his rib cage heave and cave, knowing that soon it would seize up; that those thick fluids moving around would stop churning, and the man he loved most would choke to death.

On May 1, 1929, with his wife and teenage son sitting beside him, Arthur took his last breath. Three days later, on a gloomy morning, Robitzek followed his father's casket, draped with sprays of roses, lilies, gladioli, and carnations, through the vast acres of Woodlawn Cemetery in the Bronx. There they laid Arthur to rest in the same ground as Herman Melville, Nellie Bly, and suffragist Elizabeth Cady Stanton.

His father's death was wretched, altering the course of his life. Instead of pursuing a degree in accounting and joining the family business, he took premed courses at Colgate University. After graduating, he enrolled in New York's Columbia University College of Physicians and Surgeons to study chest diseases. It was there, while struggling with an organic chemistry class, that his professor told him, "You will never be a doctor," a remark Robitzek never forgot.

He finished in 1938, graduating with top honors, and took a rotating internship at Fordham University. As part of his training, he spent a year riding in ambulances.

The new Ford ambulance was sleek and streamlined, able to cut through New York City's congested avenues fast. Its siren was loud, blaring over the constant clamor of horns, trolley bells, jackhammers, and elevated trains that blanketed the city. Robitzek worked night and day—in 1938 alone there were over four hundred thousand ambulance calls in the city. He attended to car accidents, heart attacks, robberies, stabbings, domestic fights, children tumbling out of windows, and fires.

Sometimes he would watch as firemen swung their ladders ten or twelve stories high and, laden with equipment, climbed up into burning buildings. Minutes later, they'd emerge with limp bodies draped in their arms for him to save. Kneeling above the victims, Robitzek would cut open their shirts and perform chest compressions and mouth-to-mouth resuscitation, his own mouth filling with the taste of smoke and ash.

Other times, he was called to terrible accidents where bodies were pitched and tossed, their bones snapped in half. He managed the victims' pain and secured the broken bones with splints. At night in bed, his back ached from lifting hundreds of pounds of dead weight onto stretchers and loading them into the back of the ambulance, and then crouching under its low-pitched roof, trying to keep the victims alive. But he was grateful for the experience: "It exposed me to everything medical," he said.

He finished his ambulance service in 1939, the year Hitler marched into Poland and instructed his generals to "darken the skies over Warsaw with falling bombs and drown the people in blood." Seeing the devastation wrought by the German Heinkel and Junkers bombers, many American doctors felt compelled to offer their service either abroad or stateside.

The young Robitzek immediately joined thousands of his colleagues and registered for the draft, hoping to serve his country as a medic. But he learned the US military didn't want men with one good eye. The rejection outraged him: "It was the stupidest thing," he would later say. "They should know that having one eye as a diagnostician is different from having one eye as a sniper."

And so here he was, at Sea View, fighting an altogether different war. After being rejected by the military, the newly minted doctor had accepted a one-year post as a resident pathologist.

His boss at Fordham thought it was a peculiar choice for a promising young doctor with so many options. He could stay at Fordham or transfer to the prestigious Cornell University Medical College or Lenox Hill, or any hospital besides Sea View. His colleagues, too, thought it odd. Most of them avoided the hospital on the hill unless it was necessary for their training. Aside from the commute, few found pleasure in spending their days with over 1,500 infected patients for no pay.

Since its inception, Sea View had always relied on the altruism of doctors to offer their services once or twice a week in exchange for experience and research opportunities. Many turned it down. But for Robitzek, the research without pay was part of the lure: "No disease," he believed, "especially tuberculosis, should be about capital."

During his father's illness, he saw firsthand how the wealthy, his father included, were deemed worthy of good medical treatment, while others, based on their socioeconomic standing, were denied it. They were sent off to crumbling institutions like Sea View or Harlem Hospital. The disparity was grotesque, "as if disease discriminated," he'd said. In his own practice, he strove for objectivity and humility, focusing on the individual facts and how they eventually connected to a bigger picture about sickness, its manifestation, its trajectory, and its end results. At Sea View, that bigger picture was blinding.

❖

Robitzek looked at the teenage girl on the table, at her skin stretched tautly across her bones like a translucent sheath, revealing hundreds of small veins, all deflated and useless. Her ribs, or what remained of them, protruded upward like rungs on a ladder, and her arms were reed-thin and rigid. He lifted his hand and placed it on the girl's forearm. The skin was cold and clammy. Keeping it there, he moved his good eye up and down her arm, noting all the bruises, big purple blotches from the thick steel needles that had pierced and punctured her veins and muscles every day. The bruises snaked down her arm to her hands, where slender fingers led to pretty nails that the nurses sometimes helped to paint.

He was often struck by the nail polish or any other personal cosmetic choice. Every day, people deliberated over minute decisions: dark or light red lipstick, brown or black hat, long or short nails, bearded or clean shaven, black or tweed coat. Trivial decisions, really. But he knew the power of these tiny details, how they latched on to memory and later emerged in whispers of *Remember this* or *Remember that*. After his father's death, it was the bowler hat hanging on the hallway peg that often sparked his grief.

He leaned forward and sank the blade into the skin by the left shoulder and dragged the knife down, curving under the breast, to the center of the chest; he repeated the process on the right side, but instead of stopping, he continued moving the blade vertically down the middle, around the belly button, until he reached the pubic bone. There he stopped. He regarded the Y-shaped incision.

Grasping the skin flap by the shoulder, he pulled it back, and a rush of air came out. It was fetid and the stench filled the room. He reached for the rib cage, removed it, and saw the chest cavity full of straw-colored fluid, pus mixed with blood and other liquids.

Bending over the exposed chest, he slid his gloved fingers under the right lung. It slipped away. Repositioning himself, he tried again, but the organ kept sliding away from him, sinking back into the infected fluid. Eventually it gave way, and he grasped one lung, then the other, and cut them free.

He felt their weight in his palm. They were heavy and distended, like two sopping sponges, and they oozed a frothy white mucoid fluid. He placed them on a silver tray and then glanced at the other organs, the heart, which looked pale and flabby, and the spleen and liver, which both seemed smaller than normal. Later, he would pull them out and assess them, but now he wanted to look at the lungs. Wiping his gloved hand on a towel, Robitzek pulled up a chair and began his examination.

He loved this part of his job.

In the morgue, away from the clamor and rush of the hospital ward, the blue-eyed doctor fell into a reflective state; he spent long moments lingering over the organs, contemplating their final shape and composition.

Normally smooth and pink and cone-shaped, the lungs are one of the largest organs in the human body. Spread out, their surface area is the size of half a tennis court, and every day they bring in about two thousand gallons of air, enough to fill a swimming pool. This air moves through an intricate network of airways, smaller and larger passages, whose combined length is about 1,500 miles, the distance from Savannah to Staten Island and back. But beyond these facts, Robitzek was most captivated by their role in immunity.

When a microbe like tuberculosis reaches the lungs, the body mounts its defense, sending out macrophages, large white blood cells that surround, capture, and destroy the harmful organism. Ninety percent of the time, the cells manage to trap the bacteria, either killing it or holding it in a dormant state behind a kind of wall; the only sign of its presence would be a minor bump on the smooth surface of the lungs. But for 10 percent of the population, the body's defenses fail and the microbe breaks through the wall. Once free, it spreads and finds a place to settle and grow and then destroy.

The girl's lungs, splayed out, were a mess of scars, dead tissue, and cavities, giant holes where the bacteria had lived, where it chewed away at the membranes, leaving them frayed like the tattered threads of an old garment. Robitzek touched their surface. It was rutted, pock-marked with dips and hollows and voids. Of the two lungs, he noted the right one was in worse condition; the cavities were larger, and from its raggedy edge, he noticed a burst blood vessel hanging. With the tip of his finger, he touched it and followed its pathway. It led him to the center of the hole. There was the cause of death: a hemorrhage. Below it were more cavities, some tiny as pinholes and others large as golf balls; surrounding them were more dead nerves and tissue in varying hues of gray, maroon, and black.

He was awed by the power of the microbe, by its ability to mu-tilate. What had compromised her immune system? Why had she fallen ill? Why had treatment failed? These questions dogged him as he trimmed off some lung tissue. Tomorrow he would process the samples, mount them on slides, and view them under a microscope, comparing notes from previous autopsies and logging any new infor-mation. Maybe from the ruins of this girl and hundreds of others, he could help create something good and add to the science that might lead to a successful drug. He moved his feet, pushed back his chair, and placed the lungs back into her chest cavity. He repeated the procedure with the heart and liver and spleen, removing an organ and then re-placing it. When he was done, he put back the rib cage, pulled down the skin, smoothed it out, and began stitching her up.

The job didn't require intense concentration, and his mind flitted over other thoughts: his father or the disease or his wife, Katherine—he always thought of her—or the Romantic poets. He loved the works of those young nineteenth-century men and women, like John Keats, Edgar Allan Poe, and Charlotte Brontë, who penned long paragraphs and stanzas about tuberculosis as something sacred. They lauded the disease for its emotional intensity, for its power to unleash creative transcendence, for its furious fevers that became like a holy fire, inspiring them to higher realms of imagination.

Victims of the epidemic themselves, they wrote about their suffering in majestic terms: their lips trembled; their cheeks glowed; and the blood they coughed up was akin to a gorgeous crimson liquid. For the composers Giacomo Puccini and Giuseppe Verdi, tuberculosis was the operatic fate of lovely heroines. "Decay and disease are often beautiful . . . like the hectic glow of consumption," said Henry David Thoreau, another victim of the disease. And Lord Byron, the flamboyant and passionate politician turned poet, stated without irony, "I should like to die from consumption."

Now, standing in a basement morgue next to a hulking freezer full of bodies, Robitzek thought describing the disease in such rhapsodic terms seemed not only ludicrous but downright profane. He pulled up the sheet and covered the young girl.

Stopping this would require drugs. Powerful ones. Currently, pharmaceutical companies were compounding and releasing new variations of sulfa drugs, safer ones, more streamlined for specific infections. Perhaps soon they would discover one that worked against TB, one that could penetrate its cell wall, stop it from replicating, and close the cavities without poisoning the body.

But until there was something better, all he could do was pull out organs and then study them. Nothing more. He opened the freezer and slid the body inside, then shut the door.

Chapter 23

❖

Arrivals

December 1941–July 1942

At 12:30 p.m. on December 8, 1941, President Roosevelt's voice spilled across the airwaves: "Yesterday, December 7th, 1941—a date which will live in infamy—the United States of America was suddenly and deliberately attacked." For the next six minutes, he spoke about the unprovoked assault on Pearl Harbor, the will of Congress and the people, and how America was now a nation officially at war with the Japanese Empire.

Most knew that war was inevitable, but the word "war" when heard aloud from the president's lips threw open a reality that no one could escape. At Sea View, the patients and nurses took in the news, wondering how this war might affect them.

It was unlikely it would roll onto American shores. Instead, the country would follow the pattern initiated in World War I by sending its boys abroad. In Edna's immediate circle, at least half a dozen nurses had men who were of age to enlist or be drafted. Missouria's brothers and her boyfriend. Miss Evans's husband, Arthur. And Forest, but Edna wasn't too worried about him; he was older, almost forty-three, with chronic back problems, although her nephews could be called up. And Miss Gillespie, who worked the day shift on Missouria's ward. Her son, Keever, barely twenty, would be eager to register and serve his country.

Whether or not their men were of fighting age, many nurses feared the repercussions of another war. Edna did. Her teenage years had been infiltrated by World War I, and she knew how patriotism could stoke the fires of racism. During the Great War, W.E.B. Du Bois roused Black men to serve, to fight "shoulder to shoulder" alongside white men. Despite being barred from the marines and serving only minuscule roles in the navy, over seven hundred thousand Black men heeded the call to register and serve. A small fraction of them were sent abroad.

All of them went willingly, filled with pride and hope that their fight for democracy would bring them equality and put an end to lynching. But when they returned from the trenches, instead of being celebrated, they were denigrated. In their uniforms, they became targets; people chased, beat, and lynched them; in the summer of 1919, anti-Black sentiments fueled race riots that roiled across the country, resulting in bloodshed and death. James Weldon Johnson dubbed it the "Red Summer."

No one could deny that this war orchestrated by Hitler was different. The German Führer found his inspiration in America's Jim Crow laws. They shaped his decrees about anyone who didn't belong to the "master race," especially the Jews; he equated them "with bacilli," calling them the "racial TB of the nations."

His enmity for the Jews extended to his contempt for Afro-Germans and Black people, a sentiment he expressed unequivocally in *Mein Kampf*: "The Jews were responsible for bringing Negros into the Rhineland," he wrote, "with the ultimate idea of bastardizing the white race which they hate." And so Black people, like Jewish people, slid to the bottom of Hitler's racial scale, making them targets for persecution, torture, forced sterilization, and abortions. To send Black men abroad under these conditions seemed unimaginable, ludicrous, and cruel.

And then there were the homegrown troubles that would unfold. The fear. The grief. The rationing of food and clothing. The shortage of medicine and doctors and nurses. There would be longer hours and many more patients.

All these things bore down on Edna, who worked hard to replace them with happier thoughts. Recently, she had begun attending Bethel Community Church. It was a close-knit congregation led by the pastor C. Asapansa-Johnson, a dynamic man from Sierra Leone who used the pulpit to preach about social justice, civil rights, and God. Every Sunday, Edna left feeling invigorated, inspired, with a renewed faith that God was guiding and watching over her, moving her along the pathway of the virtuous. At work, things were also going well: she was being considered for a promotion to charge nurse. But the best news of all was Americus. After twelve years of separation, Edna was finally bringing her home.

Between her shifts, Edna was busy arranging Americus's room; she washed the curtains and sheets and blankets; she vacuumed and dusted, and as promised all those years ago in Savannah, she put a vase of fresh flowers on the dresser.

That morning, while Forest went to Penn Station to meet Americus, Edna stood in the kitchen slicing and dicing eggplant, sweet potatoes, onions, peppers, tomatoes, and garlic, every so often glancing at the clock on the wall. The minutes moved like hours, and then finally she heard the click of the lock. Putting down her knife and lowering the flame on the burner, she wiped her hands on her apron and hurried across the living room. Forest opened the door, and the sight of Americus caused Edna to freeze and her breath to catch. Simultaneously, as if moved by an imperceptible force, both sisters flung their arms open and fell into each other.

Edna pulled her close and felt the strength of her sister's back and arms; they were sinewy and firm, the muscles of a young woman, not the little girl she'd left on the platform. If she pressed her fingers into them, she could feel their energy and vigor. It pulsed through her entire body like an electric current.

As she held Americus there in the living room, moments flashed by and years came hurtling back: Americus learning to talk, to read; walking together by the river; cutting up peaches for the warm peach pies they used to bake; watching the races at the track; the late-afternoon thunderstorms raging in Savannah's summer sky; and all the hand-written letters, piles of them, about school and work and landscapes and feelings, all the words that tried to compensate for the years apart.

When they finally parted, Edna stepped back and placed her hands on the now-sculpted cheekbones and angled jaw. She cradled her sister's face. Americus, too, looked closely at Edna, whose eyes were duller, the lids heavier, and the corners etched with fine lines; her hair, too, was streaked with wisps of gray. But it was all worth it. Despite the disadvantages she had faced, Edna had kept her promise and brought Americus north, into their house, one with flowers, and a gas stove, and an inside bathroom.

That night, Edna, Forest, and Americus sat down at the dining room table, set with the plates and glasses and silverware usually re-served for Sundays and special occasions. In the center, Edna had laid out the platters of food. After serving themselves, the three joined hands, and Edna led them in prayer:

"Thank you, Lord, for this food," she began, and followed with more gratitude for her home, her health, her family, and her sister.

Then she raised her glass: "To Americus." And they ate and talked and stared as if their lowering their eyes might make the other dis-appear. Before clearing the plates, Edna told Americus her own good news: she was expecting a baby in July of next year.

America went to war, and the New Year arrived with unease and more sick people, who filled up the wards and surgical unit. Edna received her promotion to charge nurse, forcing her to work longer hours making daily schedules, overseeing her staff, and often stepping in to cover shifts.

One winter afternoon Miss H. arrived on the ward for preoperative blood work.

Edna needed a small amount for the lab to do a red and white blood cell count. She sat close to Miss H. and took her hand, which was pale and the skin rough, and Edna opened it palm facing up toward the ceiling. She looked at the fingers and decided on the pointer. While rubbing it with alcohol, she talked to Miss H., explaining the procedure.

It would be quick, just a tiny prick to extract two to three drops, and then they'd be done.

Edna switched out the alcohol pad for a blood lancet, pressed on the tip of the finger, and pricked it deeply, and Miss H. gasped, then coughed, and a horde of microbes filled the air.

They drifted and swirled and batches of them landed on the bed, on the lancet, and on Edna's neck and hands and face. As she collected the blood from Miss H's finger, Edna felt the wetness of the bacteria settling in the corners of her eyes, on her cheeks, and above her lips— if only Miss Mitchell had allowed her nurses to wear masks all the time, this moment might have turned out differently. Edna wiped the tiny prick and covered it with a Band-Aid. Then she went to wash her face. But all the scrubbing in the world couldn't rinse away tuberculosis.

That night, at dinner, she didn't tell Forest and Americus about the incident. But later, when she was alone, she prayed hard for herself and her unborn child.

❖

Some months after Edna arrived at Sea View she'd tested positive for tuberculosis. To keep the disease in check, she was vigilant with protocols, washing her hands, eating well, trying to rest, and removing her uniform before entering her house. Every six months, she went for her physical and biyearly X-rays, and so far, after a decade, the disease continued to behave.

But Edna knew the wiles of tuberculosis, how easily latent TB could turn active.

All it took was one trigger: a weakened immune system, close contact with an infected individual, or pregnancy, especially a high-risk pregnancy like hers. Doctors considered Edna, at age forty-two, old for a first-time mother. In 1941, women over forty accounted for only a minuscule fraction of successful births.

Her colleagues who worked on Sea View's maternity ward, one of the few housed in a TB sanatorium, talked about the need for pregnant women to be extra cautious. Tuberculosis infected babies in utero in different ways. Sometimes it crossed the placenta and discovered the fetus; other times, it slipped into the birth canal and infected that way. Edna knew treatments for pregnant women were often complicated and precarious.

The popular artificial pneumothorax was often too dangerous, and with no anti-TB drugs, doctors relied on vitamins and rest and fresh air, remedies that didn't work. With no viable solutions for treating pregnant women with either active or latent tuberculosis, many physicians told them not to have children. Those who did become pregnant might consider an abortion. Such an idea appalled Edna. The better and more practical solution was requiring pregnant nurses to wear masks and gowns, not just during surgery but for their entire shift.

The argument about masking, which reached back to 1931, continued, but it took a new turn. According to longtime mask advocate Dr. J. Arthur Myers, masking was effective and not wearing one was irresponsible. Unlike previous years, Myers was finding support within the nursing community. One superintendent wrote that nurses "have a right to expect that all reasonable precautions" are available for their protection and despite the question about the percent of germs they filtered out, masks should be used, surmising, "They couldn't hurt."

But Myers and his supporters remained outnumbered by those who believed masks offered nurses no protection. An angry superintendent penned an eight-page article arguing against the efficacy of masks: "Providing the patient with a box of disposable tissue," she wrote, "with which to cover his nose and mouth when he sneezes," would work better than a mask. To her, "the routine use of the mask is unnecessary and may lead to a false sense of security." That was also Miss Mitchell's argument and she explained why.

"My communicable disease training and experience," she said, "were too rigid for them," adding, "I was duly impressed by their inadequacy and taught the menacing aspect of their use."

For her, no Sea View nurse would wear a mask unless treating the gravely ill or in surgery.

❖

The months passed, and the United States was dragged deeper into a war that spilled across the continents. As Japan declared war on the Netherlands, and Thailand declared war on America, and the Battle of Bataan raged, Edna's legs and belly swelled. At work, while she took vitals or reinserted catheters or IV lines, she felt her baby moving and kicking.

Prior to her pregnancy, she rarely thought about getting sick, but now the prospect lingered in her mind. She tried to temper it: her mother had birthed six healthy children when illness was everywhere. Edna had watched her labor with the midwives, laywomen who learned the profession from their mothers and grandmothers. Some were brilliant; others held only the barest understanding of anatomy. They carried worn leather bags full of instruments: twine and thread, oils and herbs, teas of catnip, pepper, sweet fennel, and tansy. During labor, their hands rubbed and pressed, squeezed and pulled and eventually caught babies. After, they held the newborn, cleaned it, tied off the cord, and placed it in a crate lined with towels and newspapers. They were good women, but Edna wouldn't let them "catch" her baby. No, she would deliver in a proper hospital on Staten Island.

All winter long the voices of the radio announcers filtered into the nurse's staff room: Snow and subzero temperatures enveloped Russia, halting Germany's advance. Soldiers were losing fingers and toes; engines froze and weapons malfunctioned. Horses died upright in the drifts and mounds of snow. Closer to home, everything seemed to be rationed or in short supply: gasoline, rubber, and fuel oil; bobby pins, zippers, shoes, and nylons; supermarket aisles lacked butter, coffee, canned goods, ketchup, sugar, and even chewing gum, and tobacco shops lacked cigarettes, and the matches needed to light them.

Spring arrived, and Edna felt the weight of her growing baby.

Across the boroughs, groups of children sifted through trash, collecting scrap metal for ammunition and tanks and ships. Down at the Brooklyn Navy Yard, they were hiring women to work as mechanics. And from city hall, Mayor La Guardia told New Yorkers that the city was a prime target for German bombers; U-boats were spotted off the coast of Long Island. Sea View put together a disaster ambulance, staffed with a handpicked selection of six Black nurses and two doctors, all specially trained in case of an attack. In Times Square, the neon signs went dark, and in Washington, DC, white citizens began talking about building segregated bomb shelters.

Edna's baby was due in a month.

In June, Americus organized a baby shower and invited Edna's friends from work. She decorated the backyard and set out a table, overlain with pretty cloth and jars of fresh-cut flowers. The nurses arrived, their arms full of gifts and more food, and they passed the afternoon in merriment.

On July 11, 1942, Edna's son came into the world. He was strong and loud, beautiful and healthy, and he looked like her father, R.V. Late at night while nursing him, his tiny hands balled into fists, she sometimes traced the outline of his face with her finger. In those long, dark hours, while she held him on her breast, she vowed to raise him here, in the community she was building on Staten Island, far away from the violence of the South. His boyhood stories, she promised, would not carry the same pain as those of his father and grandfather, or the thousands of other Black men born under Jim Crow. His life would be one of joy.

After he nursed, she placed him back in his crib, pulled up his blanket, and leaned over, inhaling his smell.

"Thank you, Lord," she would say, for "keeping me healthy."

But mostly she praised Him for "His greatest gift," she said, "her son," whose name she liked to whisper: Forest Ballard Jr.

❖

Edna would never forget the year 1942. Despite her scare while pregnant, the food rations, and the ongoing news of the war intensifying, the year was bowing out with good news for Black nurses.

Mayor La Guardia had finally named Commissioner Goldwater's replacement, Dr. Edward Bernecker, who wasted no time "breaking an almost half-century of precedent." "Negro applicants would be accepted for training in every school under the jurisdiction of the Department of Hospitals," he announced. News reached Staupers and other Black leaders, who lauded his push for integration. It was one of integrity, they said, and "a step toward the building of a real democratic America."

Well, maybe . . .

Chapter 24

❖

The Prisoner

Spring 1943

The war came to Sea View in the spring of 1943. It arrived with a new patient who looked no different from the other sick men. He was young, in his early twenties, but tuberculosis had stolen the vitality of youth, turning his once-handsome face into a colorless terrain of dips and hollows. He spent his days listening to the men of Ward 64 and monitoring the little gray mouse that scurried along the baseboards of the pea-green walls, disappearing behind nightstands and reappearing under beds. Throughout the day, he coughed and spit phlegm into tissues that he balled up on his bedside table, the pile marking the passage of hours. He, like the rest of the men, wanted to go home, back to his old life.

But he was different from them. He was a German soldier, a man of Hitler's army, and most likely a transfer patient from Halloran General Hospital, a military complex less than five miles from Sea View. Newly built on 323 acres of wooded land, the seven-story building housed three thousand beds and offered preliminary care to wounded American soldiers returning from war.

Arriving on hospital ships with names like *Benevolence* and *Solace* that docked at the piers of Staten Island, the bandaged soldiers disembarked on crutches and wheelchairs while adoring crowds welcomed them by waving flags and singing "Roll Out the Barrel." The young men stopped to greet the people and share their stories with journalists.

In their clean uniforms, the soldiers recounted their experiences of being captured by SS officers who forced them to march miles in the freezing cold; if they slowed or stopped, the Nazis would jab their arms and legs and torsos with bayonets. They told stories of lice-infested prisons, of being starved and sometimes beaten until their ribs cracked and they passed out from pain. When they finished, the ambulances whisked them away to Halloran, where doctors sorted them by illness or injury and if necessary passed them along to other hospitals. A diagnosis of tuberculosis sent them to Sea View.

But those same mercy ships also carried prisoners of war, protected under the Geneva Convention. The document outlined specific provisions for wounded soldiers and sick POWs, calling for countries to provide medical facilities, personnel, and aid. Prisoners, it stated, were to be treated as honorable soldiers, objects of neither derision nor abuse.

During the war, the US government committed itself to the civilized treatment of Axis prisoners, hoping that its humane behavior would inspire its enemies to do the same with captured Americans. For many citizens whose taxes paid for the POWs' medical care, this was an outrage, especially with the Germans, who cared little about the Geneva Convention.

From the start, the Nazi on the ward disliked Missouria. When she asked him to do something, he ignored her. When she tried to touch him, he winced. The struggle happened daily.

"Good morning."

He stared ahead.

"How are you feeling today?"

Nothing.

"I'm going to take your temperature."

And then he would turn and stare at her—jaw set, eyes narrowed, lips drawn, his face a portrait of disgust. But Missouria, in her usual manner, kept doing her job. She slipped the thermometer under his tongue, took his pulse, collected his sputum, and emptied his bedpan. Afterward, she bathed him and shaved his beard, carefully, like she had for Mr. Albert. Then with her big hands, she turned his body to change the sheets, lifting the feeble, stringy mess of muscles that once radiated with spirit and determination; that might have danced in low-lit clubs before the world knew about men like Goebbels and gas chambers and camps in places called Auschwitz and Bergen-Belsen and Dachau. When she was done, he lowered his eyes, picked up an art pad, and started drawing.

He spent hours propped up on pillows sketching things, maybe battlefields, water towers, box latrines, planes, wounded men, tanks, or the cramped insides of submarines, or maybe lungs. He spoke to no one. If he wanted something, he banged on the bed rail, the metal sound reverberating in the ward: "*Krankenschwester*" (Nurse), he cried out, his voice belying the fragility of his body and startling the men of Ward 64, who wanted to know how he'd arrived here.

Thousands of miles across the Atlantic, in May 1943, American forces won their first decisive victory in Tunisia, squeezing the Germans in the Battle of Hill 609. The victory caused a delighted Winston Churchill to applaud the American-British partnership before a joint session of the US Congress. With this welcome turn, however, came a burden. Over two hundred thousand German prisoners arrived in America and were dispersed among the hundreds of newly built POW facilities, mainly in the South, the Southwest, and the Great Plains— by 1945, the number of German POWs would balloon to four hundred thousand.

Situated on the outskirts of small towns, the camps were built to the highest American military standards, making them some of the finest in the world. Georgia's Camp Gordon boasted twenty-two dormitories, each equipped with showers, toilets, hot water, and heating.

The facility also hosted ten mess halls, some of them artistically dec-orated, as well as three recreation centers, one school building, and an exquisite library. With clear blue skies above them, prisoners perceived the camp as a resort.

During holidays, chefs toiled in the kitchen, preparing special meals served on tables draped with cloths. Uncorked and decanted bottles of red and white wine stood amid the bowls and platters of food. Dressed in their green jumpsuits, the letters "PW" imprinted across their shirt backs and pant legs, the POWs sat down and filled their plates; they poured themselves wine and raised their glasses, toasting Germany or Hitler. For some, the camps were "like heaven," said one prisoner, "after living in a hell."

Alongside the impressive food and boarding facilities, the military constructed top-notch station hospitals, and the Army Nurse Corps (ANC), a historically white branch of the army's medical department, staffed them with Black nurses, who were ordered to call the POWs "sir."

At Camp Papago outside Phoenix, Arizona, a notoriously hard camp that housed 3,100 Nazi soldiers and high-ranking officials, mostly from the Kriegsmarine—the German navy—a German soldier announced to a nurse that he "hated niggers." The nurse reported him to the commanding officer, hoping he would punish him, but the officer refused. Indignant, she wrote a letter to the NACGN: "That is the worst insult an army officer should ever have to take," she wrote. "It is insult enough to be here taking care of them when we volunteered to come into the army to nurse military personnel . . . All of this is making us very bitter."

At the NACGN headquarters in New York City, Staupers and Riddle took the grievance seriously and demanded the ANC remove Black nurses from the POW camps and send them abroad. Their pleas went unheeded, and the German POWs continued enjoying their life of largesse, one that Black nurses could only imagine.

In some camps, the POWs were allowed to decorate their barracks with flowers ordered from nearby florists and were gifted with radios to listen to music while they wrote letters, read, or made art. At Louisiana's Camp Polk, two POWs created murals at a local hotel; in Dayton, Ohio, they decorated a floor with green creatures, recalling mythic Germanic trolls, and elsewhere others painted seaside landscapes and spectacular oil portraits of famous German figures. A steady stream of happy guards and souvenir-hungry townspeople bought the paintings, and the prisoners pocketed the money.

The war moved on; more men enlisted, and a labor shortage gripped America. In 1943, the government passed the Emergency Farm Labor Supply Program. Here was an opportunity for hiring Black workers, but instead POWs were hired. Every morning, the Germans boarded military trucks, and American soldiers dropped them off to work at local canneries and mills, fields and farms, where they picked beets, asparagus, and cotton, jobs previously held by Black people. Farmers who hired the POWs expressed joy at finally having laborers, even if they were "the enemy." Newspapers ran stories of employers extolling their work:

"They were just the best bunch of boys," said a Texas farmer.

Observing Germans on a peanut farm, a reporter gushed: "[T]here has been no evidence of laziness or attempts to shirk their tasks. They go about their work with a will, they sing, whistle and joke with one another in their native tongue . . . There are no weaklings in the group of war prisoners . . . Each is a fine specimen of physical manhood."

Their charm extended to local townspeople, who welcomed them into their stores and restaurants, inviting them to use the "whites only" dining sections, restrooms, and fountains. On weekends, women lined up against fences to watch them play soccer. And those exhibiting good behavior received rewards. A gentleman's agreement promising not to escape or wander over five miles from the camp secured them a trip with an unarmed American guard around sleepy Georgia towns. Some meandered into bars, savoring a beer or a whiskey with locals.

Others went to the movies and ate popcorn, enjoying box office hits like *Casablanca* and *For Whom the Bell Tolls.*

But not everyone loved the POWs. Newspapers in more urban areas warned that they were "roaming at large, pilfering from homes, stealing and displaying the Nazi swastika." With their fair skin and blond hair, the men could easily pass for all-American boys, so civilians should be extremely wary.

It had already happened. Five hardened submarine POWs, trusted to transfer camps without a guard, decided to have a little fun. Dressed in stolen US military uniforms, they tacked Nazi pins to their lapels and traveled for days on a train, drinking, and eating and chatting happily with fellow passengers. According to the story, no one on the train noticed the men were German war prisoners on the lam.

❖

But the men on Ward 64 knew who was in their space. As the months wore on, they scrutinized the German while talking about the Yankees, playing poker or checkers, or listening to the radio streaming in more bad news, love songs, and patriotic messages for the boys fighting abroad. They clustered together and in hushed raspy voices wondered: How many of their countrymen did this Nazi force to march? How many did he herd and lock into cattle cars and starve? How many had he beaten? Had he killed anyone?

They found joy in reenacting the comedy sketches of Abbott and Costello's baseball act "Who's on First?" Over and over, they played the scene until it became gibberish, word salad, and they choked with laughter. But the POW never laughed. He just watched, taking it all in, noting how Missouria never stopped them, waiting for the right moment to act.

Chapter 25

❖

"Al Hit Paydirt!"

June–October 1943

Twenty miles from Sea View, on a bright and warm June day, Dr. Selman Waksman, the soil microbiologist from Rutgers, entered the Pennsylvania Hotel in midtown Manhattan. Making his way through the lobby, he took the elevator to a high floor, where he entered a meeting room. Stepping inside, he greeted the small group of men from the Trudeau Sanatorium's Saranac Laboratory, the National Tuberculosis Association (NTA), several university labs, and Merck Pharmaceuticals, who had come together to discuss TB drugs, or lack thereof.

It was a laid-back meeting, with a quiet mood, infused with the same dour pessimism surrounding so many other meetings about tuberculosis and medications and a cure. Prontosil and penicillin and most of the sulfa drugs had been cast aside, considered useless against TB. A new group of drugs, sulfones, being tested at the famous Mayo Clinic in Rochester, Minnesota, were also proving no good; they had too many side effects.

How about the digestive enzymes of earthworms? asked Dr. William White from the NTA. Waksman straightened his back, thinking it was an impractical idea, on the verge of being comical. But as he listened, it became clear that he was an outlier. Merck and the NTA were taking White's suggestions about earthworms seriously.

Waksman interrupted. While earthworms could produce an enzyme capable of digesting the TB bacteria, he said, in humans "any enzyme system powerful enough to bring this about would certainly digest the human organs as well."

The response vexed White, a veteran doctor who'd spent his career thinking about tuberculosis. Waksman was not a physician or a chemist; the Russian doctor was a soil microbiologist whose area of expertise was protozoa and fungi, not chest cavities and the pathology of disease.

White challenged him: "How do you propose to go about this problem?"

Waksman thought for a minute.

"The antibiotics will do it . . . They will kill the bacterium not by digesting it," he said, "but by interfering with its metabolism and its growth, without injuring the host." Eyes shifted and brows raised. Antibiotics, everyone believed, were useless against the microbe.

What was Waksman talking about? Was the soil expert hiding something?

Some years earlier, Waksman had a chance encounter with Dr. Alexander Fleming, the Scottish physician who discovered penicillin. During the meeting, Fleming had remarked how the future of medicine lay in antibiotics culled from organic substances—mold and microorganisms—not synthetic substances like sulfa. Waksman was captivated by Fleming's idea of a new generation of drugs born of the earth rather than in a lab.

After their conversation, Waksman returned to Rutgers and that long-forgotten study, the one proving that something in manured soil killed tuberculosis, the same one he'd said was "very interesting but it was leading nowhere," began to make sense: if Fleming could create penicillin from mold, then maybe he could fashion an effective TB antibiotic from something in the soil.

With these thoughts, he committed to search the vast underground network of microbes and protozoa, fungi and nematodes, to find the organism capable of killing tuberculosis. But there was one problem: the disease terrified him. His solution: hire a graduate student.

Weeks later, Albert Schatz appeared at Waksman's door. Young with an old-Hollywood kind of handsome, the dark-haired twenty-three-year-old had recently returned from the war, where he'd served as a bacteriologist in the US Air Force Medical Corps. He was reed thin, penniless, and desperate to finish his PhD.

Waksman knew Schatz from his prewar undergraduate days at Rutgers and was happy to offer him a position as his assistant researching antibiotics for a stipend of forty dollars a month. It was a paltry amount, the lowest of all the graduate students, but in exchange for chores, Waksman said Schatz could live in a small side room in the plant pathology greenhouse. It was an enchanting place where students played with seeds, growing hydroponic plants that blossomed into different varieties for FDR's victory gardens.

Then Waksman let Schatz in on his secret: in the soil lived a microbe or set of microbes that cured tuberculosis. Schatz's job was to find it.

When Schatz was a boy, tuberculosis had wheedled itself into his life. Growing up poor on his grandparents' farm in rural Connecticut, Schatz saw classmates and neighbors "lose weight and waste away." He recalled how "none of them could go to a sanatorium, so they remained home, coughing and infecting others," until eventually they died.

In the air force, he'd struggled with a similar helplessness. In those field hospitals on the fringes of tiny European towns, Schatz saw hundreds of soldiers, not much older than himself, being carried in on stretchers with shrapnel dug deep into their bones and organs. They came with limbs and bodies grotesquely swollen from wounds and infections and disease: cholera, pneumonia, sepsis, typhoid, and tuberculosis. He worked hard trying to save them, using the only two available antibiotics: sulfa and penicillin. Sometimes the drugs worked, especially with pneumonia or flesh wounds, but they were useless for

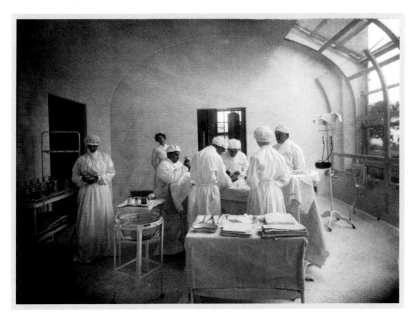

Sea View Hospital as it looked in the early twentieth century, with patients taking the "rest cure" (*above*) and surgeons and nurses at work using natural light from windows (*below*).

THE BLACK ANGELS AT WORK

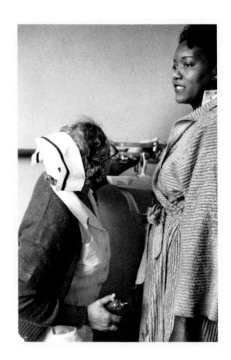

Christmas at Sea View.

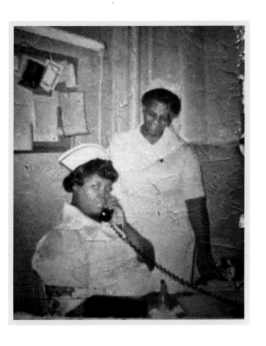

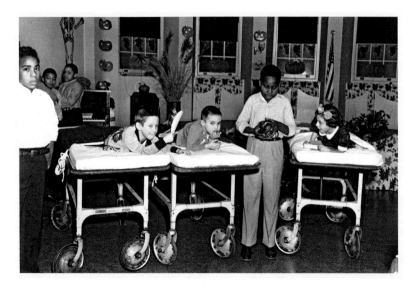

Children at Sea View.

Lungs destroyed by tuberculosis.

Dr. Edward Robitzek (*left*) and Dr. Irving J. Selikoff (*right*).

Everyday life for patients at Sea View was filled with too much time and not enough to occupy it.

The tedium of life at
Sea View took its toll.

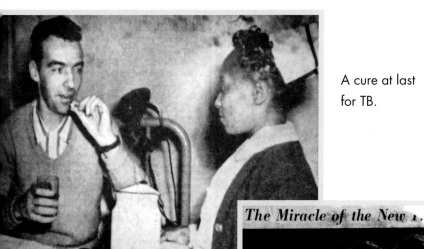

A cure at last for TB.

The Miracle of the New

Hilda Carrion eyeing the life-saving isoniazid.

Patients celebrate the cure on the wards.

Celebrating Virginia Allen, the last living Black Angel.

A mural today at Sea View remembering the nurses' work.

the more stubborn bacteria. And so, at night after his shift, he sat with the dying, comforting them just as Edna and Missouria were doing half a world away. In the soldiers' faces, he saw the anarchy of war; in their bodies, the chaos of disease; and in their last breaths, the terror of falling into a place without dimension and time.

During those vigils, he had vowed to do something to fight bacterial infections, and despite the low stipend, Waksman's offer appealed to him personally and intuitively. A "mystical sixth sense," he said, guided many of his decisions. And that feeling was now telling him that "he would find something."

Yes, he would do it.

But, Waksman explained, there was one stipulation: Schatz was never to come up to his third-floor lab with the TB bacteria. Ever.

For almost a decade, Waksman had been teasing through the soil, screening various groups of microbes to determine if any were powerful enough to inhibit the growth of different bacteria. Of the many minuscule soil microbes he found, one group had caught his attention, actinomycetes, or "ray fungi." They were curious-looking creatures that reached back four million years. A hybrid of bacteria and fungus, they were notable for their signature feature: long hyphae that branched out like the tentacles of a jellyfish and produced enzymes that could decompose dead animals and remake nutrients for plants to grow. They were versatile, easy to grow, and found everywhere—in soil, fresh water, sea water, and compost. And they gave the earth that unique after-the-rain smell.

Waksman loved them.

Some years ago, he had isolated a strain of actinomycetes that appeared to have antibiotic properties against the bacteria responsible for typhoid, plague, cholera, and salmonella. But hopes for it died when it kept killing the test mice. Although the drug would never be used in humans, it had caught the attention of Merck. Executives from the pharmaceutical giant reached out to Waksman and offered him a partnership. In exchange for funding, they asked him to search out potential antibiotics. If something came to fruition, Merck would help him research it and give him a percentage of any royalties.

In early summer, Schatz began his great dig into the recesses of the earth to find the strain of actinomycetes that might yield an anti-biotic strong enough to fight tuberculosis. Every day, Schatz rose before dawn, pulled on the same worn gray trousers and crumpled white shirt, and strode across campus. He walked with determination, passing the dairy barn where the Holstein cows grazed and the poultry house with its assortment of hens, to search the soil.

He looked under logs, around the bases of trees, under leaves, beside wild mushrooms, and in the discarded petri dishes of col-leagues. But his favorite places to dig were the mounds of decomposing compost outside the plant pathology building and in the college stables, full of fresh horse manure; the best soil, Schatz felt, was less than twelve hours old. It was rich, soft, and vibrant. And it stunk.

One mid-August morning when Schatz returned from his for-aging, his close friend Doris Jones, a graduate student studying the effects of microorganisms and antibiotic substances on fowl viruses, handed him a used petri dish. It was streaked with a swab from a healthy chicken's throat. Schatz thanked her and took the dish to his lab, a run-down room where fantastic configurations of apparatuses rose from the wooden tables bringing to life the inner workings of his mind.

Taking Jones's sample, he diluted it, then dropped it onto several petri dishes lined with nutrient agar. He repeated the process with a separate batch of soil he'd collected from the stables that morning, and then placed both in an incubator.

A week or so later, he removed them, and a universe of powdery microbial colonies in stunning shades of muted yellow, red, brown, and grayish green covered each plate. Some were surrounded by "clear zones," areas indicating that the soil microbes had successfully warded off the respective bacteria. They might make a solid antibiotic. Schatz studied each colony, and with nothing more than a hunch, that "mystical sixth sense," and what his wife called "Albert's eagle eye," he selected those that looked like germ killers.

He chose one colony from the chicken batch that his friend Doris Jones had given him. He named it D-1—"D" for Doris and "1" because they were the first actinomycetes he isolated from the agar plate. He planned to test D-1 beside another colony that came from the stables, which he named 18-16. Once each colony was isolated, he transferred it to fresh agar plates. In two weeks, a new pure colony would grow.

While he waited for D-1 and 18-16 to mature, he continued testing other soil samples, working long into the night, until his nails turned black and his hands smelled like earth and manure. Sometimes, overcome by exhaustion, he curled up on the floor and fell asleep. When he woke, he splashed water on his face and began again, despite the unfavorable odds.

"The failure rate [was] about 99.99 percent," Jones said. But Schatz ignored percentages. His drive came from a prescient sense that he, Albert Schatz, would discover something effective.

Two weeks later, on October 19, 1943, Schatz walked into his lab. It was 2 p.m. when the skinny graduate student pulled out two petri dishes—the one labeled D-1 and the other 18-16—and looked at them. In front of him, appearing diagonally across the plate, were not one but two new strands of actinomycetes.

Their color was a pale grayish-green, and under a microscope they looked like a strand of rare pearls. But they weren't just beautiful. When he tested them for antibiotic properties against a particular bacteria, each one showed wide clear zones, meaning both new strands stopped the growth of bacteria that was smeared on the petri dish. This was the first indication they might work as a drug.

In the words of Jones, "Al hit paydirt!"

Holding the two plates, Schatz walked down the long corridor, up to the third floor, and entered Waksman's office. He put down plates

D-1 and 18-16, with their clear zones. Waksman contemplated them, then instructed him to isolate them, find their food source, and begin more tests. Immediately.

❖

In the cramped lab, Schatz worked round the clock trying to produce an antibiotic from the two new strands of D-1 and 18-16, which he was now calling *Streptomyces griseus* (*S. griseus*). Similar to all bacteria, *S. griseus* needed food to flourish, and Schatz discovered that D-1 and 18-16 grew best in a meat-extract mixture. To speed up the process, he ran "endless numbers of one liter Erlenmeyer flasks" containing beef broth.

Soon batches of fuzzy, grayish-looking colonies began sprouting on the surface of the beef broth, floating around like isolated storm clouds. Schatz, in a painstaking process, removed them, and to the best of his ability, filtered out the impurities. Then he began testing them on different diseases.

Daily, he dropped diluted strains of *S. griseus* onto agar plates brushed with typhoid, cholera, and other common germs. Out they came, again and again, flaunting the much-desired clear zones. Things kept getting better. Tests showed that *S. griseus* was effective against bacteria that evaded penicillin, like the deadly and stubborn *Staphylococcus*. Now certain that D-1 and 18-16 were acting like antibiotics, Waksman and Schatz were ready to begin in vivo tests on animals.

But Rutgers housed none of the conventional lab animals used by scientists for such tests—mice, monkeys, guinea pigs, or rabbits. The only available animals were horses and chickens and Holstein cows. All of them were too big and cumbersome for a drug trial.

Waksman had an idea: chicks. Unborn baby chicks from the poultry lab.

Infecting them fell to Doris Jones, a dreadful process requiring her to use a dental drill to pierce the egg, and with a tiny syringe drip fowl typhoid into the embryo of the unborn chicks. She hated the job and the way the egg felt in her palm. Its smoothness and warmth and weight reminded her of the growing baby tucked inside it, the one she would kill.

After poisoning all the embryos, she injected a small amount of Schatz's potential antibiotic into half the eggs. The other half received nothing. Two days later, the untreated chicks died. But the ones given Schatz's potential antibiotic began hatching. Jones squealed in delight at the sight of the wobbly, furry creatures. Her joy was short lived. Waksman wanted her to kill the newborns and autopsy their tiny bodies to confirm their internal organs were disease-free. Jones started crying.

With tears streaming down her face, she slipped the scissors through their necks, cut open their chests, and examined their organs. Two days later, she announced the baby chicks were typhoid-free.

Jubilant, Waksman returned to his office and called Merck, upholding the agreement to inform the company of any prospective drugs. He had one.

It was, he said, aptly called "streptomycin," and it held "great promise."

Chapter 26

❖

"Ich Hoffe Du Wirst Krank"

1943–1944

On days the weather permitted it, the men of Ward 64 rode the rickety elevator up to Sea View's sixth-floor roof terrace to meet the American soldiers, some with clever nicknames: Wolf, the Dog, and Jack Rabbit. Leaning against the waist-high railing, cigarettes pinched between their fingers and the city sprawling behind them, the men listened to the soldiers, who gestured and cursed while recounting wild stories of fighting the Germans. They narrated gun battles in which American servicemen watched Nazis fall like rag dolls and told how tanks rolled through the streets and squares, their treads crushing trees and cracking the concrete.

Too sick to have enlisted or served, the men of Ward 64 were captivated, transported to small European towns with unpronounceable names, where they imagined the heat of bombs and the smell of scorched earth. They saw themselves standing on the decks of battleships that launched from the naval yards across the bay, looking down the barrels of enormous guns.

The soldiers kept talking, assuring them the stories were all true. They really had spent hours in foxholes, then emerged to march over fields where the ground was a tangle of bodies. They saw machine-gun fire so fast and furious that the bullets glowed phosphorus white; some men thought it was fireworks. And the planes thousands of feet in the air being chased by the Luftwaffe: artillery fire, then metal hitting metal. The plane faltering, stalling, plummeting from the sky in fiery streaks, the pilot and bombardier, navigator and gunner falling through the fuel-soaked air. Sometimes the young soldiers carried on with a cynicism too old for their age. But that was war.

In other stories, the boys bailed out of the burning planes, falling into the black night. They fumbled for the rip cord and pulled hard, and the parachute opened with a whoosh. Sometimes they landed in a tree or a side street or an open meadow, where they passed out and woke up in a field hospital. The Red Cross and Army Corps Nurses were kind white women who sat beside the soldiers and comforted them.

After hours of hearing about tanks and planes and battles, the men of Ward 64 returned to the fourth floor, their tempers flaring and sense of patriotism offended. They were angry about sharing their ward with the enemy, the German whose fellow soldiers were killing their brothers, raping women, and gassing children.

Missouria heard them, but was weary of the drama, of their indignation. She missed their banter about Wall Street and horse races, collapsing bridges, and who would die next. Now all anyone talked about was war and Nazis and violence. It seemed to have permeated the world.

In Beaumont, Texas, late spring unfurled with a rumor that a Black man had raped a white woman, resulting in a confrontation between white and Black workers at the Pennsylvania shipyard. Weeks later in Detroit, on the eve of the summer solstice, a fistfight between a Black and a white man at Belle-Isle Amusement Park turned into two days of riots that ended with twenty-five Black people dead, seventeen at the hands of police.

Then in August, on a scorching New York night, a white rookie cop shot Robert Bandy, a Black serviceman, for intervening in the arrest of a Black woman accused of disturbing the peace. As the ambulance with the injured Bandy sped to the hospital, word of the incident swept through Harlem's streets, packed with people sitting in parks and on stoops, fanning themselves and trying to find relief from the midsummer heat. Talk about Bandy's condition churned, moving from person to person. Small crowds gathered, and then came the rumor: Bandy was dead, killed by the white officer.

The smaller crowds blended together, joining forces, and Bandy, like Lino Rivera, who had sparked the riot of 1935, became the catalyst for unleashing eight new years of pent-up fury, intensified by the wartime shortages and the lingering problems of housing and un-employment that had started during the Depression. And now the mistreatment of Black people by the mostly white New York City police force and the segregation of Black soldiers added to their anger.

The image of Private Bandy trying to free a Black woman from the hands of a white officer became symbolic of everything that was wrong with America, and Harlem's rioters clung to it for two days as they smashed streetlights, shattered windows, and looted. The aftermath left six people dead and hundreds injured, prompting Walter White, head of the NAACP, along with middle-class Black folks, to denounce the violence.

Poet Langston Hughes disagreed, finding their reaction trifling and unjust: "Civil disturbances usually brought racial progress," he said. They also brought poetry. In response to the riots that summer, he penned "Beaumont to Detroit: 1943," a stark eight-stanza poem drawing parallels between Jews living under Nazi rule and Black Americans living under Jim Crow. He ended by asking, "How long I got to fight / BOTH HITLER—AND JIM CROW."

The poem appeared like an anthem for Missouria, something written for her and her fellow nurses, especially Miss Gillespie, now the supervisor of Sea View's employee clinic. Her only son, Keever, was stationed abroad.

For two years, Miss Gillespie sat at her desk in the infirmary and read his weekly letters.

"Mother Darling" or "Mother Dear," they all began, a salutation that made her smile but also brought her to tears. The seasoned nurse always dreamed of giving her son a bright future, one without strife. He was why, in 1932, she'd quit her job, packed up the car, and fled Birmingham, Alabama; he was the reason she stayed in Harlem, where he took music and singing lessons. Now her boy was writing about the fields and forests and beaches of the European war theater.

In one letter, he wrote that he was "sleeping on the ground . . . in tents in woods . . . grass for bed, stars for roof and ceiling . . . Others are writing home, some are shooting pistols, sun is going down . . . planes come at night; they attack when they see light."

But the army always vetted the letters, leaving Miss Gillespie to wonder who or what was being attacked. Over time, she came to understand Keever's writings were just descriptions, broad brushstrokes of a young man fighting in a devastating war somewhere in the world, in a place she didn't know. She read and reread them, studying the words like they were encrypted maps hiding his whereabouts.

In other letters, he asked about investing his allotment checks, or he needed his mother's medical advice "for his migraines." He couldn't get the necessary medication, or any medication, he said, and was "just sweating them out." The image of her son lying in a field suffering like that broke her. How easy sending medicine would be if only she knew his location.

But he moved all the time. A recent letter told of how he'd moved to a town. Despite the "air of treachery in this town," the young soldier wrote, "the birds sing like they do at Sea View."

❖

For almost a year, Missouria brought the POW magazines and extra pillows and propped him up to eat so he wouldn't choke. She continued to help him get dressed and take a bath and hoped he would be gone soon, sent back to Halloran Hospital or Germany. But winter came with its bellowing winds, then the New Year, spring, and summer of 1944, and he was still there, hassling Missouria.

June brought terror to the city when Emmanuel Kalytka, a twenty-nine-year-old German POW, escaped from Halloran Hospital. The FBI and NYPD joined forces and organized search parties, combing the island's thousands of acres of woods with bloodhounds. Coast Guard cutters patrolled the waters separating Staten Island from New York and New Jersey, and four-man units armed with machine guns manned the city's three bridges and five ferry docks that offered an escape from the island. Each night on her way home, Missouria passed the authorities searching for the POW.

Day one ended, and unable to locate him, the city was forced to admit it had POWs stationed within its limits, a revelation that sent waves of panic through Staten Island's neighborhoods. Shocked citizens began asking the same questions as Missouria's men: Why were US enemies being cared for in city hospitals? Why weren't they in the POW camps? Who was paying for them?

As the search widened and more people expressed their distress over Americans caring for POWs, hope blossomed: Missouria's plight might end. But on day three of the search, the square-faced, gray-eyed Kalytka turned up. He was found sitting in Halloran's mess hall, hunched over his lunch tray of mushroom soup, roast veal with carrots and potatoes, chocolate cake, and milk. Journalists reported Kalytka had spent the last two days wandering around, "just to see the good old United States," he said. At night, *The New York Times* reported, he fell asleep "in a heavy wood near Sea View Hospital."

Within days, the story and the public outrage ended, and so did Missouria's optimism for the German's removal. For now, he would remain on Ward 64, and until he either died or left, Missouria would keep working, treating him no different from the men who watched the daily exchange:

"Good morning."

Silence.

"How are you feeling today?"

Nothing.

"You need to eat."

More silence.

The routine never seemed to change until one morning when Missouria stood by his bed taking his vitals. He began to cough; it was a rough and guttural sound, and the phlegm rose from inside his chest. Higher and higher it moved, until it reached his tongue. Keeping it there, he turned toward his nurse, the woman who had washed and shaved, wiped and changed him for a year, and he took a deep breath and spit. The thick wet ball of green and yellow mucus landed on the collar of Missouria's uniform.

"*Ich hoffe du wirst krank,*" he sputtered.

"I hope you get sick," he repeated in English.

Missouria looked at him, the way Mama Amy had taught her. She wanted to hold his gaze, so he could see her. Then she finished taking his vitals and from her cart took a cloth and began wiping the disease from her uniform.

PART IV

❖

1944–1949

Chapter 27

❖

The Nature of Things

Spring–Summer 1944

It was well past 9 p.m. when Dr. Edward Robitzek left his basement office at Sea View and walked across the empty grounds toward the parking lot. Holding his briefcase, stuffed with patient files that needed reviewing for a new drug trial, he felt a dampness in the air. It was heavy and cool, blowing with an urgency that rustled the leaves and warned of an approaching storm. He quickened his step, passing by the surgical building and patient pavilions, at which he glanced and wondered who might die tonight and which nurse would call asking him to return to "pronounce" the dead and sign the death certificate.

In the parking lot, he stopped at an old green Studebaker, opened the driver's-side door, and set down his briefcase; before getting in, he looked up at the clouds and breathed in the air, filling his lungs, cleansing them from another day spent at Sea View.

On the short drive home, he listened to the radio, his mind alternating between the hours of work remaining and the cartoonish voice of an advertisement: "Delicious chocolaty Tootsie Rolls—boy, they're cram-jammed full of energy."

What a silly ad! But it was better than the daily news, full of bleak stories of death and destruction. A few weeks ago an antiaircraft accident had thrown his Staten Island neighborhood into chaos after a gunner accidentally set off a rapid-fire gun from a freighter docked at the port. For two minutes, fifty shells whistled through the icy afternoon air, crashing onto streets and in yards. Some exploded. One blasted a tree, another shattered a garage door, and another destroyed the back of a car; the rest settled beside curbs or on sidewalks. The incident took place less than a mile from his home, and the shells hit in places where he and his wife, Katherine, often walked with the boys.

Inside his apartment, he hung his hat and coat and listened to the faint words of a lullaby drifting down the hallway. Katherine. Her voice was melodic and soothing, full of a tenderness that made him ache. He walked into the bedroom, sat beside her, and took her hand. It was delicate, the skin smooth, and he closed his fingers around hers, holding it for a long moment; then he kissed her and his two boys and walked to the living room to begin working. His recent promotion from chief medical resident to acting director of pathology pulled him further away from the morgue and deeper into research at Sea View.

Sitting at his desk in the living room, surrounded by files and medical journals, he became preoccupied with thoughts of the overflow of patients at Sea View. There were so many now, and the war was sending home more and more TB-infected soldiers, who he feared might start an epidemic. Where would they go?

Sea View was already operating above capacity; beds had been packed into every available corner and down the center aisles of the wards, upping the patient population from 1,500 to 1,800, and still there were hundreds more on a waiting list that never really moved—for the 79,000 available TB beds in the country, there were only 86,000 annual admissions, meaning that 7,000 people were either being discharged or had died. The rest remained hospitalized, languishing in their beds. Such a statistic left Robitzek feeling helpless at the lack of options and the dead-end drug trials that often took place at Sea View.

Soon he would be starting a new trial on Diasone, a drug different from the soil-derived streptomycin formulated in the rough-and-ready lab at Rutgers. Diasone, by comparison, was a sulfa drug whose therapeutic properties were tested by Dr. George Raiziss. Early results were encouraging, but Robitzek couldn't ignore that since sulfa's discovery in 1937, infinite variations had been formulated and tested globally on TB-infected animals.

Although some combinations of sulfa arrested the disease in guinea pigs, rabbits, and mice, almost none proved suitable for human trials. They were all too toxic. In his study, Raiziss had admitted that Diasone caused some harm in mice and also caused some side effects, but its toxicity remained low. Overall, he believed it gave "promise of favorable clinical application in tuberculosis."

And so the orders came down: Robitzek would test it.

Despite his promotion, Robitzek didn't have much input about drug testing at Sea View. The administration had tied his hands in a kind of Faustian bargain: tuberculosis needed drugs, and large pharmaceutical companies needed patients for testing them. Under this give-and-take, Sea View received the novel drugs, and in exchange, the hospital offered up its patients for human trials. For Robitzek, it was a lopsided deal, one that ignored patient safety and skirted the ethics of medicine, but it wasn't entirely the hospital's fault.

Many, including the drug manufacturers, saw Sea View's patients as hopeless and expendable, people on the fringes of society that no one would miss. Without any federal rules governing the use of investigative drugs, these patients, desperate and willing to pin their hopes on any vaunted possibility of being cured, became perfect test subjects for pharmaceutical corporations driven by the most dangerous of combinations: monetary profits and notoriety. Everyone knew a cure would bring prominence, patents, and billions of dollars in revenue. Globally, scores of companies were researching TB drugs. They worked quickly, pumping out one potential remedy after another, and if it showed the remotest of promise, they sent it for testing.

Since Massengill's elixir tragedy, things had changed, but not nearly enough. While the FDA was more attentive to consumer safety and regulating how and what drugs came onto the market, behind the scenes, before the drugs were packaged, things remained messy. Clear drug-testing protocols still didn't exist. The American Medical Association had only "outlines" that gave "an objective, a pattern . . . not a regulation," granting doctors immense leeway. Based on their own curiosity or needs, physicians like Robitzek could arbitrarily decide trial parameters.

And in addition to the vague protocols, there were no laws stopping a drug company from giving Sea View, or any other hospital, subpar drugs—ones that were rushed and would jeopardize the lives of already fragile people. Robitzek hoped this wasn't the case with Diasone.

For this trial, he needed one hundred people, a mix of men and women all diagnosed with pulmonary tuberculosis. From the stack of folders, he lifted the top one, opened it, and, in the stillness of the room under the lamplight, began reading the case files:

Sally K., single seamstress, sick for eight years: prognosis poor.

Leroy J., married, Pullman porter, sick for ten years.

Ruth T., married, housewife, sick for two years.

In the next room, he occasionally heard his wife and sons stir as they flitted through dreams and he read into the night, his mind reeling from the dozens of summaries detailing lives and bodies in chilling states of decay: uncontrolled weight loss, chronic diarrhea, kidney malfunction, GI tracts twisting, spines collapsing, skin ulcerating and then erupting, and lungs, so many lungs ravaged by the disease. After reading each case file, he placed the folder in one of two piles: suitable candidates or not. But despite where the folders landed, all the stories reminded him of the transitory nature of things; how precarious it all was, how in an instant everything could change, and how one day his life could also come crashing down.

Chapter 28

❖

"In the Business of Dying"

Summer 1944

Missouria knew all about lives collapsing. There was one in front of her with his face frozen and his eyes flung open, the motionless pupils catching flecks of sunlight. He was young, in his early thirties, and pre-tuberculosis, his life had been spent under the hoods and bodies of cars: Fords, Plymouths, Dodges, and Chevys—his nails slick with oil and grease from changing spark plugs and steering fluid and turning valves on carburetors and shock absorbers. But now, all that was gone, finished in an instant under the blue-gray light of daybreak.

The young man, called J.R., began choking that morning while Missouria was filling out her nurse's notes. She heard the sounds, those great guttural noises of tuberculosis brandishing its power and demanding its price. Dropping her pen, she rushed to his bed, joined by another nurse, and the two women worked quickly, pulling him upright; they tried to calm him, but he was inconsolable. He thrashed and flailed; sheets twisted, and his mouth made grotesque shapes trying to clear the blood and mucus clogging his airway.

The other men on Ward 64 sprang up in bed and watched the blood from his throat ooze from his nose and splatter from his mouth. They saw his face turn shades of blue and his eyes grow wild and unfocused, and from him came a sound, a primal half-human, half-animal noise.

Then J.R. went limp.

Three years into her job, Missouria was surprised by few things. She'd managed to adapt to the rawness of the men's ward, to the crass and bawdy language; she'd learned to ignore the flaring tempers and even the racial slurs. But she could not reconcile those who died alone, without family, whose bodies were unclaimed and unmourned, sent to potter's field, the graveyard for paupers.

When it came to dying, some nurses were more practical than others. They didn't think too long about death. They came in, cleaned up, washed the body, filled out the paperwork, and readied the bed for the next person. To them, dying was just another part of life. Another aspect of their job.

"We are in the business of dying," one nurse had said.

Missouria saw things differently. Death, she believed, was a hallowed part of God's broader plan for eternal life, but at Sea View, His plan was often difficult to see. Here death didn't come quietly, draped in the garlands of holiness; here it was crude and ugly and made people gag and vomit and bleed. It turned last breaths into terrifying acts, undertaken in front of people who made morbid jokes about one another, who laughed at how old Joe wasn't "going to meet Saint Peter," or how Maurice from bed 12 "was looking gruesome," or how Harry's "bridge days were over."

Here, men hawked one another daily, watching who slept, who ate, and who used a bedpan; they counted the visitors, who showed up and how often. They kept secret notes of vitals and sputum counts and then traded information, taking bets on who would die first and how: "Richie's gonna starve to death," and "Mr. Albert's next."

When they made these predictions, their voices carried more dread than cruelty. They understood dying at Sea View meant doing it alone, in public, in front of too many eyes, on a bed and pillow where someone else had died, beside a rusty nightstand that had held letters and cards, pictures and books and trinkets of so many others. It meant life ended with the pieces of strangers, their hopes and dreams and sins all swallowed into the wide womb of some unknown world.

Missouria stepped closer to the dead man and readied herself to wash his body, a job many nurses disliked. Some found the feeling of rigor setting in and the skin turning colder frightening; a few feared the soul becoming stuck and lingering around the corpse or, worse, slipping into their own. Other nurses remained aloof to spirits and souls and rigor; instead, their concern was time away from their rounds. So they washed quickly, with detachment, a disconcerting perspective to Missouria. To her, the dead were sacred, worthy of her time and the risk that Miss Mitchell, who wanted her nurses to work sensibly and not sentimentally, might reprimand her.

With two fingers Missouria reached up and closed J.R.'s eyes, then packed his nose with cotton to stop any discharge. From a basin of soapy water, she picked up a small towel, wrung it out, and began washing his face, wiping his forehead, eyes, and cheeks, hollow spaces that dipped like small valleys. She cleaned behind his ears and around the lobes, down toward the jawbone, feeling the sharpness.

The work drew her into a quiet place, away from the din of the ward and the voices of the men who whispered behind her. In this space, where sunlight dabbled her hands as they dipped and wrung and washed, sanctifying the body, she felt close to God and her calling and began to hum "Swing Low, Sweet Chariot."

She loved this hymn, loved how the melody moved, slow and deep, bringing to life images of chariots and rivers and angels lifting one to deliverance. Mama Amy had taught it to her, along with "Deep River," "Go Down Moses," "Wade in the Water," and so many others. Faith, she had told her daughter, went beyond John or Kings or Song of Songs; it came alive in the spirituals. "They are the cries from within," Mama Amy had said, "ancient sounds of the spirit," which brought rhythm and unity to daily tasks.

Missouria first heard them at home when Mama Amy swept or

cooked, washed or prayed, and then again in church and in the fields of the Lydia Cotton Mills, where she picked each morning before school. In those predawn hours, the song began with one voice that cracked through the stillness, followed by another and another, until everyone was pulling and singing, their words vibrating through the rows of cotton.

"It was a sound full of fury and joy and sorrow," Missouria's niece said.

Now she moved the towel down his body, cleaning his collarbone and chest, scrubbing the skin caked with dried blood and crisscrossed by scars from pneumothoraxes, wound drainages, and the first of two thoracoplasties. She kept going, maneuvering the cloth over his ribs, where, inside his chest, his lungs lay dormant, distorted, pockmarked, engorged, and gray. What a terrible, terrible disease.

Missouria rewet the cloth and started washing his legs, mouthing the words: "I looked over Jordan, and what did I see / Coming for to carry me home."

She pulled it in long strokes over his thighs and calves and down to his feet, where the skin was pulled tight and the blood pooled, turning them a bluish purple, a telltale sign that decomposition was underway. It was remarkable how the body continued dying; how the inside of a corpse still had life: blood drained from smaller veins in the skin; bacteria dispensed from cells and organs; and calcium, now stagnant, stiffened muscles.

The process of breaking down went on for weeks and months, sometimes years; organs, veins, tissues, muscles, bones, and skin persisted, decaying on their own timetable. Muscle cells lived for only hours after death, but bone and skin cells lived for days. Blood took anywhere from a week to ten days to decompose, and nails and teeth remained intact for two or more weeks. A month in, the body began dissolving, but it would take one hundred years for it to fully deteriorate, for the bones to become dust, leaving behind the scant traces of humanity: teeth; corpse wax, a substance appearing during decomposition;

and nylon threads from the casket lining. And then there was the soul. Missouria believed it went on eternally. How anyone could perceive the dead as merely rotting flesh, undeserving of dignity, was mystifying.

She finished cleaning him, dropped the cloth on the tray, and picked up a fine-tooth comb. She parted his hair and rubbed in some pomade, so it shined. Then she crossed his hands over his chest and tied them together. Finally, she wrapped him in a shroud.

The aides came and pushed the gurney toward the elevator, its wheels clattering along the floor. Missouria walked alongside them, past the men on Ward 64, who watched the procession from their beds.

When the elevator reached the basement, the operator pulled open the metal gate.

The wheels of the gurney echoed loudly through the damp and winding tunnels of Sea View, used to move linens, supplies, equipment, food, and the dead. They led everywhere, including to the morgue, where the body would remain until someone claimed it or the city coroner took it away.

At Sea View, limited space prevented the morgue from storing dead bodies for an extended period; after notification, kin were expected to collect their loved ones almost immediately. This was a challenge for many, especially when the deceased was an immigrant whose family was thousands of miles away or for those with no savings.

Arrangements took time; body removal cost money, and so did burial—the average price was about $300 (equivalent to $5,000 today), an amount beyond the means of many. And so, too often, Sea View's families were forced to forsake their dead to the city.

Over the years, Missouria saw the grief of poor people who couldn't bury their loved ones. Mothers who clutched their chests and fell to their knees, sobbing, fists held up to God; grown men collapsing; and grandmothers shouting in languages she didn't understand. Some asked questions, hard questions whose answers would become family legacy: How did it happen? Was there pain? Did death come quickly? Any last words? Were they alone?

Some nurses would lie, not outward lies or tall tales, but lies by omission. They didn't talk about the choking and breathlessness, only the hemorrhaging. The rest could be implied. Missouria understood why they omitted things, but she couldn't lie. She always told the family what happened: if a person had choked, she told them they'd choked. While she spoke, some wept, and others listened stone-faced, as if they were hearing a repeated public service announcement.

Missouria and the aides reached the morgue and they pushed the gurney inside, where muted light from the windows illuminated the new freezers. They were bigger, more powerful, installed by the city to accommodate the growing number of corpses, but they still weren't enough—over two thousand people a year died at Sea View.

Seeing them, with their steel doors and industrial latches, and hearing the hum of electricity coursing through the wires to keep the corpses cold, overwhelmed the senses. Missouria handed the paperwork to the pathologist, glanced one last time at the gurney with the shrouded man, and started walking back through the low-lit tunnel.

J.R. had no family. No one had ever come to see him, and now no one would come to collect his belongings or relinquish or claim his body. For the next few days, or however long the morgue could keep him, he would remain in the new freezer, a tag hanging from his big toe, while his body filled with bacteria and gases. When no one showed up, he would officially become city property, his corpse available as a medical cadaver or for burial at New York's potter's field. Most likely, J.R. was headed for the latter.

Sea View sent hundreds of patients a year to potter's field. In the morgue that day, two men in the freezers above or below J.R. were also slated for potter's field. In the next few days, depending on the workload, the men would be processed and picked up by the city coroner.

All day and night, the hearses and coroner's trucks, came through Sea View's morgue, a flat, unassuming building shaped like a small letter "h." They pulled up to the carport and collected the dead. The hearses went to local funeral homes, but the coroner's trucks drove to the port, where the deceased continued their journey to the coroner's office.

There the coroner scrawled their names in a ledger, put them in rough pine boxes, nailed down the tops, and sent them to the City Island Ferry, a small boat that made a single stop: potter's field on Hart Island, a remote 131-acre strip of land in Long Island Sound, just east of the Bronx.

First used in 1864 as training camp for the 31st Infantry Regiment of the United States Colored Troops and as a POW camp, it quickly transformed into a burial ground for Union army soldiers. Following the Civil War, the privately owned island, renowned for its miserable conditions, was used to house the mentally ill, the destitute, the diseased, the homeless, criminals, and truant boys.

In 1867, the city purchased the land and turned forty-five acres into a public cemetery for the indigent and unclaimed bodies of New Yorkers. Two years later, gravediggers lowered the first body into the ground: that of twenty-four-year-old Louisa Van Slyke, who died alone in Charity Hospital from yellow fever. Since then, Hart Island had become the final resting place for tens of thousands of down-and-out New Yorkers.

On the island, inmates from the local jailhouse met the coroner's trucks. They unloaded the pine boxes containing the bodies of former cigar makers, cooks, construction workers, shoemakers, butchers, bellhops, taxi drivers, flagmen, dockworkers, and anyone else who couldn't afford a private burial. Many times, smaller boxes arrived, no longer than two feet. They held babies. Inmates carried those in one hand. All of them were piled onto a pickup truck that bumped its way up and down the unpaved road of Hart Island, its tires sending up little clouds of dirt and tiny pebbles, which pinged off the wooden coffins, all shifting and thumping together.

At potter's field, there were no winding roads leading to sections with names like Eternal Love, Vale of Sorrows, or For All Eternity, where granite crosses and marble angels with outspread wings and sorrowful faces guarded the dead. There were no flowers left at gravestones or benches placed under weeping willows where people could sit and remember and grieve. Here there was a wide-open space, and the dead were buried in mass graves, long trenches dug deep in the earth. Adult coffins were stacked three or four high, and the children's eight to ten. Far away from anyone in these unmarked graves, all traces of them would vanish. *The New York Times* once described potter's field as the place "where the rough pine boxes go."

It was a graveyard, one reporter said, "of last resorts," and Sea View was its purgatory.

Chapter 29

❖

Promise

Summer 1944

Albert Schatz stood at his table preparing petri dishes and flasks for a dangerous experiment. Beside him was a package containing H37Rv, the most virulent human strain of tuberculosis, sent from Waksman's two new partners. Schatz picked it up and held it. He was eager to open it and begin working with the bacteria, but not yet. First, he needed to fulfill the bargain Waksman had independently struck with his new associates.

A year earlier, Waksman had combined forces with two TB experts from the Mayo Clinic in Rochester, Minnesota. Dr. H. Corwin Hinshaw, a big, spirited man who specialized in chest diseases, and Dr. William Feldman, a tall and thin veterinary pathologist. Feldman, following many others who devoted their lives to tuberculosis, had a personal interest in conquering the disease.

Growing up, Feldman had seen his altruistic mother turn their front porch into an outdoor TB ward. Every day, entering and exiting the house, he saw bodies of people lying indolent on blankets or mattresses; they looked famished, as if they were a breath away from dying. Over the years, their collective faces blurred into a pastiche of images that impressed themselves into his psyche and eventually carved the pathway for his life's mission. His doctoral work led him in a slightly different direction: studying tuberculosis in animals. But six years ago, in 1938, on a frigid night during the height of the sulfa boom, his career path changed again.

While returning from a medical conference, Feldman found himself in the back seat of a freezing old Ford huddling next to Hinshaw. As the wind blew snow and ice at the canvas top and sides, the two doctors found solace in talking about tuberculosis. Hinshaw brought up a recently published study by two researchers who had used a sulfa variant to treat TB in animals. That drug had failed. But, Hinshaw said, a newer version was available. Maybe it would work. And then, somewhere on that dark highway, fate or karma, or whatever forces draw people together, inspired the two men to collaborate. They would test the new version of sulfa.

The deal that bleak, freezing night turned into years of testing hundreds of sulfa variations and other druglike compounds. Few made it past the lab, and despite the frustration and failure, they realized the TB microbe was stalwart but not indestructible. They agreed to keep going, looking for a cure by following any lead.

Some months ago, they had read Waksman's short introductory paper on streptomycin, listing its potential efficacy against different bacteria, including tuberculosis. Immediately, they drafted a letter to Waksman, but in one of those strange coincidental twists, he had already contacted them. Would they, Waksman asked, want to "participate in a cooperative study of the drug's potential?"

Yes, the two doctors said.

Then came the deal: The Mayo doctors would give Waksman the deadly H37Rv strain of *Mycobacterium tuberculosis* for Schatz to test in vitro, in test tubes. In return, Waksman would send them 10 milligrams of streptomycin to test in vivo, specifically in guinea pigs. Although running simultaneous tests of the drug at two separate labs in two separate ways, in vitro and in vivo, was not optimal, they agreed it would speed up the process of getting to human trials. Now they needed Schatz to cook up the streptomycin necessary for all the tests.

Down in his lab, Schatz reconfigured his table, setting up the Bunsen burners and flasks with beef broth, and to quicken the process, he set up two small stills and ran them twenty-four hours a day; he took to sleeping in the freezing basement and enlisted the night watchman to check on the stills while he slept. If they boiled below a certain point, Schatz told the watchman to wake him up. All through the fierce northeast winter, Schatz worked alone in the lab, tending to his flasks and the growing colonies of *S. griseus* that would eventually become the drug streptomycin. During this time, Waksman, his fear of TB heightened by the presence of the new H37Rv strain housed in his labs, never came downstairs. Instead he reiterated that no "pathogenic tuberculosis culture" should come anywhere near him.

In early spring, Schatz bottled and sent 10 milligrams of streptomycin to the Mayo Clinic for Feldman and Hinshaw to begin their guinea pig tests. Then he cleared his space and prepared it for in vitro testing of the deadly H37Rv bacteria.

To anyone watching, the scene unfolding was the stuff of nightmares. Schatz's lab lacked every safety protocol necessary for testing infectious bacteria. There was no inoculation chamber outfitted with UV lamps, a necessity for keeping the bacteria contained and free from contamination; the lab lacked a separate positive pressure room designed to filter out the infected air and a special incubator for TB cultures. And the old hand-cranked autoclave used for sterilizing equipment barely worked.

"If you forget it, it overheats," Schatz explained, "and *ker-pow*."

But he set to work anyway, his lab clothes as paltry as his workspace.

Without a mask or gloves and dressed only in a cracked rubber apron designed for working with soil, Schatz began transferring the lethal strain. He placed it in narrow test tubes lined with a special pale green culture medium that would promote its growth. In one tube after another, he carefully, almost mechanically, brushed the interior with the H37Rv bacteria; in half, he dropped different dilutions of streptomycin. The others got none. When he finished, he plugged the tops of the test tubes with cotton.

Sometimes, while pushing in the cotton, Schatz held his breath, afraid he would loosen a single microbe, setting off an outbreak among his colleagues. At night, Doris Jones witnessed him washing his mouth with antiseptic. The rinse did nothing, but it made him feel safer.

❖

Just before summer, Feldman and Hinshaw called Waksman with news: the results from their guinea pig study were striking. Schatz's small, impure amount of streptomycin had produced a "bacteriostatic" effect in the TB-infected pigs, meaning it stopped the bacteria from reproducing. Even better, none of the animals was showing signs of toxicity.

The drug was working.

The news excited Waksman. Their findings correlated with Schatz's results: in the test tubes without streptomycin, rough-looking, sandy-colored H37Rv TB colonies mauled the pretty green medium. But those sprinkled with streptomycin remained undisturbed, pristine.

Weeks later, the Mayo doctors traveled to New Jersey to discuss the next steps. Inside the small agricultural building housing Waksman's office, they were besieged by smells of earth and soil and other natural odors they couldn't quite place. On the third floor, they found Waksman, cheerful and in good spirits. In his office, sitting across from one another, the men exchanged pleasantries and then turned to business.

Hinshaw explained that they wanted to run a second round of tests on a new batch of guinea pigs, but they needed more streptomycin. Waksman was happy to oblige. He sent them downstairs to talk with Schatz while he waited upstairs.

Down went the two men, who found their way to Schatz's make-shift pathology lab. At the door, they stopped, aghast, and surveyed the room, taking in the test tubes topped with cotton, the archaic autoclave clanking away in the corner, and the lack of space and proper ventilation. And there in the middle was Albert Schatz, twenty-four years old, with his entire life in front of him, standing in that decrepit rubber apron, his hands and face unprotected, working with the most virulent strain of tuberculosis known to humankind.

That Schatz had accomplished anything in these primitive conditions was a marvel, but it could not continue. No doubt, he would get sick and then sicken others. And it was unlikely he could produce the amount of pure streptomycin essential for finishing their tests.

Back upstairs, they expressed their concerns to Waksman. To move forward, they needed a new arrangement. Masking his frustration, Waksman picked up the phone and called Merck, now one of America's most influential pharmaceutical companies, and arranged a confidential meeting for the following day.

In the boardroom of Merck's facility, twelve chemists seated around a table welcomed Waksman and his guests. Feldman wasted no time in presenting their case: the first guinea pig tests with streptomycin had produced excellent results; they needed more of the antibiotic to run longer and more nuanced tests.

His request was met with a firm no. The company was overwhelmed with producing penicillin for the troops.

Feldman tried again. This time, he appealed to their more emotional side, meeting the eye of each employee and telling them the drug was essential for humankind.

They understood but were unmoved.

Waksman became anxious and stood up. He made them an offer: he would come down to the lab and plant the cultures. They thanked him but declined, reiterating their need to remain focused on producing penicillin; tens of thousands of soldiers relied on it. Hinshaw, more measured than Waksman, agreed, then added a statistic: in World War I, more soldiers had died from tuberculosis than in battle. Now he had their attention. They called in the CEO, George Merck.

An industrious man, George Merck knew Waksman personally. Some years earlier, Mr. Merck had secretly engaged him as a consultant on microbial fermentation, paying him to find new ways of making citric acid. The hushed, under-the-table deal could have cost Waksman his job—universities weren't happy with professors using their labs and supplies for "private consulting" and personal profit. But Waksman had succeeded, and Mr. Merck was happy.

Streptomycin's potential was apparent to the savvy Mr. Merck. Immediately, he agreed to help, promising to build a new plant to produce the new antibiotic, an endeavor whose cost eventually topped $3.5 million. Until then, he assigned fifty workers to produce streptomycin at the New Jersey facility. Handshakes followed and everyone seemed gratified.

Later that day, before Hinshaw and Feldman boarded their train for Rochester, Minnesota, Waksman handed them a small supply of streptomycin, but followed the gesture with a portentous warning about "premature publicity." They were not, he said, to write or talk about the drug until patents were secured. Otherwise, he and Merck could lose millions in profits.

The men were confused, and his words struck them as rash; no one was talking about writing scientific papers, at least not yet. But more unsettling was his delivery. There was something menacing in his tone and his expression. They couldn't quite place it, but it was enough to awaken that niggling sense of something feeling very, very off.

Chapter 30

❖

188 Wheeler Avenue

July–October 1944

Missouria was getting ready for work when the petition arrived that July morning in 1944. She opened the envelope and her eyes darted across the page. At first it confused her, but slowly its meaning became clear.

For years, Missouria had been stashing away her money, saving for a house, and after a tedious hunt, similar to Edna's, she had found one on Wheeler Avenue, around the corner from Bradley Avenue. Wheeler was a quiet street with only five all-white families: four Italian and one Norwegian. They had known one another for years, and all of them lived happily side by side. If Missouria moved into the house, the petition explained, she would ruin the homogeneity of the street. There were plenty of other houses she could consider, just not this one. The petition was signed by a Mr. Saveno Cofano, a short Italian man who lived at 191, directly across from the house Missouria hoped to buy. Beside his signature were those from the other Wheeler Avenue families.

Missouria read the notice, once, twice, three times, and with each new pass, her indignation mounted. She had endured years of caring for the men on Ward 64 and of working double shifts to save money; she had watched the houses on Edna's street fill with Sea View employees;

cooks, technicians, groundskeepers, porters, and nurses moved in, turning it into a thriving community of Black professionals, especially women.

When Missouria had first looked at the house, the real estate agent had assured her there wouldn't be any problems. It was cheap and close to Sea View, in an unpopular area where most people were reluctant to buy, particularly Staten Islanders, who believed the air around the hospital was contaminated with tuberculosis. Supposedly so were the animals: the rabbits, birds, and even the earthworms that lived in the surrounding forest. All of them harbored the disease.

Missouria and the other nurses found it sad, and in a way comical, how people slipped so easily into believing these unsubstantiated myths, but then again, it wasn't too shocking, considering what they believed about Black people. But if they wanted to stay away, the Black nurses were happy to keep buying the old homes and empty lots. To them, the area, bound by trees and full of uncrowded streets, was lovely.

Built just a few years earlier, the house at 188 Wheeler with the pretty blue-gray siding was roomy, featuring three floors and a basement. With the extra space, Missouria could take in family or friends or anyone else in need, especially children. She had always dreamed of having a brood of kids, but a gynecological issue had destroyed her ovaries. Unable to have children, she set her sights on adopting them.

Behind the house, a huge backyard stretched into the one-acre lot next door, giving her plenty of space to plant flowers, trees, and vegetables and to erect a chicken coop. She had no interest in other homes. Her mind was made up, and no one would change it. Certainly not Mr. Cofano with his foolish petition.

She tossed it aside and finished getting ready for work, fastening her nurse's cap with bobby pins, sliding on her copper bracelet, and slipping her mints into her purse. When she was done, she picked up the phone, dialed the agent, and explained the situation. The agent listened and responded.

She was sorry, but things like this had happened before. And they never ended well. There were other houses, just as big, but on different streets that already had Black families.

Would Missouria reconsider?

"I don't want another house. I want the one on Wheeler," Missouria said.

❖

Mr. Reiman was standing behind the counter of his hardware store, his pipe dangling from his mouth, when Missouria walked through the pockmarked screen door the next day. She told him about the petition and the agent, and he puffed and listened. Reaching into one of the many drawers, he pulled out a piece of paper and jotted down the name of a lawyer. It was his friend, he explained, who'd helped other nurses in similar situations. But before calling the lawyer, Mr. Reiman wanted her to see another friend, Mr. William A. Morris Sr., president of the Staten Island chapter of the NAACP.

Morris was big and imposing, but his stature belied his disposition. At heart, he was gracious, easygoing, a family man who devoted himself to advocating for nonviolent change. But in his tenderness, there was a fierceness, a fire that recalled Mama Amy's.

She liked him immediately.

Originally from North Carolina, Morris arrived on Staten Island in 1898. In those forty-six years, he had built a successful moving business and became well known as an honest man, a character trait that earned him the respect of the white community—no small feat. While he appreciated their trust, he knew the different ways white Staten Islanders tried to push out Black people, especially those hoping to buy homes.

The history of bigotry reached back decades, but twenty years ago, in June 1924, the enmity of white Staten Islanders became public.

That year, a mile from Wheeler Avenue, Sam Browne, a mail carrier and Spanish-American War veteran, had bought a home and was preparing to move in when he received the following letter: "If you move into that house on Fairview Avenue, Castleton Hill, it will be the worst day's work you ever did. You may treat this lightly, but after you move in, it will be too late. You should know better than to move where you are not wanted. Yours for the flaming cross, 'K.K.K.'"

The letter made Browne uneasy, but he disregarded it, refusing to be intimidated. His wife was a respected teacher at the local public school, and he was a war veteran and civil servant. In his eyes, he had a right to live wherever he wanted. A month later, he moved to 67 Fairview Avenue, in the all-white "stucco and rose garden neighborhood" of Castleton Corners.

Mr. Musco Robertson, Browne's next-door neighbor, owned Robertson Development Company, the real estate agency controlling large portions of Staten Island. Within days of Browne moving in, Robertson, a Southerner, approached him and introduced himself as the "chairman of a citizen's committee." In a friendly but firm tone, he explained that Browne was "the only negro man in the neighborhood," then offered to buy the house. Browne refused, saying he "intended to make the place his permanent home."

Before he left, Robertson handed the war veteran his brochure advertising Castleton Corners: "This exceptional development is dotted with many beautiful homes and every one is occupied by a 100 percent American family." Having grown up in Alabama, Browne understood exactly what "100 percent American family" meant.

That summer, Browne spent the hot July nights sitting on his porch, shotgun perched beside him, watching his neighbors hold nightly meetings in their yards. Down south, white men used to hold the same meetings deep in the woods or in the basements of white churches or town halls. Despite their gatherings, he still refused to leave.

One night toward the end of July, while sitting on the porch, he noticed a stream of about forty people marching two by two up the street. He picked up his shotgun. The group of people, men and women, dressed in ordinary clothes, stopped in front of him and said nothing. Then they crossed over his lawn and slowly started circumambulating his home, as if the site were holy.

Browne rose and lifted his shotgun.

"Are you looking for Sam Browne?" he shouted.

The procession stopped.

"Are you looking for Sam Browne?" he repeated.

Silence.

"Cowards," he shouted at them, raising his gun and forcing them to scatter.

Some weeks later, members of Robertson's "citizens' committee" returned and spread themselves across Browne's lawn. They pelted his house with rocks and shattered his windows. Inside, the Browne family hid in terror. Minutes passed like hours.

Finally, the sound stopped, and through the window, Browne saw a brilliant orange glow rising from the front yard and turning the night sky into a sunset. It grew brighter, and he grabbed his gun, ran downstairs, out the front door, and onto the porch. Then he saw the burning cross. He spent the next morning cleaning up dried ash and burned leaves.

Soon the rocks turned to bricks, sending glass onto beds and dressers, couches and coffee tables. Browne took the letters to the district attorney, who promised to investigate the "citizens' committee" of Fairview Avenue. But most likely, he told Browne, the KKK wasn't involved in any of the property destruction; he should ignore their letters.

When the neighbors learned about Browne's legal complaint, they sent more letters with grimmer warnings: to date, they said, this was the "work of a novice," and that the KKK had "very effective methods of handling people like him." Also, they added that involving the DA meant nothing: "There are five of us for each nigger on Staten Island. Are you aware of that?" they wrote.

A year later, after his shrubs had been pulled up and his windows shattered multiple times, the NAACP threatened to sue the city for refusing to protect Browne's civil rights. In response, the district attorney indicted six men, but the harassment continued. Still, Browne refused to leave. People from outside the neighborhood joined in, forming bigger, more threatening mobs that continued to uproot plants and break windows.

The summer ended with the Manhattan NAACP, responsible for Browne's case, suggesting that Staten Island establish its own chapter of the organization. In September, Mr. Morris became president, and two years later he helped bring a criminal and civil suit against nine of Browne's neighbors for damages and conspiracy. A grand jury indicted all nine men, and three years later, the "citizens' committee," humiliated and furious, receded back into their homes.

Mr. Morris asked Missouria what she wanted to do. She could persist like Sam Browne, or she could find another home. Even with the backing of the NAACP, it could be a long, drawn-out battle—months, even years. And the families on Wheeler seemed well prepared to fight back, especially now, after the city had appraised the neighborhood.

When the real estate agent showed Missouria the house, she failed to disclose some pertinent information about the property. Beginning in 1938, the year Edna bought her home, the federal government came to appraise the area. In the report, the evaluator determined Missouria's desired neighborhood was "definitely declining" and warned homeowners that sales prices were lower than in previous years "due to slight influx of negro population."

Sea View, half a mile south, was of course to blame: "The New York City administration employs only colored help in this large institution," the inspector wrote, "and it is natural that many of these negroes will find their way into adjacent low-grade areas, of which this is one of the nearest." Because of this, he continued, "there is no apparent movement of any desirable population toward the area and the trend appears inevitably downward." In ten years, the assessor projected, the residents of Wheeler Avenue and the successive streets would find themselves trapped in a "red zone," surrounded by Black workers and their once-beautiful homes now valueless.

Missouria took in Mr. Morris's information and this system of demarcating lives. Maps and lines had defined her entire life. They were drawn throughout history, straightened, elongated, bent up and down by people who met in town halls and state capitals and now in the federal government. She had spent too many years confined inside those lines, told where to go, when, and for how long. She had come here to change her life, to live as a professional, and to put down new roots.

Some weeks later, Missouria returned to Mr. Morris's office at his moving company. She found him sitting behind his desk surrounded by work orders, with the phone ringing constantly. He was gracious, offering her water or tea, and eager to hear her response.

Yes, she wanted the house, and no one would change her mind. As promised, Mr. Morris worked alongside her lawyer, and in July, Missouria Louvinia Meadows-Walker signed her name to a deed and officially became a homeowner.

But the harassment and threats didn't stop. She moved in and more petitions and warnings arrived in her mailbox. She sent them to Mr. Morris and her lawyer and spent her days off and before work in the backyard, pulling up weeds, turning over the soil, and planting trees: apple, peach, and pear. As she worked, she sang. But the families of Wheeler weren't soothed or moved by her songs. They grew angrier. Graver threats followed. In late fall, Missouria's lawyer called and asked her if she wanted a gun.

"Get it," Mama Amy said, and then she retold the story of her ex-husband, Will Meadows, and the cow. Missouria listened, again—how Mama Amy loved that story. It made her proud.

"Get the gun," she repeated, after finishing the story.

Chapter 31

Firsts

Halfway across the country at the Mayo Clinic, the twenty-four-year-old woman lay dying.

Her name was Patricia, and she was suffering from a grisly strain of pulmonary tuberculosis that was halfway through devouring the lobe on her right lung. She had already undergone a thoracoplasty, but the operation produced nothing except the loss of a handful of ribs. Her physician grew desperate, calling on Dr. Hinshaw; maybe he could help. Hinshaw arrived and stepped into Patricia's room and encountered a ghastly scene of a skeletal being lying in bed, her eyes sunken deep into her skull, and her face and body drenched and trembling from fever. Hinshaw noted her pallor, took her vitals, looked at her chart, then confirmed her prognosis: Patricia was dying.

But he had an idea.

Currently, he was still doing the second round of large-scale guinea pig tests with streptomycin. So far, nine pigs treated with the drug showed signs of healing. Maybe he could try the novel antibiotic on Patricia. What did they have to lose?

Would she like to try an experimental drug?

"Yes," she said without hesitation.

Using his guinea pig data to calculate dosing, Hinshaw took a vial of streptomycin—it was the last of the batch sent to him by Schatz and most likely impure—and placed the tip of the needle inside. He pulled the plunger back and watched the gooey substance slowly fill the syringe's glass barrel.

Holding her upper arm, he prodded it with his fingers, trying to find her muscle. Streptomycin was an intramuscular drug, and for it to work, the injection needed to penetrate the muscle, a challenge for TB patients, whose muscles, as one nurse put it, always became "like wet spaghetti."

He found a spot and, after sterilizing it, stretched the skin, which felt thin and papery, almost like it could tear, and prepared to inject her. Carefully, he inserted the needle at a slight angle, brought up the plunger, then pushed down, and felt the tip slowly going in, descending deeper and deeper until it penetrated her muscle; then he released the gooey liquid from the glass plunger, and it filled her body.

Pulling out the needle, he held up the empty syringe to mark the moment: November 20, 1944, the day Patricia became the first person with pulmonary tuberculosis to receive streptomycin.

Now came the wait.

Every day, after logging in his guinea pig data, Hinshaw returned to Patricia and examined her, and if he had streptomycin—often he ran out and had to wait for Merck to send more—he would adjust the dosing and inject her. Each time the needle pierced that papery skin, Patricia recoiled from a pain that lasted for hours and turned her arm purple. She also suffered crushing side effects: headaches and facial flushes, sore joints, exhaustion, and sometimes fever and chills.

And yet, she endured.

Some weeks after the first dose, Hinshaw walked in and found Patricia sitting up in bed, alert and feverless. He held up her X-rays; they showed the infection was clearing, but her sputum was still positive for TB.

That was odd. Normally, if the infection cleared, the sputum would be negative. Maybe, he reasoned, the interruption in treatment was to blame. Or maybe it was how the drug worked, or maybe she wasn't healed yet; perhaps the drug was only partially working. He didn't know.

In January 1945, two months after first injecting Patricia, Hinshaw finished his guinea pig trial and sent a cable to Waksman: "Incomplete results indicate impressive therapeutic effects."

While this was good news, Hinshaw knew that if Patricia's results weren't as striking, the animal tests wouldn't matter.

❖

While Patricia continued making history, in New York City, on a freezing January afternoon, another historic moment was taking place in front of the Hotel Pierre on Fifth Avenue. A crowd of three hundred nurses, politicians, and journalists filed through its grand entrance and made their way to one of the elegant meeting rooms to hear Norman T. Kirk, surgeon general of the US Army, speak.

Kirk, a thin man with a face full of angles and a receding hairline, stepped up and began talking about the war. At present, he announced, the army was short on nurses. There would be a draft, he said.

As the crowd processed Kirk's words, NACGN president Mabel Staupers wasted no time rising to her feet. She had spent the past two years protesting the limited quotas for Black nurses and arguing against restricting them to caring for POWs. Her tenacity garnered increasing sympathy from white nurses, who were currently experiencing their own disrespect in the military, with lower pay and gender limitations. In November 1944, the same week Patricia received streptomycin, Staupers sat down with First Lady Eleanor Roosevelt. After their meeting, Mrs. Roosevelt began pressuring Kirk to increase the ranks of Black nurses.

So far, Kirk had resisted.

"Why isn't the army using colored nurses?" Staupers asked him.

"Of the 9,000 registered Negro nurses, the army has taken 247. The navy takes none."

Kirk, in his military brass, squirmed.

"There are 7,000 Negro nurses in comparison to 200,000 [white nurses] in the United States," he said. "I believe that the average share of colored nurses in the Army is equal to the total number of Negro troops."

Staupers eyed him, knowing his math was erroneous. If what Kirk said were true, there would have been "1,520 Black nurses in the army and navy, not 330 in the army." The two engaged in a verbal spar, with Kirk reiterating an earlier statement that Black nurses were equal to the number of Black soldiers.

We use them "where we can use them, but we don't mix them," he said. "We don't house Negroes and whites together."

The following day, the Kirk-Staupers exchange, as the press called it, made nationwide coverage. Almost every Black newspaper splashed it across their front pages: "Urge Roosevelt Act in Snubbing of Our Nurses," *The New York Amsterdam News* proclaimed.

Less than a week later, a congressman introduced the Draft Nurse Bill to fill the ranks, and the Kirk-Staupers tension intensified, setting off a nationwide public outcry. People demanded to know why young soldiers were in field hospitals, injured and sick, with a threadbare staff of nurses. They asked how many men had died because of subpar care and how many had suffered needlessly, waiting too long for medicine. And all along, the country had nurses, thousands of them, ready to serve, but they were being turned away because of their skin color. No one, not the military or President Roosevelt, expected such a response.

Staupers, as always, seized the moment and went public, harnessing the national anger and America's sympathy. She urged everyone to march into Western Union and send telegrams to President Roosevelt and Kirk protesting their racist policies.

The telegraph wires hummed.

Every day, Roosevelt and Kirk woke up to piles of mail and a never-ending cascade of telegrams arriving at the White House. They came from a myriad of organizations—the NAACP, the Catholic Interracial Council, and the American Civil Liberties Union—as well as politicians, nurses, doctors, and ordinary citizens. They were scathing, full of fury at the military quotas imposed on Black nurses and their consignment to care for only POWs and Black soldiers.

Unable to escape the mail or the wrath of Americans, including his own wife, Roosevelt was forced to end the quota system and exclusion of Black nurses from the military. On January 20, Kirk announced the Army Nurse Corps would accept Black nurses, officially dismantling decades of segregation.

It was a pivotal moment for Staupers, ten years in the making, and she hoped the American Nurses Association would follow suit and finally integrate Black nurses into the organization. But, as usual, enough white nurses scoffed and scowled at the prospect of taking down the racial structures that kept their organization free of Black women.

And so, once again, nothing happened.

The ANA's refusal to change was discouraging, but it didn't diminish the victory. Thousands of Black nurses lined up to register and serve, including Olive Lucas and Petra Pinn from Sea View. Their pending departure irked Miss Mitchell, but she could do nothing to stop them. This time, in a rare moment, America raised its voice and spoke on behalf of Black nurses, and everyone listened.

❖

As Congress considered the bill allowing Black nurses to serve, Hinshaw was studying Patricia's most recent X-rays. They showed a clearing of the disease, which was good news, but her sputum results were still coming back positive for tuberculosis, leaving him perplexed.

He informed his colleagues, who didn't seem concerned. Maybe the new drug cured but left a false positive or maybe Patricia still had residual traces of the disease that in time would clear. Whatever the reason might be, for them, the current moment called for a celebration, not hesitation.

Hinshaw was unconvinced. Something was wrong, he knew it, but couldn't do a thing. He was powerless, unable to stop the global frenzy brewing, the one he'd set in motion on November 20 when he first injected Patricia with streptomycin.

Chapter 32

Dark Places

February–April 1945

Cures and victories were not yet happening at Sea View. Instead, there were staff shortages, long wait lists for beds, and devastating relapses from patients, including Hilda Ali.

Several months earlier, after a three-year respite, the longest of her brief life, Hilda, now thirteen, had been readmitted. This time, her intake read "far advanced pulmonary tuberculosis," a somber change from her initial diagnosis of advanced pulmonary tuberculosis. But Sea View's nurses didn't need a chart to tell them Hilda was sick, very, very sick.

Hilda, who dreamed of a life beyond this, now spent most days in the incurable room, the one where Salaria Kea used to work, drifting in and out of consciousness, her eyes opening occasionally only to see shadows of people—nurses, doctors, her mother—shifting around her. But even those brief moments of waking overwhelmed her lungs, full of microbes hell-bent on obliterating every tissue and nerve and vein. Daily they kept multiplying, creating more necrosis and a heaviness, a pressure akin to a giant hand pressing down on her bony chest, aiming to flatten her. She tried to speak, but the words became lost, tangled in her vocal cords; she wheezed and made squealing noises that swished around the fluids in her chest, causing her to choke and spit up blood and phlegm and bile.

Her mother sat bedside, impotent and helpless, while an ugly, driving fever consumed her daughter. It matted her hair to her face and coated her body in sweat, leaving a sheen that made her skin glisten as if someone had covered her in grease. Her mother watched as the nurses came in and took Hilda's pulse, adjusted her oxygen, and then changed her nightgown and linens. They lifted her up, her body slouching here and there, and pulled off her soggy nightgown and worked, pretending they didn't notice her ribs bulging and her vertebrae rising from her back like a small emerging fin.

It was these images that sparked a universal dread, one that struck parents whose children lived with chronic illness. Hilda's mother came every day because she worried about her daughter dying alone and about forgetting how her daughter's lashes curled or how her face looked when she slept or how she smiled, though that rarely happened now. She came to remember all of it, all the horror, the pain, the smells, the sounds, and the sights of piles of people suffering, including her own child, Hilda Ali, who prior to this admission had spent five of her twelve years at Sea View, or 1,702 days, officially making her a lunger. Hilda Ali, who was trapped in an old and broken body.

To try to save her, doctors wanted to perform a lobectomy, a high-risk surgery that would remove one or two diseased lobes from the lungs in an attempt to stop the spread of TB. At that moment, however, Hilda was too sick for any procedures.

But if Hinshaw's human trials with streptomycin generated positive results, then everything would change for Hilda and so many others whose lives had become one long meditation on dying.

❖

By February 1945, talk of the novel antibiotic streptomycin was weaving its way through the offices of pharmaceutical companies, labs, and hospital wards. It was the good news Dr. Robitzek needed, and he celebrated with his wife, hoping the year would be bright for them, the future of medicine, and his Diasone trials.

After months of scrupulous planning, the nurses had recently given the 106 patients their first dose. Every day for the next few weeks, they would chart their sputum counts, temperature, blood pressure, and pulse while looking for rashes or signs of jaundice. Then they'd ask about side effects: Did they have any constipation, incontinence, or headaches? Heart palpitations? Anxiety? Insomnia?

The work was exacting and repetitive and one misstep could throw off the trial, but Robitzek, unlike many doctors, had faith in Sea View's Black nurses; they "ran the wards," he said, and without them, "I wouldn't have a job."

After evening rounds, he collected their daily data and compiled it, a job that took hours, keeping him at Sea View well into the night. He stopped occasionally to stand up and stretch or give his eye a rest, and also to call his wife and wish her good night. "I love you, Katherine." He always told her that.

On the night of February 11, when they spoke, she didn't mention the headache. She saw no reason; it seemed ordinary, no different from the other ones. After putting the boys to bed, she took an aspirin and lay down. Hours later, when Robitzek came home, Katherine was asleep. He kissed her and slipped into bed. In three days, it would be Valentine's Day, and he planned to buy her a card and a big bouquet of flowers.

Morning broke, and Katherine woke up confused. Her vision was blurry, and her chest ached. Robitzek called an ambulance, sent the boys to a neighbor, and returned to his wife, trying to keep her awake and alert, but she was woozy, her eyes straining to stay open. The paramedics arrived, and in his robe, he watched them working, their hands moving quickly, reminding him of the days when he went into people's homes to save them. He knew the pressure of making split-second decisions, choices that meant the difference between life and death.

The two men lifted Katherine, placed her on a stretcher, and covered her with a blanket, then disappeared down the hall, out the door, and into the building's elevator. As the ambulance raced down Victory Boulevard, its siren blaring, echoing through the familiar neighborhoods, inside its cabin, thirty-one-year-old Katherine fought to stay awake, but midway to the hospital, she blinked and then closed her eyes.

By the time Robitzek arrived at the emergency room, Katherine was unconscious, in critical condition, with her blood pressure soaring, and no one knew why. For the next forty-eight hours, he sat vigil beside his wife, watching her breath and keeping track of her vitals. He wet her lips with ice chips, stroked her hair, and talked to her, telling her things. But she was too far away to return, and on the second day, when Budapest fell to the Red Army and winds gusted across the city, he knew Katherine was never coming back. She died the next day, on February 14, 1945, Valentine's Day. In a haze of grief, the newly widowed doctor planned a funeral and arranged to bury her at Woodlawn Cemetery in a plot beside his father.

The weeks following her death were impossible. Being inside the small apartment with all of its trappings of Katherine—drapes, rugs, chairs, pictures, vases, lamps, glasses, napkins—pulled him into fresh places of grief. He sat on the couch, the one she had chosen, for hours and listened to the kitchen clock ticking or the wind whistling outside. In the mornings, he lay in bed and watched the sunrise, the rays swooping through the window, reaching the space where she used to sleep. Sometimes he turned over to grab her. He missed her voice, ached for her scent. Traces of it still lingered on her clothing, the bedsheets, and the pillows, but soon it would fade.

Taking care of the boys seemed an insurmountable task. He called his mother, who traveled from the Bronx to help him. While he worked, she cooked and served dinner on Katherine's plates; she cleaned and watched her grandsons, now two and three, who missed their mother. But despite all her efforts, things still seemed out of order. The boys were anxious, edgy, unsettled.

Some nights when Robitzek read to them, they took too long to fall asleep, and other nights while trying to work in the living room, he was interrupted by their chatter about boats and planes and animals and Mommy. The word infiltrated his brain and dominated his thoughts.

After talking with his mother, he realized they would be better off living with her in the Bronx. He packed up their things—the clothes and diapers and stuffed animals, the blocks and pull toys—and headed for the ferry. From his rearview mirror, he caught glimpses of his two young sons in the back seat prattling on, saying words he didn't understand. Katherine always seemed to know what they were saying. But the boys would remember nothing of their mother. Memory would erase all of her. It was like that.

He arrived at his childhood home on Billingsley Terrace. The boys ran inside and through the kitchen, where pots boiled on the stove, to the living room and past the space where Arthur Robitzek, the grandfather they never knew, had died. Robitzek followed them, taking them upstairs to his old bedroom, their new room for now. Sitting on his boyhood bed, he unpacked their things.

And then he left.

As he drove back to the ferry port, the car seemed too big and too quiet. He could have turned back, but he kept driving, moving through the city with its neon signs illuminating the busy streets and sidewalks full of people. Waiting at the stoplights, he saw the crowds stepping off curbs, men and women with their heads down and coats pulled tight, hurrying to reach a destination. None of them knew what had happened to him and his family. They, like the rest of the world, kept moving. If only he could bring the entire city into his sadness, let the people of New York feel the loss of Katherine Robitzek, maybe he could find some relief.

At home on Staten Island, he lay awake in the clear darkness, with images of his late wife appearing and disappearing in his mind. There was too much sorrow in the world, especially at Sea View. Every day, people died by the handfuls. In the morgue, bodies amassed. He had spent years opening them up, reaching inside, pulling out lungs and spleens and kidneys and brains in search of the precise reason that life had ended—tuberculosis or something else.

The medical coroner had opened up Katherine, sliced off tissues from her heart and lungs and brain, to uncover why she had died. Weeks later, Robitzek received the report: a cerebral aneurysm caused by chronic hypertension, or, in layman's terms, undiagnosed high blood pressure. Knowing the cause changed nothing. In some ways, it made things worse. He wondered if each headache or moment of fatigue was a warning that he, Dr. Edward Robitzek, acting medical director of Sea View, had missed.

To assuage the guilt and sadness, the inability to sleep and the memories that their home aroused, he shaped a new routine: he arrived at Sea View early in the morning and sometimes left well past midnight. Work was the only thing that distracted him from thinking about Katherine. He grew more determined, pouring all his energy into his research, into finding a remedy, a cure for tuberculosis, something that would avenge his father's death and make his wife's passing meaningful.

But his mission was proving difficult.

In May, three months after Katherine died, Robitzek sat in the pathology lab, a low brick building behind the pavilions, with a stack of folders and a legal pad. He was tired but determined to finish an article on the Diasone trial for the Sea View *Quarterly Bulletin*, the journal he edited.

With his fingers, he flipped open the folder and pulled out a batch of papers on the trial, the one he'd started weeks before Katherine died. It had kept him away from his family, kept him here working late, cross-checking data and making charts, and now he would determine the results. His good eye moved across the pages, synthesizing pertinent information that he jotted down in his doctor's scrawl on the legal pad.

Duration: four months. Some continued to six months.

Patient numbers: 106.

Complications: headache, anorexia, cyanosis, nausea, tremor, vomiting, weakness, skin lesions, palpitations, tachycardia, epigastric pain, visual disturbances, nervousness, polyphagia, hepatitis, jaundice, and lymphadenopathy.

Seeing the side effects strung together on the page like a garland of anguish alarmed him, especially the section on "R.P., a 17-year-old colored female."

Twenty days into the trial, R.P. had woken up with her lips swollen and bleeding and full of herpes-like lesions. The nurse called Robitzek, who examined her and ordered a lower Diasone dosage. He left, and hours later the nurse noted a temperature of 104 degrees. Under layers of blankets, R.P. shook with chills, and soon a rash covered her tongue and palms and feet. The nurse called him again, and this time, hoping to stop the reaction, he discontinued the drug and called for a blood count, which revealed leukocytosis, a high white blood cell count. He ordered a transfusion.

Two days passed and R.P. was getting worse. She could barely swallow, and her entire body was awash in "cherry sized" blisters that sent pus and blood trickling down her arms and legs, chest and torso, soaking the sheets and blankets. Nine days after the first symptom had appeared, R.P. died. Blood tests revealed that the cause of death was Diasone.

There it was, in writing, his original fear come to pass, the dread that the drug was not safe enough, that it had not gone through extensive animal tests, and that there needed to be stricter protocols, oversights, and regulations before starting any human trials. This experience left his mind full of unanswerable questions: Was R.P.'s death preventable? Was the fault his own, the drug's, or something beyond anyone's control? These musings would stay with him for a long, long time.

In the other folders, he read through the nurses' charts that listed the weight gains and losses, bacillus counts, and tabulations on positive and negative sputum: "Their work was masterful," he would later say, and he was grateful for their dedication to the other patients who had volunteered for the trial and who might have also died without their expertise.

After reading all the information, he brought it together, building paragraph upon paragraph describing how the study was conducted, the ages and genders of the patients, their reactions, and the dosing history.

In between thoughts, he paused and rubbed his neck, leaning his head back. Above him were rows of shelves stocked with lab equipment, all reminders of the late nights he'd spent away from Katherine, amassing data, hoping that it would yield a good outcome and that Diasone would emerge "favorable in clinical application," as Dr. Raiziss claimed. All of it now seemed wasted. He lowered his head and penned the sad reality: "Our results clearly indicate that Diasone does not cure chronic pulmonary tuberculosis in human beings."

He put down the pen; there was nothing left to say.

As he stepped out of the lab and into the warmth of the spring night, his briefcase in hand, he saw the pavilions across the way with the nurses inside, silhouetted against the ward lights. They were getting patients ready for bed. One lifted a pitcher and poured a glass of water, another bent over a man, and at the far end, one was adjusting a blanket. Their figures framed by the windows recalled the old black-and-white shadow theaters.

Much of life at Sea View was like a theatrical performance, an endless drama in which everyone played their prescribed role. Nurses worked to keep dying people comfortable and optimistic, reciting aphorisms that Miss Mitchell forced them to memorize. Sometimes on his rounds, Robitzek heard the nurses repeating the sayings, and saw they didn't work. Neither did the crafts from occupational therapists or the movie nights. He, too, was culpable, continuing to prescribe more bed rest and invasive surgeries or trial drugs to half-dead patients and the lungers, with their terminal prognosis and endless cycle of admittance and discharge. Everything was a Band-Aid fix done to prolong life, not save it, and many of the patients saw through the lie. And yet doctors and nurses all kept up the "compassion pretense," as Robitzek called it, pretending that Sea View's sick could be fixed.

Some of the patients grew angry, finding the deception egregious, and lashed out at the nurses or one another. Recently, on Ward 62, a shipyard worker had fatally stabbed a man in his bed with a long pocketknife, claiming the man was keeping him awake at night. But no one really believed the root cause of the stabbing was snoring or anything else. It was Sea View.

Robitzek understood their fury at being sick and cooped up here, away from the energy of the world. It pushed them into dark and unknown places. Once there was a woman who used to sit in bed making charcoal drawings of patients eating, crying, praying, sitting in wheelchairs, and staring at nothing. She spent whole days sketching them, filling in their bodies and faces until the drawings properly captured the reality of what she called "this hell on earth," a reality Robitzek started to believe might never end.

Chapter 33

❖

A Brighter Future

June–December 1945

Back on Wheeler Avenue, Missouria never got the gun. Instead, she bought more seeds and planted them in her front yard, which bloomed with flowers, casting off the scent of roses and geraniums, gardenias and honeysuckle.

Inside, she replastered, painted, drilled, and hammered, hanging pictures and shelves and making it a home—"the place I built," she said. Then she drove to South Carolina and brought up her sister Frances, who moved in downstairs. But Mama Amy, despite Missouria's pleading, stayed in Clinton. She was remarried and running a boardinghouse and "it was too late to leave," she had said.

The more Missouria filled out her home, the more it upset the neighbors, especially Mr. Cofano, who stood at his living room window watching all the renovations with an expression that said "I hate you." Missouria saw him, felt him looking at her, but pretended he didn't exist. Between work, she continued building her life, and soon, in the Black community, her house became known as the place for "anyone and everyone," her niece said, especially her family.

Teresa and Henry showed up first. They belonged to her older brother, who had eight kids. Then came R.B., Missouria's first cousin. A World War II vet, R.B. had lost his leg in an accident and was prone to wild mood swings. Sometimes he turned nasty. Missouria didn't like it and wanted him to leave, but he had nowhere to go. She gave him a room upstairs, where he sequestered himself and spent his days eating and in the years to come lazing in front of the TV, watching sports. Every so often, when something excited him, R.B. would spring up from the chair and jump, and his wooden leg would hit the floor like a hammer, the sound blasting through the floorboards.

In rare moments when she could sit alone, Missouria relaxed by reading magazines or poetry or novels, the words creating images that erased Mr. Cofano and his animosity and the hectic days in the men's ward. She fell into new worlds with new people. Zora Neale Hurston invited her to walk Florida's dusty road and listen to music alongside Janie Crawford, the protagonist in *Their Eyes Were Watching God*. Few books touched Missouria like this one. She found a kinship in Janie, in the burden she carried, one caused by history, but also in her journey from "a vibrant, but voiceless, teenage girl," as one critic said, "into a woman with her finger on the trigger of her own destiny."

In late summer, the neighbors' threats grew more violent, compelling her lawyer to serve each one with court orders. The Norwegian family, who kept an old winter sled on their front lawn, moved. But the rest remained, menacing her from across the street. During the day they sat on the stoops, and at night they peeked from behind drawn curtains, surveilling the first Black woman of Wheeler Avenue. They tracked who came and went, what she did, and when she returned home from the hospital, a place that they believed further contaminated their block. Many years later—after Missouria would help shut down Sea View and then witness Mr. Cofano's own tragedy—the Wheeler families would come to see things differently. But until then, they "kept watch on Aunt Lulu," her niece said, "every day."

On August 15, 1945, weeks after Missouria found peace from the written threats, Imperial Japan surrendered to the United States, officially ending World War II. The news wrapped itself around the globe.

At Sea View, there was a collective feeling of joy that spread through the pavilions. Once again, patients turned on radios and listened to an announcer who in a quick, near-breathless voice described the revelry unfolding outside the ward.

Across the bay, in the winding alleys and narrow cobblestone streets of New York's Little Italy, there was music and dancing. Less than a mile away, in the Garment District, confetti, fashioned from cloth scraps, drifted down from the tall buildings and onto the avenues. In Times Square, reports estimated, two million people were packed into a ten-block area: when the official announcement proclaiming V-J Day flashed across the electronic news crawl on Forty-Second Street, a celebratory roar erupted. It lasted for twenty minutes and incited a spate of spontaneous hugging and kissing and picture taking—*Life* magazine photographer Alfred Eisenstaedt clicked his camera and, in that split second, immortalized an American sailor embracing a random nurse and kissing her on the mouth. The image became iconic, symbolizing the end of the war and the heroism of young veterans and the nurses who cared for them.

Uptown in Harlem, one hundred thousand people cheered and shouted, whistled and prayed; cars honked their horns, and impromptu parades sprang up. Residents ripped up the pages from telephone books, leaned on their windowsills, and tossed out handfuls of yellow and white paper; they cheered and blew noisemakers as the torn-up names and addresses of New Yorkers floated through the summer air.

At the nightclubs, champagne flowed, and people drank and danced to a new up-tempo style of jazz called bebop. It seemed to suit the mood. One journalist said that such a celebration "had never been seen here since Father Knickerbocker stood on the banks of the Hudson River and said in effect, 'Let's build New York City.'"

In many ways, the city had been rebuilt by the war, which had killed seventy-five million people worldwide. Before Hitler invaded

Poland's skies and erected his camps, killing six million Jews, the city was still tottering its way out of the Great Depression. Now, just six years later, it was rejoicing in unthinkable prosperity.

The subways moved two million people a day. Factories, over forty thousand of them, employed a million workers. They churned out fabrics, hats, shoes, fur coats, glassware, soap, furniture, boxes, balloons, and more, reigniting Gotham's economic engine and transforming New York into the manufacturing capital of the world.

Its ports, so crucial during the war, now handled 40 percent of the nation's waterborne freight, 150 million tons a year. And Wall Street, overlooking the harbor, rebounded too, with daily trading reaching hundreds of millions of dollars. The United Nations joined General Electric, US Steel, Union Carbide, and JPMorgan Chase in choosing New York as its headquarters. "New York is not a state capital or a national capital," the writer E. B. White observed, "but it is by way of becoming the capital of the world," and everyone seemed to want a part of its energy.

But not everyone celebrated.

In Harlem, Black workers worried about losing wartime jobs: "I am scared to death," said one civil servant.

"I'm sorry that it's over," remarked another resident. "Now they'll start pushing the Negro around in grand style, as usual."

Their fears came to pass almost immediately. When a million military personnel returned home, and unionized vets resumed working, they forced out longshoremen like Forest, who once again loitered around the pool halls, this time in Staten Island, betting on games while waiting to hear about potential jobs. By September 1, 1945, over seventy thousand Black workers in six southeastern states were facing layoffs, and although predictions for new jobs remained high, it was little consolation to the newly jobless.

But outside the affected communities, few noticed the unemployment claims rising. With the wartime celebrations finished, life simply returned to normal: the antiaircraft guns and the ships positioned all along the harbor vanished; husbands came home after work; ration coupons were gone; the shelves of King Kullen and Piggly Wiggly markets were once more stocked with butter and bacon, coffee and sugar; and in the frozen-food aisles, shoppers discovered a new item—frozen meat pies.

Around the boroughs, department store windows flaunted spring fashions and nylon stockings, the most anticipated postwar item. During the war, the thin, sheer leg coverings disappeared from shelves, as the material was used to create glider towropes, aircraft fuel tanks, flak jackets, shoelaces, mosquito netting, and hammocks. Now they were back, and their presence sparked "nylon riots."

In Pittsburgh, a mile-long line formed as forty thousand people, mainly women, stood, hoping to own one of the thirteen thousand pairs of stockings; in Augusta, Georgia, crowds overturned displays and knocked down shelves looking for nylons; in San Francisco, ten thousand shoppers converged on a store, forcing it to stop sales; and at Macy's, New York's famed department store, a clerk made a fatal mistake: he posted a sign advertising nylons. Within hours, the Herald Square store was overrun by twenty-five thousand women who hoped to grab a pair. "It's what American women have been waiting for," said a salesclerk.

❖

As women scooped up nylons and New Yorkers enjoyed concerts and parades, at the Mayo Clinic, Hinshaw marked the end of the war by celebrating streptomycin.

Patricia had made a full recovery, encouraging him to abandon testing the drug on any more guinea pigs. Instead he turned his attention to human trials. In one month, he had treated several dozen patients suffering from advanced pulmonary tuberculosis with streptomycin. His preliminary results showed that the drug "did not appear to have any rapidly curative action," but it trended toward prompt improvement of recently developed lesions.

On August 25, Hinshaw wrote Waksman a letter updating him on the trials: "We have now treated a total of thirty-three patients . . . and continue to be quite optimistic . . . early, extensive lesions are reversed to an unmistakable degree."

In the same letter, Hinshaw mentioned the results had impressed two US Army doctors, Esmond Long and Henry Sweany. They were now planning to use streptomycin in a large-scale study on veterans with extrapulmonary tuberculosis—TB that originated in the lungs but had spread.

Days later, a uniformed postman delivered the letter to Waksman, who read it with enthusiasm, realizing that streptomycin was about to become a life-changing antibiotic.

But then he remembered his agreement with Merck.

In 1939, Waksman had signed a contract with Merck granting them exclusive rights to any drugs he discovered; now, on the precipice of success, he questioned their ability to meet the impending demand. In his third-floor office, he reasoned that if several companies manufactured the drug, then demand could be met and prices kept low. He called Merck, shared the good news, and requested a nullification of their agreement.

While Merck deliberated and Waksman waited, Hinshaw penned another letter: "Observations regarding the clinical application of streptomycin continue to be cause for enthusiasm. New information is constantly being assembled."

But further down, the good news shifted. Hinshaw explained how the War Production Board, responsible for overseeing the army's trials, had taken over distribution of the drug, cutting off or curtailing the supply to any civilians, except himself. While he was grateful, the restriction barred anyone else from running trials; fewer trials meant less information and more possibility for error. But his hands were tied. He could do nothing. For now, he told Waksman, he would continue running his tests and sending updates.

In early October, Hinshaw's letter arrived on Waksman's desk. He read it, seemingly unbothered by Hinshaw's concern about the army restricting distribution. To him, all the news was good. The US Army was using his drug, and it was working. But the more celebratory news: Merck agreed to nullify their 1939 agreement, provided everyone involved could reach a new one.

Merck's new offer was charitable: it would give the patent rights of streptomycin to Rutgers and accept a nonexclusive license to produce the drug. In return, the company requested a "rebate on royalties to compensate" for the monies spent on developing the antibiotic. Merck's generosity was praised, and all parties were happy with the settlement. Soon Merck's new plant in Elkton, Virginia, and the plants of half a dozen other pharmaceutical companies prepared their enormous steel tanks for mass production of Waksman's drug.

The year ended on a high note with a final letter from Hinshaw: "I believe that we now have undeniable clinical and pathological evidence that streptomycin modifies the course of tuberculosis in man in a favorable direction."

But despite the positive results, Hinshaw remained guarded, telling Waksman how "the magnitude of this effect, its permeance and its applicability" could not be decided until the army lifted its restrictions and allowed widespread distribution and testing. Then hospitals could run multiple trials, charting any long-term effects, all of which were still unknown. Hinshaw finished by urging extreme caution in touting streptomycin as *the* cure, stressing how misrepresentation could have horrendous effects.

Then he sealed the letter and prayed Waksman would listen.

Chapter 34

The Second Call

Summer 1946

As the streptomyces multiplied in fermentation tanks, the nurses at Sea View were busy closing wards. The shutdowns happened slowly. First, they closed one, then two, then three and four; by late spring 1946, the number of shuttered wards had reached ten. To an outsider, the empty spaces, with their neatly made beds and inactivity, looked like hope. But to the nurses, whose patient load had doubled, increasing from ten patients to twenty, the image was jarring, a stark reminder of the worsening nurse shortage.

As the summer moved on, talk among the nurses revolved around the crisis. Almost daily, articles flaunting alarming statistics and warnings rolled off the presses: in July, *The New York Times* reported, "The acute shortage of nurses has kept at least 1,235 beds in public and voluntary hospitals in New York City empty." Some paragraphs later, the reporter claimed, there was "no immediate solution to the problem," adding, "There are 6,000 vacancies on the nursing staffs of hospitals."

The mayor gave more shocking figures, breaking down the collective numbers: there were 2,904 nurses to care for 17,200 patients, and the list of hospitals shuttering wards kept growing. Throughout the five boroughs, the triage areas swelled, but upstairs on the floors, thousands of beds remained unoccupied: 300 at Welfare Island, 400 at Manhattan Hospital, and close to 200 at Sea View. In Brooklyn, two hospitals shut down their maternity wards, and Kings County Hospital's new psychiatric wing, housing 386 beds, simply could not open. And on Long Island, local reports said it took twenty-five to thirty calls to find a single nurse for an emergency.

Reasons for the shortage varied: overwork, poor pay, and health concerns. But many nurses returning from the war wanted better opportunities. Initially, the health and hospital administrators took the staff losses in stride, believing the situation would right itself. However, a year after the war, the shortage was growing bigger, and the nurses who kept working were now complicating the situation by demanding change. They wanted a voice in framing policies, social security benefits, and unemployment insurance; shorter hours, more pay, and better working conditions, including less arduous patient loads. If their needs weren't met, they, too, would leave.

The NAACP embraced the moment and joined in amplifying the voices of Black nurses: it was finally time, they said, for the American Nurses Association to raze its racial barriers and admit Black nurses. But currently, the ANA wasn't concerned with crossing the color line; it was busy trying to save its profession from complete collapse. Even doctors, usually reticent to involve themselves in nursing issues, made a public declaration: "Doctors and nurses are members of the same family," and the shortage had "greatly hampered the entire medical profession."

But not everyone empathized with the nurses' plight.

The superintendent of Lenox Hill Hospital, Dr. John H. Hayes, blamed Black nurses for the mass exodus. City nurses, Hayes believed, were already properly paid, and they enjoyed the same leisure hours and benefits that other professionals enjoyed. As he saw it, the nursing shortage was a result of a greedy, mostly Black minority intent on convincing their colleagues that nurses were being exploited.

Solving the crisis, Hayes said, was simple: hospitals should hire and train nurses who were prepared to "live a life of service." And to him, Black nurses were not and never would be committed to such a life. His remarks were ignorant and obscene, and would have been laughable under different circumstances, especially when discussing Sea View.

Tuberculosis care had never been a lure for white nurses, and in recent years, the working conditions had become abysmal, adding to the hardship of hiring and keeping even Black staff. One look around the decades-old sanatorium told a grim story of what Edna and her colleges endured every day: broken beds, rodents, outdated elevators that were small and slow, and too many patients.

At the children's hospital, where many of Edna's friends worked, things were worse: nurses were overseeing two wards instead of one, for a total of twenty-five to thirty beds. For an adult ward, the undertaking was overwhelming, but in pediatrics, the task was Herculean. The nurses' log became a book rife with entries that told of children whose pain had turned to fury.

"Alfonso found sitting on the crib, legs dangling on the outside. When restraint was put on him kicked and screamed, tore linen + threw everything off crib mattress on floor."

Bobby Kelly likes "to throw feces around."

Lionel Dunlap "went into temper tantrum" and "spit at nurses, threw all bed clothing on floor, kicked and screamed."

Edna Zebrowski was a "mess," and orders were "to keep restraints on arms and give her some phenobarbital."

Line after line told of so many unhappy children, little beings whose days passed in varied stages of outrage and distress, screaming for "this toy" or "that thing" or "no needle" or "hugs," or just "NO." More nurses might have avoided these situations and ameliorated some of their suffering, but at the moment, hiring them was a moot point.

Recently, the secretary of the New York City Nursing Council had crunched its numbers: Nursing schools needed six hundred more students by registration day, September 15. Anything less, the secretary warned, and the nursing profession would become "totally disintegrated."

These words, this possibility, taunted Edna, Missouria, Janie, and the other Black nurses working at Sea View, mocking them, hemming them in, threatening everything they had fought for: their jobs, their homes, their careers, their families. How sad that it might all end this way.

In Harlem, however, the Black papers didn't see an ending; they saw a watershed moment, a new beginning for Black nurses: "Every negro nurse who wants to work has a job," *The New York Age* declared. And with all city hospitals hiring Black nurses, "negro young women" had new opportunities. Rise, the paper suggested, and own this moment.

And that is what Edna and Missouria, Janie and Clemmie, and so many others did.

They reasoned: if the white nurses refused to work at Sea View, as they had twenty years earlier, then once again, Black nurses would step in and fill the ranks. All of them had friends and family who needed jobs. Between them, they could recruit dozens of employees—if not nurses, then aides, those often overlooked assistants so critical for keeping the wards running. Missouria thought of her niece and nephew, Teresa and Henry, who needed work. They would make excellent aides. Janie also had a relative who wanted a job; she, too, grabbed an application. Clemmie wrote to unemployed friends in Savannah. In no time, word spread across Staten Island, and Marjorie Tucker Reed, an eighteen-year-old single mother, came. It moved down the eastern seaboard and once again into the southern states: Sea View was hiring and offering potential nurses free schooling and housing and on-the-job training.

In August, Edna dialed her niece in Detroit, Virginia Allen, the precocious little girl who had followed her around at Amy's funeral asking about white uniforms and nurses' caps.

"Would you like a job?" she asked.

Chapter 35

"Magic Germ Killer"

Late Summer–Winter 1946

After the war, soldiers arrived at veterans hospitals in droves. They came wheezing and weak, their lungs suffused with tuberculosis, the infection now the price for liberating Hitler's camps, places so grisly many were shell-shocked. Those who talked told chilling tales: in Dachau, one of Hitler's most notorious camps, soldiers were confronted by a suffocating air, a peculiar otherworldly stench they compared to "feathers being burned off a plucked chicken." But once they stepped inside the camp, the smell receded, replaced by the reality of Hitler's darkest imaginings.

Thirty thousand prisoners, mostly Jewish men, save for a handful of women the SS kept in a brothel, were scattered around the dank and dark and filthy compound. They were splayed and crouched, crammed into corners and wooden barracks, bone upon bone. The "well, the sick, the dying, and the dead," said an army captain, lay next to each other, their bodies racked with typhoid, dysentery, and tuberculosis.

American soldiers were confounded but had no time to stop and process the situation. They had been sent to stop the spread of disease. They worked round the clock, tearing out SS partitions and scrubbing the walls and floors of the camps with powerful disinfectants, although all the bleach and creosote and DDT in the world couldn't cleanse them. They set up cots and created two hospitals with twelve thousand beds. Within days, these camps-turned-hospitals filled with former prisoners, whom military medics triaged and separated by disease and prognosis. But nothing they did could stop the spread of tuberculosis. With haste, it found willing hosts in the bodies of the American soldiers, and soon infection rates soared, doubling from four thousand veterans in 1940 to eight thousand in 1945.

In the States, the army tracked the rising numbers and thought of one word: "epidemic." Immediately, they hired Dr. John Barnwell and Dr. Arthur Walker, a dark-eyed, half-balding TB expert, to manage the influx of sick veterans. Scrambling to keep the disease contained, the two men had an idea: Hinshaw's reports on streptomycin were assuring, but his trial was small, hardly sufficient to merit widespread use. Now, with thousands of sick vets, many willing to try any drug, they could initiate those much-needed large-scale clinical trials of the novel antibiotic. Even if the drug wasn't perfect, and even if it caused a relapse, administering it would give them some control over the spread, and at the very least, they reasoned, they would learn more about dosing and its side effects.

Throughout the summer months, multiple times a day, the men rolled up their sleeves, pulled aside their hospital gowns, and endured intramuscular injections that made them squeeze their eyes and clench their jaws. As the thick liquid coursed through their bodies, it caused vertigo and tinnitus, fever, chills, rashes, and nausea. Men slept away entire days, but soon they felt better. Walker was relieved, believing they had thwarted the spread, and shared the initial results with Hinshaw: streptomycin was working.

Waksman was elated, and either forgetting or forgoing Hinshaw's warning to be cautious about calling streptomycin a "cure" or misrepresenting it while in trial stages, he capitalized on the moment.

In front of the camera, Waksman was charming and articulate. Newspaper and magazine journalists adored him, writing long stories about the previously unknown immigrant soil doctor from New Jersey and the groundbreaking discovery of streptomycin. While journalists recorded his words, photographers snapped away, capturing staged images of him: in a lab peering down a microscope; with a "cured" patient; or standing beside the colossal steel vats at the Merck facility where his life-changing antibiotic was fermenting.

Collier's Weekly, a national magazine known for publishing investigative journalism focused on social reform, had recently run a feature on Waksman titled "Magic Germ Killer." The opening line declared that streptomycin was a "miracle drug, effective against diseases which penicillin won't touch," including tuberculosis; another was typhoid fever, a bacterial infection spread through contaminated food or water.

The article introduced "Mr. B," a middle-aged man stricken with typhoid from an "irresponsible . . . carrier" who had infected a batch of custard puffs. Within days, Mr. B's temperature hit 105; the fever caused delusions and mental confusion; and in his gut, his intestines, large and small, were hemorrhaging. Doctors said Mr. B was approaching death, and as a last resort they gave him an intravenous drip of "a cloudy tan liquid": streptomycin. Thirty-six hours later, Mr. B's fever had abated, and his intestines had quieted and de-swelled. Shortly thereafter, the custard-eating man recovered, "as from a bad cold—a far-from-common pattern in typhoid recovery."

The reporter continued extolling the miracle of streptomycin, how mice and guinea pigs and baby chicks made complete recoveries from an assortment of diseases: dysentery and salmonella poisoning; tularemia, a deadly infection caused by rabbits or deer ticks; undulant fever, a zoonotic disease sometimes passed to humans; pneumonia; and, of course, tuberculosis.

Waksman echoed the journalist's enthusiasm. Maybe one day, streptomycin could become part of "a salt so effective against so many diseases that the need for diagnoses would almost disappear," he said, "and many courses in medical school could be abolished."

The article caused a stir, casting Waksman into the spotlight and making him the unofficial spokesperson for the novel drug. Soon, more articles appeared, and in his office, the phone rang with invitations to give talks here and abroad.

Overcome by the moment, one he'd dreamed about as a boy in his rural Russian town with the black soil, Waksman embarked on an international tour to talk about antibiotics and the wonders of streptomycin. Crossing the globe, he visited hospitals in war-ravaged places: Moscow, England, Denmark, Switzerland, and Italy, where he gave lectures and the daily papers captured him hugging children made well by his drug. In Paris, he stopped at the world-renowned Salpêtrière Hospital and visited wards with the chief of its TB clinic. On the pediatric ward, two charming children, five-year-old Michael and seven-year-old Janet, dressed in French national costumes, greeted Waksman. Each held a bouquet of pretty flowers.

Months earlier, ambulances had transferred the two near-comatose children from distant regions of the country. Each one was treated with streptomycin, and now here they stood, rosy-cheeked, all smiles and joy. Janet stepped forward and curtsied and handed Waksman her bouquet. Then she kissed his hand; her younger partner followed. Waksman stood above the two children, and as he leaned over and patted their heads, he said, "I felt like crying. These two children had, surely, been saved by streptomycin." It was a powerful moment, one signifying the boundless potential of antibiotics to save lives.

Back in the States, the impact of Waksman's whirlwind medical tour came in mountains of mail addressed to Hinshaw at his office in Rochester. Mail sacks full of letters arrived daily from frantic parents, friends, physicians, and surgeons addressed to any name mentioned by the media: Waksman, Schatz, Feldman. They bore global postmarks, from South America, Asia, Italy, France, Australia, and Eastern Europe, and many from places in America. Men, women, children, laborers, lawyers, soldiers, printmakers, salesmen, lifelong TB sufferers, and even those with other diseases picked up a pen and wrote. All of them were inspired by the articles on streptomycin, which began as cautious but eventually spun it as fantastic—streptomycin was a "wonder drug" harboring the potential to cure a surplus of infections. But for tuberculosis, it wasn't a drug that might cure. It was *the* cure.

For Hinshaw, each letter begging for the drug caused him more distress. He wasn't sure streptomycin held that much power. The drug certainly did work, but whether it could keep tuberculosis permanently in remission no one knew. And yet, he could do nothing. To the media and sick people around the world, at this moment, tuberculosis had been cured.

Meanwhile, in London, the Medical Research Council (MRC) was dogged by the question of whether streptomycin was a temporary or permanent fix. Grappling with a postwar epidemic of tuberculosis that was moving through their country, the British government asked the United States for large quantities of the drug. America refused.

During the war, the United States had given a small amount of streptomycin to Britain and France to use in case of germ warfare. The British still had those few vials, but the amount was too paltry to distribute among the lay population. They were incensed, but what angered them more was America's lack of knowledge about the drug's efficacy. Although the United States had tested the drug on thousands of vets, those trials were short in duration, running months, not years. At no point had it run a long-term controlled clinical trial. Now, with the whirlwind surrounding streptomycin, such a trial in the United States seemed impossible. But without one, no one would know the usefulness of the drug: Was it a long-term drug or one for short-term interim treatment? Should it be used with something else or be shelved? The MRC found this wait-and-see attitude ludicrous.

Rather than let its few vials expire, the MRC decided to use them to conduct the first-ever long-term controlled clinical trials to determine its worth: in this trial, one group would receive the drug, and the other group would receive a placebo.

And so the MRC recruited 109 patients, all suffering from acute pulmonary tuberculosis. In eighteen months, for better or worse, their results would alter the course of history.

Chapter 36

New Beginnings

August 1947

In August 1947, Edna's niece, Virginia Allen, arrived at Sea View from Detroit, Michigan. She was sixteen, newly graduated from high school, and had no experience with children aside from babysitting her two younger brothers. But she was charismatic and easygoing, with a playful imagination. These qualities, along with the demand for nurses, impressed the head nurse at the children's hospital. Virginia was perfect for pediatrics.

A decade old, the children's hospital sat on an isolated section of the property, behind the original complex. Surrounded by a densely wooded slope, it was a grand structure, sleek and modern, finished in cream-colored brick and limestone trim. Rising five stories high, it insinuated itself into the landscape, making it both part of the complex and its own entity.

Inside, Virginia walked down broad hallways, the antithesis of the narrow pea-green corridors in the pavilions. She marveled at the terracotta tiles and the floor-to-ceiling windows that lined each side. They lent the wards a lofty, airy feeling, but one glance left or right and the buoyancy of beauty led the eye to an endless row of cribs and beds. Walkers and wheelchairs sat in the corners, and children's toys—

stuffed bears and rabbits and rag dolls, little cars and crayons and coloring books—were scattered on the white Sea View blankets or tossed under and around the beds.

Then came the noise, so much noise. A dissonance of sounds—crying, giggling, babbling, whining, moaning, and always one of those openmouthed wails, those screeches that stilled a room. At first it was shocking, but once Virginia fell into the rhythm of work, the clamor receded.

In those first months of training, she learned that tuberculosis in children often made them susceptible to secondary conditions like diabetes, measles, chicken pox, and impetigo, an infection that created a maze of rashes and bumps and pus-filled blisters on the skin. Calamine lotion and other topical creams did little; sometimes sulfathiazole, a sulfa drug, worked. But until the rash subsided, the children spent hours itching and picking at the scabs with their tiny fingers. Some blistered and bled and became infected, causing larger wounds that festered, requiring penicillin or their hands to be wrapped in gauze.

Comforting them, Viriginia realized, was difficult. They were fussy and wheezy and upset, and some threw their food, toys, or pillows and then sniveled for hours, a constant low, nasally whine punctuated by crackling and hacking coughs. The sound, similar to the hum and buzz of a loose electrical wire, grated on the brain.

A good handful of the children fumed, their faces and necks turning red and their fingers clenched into small fists; they shouted and thrashed and threw long-lasting tantrums. In the daily logbook, the nurses tried to pinpoint why the children acted out: "Quite miserable, uncomfortable . . . listless + helpless . . . purulent mucus . . . many lesions on face-body crusted . . . infected lesions . . . new impetigo . . . infected left foot . . . fever spiked . . . appears quite ill—appears partially paralyzed."

Those daily notes, however brief, taught Virginia how physical pain was a handmaiden to an excruciating parental ache. In between the lines of rage, a different story emerged. Nurses wrote about children who missed their families. Here was Richard, Ruth, Anita, Eleanor, Jack, Robert, Cheri, Michael, Louie, and many others: "Usual day homesick . . . depressed wants to leave . . . misses home . . . wants mom . . . lonesome . . . despondent . . . worried . . . calls for mama . . . dad left . . . mom died . . ."

And on went the somber, evolving narrative of yearning and sorrow that no amount of singing and reading or playing with puppets or cars or paper dolls could eradicate.

Each age brought its own despair, but for Virginia, the toddlers were the most heartbreaking bunch. They were in between baby and little kid, language and babble, and satisfying their needs was a grand challenge. She spent a long time holding them, cradling their bodies, and wiping their cheeks, often red and inflamed, and their noses dripping with green snot that dribbled onto their stuffed dogs or bears or bunnies, tangling up their fur. On days when the fussing stopped, she read them books from the library cart. They loved the new Little Golden Book series, featuring *The Poky Little Puppy*, *Johnny Appleseed*, and *The Color Kittens*, a story about two little kittens who make all the colors in the world.

These days brought hope.

But they came infrequently, and sometimes Virginia needed to step away, to gather herself, to find a space to process the weight of human sorrow. The more seasoned nurses mentored her, explaining how the children's hospital existed in a time and space all its own; how working there collapsed the normal pattern of thinking that children got sick and went to the hospital and fully recovered. That rarely happened at Sea View.

A better way of thinking, they said, was to look at how medicine had progressed in the past two decades. Prewar they had nothing. There was no sulfa, no antimicrobials, no penicillin, only sunshine and bed rest, and compounds of gold cyanide, chlorine gas, gambine (used in antifreeze), and lots of elixirs, such as iron quinine and strychnine.

There were also quacks and medicine men who brewed tonics and anti-dotes in giant cauldrons in their kitchens: wolf liver boiled in wine, mice boiled in salt and oil, or the hot blood of young calves. Drinks of pet-roleum and turpentine were offered, so were slices of dog fat and small piles of Saharan sand. Ground-up human eyeballs. Opium. Cod-liver oil. Tanner's oil (the runoff from slaughterhouses). Bloodletting.

Edna told her niece that patients had died from these sham cures and from now-treatable skin or strep infections. She also shared how some had woken up during surgery because no one understood the finer workings of anesthesia.

Now Virginia's generation of nurses had antibiotics and new anes-thetics. Electric lights had replaced the skylights that once lit the op-erating room, and every day more drugs were being discovered and tested. Recently, the army had finished its trials on streptomycin, al-lowing the government to lift all restrictions on the drug, and it had arrived at Sea View.

"It was like a new beginning," one nurse said.

"Like a fresh start," another added.

Almost overnight, its presence swept away a collective despair. Here was the drug that arrested tuberculosis, not just masked the pain. Each day, nurses up and down the wards pulled the thick liquid into syringe barrels and injected it into patients, who now sat up, daring to imagine a life after Sea View. They shared their dreams; some were grand: marriage, a new job, maybe college or kids or a career. But sickness had humbled too many, reducing their wants to sim-ple gestures: brushing their teeth, tying a shoe, bathing alone, walking without falling, and, for one patient, to "pray without praying to die."

On the men's and women's wards, nurses noted the side effects, which for many were almost unendurable. But they knew the paradox: either tolerate the experience or die. Doctors faced their own issues with cost and supply. Streptomycin was expensive, and it passed through the system quickly, requiring re-dosing every six hours. With their limited funds, many hospitals stocked only several weeks' worth, forcing doctors into making punishing decisions: who would and wouldn't be treated. In Michigan, a $400,000 shortage, the total cost to treat all TB patients with streptomycin, ensnared lawmakers in a heated debate: Was their duty saving money or lives?

Robitzek hoped to avoid these ethical dilemmas. But each day drew him closer to one.

From the wards abounded stories of patients feeling better. They came from the young and old, the newly diagnosed and the lungers, like Missouria's patient Philip Thompson, "the old hand at TB," who had spent almost five years in and out of the hospital. This time, the thick, painful shot might save him. The good news also came down from the children's hospital.

First, a visiting physician had aerosolized streptomycin, allowing it to reach the lungs quicker and in heavier doses. The only downside: administering it took over an hour and required someone to hold the inhaler over the child's mouth. Virginia and the other aides were being trained to hold it, and soon babies as young as eight months old could be treated.

But the big news was about two patients. The first was Hilda Ali, who, much to everyone's surprise, had survived and become strong enough for doctors to operate and perform the much-needed lobectomy, where they removed a portion of her lung. The surgery was a success, which allowed her to receive streptomycin. The drug worked, and after three and a half consecutive years of being at Sea View, Hilda Ali was finally going home. Her medical card now read "far advanced pulmonary tuberculosis: arrested."

The second patient was a wispy four-year-old, languishing from miliary and meningeal tuberculosis, the latter inflaming his brain, causing him to lose muscular coordination and experience punishing headaches. Days after he started streptomycin, his headaches tapered off. He stood without falling and chewed without choking; his cheeks and ribs filled out. And he asked to play.

❖

With more and more success stories, journalists found a niche: feel-good stories. In Atlanta, they discovered Mr. Frank Edwards, who two months earlier had been planning his funeral: "He was going down steady," his ward mate said, "but by George, he really came out of it when he took that new stuff." At the Glen Lake Sanatorium near Minneapolis, the drug saved the lives of Anna Olson and her sandy-haired six-year-old, Jimmy Olson, stricken with TB meningitis: "Without streptomycin this was rapidly fatal," said Jimmy's doctors, adding that if external organizations didn't pay for the treatment, which topped $900, Jimmy would have died.

Even those who worked at one of the eleven companies processing the drug celebrated: at a Pfizer plant, employees covered the walls with morale-building placards and posters showing patients being injected with streptomycin. In Pennsylvania, the *Gazette*'s headline was simple: "Streptomycin Conquers Tuberculosis."

These stories, all of them, painted a bright, longed-for future, one without tuberculosis. But away from the wards and the public anecdotes of people recovering, Robitzek and the nurses knew something was amiss. First, they noticed that the drug worked fast; while that was good, no one had determined how or why it was working. All of it, the dosage and frequency, was guesswork, and to Robitzek, administering drugs by chance was courting disaster. He knew any scientifically effective treatment, especially one considered curative, needed strict regulations, and more important, he wondered what good was a cure that few could afford.

For Robitzek, cures that cost money weren't cures but rather options for those who had funds and torture for those who didn't. To him, any medicine that promoted healing, especially for this disease, should be free; no one, he believed, had the right to capitalize on illness. But the endless reports of streptomycin's expense were now forcing him to think about cost versus treatment and how the drug was becoming a kind of boutique medication, available for some but not all. These days, he was reading more frequently about people like Arthur T., who was stuck in a municipal hospital no different from Sea View. A lack of funds had forced a rationing of the drug, and Arthur wasn't chosen. He subsequently died, repeating, "I need streptomycin."

It was only a matter of time before this happened at Sea View.

Chapter 37

❖

"If One Had Some Streptomycin"

February 1948–Early 1949

In Scotland, Eric Arthur Blair, better known as author George Orwell, lay in a sanatorium close to death from a highly infectious strand of pulmonary tuberculosis. He was nearly anorexic and racked by night sweats and wild fevers, so doctors put him on total bed rest. It was a nightmare for Orwell, who was hankering to retype his novel, tentatively titled *The Last Man in Europe*.

When bed rest failed, doctors collapsed his lung; the excessive air in his body and his inability to write made him miserable. Six weeks into his stay and believing his progress was too slow, Orwell took matters into his own hands and wrote a long letter to his close friend David Astor, reiterating his doctor's suggestion. "It would speed recovery if one had some streptomycin," he wrote, continuing: "This is obtainable in the USA . . . He suggested that you with your American connections might arrange to buy it and I could pay you . . . for it is a considerable sum and of course the hospital can't pay it."

Astor bought the drug and shipped it off to Scotland, where Orwell's doctors remained skeptical of its efficacy on his type of tuberculosis. But Orwell, like thousands of others who were wrecked by tuberculosis, didn't care. Sickness had changed him, turned him into a desperate man willing to take any gamble to get well. If the drug worked, fine; if not, then his only loss was money.

The package of streptomycin arrived at an uncanny moment, shining a bright light on Robitzek's worries about who would and wouldn't be saved. In Glasgow, a young boy had recently died after the American government denied an appeal to send him the antibiotic. The boy's death made Orwell the first layperson in Scotland to receive Waksman's "miracle drug."

For weeks, the author was injected, enduring the slow spill of the drug into his muscles. Soon he was feeling better. But day fifty arrived and the base of his fingers and toenails became discolored and began disintegrating at the roots; his face turned red, and the skin flaked off, and a rash appeared over his body. Painful blood blisters lined his throat, inner cheeks, and lips. At night when he slept, they erupted, leaking blood into his mouth, where it dried, and, like a glue, sealed it shut. Then his hair started falling out.

Orwell's response was atypical from anything described in American medical journals. Fearing he had an allergic reaction, his doctors discontinued the shots; the author donated the remaining drug to the wives of two physicians, who recovered. But despite Orwell's startling side effects, it appeared streptomycin had worked: "It's all over now," Orwell wrote to his publisher. "Evidently the drug has done its stuff . . . It's rather like sinking the ship to get rid of the rats, but worth it if it works."

Doctors released him and he returned home to finish his book. Sitting in bed wearing a frayed dressing gown, he "chain-smoked black shag tobacco in rolled up cigarettes" and typed and retyped the "last stages of this bloody book," he said, "about the possible state of affairs if the atomic war isn't conclusive." Adding to his misery was the feeling that however much he rewrote and edited, his manuscript was "unbelievably bad" and without a permanent title.

Meanwhile, back in the United States, early June broke with warnings about streptomycin: *The New York Times* printed Hinshaw's cautioning to doctors about replacing "proven methods"—bed rest—with the novel drug.

A Wisconsin newspaper advised that streptomycin, when given over a long period, can cause the TB germs "to build up a tolerance" to the drug. A Texas paper declared that streptomycin was "oversold at the start, much as sulfa drugs were," and a Columbia University doctor surmised, "Streptomycin is no sure-fire weapon against tuberculosis."

As the summer passed with mounting warnings, Orwell, deep into rethinking words, shifting sentences, and moving paragraphs, began coughing and spiked a fever. But he refused treatment, staying in his old iron bed to retype the manuscript and finish the description of the body of Winston Smith, his protagonist, after being tortured and starved: "The truly frightening thing was the emaciation of his body," he wrote. "The barrel of the ribs was as narrow as that of a skeleton; the legs had shrunk so that the knees were thicker than the thighs . . . The curvature of the spine was astonishing."

Some speculated that Orwell was describing his own physical demise, as tuberculosis was consuming him from the inside out. Pale and wasted and barely able to sit up, he finished the book and titled it *1984*, an inversion of 1948. Then he went to a sanatorium, where his doctors once again tried streptomycin. The first dose "had ghastly results," Orwell said. He wrote a letter to his friend wondering, "What had gone so dangerously wrong?"

Back at Sea View, Robitzek was asking a similar question.

❖

In the children's hospital, the four-year-old boy once again began waking at night, clasping his head and writhing in agony. Nurses gave him aspirin, then opiates to ease his pain. They brought him juice and ice cream, but he stared at it glassy-eyed and apathetic, watching as the scoops melted into a soupy mess, and his brain swelled until one morning he stopped breathing.

At first, his death seemed an isolated incident, but when news reached the adult pavilions, perceptions changed. Nurses reported that patients who received streptomycin were experiencing Orwellian symptoms: nausea, dizziness, skin rashes, mouth blisters that popped and bled, hair loss, and tinnitus. Some nurses added that the drug appeared to stop working almost overnight.

Questions abounded:

Was streptomycin to blame?

Were those patients who'd died given too much?

Were these allergic reactions?

Maybe the sicker patients needed a higher dose. Or maybe it should be given in combination with something else. Whatever the reason for the symptoms, Robitzek lacked sufficient information to stop using it. Until he could prove something concrete was causing these reactions, he directed nurses to keep administering it, logging every observation and patient complaint. Alone, however, he worried about his decision, afraid it might cause more people to die.

The warnings about streptomycin and the mounting death toll cast a pall over Sea View that grew and grew, inching its way across every pavilion, and two weeks before Halloween 1948, it entered the children's hospital.

Frankie Gadsen, a five-year-old Black boy, was nearly asleep when four boys slipped from their beds and ordered him to get up and follow them. The group made their way through the ward to the patients' bathroom, sneaking beneath the decorations Virginia had helped hang, paper ghosts and pumpkins, spiders and cobwebs. Once inside, they prepared to "initiate" him into their "hospital club."

One boy shackled him to a pipe, while another turned on the hot water, and then all four watched as the stream surged down, scalding his arms, legs, and torso. He screamed, but no one heard except the boys, who kept watching. Fifteen minutes went by, and finally satisfied, they shut off the water and left him crying on the white-tiled floor. Time passed, some reports said hours, but eventually one of them returned and freed him, and Frankie walked back to the ward, past the smiling ghosts and pumpkins and cobwebs, and crawled into bed with his body burning. Six hours later, a nurse found him shivering, the burns raw and blistering. Doctors transferred him to another ward and placed him on the "critical list."

In the morning, the situation worsened after hospital officials bungled the response by refusing to tell his mother what had happened. She said that his "body and face were nearly cooked and . . . [he] failed to recognize" her. With her emotions volleying between despair and rage, she contacted the NAACP, which wasted no time opening an investigation into Sea View, arguing criminal negligence. No one denied that at some point during the night, the ward had been unsupervised, but the reason wasn't neglect. It was a shortage of nurses. Normally, each ward had two nurses; that night, a lack of staff meant that a single nurse was overseeing two wards, each with more than twenty children.

The story moved through Sea View, leaving a trail of horrified nurses, who had foreseen something like this happening. They had tried to fix the situation themselves by recruiting friends and family to work, but the deficit was too big and too widespread. The country still needed thousands of nurses, and a good many at Sea View.

While Miss Mitchell and the administration scampered about trying to solve the nursing problem and avoid another Frankie situation, Dr. Robitzek was in his office, the most recent issue of the *British Medical Journal* laying on his desk. Inside were the results of the controlled streptomycin study undertaken by Britain's Medical Research Council (MRC).

He lifted the journal and sat back in his chair. Often before settling in to read, he would look out the window to clear his mind. The day was cool, and the late-fall wind swayed the trees, picking off the remaining leaves. He enjoyed watching them fall; so had Katherine. This was the third autumn without her.

In the distance stood the pavilions, their porches filled with patients watching the leaves and breathing in the crisp autumn air. Even though the rest cure was long defunct, the ritual of taking patients outside remained. Seeing them now wrapped in blankets, seated on chairs and beds, he knew they were counting on streptomycin to cure them. He opened the journal.

For eighteen months, Britain's Medical Research Council had run the most thorough and unbiased clinical trials testing the efficacy of streptomycin on TB meningitis in children, tuberculous bronchopneumonia, and pulmonary tuberculosis. For eleven pages, he studied every chart, read each word, sometimes twice, and, as always, underlined key sentences and paragraphs, each one more heartbreaking than the last.

Frequently, he found himself nodding, agreeing with the results of the MRC study. The words confirmed what many of the nurses had observed in patients who took Waksman's drug: toxic effects including giddiness, persistent dizziness, unsteadiness of gait, nausea, vomiting, and severe inner ear and urinary issues. The British clinicians also corroborated the fluctuations in weight gain or loss and, in females, amenorrhea, the absence of menstruation.

Each page painted a clearer and more bitter picture of streptomycin. Six months into treatment, data showed, patients who received streptomycin were no better than those in the placebo group. The heartbreak grew when clinicians discovered that many strains of TB had become resistant to Waksman's antibiotic. And the microbes were not only defiant, but sometimes they downright enjoyed the drug, preferring it to their customary food and leading the patient to a quicker death.

Then came the last paragraph: "It seems probable that streptomycin resistance is responsible for much of the deterioration seen in S [streptomycin] cases after first improvement."

The researchers concluded that "no clinical cures had been achieved."

After Robitzek read the report, Sea View's deaths no longer appeared arbitrary. He started planning out the next steps: a meeting to inform the medical staff about the latest findings and then to determine whether to discontinue the drug.

For Robitzek, it seemed like the center of the earth had opened up, and he was staring into an great abyss simmering with Sea View's ills: there was little Frankie Gadsen with his charred and brutalized body, the nursing shortage, the violence lurking in the wards, and the unceasing human despair. And now, these trial results, confirming what many knew but feared uttering aloud. Streptomycin had been a wonderful breakthrough, but it wasn't a "miracle drug," the cure for tuberculosis. Instead, according to one doctor, because of its failure "the progress in the chemotherapy of tuberculosis seemed to come to a standstill."

There was nothing left to try.

PART V

❖

1949–1952

Chapter 38

❖

Rumors

Fall 1949

On an autumn day in 1949, the RMS *Queen Mary* eased from its slip at Pier 90 on New York's West Side and turned its thousand-foot body toward the North Atlantic. As the grand liner moved through the choppy waters of the bay, excited passengers stood on deck and watched the city recede. Among them were Dr. Walsh McDermott from Cornell University Medical College and Hinshaw from the Mayo Clinic.

Dressed in stylish suits—loose double-breasted jackets with broad shoulders and drapey high-waisted trousers—the two men were headed to Germany to investigate a rumor rippling through the medical world. In the war-ravaged country, supposedly, a doctor had developed a synthetic chemical that cured tuberculosis.

Rumor said the drug was created at Bayer during the height of the war. Only a decade earlier, Bayer had been the largest chemical and pharmaceutical company in the world, reaping huge financial rewards from patents in Europe and the United States. Known globally for its drug innovations and its impressive list of Nobel Prize–winning scientists, the company was associated with greatness. But no more.

During the war, Bayer's parent company, IG Farben, had struck a deal with the Third Reich to construct a chemical plant in the Polish town of Oświęcim, known in German as Auschwitz. Called "Auschwitz III," the plant was a monster of a factory where thousands of mostly Jewish prisoners worked around the clock, churning out synthetic rubber and high-performance fuels, including aviation gasoline and fuel oil for naval use, various plastics, stabilizing agents, resins, methanol, and pharmaceuticals. Anyone idle or refusing to work was sent next door to Farben's concentration camp, Buna-Monowitz, the first camp constructed and financed by private industry.

But Farben's investment with the party went beyond Auschwitz III. It reached into the vast supply of new and existing drugs, handing them to the Reich. Prisoners, over 7,200, became human guinea pigs for Nazi doctors, who used Farben's experimental drugs to test potential cures for an array of diseases: typhus, malaria, yellow fever, infectious hepatitis, and tuberculosis. Many of the experiments left the victims permanently scarred or in unbearable pain. Despite the sordid details of its wartime work emerging, the company was still in business making drugs and profits.

When the two doctors disembarked on the German coast some days later, a chauffeur met and escorted them to a limousine, compliments of the Allied forces. Their first stop was the town of Elberfeld, tucked in the northern Rhine region on the Wupper River, to pick up Dr. Gerhard Domagk, one of Bayer's most celebrated scientists.

In 1927 Bayer had hired him to head its state-of-the-art pathology lab. In just five years, the hardworking, methodical, and unusually observant scientist—some described him as having an "ability to *see* beyond the physical world"—discovered Prontosil, the radiant red powder that became the first antimicrobial drug in the world, saving FDR's son and kicking off the sulfa boom. It had earned him a Nobel Prize.

Now Domagk had a new drug, one he claimed cured tuberculosis.

Sitting in the back of the limo during the long drive to Domagk's town, the American doctors gazed out the window at the landscape.

Four years after the war, many parts of Germany were still in a state of devastation, laying bare a cataclysmic loss of life. Farther out from the city limits, the limousine drove by small groups of people walking on the side of the road, carrying suitcases or sacks stuffed with their belongings; around them blackened trees with charred branches stretched across the bombed-out land.

They arrived in Elberfeld, where much of the once bucolic town was still in ruins from the night of May 30, 1943. That night, Britain's Royal Air Force filled the sky with over seven hundred planes. For a full hour, the bombs fell, setting the ground ablaze. Wind from the valleys fanned the flames, which moved in fiery waves across bogs and forests, valleys, and city streets. Aloft, British pilots steered their flights through the summer sky. "The place seemed on fire from end to end and smoke came rolling up to us," one British pilot said. "It must have reached a height of three miles."

When the American doctors arrived at Domagk's house, they were greeted by a tall and gaunt man with pale blue eyes who joined them in the back seat. He was pleasant but reserved, the war having dulled his once-vibrant spirit. As the limousine pulled away, it passed beneath the Bayer factory, which was situated on the hill above the town. The sprawling complex covered several blocks; half of it was destroyed.

Domagk settled in and started telling them about his new drug. So far, he said, it had cured over seven thousand people with TB. And soon, in the sanatoriums they were scheduled to visit, the two doctors would see for themselves.

In 1943, at the height of the war, Domagk had become alarmed at the rising rates of tuberculosis in Germany. Fearing a global TB pandemic, he rose each morning and made his way through the wreckage of Elberfeld. Avoiding the SS officers combing the streets, who, he said, "strutted about like a cock on a dunghill," Domagk made his way to the Bayer factory. The library was scorched, the labs were blown apart, and the test animals had been incinerated in their cages. In fits and starts between the air raids and falling bombs, with gas masks and threadbare clothing, he and two colleagues worked to perfect this "synthetic chemical," a fine crystalline powder with a bitter taste that he named Conteben.

He first tested the drug at the Hornheide Sanatorium near Münster, a place devoted strictly to treating *Lupus vulgaris*, a dreadful and incurable version of tuberculosis that attacks the skin and face. There Domagk met Katharina F., a fifty-four-year-old woman.

For the past twenty years, Katharina had watched the slow-growing ulcerations fester and pick away at her beauty and youth, devouring the skin and tissue of her nose and eye sockets and part of her jaw. Her face resembled half a skull. Before Domagk arrived, doctors had tried every available treatment: electric cautery, diets, ointments, homeopathy, radiotherapy, and reconstructive surgery. Nothing worked. Depressed and suicidal, she refused to leave her room.

But three weeks after starting Conteben, Domagk said, the ulcers by her eyes were healing, and the ooze from the wounds had stopped. And, he added, Katharina experienced no side effects. None.

The proud German could vouch for the drug's safety: the first person he had tested it on was himself.

The road through the northern German countryside was bleak. The asphalt was shattered and littered with debris, and flanking each side were more camps full of evacuees. But once the limousine turned off the main road toward the sanatoriums, the scenery changed to lush forests of evergreens that echoed with wind and trilling birds. In many of these far-flung places, it seemed time had stopped, as if the war had never happened. At the hospitals and sanatoriums, Hinshaw and McDermott visited floors of patients afflicted by all forms of tuberculosis— pulmonary, brain, bowel, uterus, joint, blood, brain, and kidney; they saw tuberculosis of the vertebrae, lymph nodes, and female genitals. The

German doctors were gracious, allowing them to examine their patients and study their charts before and after treatment with Conteben.

In one hospital, they learned the drug seemed to cure blood-borne TB. It was also effective for TB of the throat; victims could speak and swallow again. Intestinal sufferers were eating and putting on weight without chronic diarrhea and dehydration. And for those whose vertebrae the microbe had sheared, Conteben cleared the way for new bone to develop.

And for pulmonary tuberculosis, most of the trials had showed great promise. Hinshaw and McDermott were impressed with Domagk's ability to conduct such extensive studies while his country was being annihilated. After their sanatorium tour, the Americans were convinced the evidence in favor of the drug, unknown outside Germany, was "overwhelming."

Prior to boarding the RMS *Queen Mary* back to the States, Domagk gave them a small supply of Conteben. The impetus for the gesture wasn't charity but resignation. Domagk knew Bayer could no longer protect its medical discoveries. After Germany lost the war, the Allies were scavenging the company's secrets and records.

On the ship, with the drug safe in their bags, they relaxed. The grandness of the liner was a welcome change from the rubble and ash and the patients, especially the unforgettable Katharina with her blistered and half-eaten face. And the drug seemed to work. Still, both knew the wiles of the microbe, how artfully it evaded drugs, and after Hinshaw's recent experience with streptomycin, neither wanted to take any chances. They would remain reserved.

❖

Two months after returning from Germany, Hinshaw stood at a podium looking out into a room filled with three hundred men sitting in pressed trousers, shirts, and neckties with fat knots. After greeting the crowd, he told them about his recent trip to Germany with McDermott. He described their hours of riding through the shattered country, visiting over three hundred hospitals, and seeing firsthand the results of Conteben, now renamed TB-1. In the long and difficult race for a cure, the drug was an exciting find. It offered hope, a promise that tuberculosis might be conquerable.

He explained how he and McDermott, after returning, had tested the drug at veterans hospitals across the country. But the results of their short, two-month study were disappointing. Unlike Domagk's German studies, theirs showed that TB-1 led to some side effects—loss of appetite, malaise, and skin eruptions resembling measles. It was also proving more toxic than streptomycin and para-aminosalicylic acid (PAS), an aspirin derivative recently discovered in Sweden. But the side effects were brief, and the TB bacteria didn't appear to develop resistance, meaning, unlike streptomycin, treatment with TB-1 could possibly span months or even years.

Regardless of the side effects, Hinshaw believed TB-1 had "good antituberculosis activity." With the disease killing one person every fifteen minutes in the United States, a drug with such strong anti-TB activity and mild toxicity "would be an important addition to currently available germ-fighting chemicals," Hinshaw said.

Many in the room were inspired by Hinshaw's talk, which incited in them a new sense of hope—not for the drug itself, but for the "antituberculosis activity" in its chemical makeup. And they understood "antituberculosis activity" meant that something in TB-1's composition warded off the bacteria. If they could unlock the ingredient, then they could develop an even stronger, more effective drug.

The following week, *Time* magazine ran a short article titled "War Booty." It recapped the meeting and the optimism people felt after leaving it. But the second-to-last line was especially exciting to pharmaceutical companies: "Because the drug was developed during the war, the German patents are no good and any US manufacturer can make it." This, for them, was the real "war booty"—what we would now call "intellectual property."

❖

Almost immediately, chemists raced to their labs and began deconstructing TB-1, hoping to find its antituberculosis ingredient. At F. Hoffmann–La Roche in Nutley, New Jersey, Dr. Herbert Fox worked with a ferocious urgency. Sitting at his bench in his lab, surrounded by flasks and beakers and test tubes, he was at ease shifting molecules, breaking them apart and re-forming them, to create new drug compounds. In his six years with the prestigious pharmaceutical company, Fox, with his round black glasses—a fashionable staple for scientists in the postwar period—and boyish grin, had carved out an impressive reputation. Words like "genius" and "mastermind" were used to describe him, but, like Schatz, he relied on his intuition to understand the inner workings of chemical compounds.

After Hinshaw's lecture, he turned his attention to TB-1. Day after day, he spent hours tweaking its composition. He attached new molecular chains to it, hoping each new synthesis would become the combination capable of killing the TB microbe without poisoning the body. He sent all his permutations up to La Roche's chemotherapy lab, run by two renowned chemists: Dr. Robert Julius Schnitzer, who had once headed Farben's chemotherapy department until he was fired by the Nazis as a non-Aryan, and Dr. Emanuel Grunberg, a Yale alumnus.

The two chemists followed a strict regimen for testing all compounds in mice: infect, inject, and then watch. One of two things always seemed to happen: either the drug had zero effect on the disease, or its effect was eventually eclipsed by debilitating side effects or toxicity. Whatever the reason, the outcome was always the same: the animals died.

❖

While Fox fine-tuned the drug and the chemists autopsied mice, twenty-five miles south, at Sea View, Miss Mitchell's tenure was coming to end. After twenty-three years of service, the superintendent of nurses, responsible for training so many stellar Black nurses and, too often, for making their lives difficult, handed in her resignation.

She was sixty years old when she walked out of Sea View with her white hat, starched and upright, and her signature blue cape trailing behind her. Some of the nurses would miss her. But many, including Edna and Missouria, both recently promoted to head nurse, were looking forward to working under Miss Anne Giles, the interim superintendent, a more generous and gentle woman, and soon to be the last white supervisor at Sea View.

Chapter 39

Mamie

March–September 1950

The hospital was over capacity when the nineteen-year-old local girl from Stapleton, one of Staten Island's historically Black communities, arrived. Barely able to stand, thin, frail, and coughing blood, she grasped at the arm of her sister. Nurses brought her inside, where she was quickly admitted to Pavilion 4's "incurable ward" with the glass windows. Her name was Mamie Blair. Her diagnosis: severe pulmonary tuberculosis. Her prognosis: very poor.

Janie B. Shirley, her nurse, the one who'd inspired Edna to buy her house, began treating Mamie with a combination of two drugs, streptomycin and PAS. Recently, the British Medical Research Council determined that combining both antibiotics had a more powerful reaction. She also gave Mamie cod-liver oil; despite it having no proven effect against TB, many still believed it had curative properties.

As March turned to April and the flowers bloomed, the young girl grew sicker; her body became thinner, and her fever went higher. Mamie could do nothing but lie in bed and look out the window. The angle allowed her to see only a sliver of sky at the top of the frame. Throughout the day, it shifted and changed. Sometimes it was dull and heavy, with rain that would tap at the pane. Other times, it was blue, with stark white clouds that would inch across the sky.

Three times a week her mother, Ruby Lee Blair, came to visit. Her arms, like Hilda's mother's, were laden with homemade food that Mamie never ate. Ruby was a gentle woman, kind and simple in her ways, but nothing "got by her," Mamie said. "She saw everything."

Sitting bedside on a wooden chair, the food growing cold, she watched her daughter's chest heave and hiss. And she prayed. The days she wasn't with her daughter, Ruby visited her toddler son, George, who had tested positive for tuberculosis and was also being cared for at Sea View, in the children's ward just across from Mamie's pavilion. In the evenings, Ruby left Sea View and went to work at the Marine Hospital in Stapleton, where she took care of sick veterans. Sundays, she woke and went to church and implored God to make her daughter well and for Sea View to release her son.

Ruby didn't understand why they were keeping little George. Although his sputum was positive, he wasn't sick. Many people, including the nurses, tested positive but weren't ill. When she asked why her son couldn't leave, the doctors told her it was "preventative."

Here the boy was safe and well nourished, they said, cared for like children in preventoriums, those sanatoriums in the early part of the century designed for children who were infected but not sick.

But Ruby didn't know that many preventoriums targeted children from poor families and non-English-speaking immigrants, perceived as dirty and naïve about practices that spread disease. They also went after poor Black people, who, like immigrants, were considered incapable of caring for their children.

Once removed from their homes, the kids were monitored by a nurse, who ensured they were eating good "American food" and getting a proper education. She also disciplined them to become "proper" citizens with the "right" hygienic practices. When the staff felt certain the kids had been trained, they were discharged.

After months of haggling with Sea View, Ruby was unable to persuade them to release her son. So she stopped asking. If Mamie could speak, Ruby knew she would've advocated for her brother going home. For now, though, all Ruby Lee Blair could do was keep visiting and praying.

❖

Sometimes at night, Mamie's thoughts would shift to 1938, when she fled the plantation in Shorterville, Alabama, with her mother and seven siblings. She remembered the movement of the train, how its steel wheels rolled across hundreds of miles of track, hurtling toward Staten Island, this unknown place where her father had landed. On the narrow seats in the Jim Crow car, she sat next to her mother, eating fig bars and looking out the window at the country rolling by, at those great open fields like the ones that her parents had tilled. As the day wore on, she saw the sunset and the sky turn dark, and then fell asleep watching the moon following from above. When she woke up, they were in Baltimore, at the Mason-Dixon Line. The family got off to switch trains, and for the first time in her life, Mamie sat on an integrated train.

Her mind wove deeper through the years. There she was starting school at PS 14 in Stapleton, where she learned to read and fell in love with books. After school, on Gordon Street, that run-down block with its rows of houses that leaned left and right, she saw kids playing on the street. On one end, the jump ropes from double Dutch turned and girls ducked into them, jumping simultaneously; on the other, serious hopscotch games played out. She loved tossing the old bottle cap and skipping through the numbers. Then came the rain, and as the water gathered around an overwhelmed gutter, the kids jumped and splashed like they were in a wading pool.

But mostly she remembered reading: leaving her house to walk the eight blocks to the library to check out books, and then running home to find a hidden corner to enjoy them. Her favorites were the Nancy Drew series. The blue illustrated covers with their orange titles, *The Hidden Staircase* and *The Whispering Statue*, thrilled her, and the heroine female detective made them more appealing. Each book she finished brought her closer to her dream of becoming a teacher or librarian, but before her high school graduation, the principal called her into his office. She had top grades in English and accounting, but she would not be receiving the accounting award.

"You could never be an accountant," he said. "You do understand what I mean." At the ceremony, he handed her a diploma and a cooking award instead.

Her parents were still proud—neither of them had graduated from high school. Her mother could read and write, but not her father. While Ruby took care of the kids and picked up odd jobs, her father worked as a gravedigger at Frederick Douglass Memorial Park, in the Oakwood section of Staten Island, where he'd buried thousands of Black bodies. Some were notables, including Mamie Smith, the first Black singer to cut a blues record, and King Solomon "Sol" White, a pioneer in the Negro Leagues, but most were ordinary New Yorkers.

One summer when Mamie was six, her father took her to the cemetery's Memorial Day celebration, a yearly event that brought in people from the five boroughs. She and her father worked under a tent, selling barbecue sandwiches and soda, and he talked about the plotless people who couldn't afford their own graves. Many came from Sea View and were buried with strangers.

"The graves are stacked up five high," he said.

Mamie spent entire nights in TB-induced dreams, wandering the recesses of her memory and believing she would never leave the bed; that she would die here and someone like her father would dig her grave. Women died around her all the time. Then the Bone Man came and took them away.

"It was normal, like coughing," she said. "You closed your eyes and woke up in the morning, and the bed next to you was empty."

❖

At Hoffmann–La Roche, Herbert Fox had a moment of clarity. One day, while contemplating the structure of TB-1, he recalled a small French research study on vitamin B, prompting him to return to the molecule niacin, or nicotinic acid. Something clicked, and years of examining chemical reactions pooled together in his mind. On a hunch, he took some of the structure of niacin and some of the structure of TB-1 and fused them together, creating a single compound. On July 7, 1950, he registered the compound internally as Ro 2-3973 and sent it up to La Roche's lab to test "for antituberculous effect."

Throughout the summer of 1950, as the Korean War raged on and Mamie lay dying, Schnitzer and Grunberg tested Fox's substance in mice. They injected the deadly H37Rv strain of tuberculosis into their tails and split them in two groups: one group received Fox's new compound, Ro 2-3973. The control group got nothing. Then they waited.

Soon the control-group mice grew lethargic and sick, but the mice with Ro 2-3973 remained healthy and peppy. Schnitzer and Grunberg moved to the next phase of treating the healthy mice with a "medicated diet," which required injecting them with the drug for three weeks, and then withholding treatment for another three weeks to test for side effects. After the six weeks, they killed the mice and autopsied them. They made tissue sections, stained and mounted them, and then inspected slide after slide under the microscope. They repeated the tests until their vision blurred and their backs ached. They called up Fox and invited him to peer into the eyepiece of the microscope and view the slides from the mice given Ro 2-3973. He bent forward and looked, and his eyes grew wide. In all the years of testing tuberculosis, not one drug had left mice disease-free.

Until now.

That afternoon, Fox filed a report to La Roche management: "One compound, Ro 2-3973, appeared to be of outstanding activity," he wrote.

Chapter 40

The Carnation

October 1950

The phone rang early in the afternoon of October 5, 1950. Edna lifted the receiver and a voice on the other end told her to come to Brooklyn Hospital. Forest Sr. had suffered a heart attack. She took in the words, but they didn't really register.

On the ferry to Brooklyn, Edna sat inside praying. Feeling the vibrations of the engines as they moved the vessel across the bay, her mind began freewheeling. His laugh. The jazz clubs. Strolling down Seventh Avenue. The boarding room. His fedora. His smile. The riots. The late-night ferry rides. Those days were long gone, distant images of a life, of a young man and woman, who were also gone. Her lithe legs were thicker, streaked with veins from years of standing, and her eyes dimmer. Imagining a life without Forest Sr. was hard, but harder still was imagining her son without a father.

At Brooklyn Hospital, a doctor greeted her and took her into a room, where he delivered the news: Forest Sr. had died. He was fifty years old.

Standing above his body, she found it hard to believe he was gone just like that. All her life Edna had encountered death, every day for two decades at Sea View. Dead bodies were routine; they didn't scare her or really faze her anymore. But seeing her husband on the gurney, his shirt torn open and his body bruised from the chest compressions, crushed her. Edna without Forest was an incomplete equation.

On Bradley Avenue, the living room filled with nurses and friends who brought food: casseroles, biscuits, fish, green beans, spaghetti, pies, and cakes. What else could they do? they asked. Could they take Forest Jr., who liked to sit under the table and watch the ongoing stream of women coming and going, the women who wept alongside his newly widowed mother, who murmured about things that eluded him: finances, wills, plots, services, announcements, and obituaries.

He watched as hands, some with long nails, offered his mother tissues, a cup of tea, a plate of food. "Eat," they said.

But Edna didn't want food. She wanted Forest Sr. Her son saw her put down the plates and teacups and move about the room, wringing her hands, as she retold the story, the call, the ferry ride, the gurney, his body.

That week, Edna planned the church service, and she shopped for a coffin at Billups Funeral Home, one of two Black-owned funeral homes on Staten Island. The coffin she picked cost $700, leaving nothing for a gravestone, at least for the moment.

At Frederick Douglass Memorial Park, where Mamie's father used to dig the graves, Edna chose a plot under a small group of trees. It was serene but not too far out of the way—Forest would like to be close to people.

On the morning of the funeral, Edna and Americus, wearing black dresses and wide-brimmed hats, stood beside the casket of Forest "Snake" William Ballard. The two women greeted the long line of mourners who came through to pay their respects. There was Clemmie, Janie, Missouria, Miss Demby, Marion and Arthur Evans, Miss R., Forest's friends from the docks, and his Friday-night poker buddies: Mump Fudge, Dirty Johnson, and Jim, who worked in the belly of the ferry, collecting the tickets for cars. The men shared stories of their all-night card games and pool-hall escapades. Arthur wept openly over his good friend's death.

Young Forest, just eight years old in his new suit, grew restless. The service was long, and although he understood his father had died, he wanted it to end: the grief of all these people was too much.

"Settle down," Americus told him.

In the last few years, she had stepped in as a second parent, becoming the primary disciplinarian. She cooked for him and, when he came home from PS 30, oversaw his homework. While Edna mostly spoiled her son, Americus, two generations younger, was wary of the crowd Forest Jr. might fall in with—the boys who smoked and drank and started fights; who dated nurses and didn't offer to open doors or pay for their dinners; who shrugged off God. Those who had no job—"grifters," she called them. She worked hard to teach him the "old ways": responsibility, respect, a good work ethic, and, most important, faith.

Forest Jr. was dutiful but not obedient. Americus told him that he came into the world with "a twinkle of mischief in his eye." He rode his bike too fast and played a little too hard. When he was three, he demolished his tricycle, trying to ride off a ramp. He often sneaked into the neighbors' kitchens and grabbed cookies, pieces of pie, biscuits, and whatever was off-limits. Once he sat in Arthur Evans's car and released the clutch. The car went rolling down the street, straight into a lamppost. Fortunately, no one was hurt.

He often talked back, but Americus "shut him up quick," he said. Over and over, she told him, "Your mouth is gonna get you nowhere but shining the shoes of Bobby Cook," Bradley Avenue's local bad boy.

Now, staring at the spray of flowers draped over his father's coffin, little Forest took the hundreds of memories and stuffed them down deep, where his father's loss would hurt less. But one memory he refused to lock up: Christmas Eve.

Some years earlier, he had peeked through the keyhole of his bedroom and watched his mother and father put up the Christmas tree. It was big and fresh and filled the room with the scent of pine. His parents whispered and laughed while they decorated and wrapped gifts. In the morning, they told him Santa had brought the tree. Forest never told them he knew the truth, a truth that was better than believing in Santa.

The limousine followed behind the hearse holding his father's body, and the funeral procession made its way up Victory Boulevard toward Bradley Avenue, so Forest Sr. could pass his home, a place he loved, one last time. Young Forest looked out the window as they drove by Benny's luncheonette, Joe and Pat's candy store, and Miss Demby's house, and wondered if his father could see them.

At the grave site, Edna wept so hard her shoulders shook. Americus held her sister by the elbow, keeping her steady. Then together they walked to the coffin, and Forest Jr. watched as his mother leaned over and placed a single carnation on it.

Chapter 41

❖

On the Open Ward

By late fall, Mamie's condition had improved, and she moved from the small six-bed unit to the open ward with thirty other women, most of them from Harlem and the Bronx. Her mood lifted, and so did her fever. She was awake and lucid, and her mind eased from the fiery whirlwind of memory.

To pass the hours, those who were feeling well enough could write letters, crochet, draw, or read. But some wanted to be alone, and others, Mamie said, "had gained strange habits": one rocked back and forth in bed, and another spent hours washing her hands at the sink. She would wash them, dry them, and walk back to bed; fifteen minutes later, she would get up and repeat the ritual. Her skin had turned raw.

Mamie befriended a small group of four women. One had a transistor radio, and at night they broke the rules and gathered on the bed of Mama Perez, a white-haired woman in her mid-fifties who never had visitors. But, Mamie said, "she became everyone's mama." Huddled around the radio's speaker, they turned the volume low and listened to music—Nat King Cole and Billy Eckstine, a Black pop singer who was known for his debonair looks and smooth baritone voice.

Sometimes they tuned in to radio programs like *Abbott Mysteries* or the new drama *Night Beat*. But the big thrill was listening to the popular blues disk jockey Harold "Mr. Blues" Ladell on his radio show, especially if they'd requested a song. The four women had started a tradition of writing to Ladell when someone was about to be discharged: "Mr. Ladell, can you please play this song for my friend?" they'd write.

They wrote and called so often that Ladell began introducing the songs with a lead: "This is for my greatest fan club in Staten Island," he'd say, his voice filtering into the ward. The women always laughed at his acknowledgment.

"He never knew we had *that* disease and were dying," Mamie later said. "It made us feel normal . . . for a little while."

December came and Nurse Janie Shirley brought Mamie good news. Her sputum was negative. She could have a pass to leave and spend Christmas at home. So her sister came and took her back down to Stapleton, and the family prepared for the holiday. Only little George was missing. He remained at Sea View. No, he could not have a pass, they told Ruby Lee.

For Mamie, the holiday was still joyous. The Blair family ate and told stories and opened gifts, and that night, for the first time in almost a year, she slept in her own bed with the brilliance of the city lights glowing outside her window. "They were so close," she said, "but I knew soon they would fade away."

Chapter 42

A Funeral to Rejoice

January 1951

Forty-three years after Minerva Franklin and a handful of nurses walked into St. Mark's United Methodist Church in New York and established the National Association of Colored Graduate Nurses, the current leaders of the organization returned to their symbolic birthplace. There on a wintry day in January 1951, the board of directors voted the organization out of existence.

Shortly afterward, Mabel Staupers and the new executive secretary, Alma Vessels John, issued a press release announcing the disbanding of the NACGN. In it, they justified the reasons for the organization shuttering: over the last few years, they had made significant progress. The number of state nursing associations prohibiting Black nurses from joining had dropped from seventeen to five, and the number of schools admitting qualified Black nurses had risen from 28 prewar to 330 by 1950. Hospital staffs and health agencies had also integrated.

"The doors have been opened," Staupers said. "We are now a part of the great organization of nurses, the American Nurses Association." This was the victory Staupers had been working toward for seventeen years: integration into the all-white organization.

The moment was bittersweet: this was the first major Black organization to end its work, she said, "because it feels that its program of activities is no longer necessary." To celebrate, the NACGN leaders invited more than a thousand people to a closing "testimonial dinner" on January 26.

It was a brisk night, but for the people in gowns and tuxedoes strolling into the forty-four-story Essex House overlooking Central Park, the wind and cold didn't matter. Inside the art deco lobby, well-known Black and white guests, including Staupers and her former colleague, the stylish Riddle, NAACP president Walter White, and other distinguished citizens nibbled on hors d'oeuvres and drank champagne from fancy glasses. When the dining room filled, Ralph Bunche, the first Black ambassador to the United Nations, stood up and welcomed the crowd: "This is a cause for rejoicing, for this is evidence of American democracy reaching its maturity."

The room filled with applause. Then Bunche introduced the keynote speaker, the Honorable Judge William H. Hastie, the first federal Black judge, who stepped up to podium: "The passing of an organization can be only somewhat less sad than the death of a human being," he said, "but in this case I rejoice."

Over the course of the evening, every speaker praised Staupers's leadership; they honored her with accolades for her guidance and courage in choosing to dissolve the organization that had fought for assimilation and equity and broken down so many barriers for Black nurses.

One writer summed up her achievement with the NACGN from 1933 to this moment. It was "the symphony of the nursing world," she wrote, "of which Staupers was apparently composer and conductor."

For Black nurses in America, it was a pivotal moment. They were now free to join state associations and become part of the American Nurses Association. At Sea View, too, there was joy. The new generation of Black nurses, Virginia and her friend Marjorie Tucker Reed and Curlene Jennings and many others, would have opportunities that Edna and Missouria and the nurses who answered the earlier calls only imagined. There would be promotions and access to jobs, and they had a national organization backing them.

Now, Riddle said, they were American nurses, not "Negro nurses."

But in her tempered way, she added that problems persisted— salary discrepancies based on race and tokenism. Except now, those problems were no longer consigned to the NACGN. They were now the business of the "entire nursing profession."

The next day, Walter White told the newspapers, "For the first time in my life, I have enjoyed a funeral."

Chapter 43

❖

The Apparitions

January–April 1951

After Christmas, Mamie returned to Sea View with a cold that had settled in her chest. Shortly after the NACGN farewell gala, it worsened: Her lungs swelled, and her chest cavity filled with fluid, and every breath sent a searing pain through her body. "Pleurisy," an inflammation of the lungs, the doctor said, and put her back on bed rest.

In the spring, when the wisteria curled itself around Sea View's pergolas and fences, Mamie began to decline. As predicted, the streptomycin-PAS combination had stopped working, and now the pleurisy caused the disease to flare up. Her eyes became glassy, and fever turned her skin hot. The hacking cough returned, and once again, doctors and nurses made a frantic effort to save her life.

She needed a bronchoscopy, a procedure in which doctors inserted a long metal rod fitted with a camera down her throat toward her lungs to assess the damage. It required that Mamie be completely still, sitting with her head back and mouth open while the surgeon pushed the tube deep into the airway. Most patients gagged, bringing up bile; unable to spit it out, they swallowed it and gagged more.

Nurse Janie Shirley wheeled Mamie through the covered corridor, past a group of men smoking cigarettes, and into the surgical ward. But once in the room, Mamie refused to remain still.

"I was scared of the iron pipe," she said. "I thought it was going to stick in my throat and break my neck."

Nurse Janie Shirley reassured her that wouldn't happen and promised to stay with her through the procedure. But Mamie refused, so Nurse Janie turned the wheelchair around and wheeled her back to Pavilion 4. Back in the side ward, Mamie returned to her TB-fevered dreams beside Lena Meller, a thirty-seven-year-old mother who, with her husband, had escaped being put in a concentration camp and used to write long letters to her daughter, Evelyn, but stopped when she became too sick to sit up.

While the two young women slept, the nurses updated both charts to "critical."

They came at night when everyone was asleep, Mamie said. Most of the time, they were women in all white who stood or sat at the edge of the bed. Sometimes they had no face, but if they did, their eyes were big and wide. When they came, she said, they never talked or moved. Except once, when one of them stood on the bed, her hands high above her head and her palms splayed open facing the heavens.

Some of the women who saw them screamed and cried out, and the nurse on duty would arrive and comfort them: "There is nothing there," the nurse would say, walking to the end of the bed.

But the women agreed there was something, something only the sick could see. Some called them visions or visitors; others called them apparitions or spirits or ghosts; others said they were "waking dreams."

"Not everyone saw them," Mamie said. Some of the women laughed at the stories of ghosts, but not Mamie. She knew they were real. The white women had come to her. "They appeared at the foot of the bed alongside the angels and Mother Mary," she said. "And floating above them were the words of John 14:1: 'Do not let your hearts be troubled. You believe in God.'"

Mamie was simultaneously awed and terrified of the apparitions. She tried to will them away, but they still came. Night after night, they arrived and woke her. She would open her eyes and see the vision, and each time she would believe it was a dream. "I would turn on the radio, but it wouldn't go away," she said. "Then I knew they were back."

Maybe, she thought, they were bringing her a message, or maybe they were waiting to take her away. She didn't know.

Chapter 44

A Trial of Five

January–October 1951

During the year that Mamie slipped in and out of life, Herbert Fox continued working on his new drug, Ro 2-3973, the compound that killed tuberculosis in mice. In January 1951, Fox and his company, Hoffmann–La Roche, committed to six months of testing it. They said Ro 2-3973, which belonged to a class of drugs called hydrazides, had "outstanding activity" and called it isoniazid, soon to be known as Rimifon. They also continued refining a derivative, called Marsilid, which they had been testing on TB-infected monkeys, guinea pigs, dogs, rats, and mice. But now everything depended on a human trial.

Fox needed a lot of patients, diverse in gender and age, and sick with different forms of tuberculosis. They needed to be hopeless, meaning all other treatments—bed rest, combination drug therapy with streptomycin and PAS, and surgery—had been tried and failed. Choosing incurables assured Fox of two things: If they improved, it would be from the drugs and nothing else. And if things went wrong—a genuine possibility—this population would draw little public attention.

Only one hospital could satisfy all his needs: Sea View.

It was perfect.

With 1,800 patients, ranging from infancy to old age, its wards boasted every variation of the disease in different stages. Testing the two drugs there would guarantee a substantial set of results. And it had excellent doctors—Robitzek, for one—who knew the disease from the inside out and who were experienced in running drug trials. But beyond the doctors, it had the Black nurses.

Decades of being immersed in everything tuberculosis had given them an intimate knowledge of the patients and their needs, an understanding that was separate from Robitzek's. They knew how the disease ebbed and flowed, how it cloyed, then let go; they knew its moods and how vicious it became, its arrogance and disregard for human life. They picked up its nuances, the way it affected not just the diseased area but the whole of a person. And they had experienced firsthand how treatments had changed. Edna easily recalled a time before any drugs when the only hope was invasive surgery, with the galling terror of secondary infections. Missouria and Nurse Janie Shirley, too, remembered the days of applying external ointments made from oils and extracts, hoping to stop bacterial infections.

No one was more qualified than these nurses to assist Robitzek and the other doctors with a trial of this magnitude.

❖

On a late spring morning in May 1951, Fox's colleague, Dr. Roger A. Lewis, picked up the phone and dialed AR4-6656.

Eight miles away in Paterson, New Jersey, at the private practice of Dr. Irving Selikoff, the phone rang. Selikoff, a stocky, strong-faced lung specialist, was in the middle of his day examining patients. For the past six years, he'd spent several days a week at Sea View working alongside Robitzek. Both men were deeply invested in finding a cure and had become a well-known team.

When Selikoff answered, Lewis, a forthright man, began talking. La Roche's lab had just finished testing three new drugs, and their efficacy in mice, dogs, and guinea pigs was unusually high, twenty times higher than that of the failed streptomycin, and over ten times higher than that of TB-1.

"Things look better than ever. Would you be interested in doing some research on humans at Sea View?" Lewis asked.

❖

Two days after the call, Drs. Robitzek and Selikoff, along with Lewis, sat at the long oval table in the conference room in the administration building, poring over La Roche's animal trials. They were impressed with the results, and asked permission from Dr. Ornstein and the medical board at Sea View to start a trial. Without hesitating, they said yes.

Robitzek called a meeting with the nurses, who would be on the front lines, doing much of the day-to-day work. Missouria and Edna, Janie and Clemmie, and their colleagues Miss Newton, Miss Whitted, Miss Giles, Miss Alvarez, Miss Morejon, and Miss Stiversa Bethel, the first Black nurse to become assistant supervisor of nurses, filed into the conference room and found seats at the oval table.

And then he explained the trial, or, as one journalist later said, "the most grandiose experiment ever undertaken in the history of medicine."

Once a day, the nurses would inject a predetermined dose of the new medication into the patients—it was important that patients received this drug and nothing else, no streptomycin, no PAS, no vitamins. Any additional medication could throw off the trial or, worse, kill someone.

Robitzek trusted them—he knew their work ethic—but they were all in uncharted territory with this new medication. Past drugs had already been tested on humans, but not Rimifon or Marsilid. They, the Black nurses, would be conducting the first human trials using the new compounds on patients handpicked by him and Selikoff; the risks all around were vast.

Following Fox's criteria, the two doctors had sifted through heaps of folders looking for "patients with extensive disease . . . the so-called hopeless cases whose death was imminent."

To begin, they explained to the nurses, they had chosen five people, all of them lungers, diagnosed with bilateral severe pulmonary tuberculosis; in addition, they all were suffering from secondary conditions—high blood pressure, diabetes, anorexia, heart problems, impetigo, and various other infections. Most of the nurses, he was sure, knew these patients, who'd been in and out of Sea View for years. They were Hilda Ali, now Hilda Carrion, along with Richard Powers, Daniel Murphy, Lucille Donnes, and Edith Johnson.

Before ending the meeting, Robitzek cautioned the nurses "not to say a thing" about this new drug or the trial to anyone, including their families. He dreaded the rumors and misinformation that always happened. And if the drug showed promise, he feared hearing that go-to phrase "wonder drug," or "miracle cure"—two words he later said, "I came to hate."

On the women's ward, Robitzek walked to the bed of Hilda.

She was now nineteen, and despite everyone believing she had been cured in January 1950, months before Fox discovered isoniazid, she was readmitted. During her three-year respite from Sea View, the longest of her life, she had begun living as if tuberculosis were behind her. She had graduated from high school, married, found a job as a curtain maker, and recently had a baby, a boy named Robert. But soon after his birth, the disease reappeared with a vengeance. In the critical ward, beside Mamie, Hilda stared and prayed and slept.

Pulling up a chair, the one reserved for visitors, the one Hilda's mother and Ruby Lee knew so well, Robitzek sat down and moved closer to her. He heard the jangling of disease that swished fluids around her lungs, infected liquid that would eventually drown her.

He explained the secret trial and the new drug that seemed promising. It did not guarantee life—he made this clear to her and all the patients—and the risks were high, but it was her only option.

Would she do it?

She looked at him. Of course she wanted to do it, of course she didn't want to die. She wanted to grow old and see her son grow up, but she was afraid the drug would fail or make her sicker, the way all the others had done.

He couldn't give her concrete assurance. But this, he said, was her only option.

"Yes," she said, her breath full of disease. If TB were visible at that moment, it would have blackened the room.

After Hilda, Robitzek went to the beds of two other women, Lucille Donnes, whose mother had died at Sea View twelve years earlier, and Edith Johnson. They also said yes. And Edith later added: "If he offered us arsenic, we would have taken it."

Then he took the rickety elevator with the gossipy operator to the men's ward and found Richard, a boisterous and gruff man who enjoyed sneaking liquor onto the ward, and the more subdued Daniel. To each, he repeated how the drug was new but it was their only chance for life.

Richard and Daniel didn't hesitate to agree and sign the consent form. Robitzek knew the desperation to live, to be in the world, to feel its life-force, drove each of their answers.

He, too, wanted to see them live. In fact, all the Sea View staff members were longing for this scourge to end, for the Bone Man and the Grim Reaper and the apparitions to cease shadowing their lives, and for the doors to this "magnificent institution," built so many years ago as a testament to the human spirit and to its will to survive, to finally close.

And maybe that's why they all shook hands, the Black nurses and white doctors and dying patients, and together leapt into the forward movement of the moment, that perpetual motion needed to keep life going.

❖

Two weeks later, on June 19, 1951, Missouria stood at Daniel's bed and prepared to administer his first dose of isoniazid. Daniel, a sixty-one-year-old car waxer, suffered from a rare case of tuberculosis of the tongue, causing it to swell enormously—the tip hung from his lips and the interior was stuck to the roof of his mouth. Unable to eat, he had a feeding tube that snaked down his nose and into his stomach and kept him alive. The tube and his tongue made it impossible for him to talk or laugh or cry or scream.

Every day for six weeks, Missouria would give him the drug, then monitor him. Afterward there would be a six-week waiting period, time for the doctors to gauge the drug's efficacy. This was followed by time off to watch for toxicity and disease spread. If, after the full cycle, all went well, Robitzek would add more patients and continue the trial.

The stakes were high; money and time and lives were on the line.

Missouria pulled up Daniel's pajama sleeve and prodded his upper arm muscle. The laxity of it felt like liquid between her fingers. Then she cleaned the area, stretched the skin, and injected him; he winced, and she rubbed the spot. The routine was the same with Richard. Previously, he'd spent years three years on Missouria's ward, most of them causing trouble. Now he was too sick to walk or think about making noise.

On the women's ward, Nurses Janie Shirley and Clemmie were overseeing Hilda and the other two trial patients. One, Lucille, lay some beds down from Hilda. Her life had also been punctuated by long stays at Sea View. Now at twenty-two, after a decade of tuberculosis, Lucille's X-rays showed a smattering of functioning lung tissue. Her weight had plunged to seventy-six pounds, and she maintained a fever of 104 degrees. Unable to sit up or talk, she had receded into herself, preparing to die by giving away her things: her crochet needles, a favorite sweater, and a prized fruit bowl.

Now Nurse Janie Shirley was bringing her hope. She rolled up Lucille's sleeve and cleaned the area and injected her. Then she moved her cart with the final syringe of isoniazid to the lone newcomer, twenty-eight-year-old Edith, who arrived two years ago as a "hopeless case."

Each day on their respective wards, the nurses injected Daniel and Richard, Hilda, Lucille, and Edith with an amount of the drug keyed to their specific body weight. Following the shot, the nurses took daily urine and sputum samples and logged temperatures and pulses. Three times a week they tapped arms, hands, fingers, legs, and between toes, looking for healthy veins to draw blood, which was used to count red and white cells and measure inflammation in the body.

While bathing and changing them, the nurses examined those bodies, with their sharp and brittle bones, looking for bruising or rashes, or signs of swelling around the joints, limbs, or abdomen. Then they asked questions: How were they feeling? What were they thinking? Did anything hurt? Were they dizzy? Tired? Nauseated? They noted their voice and tone, gauged their moods and emotional stability, and looked for signs of jaundice or neurological issues.

In the nurses' room after their shifts, they wrote their observations in the logbook that Robitzek and Selikoff collected each night.

June rolled into mid-July, marking the first six weeks, and the news at Sea View was good: the nurses' reports informed Robitzek of a positive trend. In all five, the fevers had abated, and their notes read, "The hopes of these patients rise day by day."

This was especially true of Hilda: after only two weeks, she was sitting up, eating, and talking, fever-free. Robitzek gave her permission to get up and walk around the ward. She was thrilled. On visiting day, she put on her bed jacket and slippers and walked to the window to see her husband and two-year-old son, who waved and grinned at his mother from down below. Maybe this would cure her.

Soon Robitzek gave the same order for Edith, who had gained so much weight that she joked her "clothes barely fit."

Richard said that he "felt like a new man."

And Daniel? Well, he, too, was showing progress. Slowly, his tongue was de-swelling.

On August 1, Robitzek stopped the drug for the six-week no-dose period to ensure there were no lingering side effects. As each week passed, he sighed in relief when the nurses informed him they weren't seeing any negative reactions or signs of regression.

By mid-September, the end of those six weeks, all the patients were status quo. While this was a positive sign, Robitzek remained reticent. Past trials, most recently the British ones on streptomycin, proved that side effects could appear later than six weeks; sometimes they took months. But he couldn't wait that long. Without continued treatment, he feared the patients could relapse. Feeling the odds were in his favor, he gave the order: re-dosing would begin immediately, and it was time to test on a larger scale.

❖

And so in late September, the great move began. In Pavilion 1, the floors and walls rang with the sound of wheelchairs and gurneys rolling through double doors, down hallways, and in and out of elevators as two wards were cleared and their patients redistributed throughout the hospital.

Needing to keep things contained and clandestine, Robitzek and Selikoff arranged for the trial patients to be housed in Pavilion 1 and separated by gender on two wards: Ward 11 for men and Ward 13 for women. For this larger group consisting of ninety-two patients, Selikoff said they would use the same criteria for selection: "hopeless cases . . . on whom every other known treatment had been tried, with no results." Robitzek reiterated it more bluntly: "Death had to be imminent."

Mamie Blair, the local girl who loved to read, was sick enough to qualify. They placed her in women's Ward 13 with Hilda, Lucille, and Edith. Joining them were Myrtle Stewart, who had a five-year-old boy, and Lena Meller, who longed to see her daughter, Evelyn. By her bedside was a valentine from her husband and a photograph of the girl at age four. Now she was seven. Haunted by her daughter's face, and the last time she saw her at Sea View through the ward window, Lena "cried day and night." Also chosen were Milagros Delfaus, a twenty-two-year-old immigrant from Puerto Rico, who said that "the sickness brought shame to her family." She hoped the drug would make her well so no one would ever know.

In Ward 13, emotions ran high. The three original women were well enough to get dressed, and their hair was shiny and styled. They walked around feverless and bright-eyed and happy to be alive. The newcomers, whose complexions were still pasty and their skin dry and flaky, stared with envy at Hilda and Lucille and Edith. Would the drug help them, too? Would it stop the apparitions?

On October 2, each new patient on Wards 11 and 13 received the first dose of La Roche's two isoniazid derivatives, Marsilid and Rimifon. The dosing this time was heavier, and the drugs had been compounded into little white pills. Each morning, afternoon, and evening, in the medicine room, the nurses separated the tiny white pills into individual disposable cups.

After each patient received their medication, the nurses recorded their vitals—pulse, blood pressure, temperature—and collected their sputum. Again, they checked their extremities for bruises or rashes and their eyes for jaundice or any other abnormalities; they talked with them, asking about their moods, their appetite, and whether they had any side effects. Then they transported patients to their X-rays, electrocardiograms, bronchoscopies, and any other necessary tests. Then they spent a long time filling out copious amounts of daily paperwork for Robitzek and Selikoff, who would meet in the conference room, now the headquarters for the trials, and assess what the nurses wrote.

The two men teased through the nurses' case reports on the physical, emotional, and mental state of each patient, reading how many were gaining back strength, how they were fever free, how coughs were "markedly reduced," and how in some there was "barely enough sputum for bacteriologic examination." They also read about side effects. Most complained about vertigo; a few had dry mouth and a skin rash and "disturbed vision," while some felt a "weakness in their legs." One or two had shortness of breath. When the doctors were done, they filled in their graphs of statistics and toxicity tables listing the symptoms and number of weeks each patient was on the drug. This information from the nurses and certain lab tests helped them readjust the dosing up or down to achieve better results. But they knew that each tiny tweak, however small, held the possibility of causing a critical reaction.

On the wards things continued to run smoothly with the nurses doling out the little white pills to the chosen ninety-two, and then charting their conditions. To be closer to the patients, Robitzek began sleeping at Sea View. In the morning, afternoon, and now at night, he would walk the two wards, checking on them.

Standing by Hilda's bed, he saw a young woman who was feeling better. There was a clarity in her eyes and a youthful flush in her cheeks. She was talkative and wanted to go home. There was no doubt every pill she swallowed insinuated itself a little more into the waxy coating of the millions of microbes living inside her and prevented them from reproducing.

Deep inside Mamie's body, things were also changing. The bacteria were dying, and her lungs relaxed and filled with more air. For the first time since Christmas, she was sitting upright and reading a book. Her eyes no longer burned or blurred when she looked at words. And when her mother came, she got dressed and walked around outside and wanted to eat the home-cooked meals that Ruby Lee transported in glass mason jars.

Under the autumn sun, Mamie began thinking about restarting her life, but she shared the same fears as Milagros, being ostracized or, worse, the disease returning: "I thought, 'What if it's my turn to die?'" she said. But Ruby Lee Blair would have "none of that talk," she told her daughter.

On the men's ward, Timothy Harnedy, a steamfitter, was also elated. Months earlier on two separate occasions, he'd requested a priest to anoint him and administer last rites. While the holy man daubed him with oil and recited prayers, the sick Harnedy hallucinated and at one point believed he had died. To his ward mates and anyone else who saw those moments, there was no doubt the Bone Man was looming beside him, waiting to snatch his soul. Now the Bone Man had moved on from Harnedy's bed.

But the most extraordinary case was Daniel. The drug found its way to his swollen tongue and began breaching the bacteria that glued itself to his cheeks and esophagus. Slowly he felt his tongue deflating, detaching itself from the roof of his mouth, and retracting from its position between his lips. He couldn't believe it. Sitting up in his striped bathrobe and matching pajamas, he told the nurses, or anyone who'd listen, how he yearned to eat real food, not the liquid that slithered down the "awful feeding tube" in his nose.

Four weeks into the trial, mealtime had taken on a different feeling. Patients stopped pushing away their plates.

"They scrape them clean and request more," one nurse said.

In the women's ward, the ladies joked about their growing waistlines and hips and not fitting into their clothes. To mark the occasion, one nurse hung a plastic bag full of eggs from a hook on the wall. It was to symbolize "new life," a rebirth that could no longer be denied. It was palpable and the nurses wrote it down:

"Patients who had been bedridden for as long as 2 years rapidly regained strength and energy and are now ambulatory. No 'bed cases' remain. The wards have a completely new appearance."

Whispers began trickling through the pavilions about the patients in Wards 11 and 13. They were being given a "miracle drug," and it was curing them.

The secret was out.

Chapter 45

❖

"Do Not Say a Thing"

November 1951–January 1952

By November, words like "splendid," "dramatic," "profound," "striking," and "potent" soared through the offices of Hoffmann–La Roche in New Jersey and at the headquarters in Sweden. In hallways, people stopped and leaned close and used them to describe the news coming from Sea View about Herbert Fox's new drugs, the magnitude of which everyone was just beginning to grasp.

Preliminary reports detailing the trials said the drug had "a profound and important therapeutic effect in human tuberculosis." And the "mortally ill" were now showing results "far beyond anything we have ever seen" with chemotherapeutic or antibiotic drugs. In the twelve-page single-spaced report, they told of E.M., whose body was toxic but, weeks after taking Marsilid, produced negative sputum. Another patient, B.V., whose weight had dropped from seventy-five to fifty-six pounds and was frail and toxic, now had gained ten pounds and showed a "renewed vigor." There was no shortage of short paragraphs describing patients who were no longer "mortally ill." It was inspiring and humbling, a moment people had dreamed about for almost one hundred years, and although the trials were still in the early stages, the data was irrefutable, pointing to one conclusion: a cure.

Hoffmann–La Roche began to prepare for a possible maelstrom.

At Sea View, the frenzy had already started. Since October, the drug had allowed Lena to sit up in bed and eat and spend her days knitting and, once again, writing long, detailed letters to Evelyn. "Dearest Evelyn," she began them all. Then she told the young girl to do well in school and that she was improving and would be home soon. But one morning in early December while she wrote, her thoughts trailed off; her sentences became disconnected, and her handwriting stilted and jagged. She paused and the momentary lapse passed. But in the days that followed, it happened again, each time for a little longer.

Unbeknownst to Lena, some beds down from her, another patient was also experiencing slips in her thinking. But for this patient, they came with a strange sensation, an unexplained dizziness that made her nervous. In Ward 11, some men, too, were having bouts of anxiety that they couldn't shake.

Nurses started talking among themselves, discussing Lena and Richard and others whose reactions were troubling. Joy from feeling better was one thing, but the medication seemed to incite a giddiness, a kind of near mania: Was their elevated mood atypical? the nurses wondered. Maybe their perception was skewed from decades of being surrounded by sad and often angry people. Perhaps these periods of excitement seemed extraordinary because they were not used to seeing them. For now, the nurses kept these observations private, confined to the logbook and themselves.

January brought with it a dramatic shift in weather—frost and snow and ice. Inside the hospital things were also shifting. Almost all the patients had vertigo and were bloated, their stomachs distending from constipation that lasted weeks; urinary issues followed. Some couldn't start urinating and others couldn't fully empty their bladders. A few confided to the nurses that when they held a fork or a pen, they "got the shakes"; others began making strange jerky movements or twitching in their sleep.

As the month went on, the nurses noted two patients who appeared to relapse. Doctors confirmed their suspicions. Robitzek was concerned but remained confident, believing the drug was succeeding more than failing. The results so far were "distinctly better than with patients using streptomycin over this time period," he said. The trial would continue.

By late January, the nurses were sure their initial instincts were correct: the joy *was* mania. On Ward 11, Missouria witnessed patients acting peculiar; they were easily excited, nervous, and unsteady. The mood swings, she noticed, were unlike any she'd seen in almost twenty years on Ward 64. These came on swiftly and escalated in a flash, with a ferocious, nearly uncontrollable fury.

Daily, minute arguments over small things turned into shouting matches, where men cursed and spit and yelled at one another. On one occasion, two men, both previously near death, stood face-to-face, their cheeks flushed with outrage. In their robes and slippers, they moved toward each other, fists clenched, one daring the other to fight. In another instance, a minor disagreement turned ugly when one man flew into a wild rage. Screaming obscenities, he picked up a metal cup from his nightstand and hurled it across the ward, hitting his opponent's face with a thwack.

For the first time in two decades, Missouria grew worried about her safety. So did the other nurses. One of them threatened to resign several times but stayed "to see how it all turned out."

Each day chatter about the drug grew more widespread. It floated down the hallways, making its way into the elevator, where the gossipy operator delighted in bringing it to other floors. There it found new life, and the story, inevitably, took on broader dimensions.

It was a familiar pattern, these whispers about "wonder drugs." It had happened with Prontosil and sulfa and streptomycin. At first they seemed to produce miracles, breathing life into the near dead. But eventually their wonder faded because of wicked side effects: vertigo, neuropathy, deafness, tarry stools, hives, numbness, and others. And they failed to stop the disease.

Still, no matter how many times the cycle happened, the human need for something to cure this disease, to finally stop it, outweighed the possibility of failure. To the sick, every new drug bringing a sliver of hope was a miracle cure, a wonder drug. And while Rimifon and Marsilid had side effects, some better but most no worse than previous drugs, they were still working, disrupting the microbe and preventing it from reproducing. Maybe this time the whispers making their way around Sea View would prove to be true.

At La Roche's headquarters, Fox was taking in the most recent news: Squibb Pharmaceuticals, its competitor, had produced its own derivative of isoniazid called Nydrazid, and was testing it with Dr. Walsh McDermott at Cornell University Medical College. After learning the news, La Roche executives told employees to "fast track all work relating to Rimifon." Then they arranged to meet with Squibb.

Since both Robitzek and McDermott were working with offshoots of the same drug, they came to a gentlemen's agreement: any announcement on the discovery and success of Marsilid, Rimifon, or Nydrazid should happen simultaneously. The two firms settled on an early April publication date to "announce the results of our work to the medical world." But the human trials, they agreed, should remain secret to avoid arousing false hopes and inciting a public frenzy, like Waksman had done with streptomycin.

While the two pharmaceutical companies were happy with the agreement, the National Tuberculosis Association, the organization behind McDermott's study at Cornell, was not. The NTA was concerned about its reputation being tarnished. As an organization, it was widely respected for its public service announcements, its Christmas Seal campaigns, and *The Constant Invader*, a series narrated by Vincent Price and Henry Fonda dramatizing the life of TB sufferers and imploring people to take precautions against the disease. Early on, Squibb, McDermott's supplier, had lagged in producing its version of isoniazid, resulting in Sea View beginning the trial before McDermott.

The early start gave the Sea View team an advantage of finishing first. If the drug did work, they would be credited for finding a cure.

For the NTA, that Sea View, the municipal hospital full of New York's impoverished patients and Black nurses, might find a cure first was mortifying. It couldn't happen. To ensure Robitzek's and Selikoff's silence, the association sent a representative to talk with them and guarantee the doctors understood that the cure should not be tied to a city hospital.

Robitzek was aghast. Here was an organization that pledged to support research, and now at this critical moment when a cure seemed promising, those in charge wanted to suppress the information coming out of Sea View and put their own interests before those of the public and those who were dying.

Subduing his morality, Robitzek agreed to remain silent. So did Selikoff. Both understood the stakes were too high to begin an ethical fight with the most powerful medical fraternity.

But despite their promises, the situation at Sea View was already beyond their control. Everywhere in the hospital, it seemed that everyone knew "something was happening" in Wards 11 and 13, and that phrase Robitzek loathed, "miracle drug," was being tossed around with impunity. He grew nervous, very nervous.

Many of Sea View's nurses knew people in the press; perhaps they would slip and say something. Or maybe a family member who came to visit might say something, or even another doctor, or an aide, or anyone related to Sea View. But Robitzek's fears went deeper.

Before the NTA representative left Sea View, he cautioned the two doctors: No information should be released, he said, until the NTA talked to the press first. Otherwise, the organization threatened them with ruin and insinuated that they could be drafted into the army, and, as a result, "might find themselves on a plane to Korea."

Robitzek and Selikoff called a meeting.

"Do not say a thing," they reiterated to the staff.

Across the harbor, reporters were already prowling hallways, pulling aside credible sources to verify tips that a cure might have been discovered. But no one was talking. The press secretary from the Health Department told Arthur Gelb from *The New York Times*, "Please don't even ask me about this," then walked away.

Gelb took the ferry to Sea View and asked several doctors. All "claimed ignorance." Frustrated, he called the director's office—it's unclear whether he called Robitzek or Ornstein—but whoever answered the phone refused to identify himself: "The phone is probably tapped," the man said. "I'd be fired if it was learned I was talking to a reporter." Then he hung up.

Chapter 46

❖

The Wonder Drug

February 1952

In the early hours before dawn on Thursday, February 21, 1952, news trucks rumbled down city streets tossing bundles of freshly printed papers from the open back doors. They landed with a thump in front of newsstands not yet open, and on corners where young boys in caps and coats would soon stand shouting the morning headlines. That morning edition of the *New York Post* carried the banner headline "Wonder Drug Fights TB."

Inside, the lengthy article discussed the marvels of isoniazid, the "new wonder drug," and it explained how Sea View patients were brought back from the brink of death, how its lack of toxicity and ability to destroy the microbe set it apart from all previous drugs, and how it "cured tuberculosis." There were paragraphs on who discovered it and how, and an overview of the trial's success. It was "better than anything so far to treat the worst killer among contagious disease," the journalists concluded. And it happened right here on Staten Island.

The story was out now. How it broke or who leaked it to *Post* journalists Joseph Kahn and Malcolm Logan was anyone's guess. Some later speculated it was a Black nurse who was dating a reporter and fed him the story over months; others blamed it on a patient who wrote to one of the papers; and others pointed at Robitzek and Selikoff.

But knowing would not have changed what happened next, when New York awoke to the morning news.

By the time the sun had crested over Manhattan's east side, journalists from other papers—*The New York Times*, the *New York Herald*, the New York *Daily News*, *The New York Age*, the *Brooklyn Eagle*—were rushing to investigate the breaking news. Some now waited in line at the Staten Island Ferry. They stood out among the crowd, dressed similarly in collared shirts and ties, loose trousers, and matching jackets with single-breasted woolen overcoats. Underneath their hats, their hair was short and neat.

At 9 a.m. the ferry pulled out of the South Ferry–Whitehall Street terminal and began its twenty-five-minute trip across New York Harbor. On board the reporters mixed in with the regular passengers, women in long coats and men holding briefcases, who sat along the wooden benches or made their way to the concession stand, where they leaned against the sleek chrome counter drinking freshly brewed coffee while talking or gazing out the windows as the boat pushed past the now-shuttered Ellis Island.

Others read their papers, pausing at different articles: Elizabeth Taylor's recent London wedding. Truman's delight in being president. Some noted the opening of *Snow White* in Technicolor or the wild story of how the notorious bank robber Willie Sutton was captured up by Sea View. And those who held the *Post* read about the cure.

Shortly after passing the Robbins Reef Lighthouse, the boat cut its engines and docked at the St. George Terminal. The deckhands opened the gate and the crowd dispersed, their footsteps resounding in the newly rebuilt terminal. Stepping outside, the ferry passengers felt the air shift; it was cold and raw, and the wind was laced with the scent of brine.

The journalists hailed taxicabs and headed up the hill toward Sea View, where the nurses and doctors were already hours into their day. On a non-trial ward, a nurse was noting how one woman's night was filled with "paroxysms." Another patient still had leg pain and headaches.

In another ward, a woman had hemorrhaged, soaking the sheets in blood, and across at the children's hospital, Virginia was tending to a child suffering from a skin rash. In the surgical ward, Edna, in her new role as a head nurse, was overseeing her staff, who were busy prepping patients and equipment for surgery.

On Ward 11, Missouria was preparing her cart—syringes, alcohol, iodine, fresh cloths, water pitcher, sputum cups, and the little white pills. All of the nurses were oblivious to the reporters sitting in the back of taxis making their way up Brielle Avenue.

The journalists arrived at Sea View, where a gauzy fog was draped over the bare trees and pavilion roofs. Inside the administration building they were met by a doctor who would accompany them on the wards. Stepping onto the elevator, the operator greeted them, pulled the gate shut, and took them to Ward 13, the women's trial ward, on the fourth floor.

When the door opened, sounds of laughter and music met them; it resounded off the pea-green walls and the ceiling. In the middle of the corridor stood Hilda, Lucille, Myrtle Stewart, and other women wearing long, pretty cotton nightgowns. With their bodies no longer emaciated and their lips and cheeks made up, they radiated health. And they were happy. Nat Fein, the renowned photographer from the *New York Herald Tribune*, asked them to jitterbug and then snapped an iconic image of them singing and dancing. Elsewhere on the ward, they banged on pitchers and bedpans, celebrating the morning's headline that announced the little white pill they were taking was *the cure*.

The reporters looked at them. These were the people the newspapers had called "incurable, hopeless, dying." But here they were, revived and rejoicing.

The women smiled; flashbulbs popped. The journalists walked past the Black nurses toward the happy women, eager to hear their stories. Edith was excited to tell them how she'd arrived at Sea View two years ago with TB in both lungs and a temperature of 105.

"There was no hope for me. They wired my mother to come, that I was dying," she said.

But now things were different. She weighed 160 pounds, and her sputum was clear of TB.

"I would like to leave now, but they don't let me," she said.

"Patience," said the doctor accompanying the journalists. "We are not that far yet."

On Ward 11, Missouria's quiet morning had also turned to chaos. There, too, men clean-shaven and wearing ascots were milling about in the hallway when the doctor and journalists arrived on the floor.

They stopped to interview two men who were bantering about sports and their sixty-pound weight gain. Another reporter found Richard sitting on his bed.

"I feel like a new man," Richard told him.

Next to him, Philip, who had spent so many years on Missouria's Ward 64, chimed in, "Brother, I was feeling pretty low and then came this new treatment."

But it was Daniel's room that reporters clamored to enter. Everyone wanted to know about the man with the once gigantic tongue. Upright in a chair, eating a steak, he commandeered the space. Full of energy and joy, Daniel pushed his tray aside, stood up, danced a few steps, and stopped. Looking at the reporters, he grew serious and began talking about the tubes doctors had passed through his nose and into his throat to feed him. They jotted notes while he kept talking.

"I could not live and I could not die," he said.

"And now?" asked a journalist.

Daniel paused and returned to his chair: "I believe that never in my life had I such a good appetite," he said. "I am sixty-three now and I will become ninety now I am sure."

"Yes, yes," the doctor said. "It's true, his tongue is cured."

And on they went through the ward, the doctor occasionally pointing to another patient.

"Tuberculosis of the hip joint . . . tuberculosis of the knee joint," he said. "They were more or less paralyzed. Now they are up and walk."

The journalists listened and wrote and kept walking.

"It seems uncanny to us . . ." the doctor continued, then paused.

"Actually, we should not have let you in as a man of the press," he said.

The journalists said nothing.

"But we could not stem the onrush . . . and now imagine what will happen if this gift from heaven turns out to be a hoax?"

The men looked at each other.

"If these damned TB bacilli," he started again, "become used to the new drug? What then, dear sir?" But the journalists weren't interested in speculating about the future, they wanted *this* story. Right now.

❖

On through the halls the reporters went, again passing the Black nurses, while searching for the masterminds they believed orchestrated the trial, Robitzek and Selikoff. Where were they? They asked around, but no one knew.

Stunned at the scene unraveling upstairs, Robitzek and Selikoff had locked themselves in the conference room, huddling amid the wall charts and notebooks and piles of folders stacked like building blocks on the lacquered oval table. For Robitzek, this was his nightmare. The trials were unfinished and inconclusive, and he lacked data to prove that Rimifon and Marsilid were safe and effective.

There was no risk assessment data on patients who stopped treatment. Would they continue to improve? Would they relapse and get sicker? Did the drug prevent people from dying, and if so, at what cost? And all the questions about proper dosing—how often to administer it, for how long, and in what amounts—remained. Recently nurses had been reporting more serious side effects: more rage and rashes and deafness and problems with equilibrium. In a few patients, they wrote that the higher dosages were causing mania bordering on psychosis.

And then the NTA, with its threat to ruin their livelihood. For Robitzek, the prospect of his medical career collapsing and newspapers accusing him of being an unethical and undiscerning doctor who ran rushed, haphazard medical trials made his stomach turn. He imagined himself, once turned down by every military agency in the United States because of his eye, on a plane to Korea to fight, or sitting home jobless, his reputation tarnished because someone had leaked the story. In those long hours of hiding, Robitzek concluded, "This was one of the darkest days of my life."

From then on he would refer to it as "Black Thursday."

The dark day carried on, each interminable hour spreading more unfiltered news of the "miracle drug" discovered at Sea View. It reached the headquarters of Hoffmann–La Roche, where tempers flared, and telegrams flew through the wires.

"It was premature," executives said, an "indiscretion" on the part of the Americans. In the early evening, the commissioner of hospitals emerged from his own kind of quarantine—he, too, had been blind-sided by the story in the paper—and held a press conference. Standing in a room jammed with more than thirty fast-talking reporters and the buzzing of rolling TV cameras, he was measured, discerning, and careful not to feed the mounting sensationalism.

"Whether the two new drugs have actually cured TB, the nation's biggest infectious killer, is too early to say," he explained. "But they look better than anything so far."

Hoping to control the hyperbole, he warned them about the unknowns, the long-term effects, the efficacy of the drug, and the un-deniable possibility of bacterial resistance.

The papers acknowledged his caution but continued to print tri-umphant stories about the "wonder drug." Each day a new set of jour-nalists, including those from magazines like *Life* and *The Saturday*

Evening Post, joined the daily newspaper reporters and came to Sea View to capture more photos and stories of recovered patients.

❖

Hilda's story in *Life* magazine featured a black-and-white image of her sitting up in bed, wearing a delicate satin bed jacket; her dark hair, in a pageboy cut, framed her high cheekbones and big eyes. The accompanying story, which detailed her twenty years of torment, was retold in hundreds of papers across the country, from the *Daily Herald* in Utah to the *Greensburg Daily News* in Indiana.

"I am one of the happiest of TB patients," she told Steven M. Spencer of *The Saturday Evening Post*. "I now feel wonderful . . . I'm hoping and praying that I will be cured soon, and I have faith that I will be cured."

In the days following, she received ten letters from other TB sufferers; one simply addressed to Hilda Carrion, Sea View, had arrived from Greece. And on Ward 11, Timothy, who had called a priest for last rites, had also received letters, one from an Irish girl, a fellow TB sufferer, who'd seen his picture in the paper. They were now in the middle of a pen-pal romance.

Here and abroad, the presses continued roiling, churning out stories with an excitement that seemed interminable. In Germany, shades of America's exuberant rhetoric were splashed across daily headlines: *Das Ende Der TB* (The End of Tuberculosis). Even the staid German paper *Stadt Anzeiger* fell into breathless descriptions, detailing how the drug had miraculously saved Sea View's "hopeless cases."

Robitzek and Selikoff were thrust into a whirlwind of press conferences and radio interviews. While they did their best to qualify their work, to insist the drug was still in a trial phase, at some point they gave up; reporters continued to besiege them about the miracle drug or, as patients had called it, "Robisellin"—a hybrid of Robitzek's and Selikoff's names. The term especially unnerved Robitzek, who found it idiotic and unprofessional.

"There is no such drug," the blue-eyed doctor chastised a reporter. "Don't use that word in the paper."

Over at Cornell, McDermott read the headlines and articles about Sea View's patients being cured and was perplexed. They had agreed to wait until April to publish the results, and to do so jointly. By sharing the announcement, both La Roche and Squibb could've competed fairly for a majority stake in the drug. Now the developing hysteria meant that all of it—ownership of the drug, Cornell's reputation, and McDermott's own standing—was in question.

In Europe, meanwhile, Dr. Gerhard Domagk was also reading the headlines and was confounded. A year earlier, the Nobel-winning scientist had come to New York for a three-day conference on tuberculosis. While there, he had met with several Americans, including McDermott and Fox from Hoffmann–La Roche. He had disclosed to them his newest discovery: a derivative of Conteben, known in the United States as TB-1, which he was excited to begin testing. Upon his return to Germany, he began a trial with a Bayer-made version of isoniazid inspired by Conteben. His results, like Robitzek's and McDermott's, were also promising, and he, too, had been preparing to publish a report in April.

Domagk's disbelief at the news soon turned to anger. This was no coincidence, no serendipitous moment. No, he was convinced the American scientists had stolen his work. Frantic, the German sat in his office and penned indignant and accusatory letters to his American counterparts. Soon the scientific world was abuzz with rumors of international lawsuits.

At stake were both riches and fame: isoniazid would make a fortune for the pharmaceutical company that could claim it, and it would bring international acclaim to the accompanying scientist or doctor. Already, Robitzek was receiving calls from doctors worldwide begging to purchase huge quantities of Rimifon and Marsilid. One called asking if the plans for a new sanatorium should be canceled.

While Robitzek manned the phones and nurses supervised the wards, all three companies—La Roche, Squibb, and Bayer—scrambled to file for an exclusive patent on the drug.

❖

At Sea View, no one was thinking of patents. Mere weeks after the press introduced Hilda to the world, turning her into the poster girl for hope and healing and tuberculosis, she took a turn that no one could have anticipated.

On the morning of March 31, 1952, Hilda, who had spent almost four thousand days of her life at Sea View, almost ten of her twenty years, who lived life in bursts but refused to give up despite the odds, suffered a fatal hemorrhage. This time, there were no reporters to witness her story. It happened in the way so many Sea View lives ended: suddenly, messily, painfully. Sometime later, Lena's letters to her young daughter became incoherent, as she slowly tumbled into psychosis, an apparent side effect of isoniazid. On Missouria's ward, Daniel's fevers returned, and the nurses watched his tongue swell and swell, until once again it filled his mouth. And another woman, who had boasted about eating "four eggs, four bowls of cereal, two quarts of milk, a pint of eggnog, and four slices of toast for breakfast," stopped eating.

Robitzek and Selikoff scoured the nurses' daily reports. They knew the warning signs and how easily the microbe became drug-resistant; they visited the patients, asking about side effects, and added their notes to those of the nurses; they took more X-rays and tacked them onto the light box and studied them, pointing at the diminishing white spots. The drug did arrest the spread of tuberculosis, but it did not, it seemed, heal damaged tissue. They concluded that it could buy time and help patients become well enough for surgery. That's what it was doing for Veronica Hall.

On May 3, 1952—three months after Black Thursday—Dr. Robitzek signed the official discharge papers for the forty-five-year Veronica Hall, who had been admitted in 1950 with large cavities in one lung and an infiltration of TB in the other. Robitzek hoped that with the TB arrested, Veronica would stay strong enough to tolerate surgery to fix her lesions.

Standing beside a line of nurses in the courtyard of the administration building, Robitzek joined them in clapping and cheering as Veronica stepped out into the lush spring morning. Before getting into a Manhattan-bound taxi that would take her home, she paused in front of the lanky doctor and the nurses. She hugged each one and then thanked Robitzek, who smiled.

The next day, Veronica's story appeared in *The New York Times*.

"I owe my life to Isoniazid," she told reporters.

Reports of other discharges followed: some weeks later, two more women from the trial walked out of Sea View. Executives at Hoffmann–La Roche eagerly greeted the news. To them, anecdotes touting the success of Rimifon or Marsilid meant more public support, and everyone knew that public perception could make or break a drug. This was not lost on representatives from Squibb or Bayer. At all three firms, accountants punched in numbers, calculating potential profits from the patent rights.

Unlike streptomycin, which was difficult and expensive to produce, these drugs were easy to make. Synthesized from coal tar, their production came out to about fifty cents a pill. With TB affecting millions worldwide, the revenue for the company that controlled the supply would be staggering. And for Bayer, the prestige of finally providing a cure for tuberculosis might even redeem its war-sullied reputation.

But as the three drug companies worked to establish their claim on isoniazid, they stumbled on a historical curiosity. In 1912, two graduate students in Prague, Hans Meyer and Josef Mally, had already synthesized the chemical compound. Meyer and Mally had no inkling about the drug's effect on tuberculosis. At the time, they were not looking for a medical therapy but simply satisfying a requirement to finish their respective PhDs. They had published their findings in a dissertation, then moved on.

In the ensuing forty years since Mally and Meyer's discovery, tuberculosis had claimed more than sixty million lives globally and left scores of others permanently maimed and their lives scarred. Scientists had risked their own health working in ill-equipped labs and morgues, digging into cadavers and studying diseased organs to understand how the bacterium might be stopped. Nurses, too, had risked their lives on the wards every day, working without masks or gowns or gloves. They fell sick and many died. And governments had invested billions in long-term care facilities and in the difficult-to-manufacture streptomycin; in the United States, the estimate for the care of a single patient had grown to $3,500. And all this time, the cure had been sitting on a dusty bookshelf.

The revelation blindsided the companies that were determined to profit from the cure: the compound isoniazid was unpatentable. And in a blink, the potential windfalls for the pharmaceutical companies vanished. There would be no monopoly or preeminence in tuberculosis care. Now any drug company could manufacture the drug. Isoniazid could reach patients around the world quickly and cheaply, and it would have no gatekeepers.

The irony wasn't lost on pharmaceutical executives and scientists. Although Domagk prided himself on "working for the good of mankind," on principle he still believed the patent belonged to him. McDermott, who was making plans for a broader long-term isoniazid trial on the Navajo reservation in Arizona, was sanguine.

"The history of science is filled with instances of independent and simultaneous discoveries," he later wrote. "Yet no matter how often this phenomenon occurs, it is a cause of wonderment."

Robitzek, for his part, was delighted. His efforts had always been altruistic: all these years he had continued working for free, and finally he had vindicated his father's death and turned his grief for Katherine into something good and lasting. Now free from the pressure of the NTA and La Roche, he could celebrate how Sea View, the under-resourced municipal hospital on an isolated hilltop, had helped bring the world a cure; how his patients, their bodies so often dismissed for lack of privilege, had enabled a remedy. And how the Black nurses, long rejected as inferior professionals, had proved America wrong.

Chapter 47

❖

Breaking Glass

November 1952

Ruby Lee Blair was right to tell Mamie to stop talking about bad things. In November 1952, Mamie's sister drove up to Sea View to take her away from "no-man's-land." Dressed in a simple print dress, with buttons and a mid-calf pleated skirt, Mamie held her bag of possessions in one hand and a glass mason jar she used for drinking water in the other. A month earlier, Philip, "the old hand," had finally been discharged. Then Richard was sent home, followed by Myrtle.

Today was Mamie's day.

As Mamie walked down the hallway, her ward mates and the nurses clapped and cheered until she entered the elevator. When the doors shut, they moved to the balcony and waited to watch her perform Sea View's curious ritual.

Outside, she stepped into the grassy courtyard between the pavilions. She stopped at the center, beside a large round concrete base with a flagpole that hoisted the American flag, and looked up to see her friends leaning on the railing in their pajamas and robes, smiling and waiting.

Then she turned away and raised the hand holding the mason jar. No one saw how it trembled before coming down in one vicious gesture and hurling the jar toward the concrete. The noise of glass shattering drowned out the cheers of the nurses and the patients watching Mamie, who stood there beneath the billowing flag staring at the broken jar.

"I smashed it to smithereens," she thought to herself, her eyes welling with tears of disbelief and joy "and praise to God."

Mamie Daniels had waited years for her turn to break her glass, to make, she said, "that symbolic gesture that life at Sea View was now behind you."

Some eight months after the trial, Daniel died with his tongue filling his mouth. So did Lena, who was eventually transferred to Bellevue Hospital for a psychotic break—most likely attributable to isoniazid. And yet, despite their deaths, they had all experienced a small gift, a brief respite from years of suffering. They had simply been too sick for the novel drug to help them.

Drs. Robitzek and Selikoff pressed on with other Sea View patients, tweaking dosages, cross-reading charts, and studying side effects. Soon La Roche refined the compound, and Robitzek tested it again and again, alone and in combination with other drugs, and discovered that a cocktail of treatments—isoniazid alongside streptomycin and PAS—was not only safe but almost 95 percent effective at ensuring a patient's survival.

And so, one by one, the patients began to leave. It was a slow trickle at first, but the nurses noticed it. Beds that remained empty, wards that were no longer overcrowded, schedules that no longer required double duty. Patient admissions began to drop—by a dozen one year, twice that the next, and so on. Those who did enter the hospital didn't stay as long. And less barbaric surgeries were required.

Missouria saw it too. There were fewer men on the ward, fewer hemorrhages, and fewer bodies being sent to the morgue. To her, how the events unfolded was remarkable: the trial, the drug, and now the emptying of wards. It had begun here at Sea View. And soon hospitals in other cities were treating patients with the drug, and their wards began shuttering; the trend continued across the continents, and in less than ten years, tens of thousands of lives had been saved. No one could deny that she and her colleagues had played a part in what many once considered impossible—stopping tuberculosis. And ironically, they had probably worked themselves out of a job.

But they knew their achievements: Sea View now had seven Black head nurses. The younger ranks, including Edna's niece, Virginia, were also moving up, beneficiaries of Sea View's schooling. Marjorie Tucker Reed, the single mother who'd arrived during the nursing shortage of 1946, graduated as an LPN and was now a surgical nurse in Sea View's children's hospital. And now Black nurses could choose from 337 training programs to advance their skills and education. Miss Gillespie, whose son had returned from the war, was planning to attend graduate school at New York University, as was Janie B. Shirley.

In the years since Edna had bought her house, Bradley Avenue had changed. Gone were the empty lots and scraggly yards, the crooked fences and homes with outhouses. Thanks in part to James Brown, a Black real estate agent who lived at 261 Bradley, the barriers to buying property were falling, allowing Edna's community to stretch into a four-block radius that was full of Sea View staff and their families.

In the afternoons, kids would pour into the streets and hop on their bikes. Forest Jr. loved his red Rollfast cruiser, with its working light and mudguard fenders in chrome, which he rode to the woods beyond Livingston Avenue. There the children would tramp around, playing games or picking blackberries until their hands turned purple. Other days, the pack of them would dash across yards or speed down Bradley, one behind the other, to the creek, where they stopped to catch tadpoles or look for snakes. Sometimes they rode down to the stables on Willowbrook Road to see the horses, stopping on the way back at Joe and Pat's candy store, where they drank Coca-Cola and ate candy, lollygagging on the corner until the Irish cop sent them home.

Many of the neighbors had also softened toward the nurses. With the advent of a cure, the women in white were no longer seen as a contagion, and it was impossible to deny the vibrancy they had brought to the once-desolate area. Doors were unlocked and windows stayed open; in the summers, kids roamed freely from house to house.

"No one talked about color," Forest recalled. "No one."

Until he was a teenager, Edna's son believed he was Italian. "Some of my Italian friends were darker than me," he said.

His mother never bothered to correct him.

Edna became known in the neighborhood as "Mother Goose." She loved to cook, and on her days off, she invited people to her backyard and served up platters of sweet potatoes, string beans, collard greens, spaghetti, and her famous fried chicken, made from chickens she had raised. Americus, who had finished nursing school and was working in the city, made the desserts: peach cobbler and sweet potato pie.

Edna's very favorite day to cook was Christmas. Even after Forest Sr. died, she insisted on putting up a magnificent tree and hanging every card she received. There were hundreds of them, and their images—angels, poinsettias, gold-glitter candles, Santa Claus, trees with garlands, glowing fireplaces, little drummer boys—turned the room into a Christmas wonderland.

Many of the cards came from family and friends, but most of them were sent by former patients. In careful handwriting, they wished Edna a Merry Christmas. And then—invoking a term coined by some patients for the nurses who had cared for them when others wouldn't—they expressed their gratitude: "You are my Black Angel."

❖

Epilogue

At night, the sky above Sea View is coal black, and the pavilions, no longer lit, are indistinguishable from the landscape. Inside the buildings, the wards have decayed, and in recent years, workers removed most of the beds and wheelchairs, desks and bookshelves and medical equipment. They swept shelves, tossing trays and medicine and bandages into large bins; whatever missed the containers or fell to the side remained on the floor, creating mismatched piles, remnants of a bygone time. In the basement, they overturned filing cabinets, spilling tens of thousands of medicals records onto the floor. From end to end, the folders sprawled, knee-deep, one life heaped upon another. Rain fell and seeped in and turned the pages to pulp.

Today the buildings continue to deteriorate; whatever windows remain dangle from their frames, and entire floors have collapsed. Now, sometimes at night, Virginia hears the patrol dogs barking, and the voices of urban explorers and curious teens scouring the abandoned buildings and acres of woods for stories of ghosts and witches and child killers with names like Cropsy and the "Gray Man." Maybe the Bone Man too.

The former Sea View nurse recently turned ninety-one, and believes she's "the last living Black Angel." After a long career in nursing and fighting for labor rights, she finally retired in 1995. When she moved back to the restored nurses' residence in 2008, and saw the pavilions and the skeleton of the children's hospital every day, she began to crystallize what her aunt Edna and all the women had accomplished.

"They helped cure tuberculosis," she said, "and close down the hospital."

In 1961, the last patient walked out of Sea View Hospital, a mere decade after the start of the isoniazid trial. Since then, the drug has become the gold standard for treatment. In 1955, Edward Robitzek and Irving Selikoff, together with scientist Carl Muschenheim from Hoffmann–La Roche and Walsh McDermott, were awarded the Albert Lasker Clinical Medical Award, also known as the "American Nobel," for their medical research on isoniazid drugs.

Dr. Robitzek eventually remarried and, together with his second wife, raised his sons while running a successful private practice and continuing to volunteer his time, this time at the Mariners Hospital. He retired in 1973 to Baltimore, where he lived the rest of his life.

But through all their work and research, the doctors and nurses live on. Unlike smallpox, tuberculosis has not been vanquished: it remains the second leading infectious disease in the world, responsible for over 1.5 million deaths annually. Isoniazid has blunted the bacteria's effects; they are no longer as powerful, and since 2000, the combination therapy has saved 66 million lives. But the microbe remains resistant and elusive, and scientists are always looking for new ways to understand it. Now that COVID-19 has shaken the world, they have turned to the ancient disease to try to conquer this one.

For Virginia, all the progress brings joy, and she often wishes that her aunt Edna and the other nurses could see the legacy they created. After Sea View, Edna Sutton found another nursing job and remained active in her church and in her community: she started a nurses' club and was a card-carrying member of the Urban League, the NAACP, and the ANA. She hosted fundraisers for scholarships at her home so that Black women could attend university. She also brought up more family: cousins and nieces and nephews. Americus received her nursing degree from the St. Philip School of Nursing in Virginia. Though she almost married twice, both engagements ended in tragedy when her fiancés died unexpectedly, and so, believing it "wasn't meant to be," she remained single, living with Edna all her life. Forest Jr. married and then served in the navy during the Vietnam War.

On December 22, 1988, Edna was admitted to the hospital for cancer; it was the first year she didn't put up a tree. She died on Christmas Eve and was laid to rest beside her husband in Frederick Douglass Memorial Park.

Mamie Blair, now Mamie Daniels, has never forgotten Sea View or the nurses or the disease that almost robbed her of life. She turned ninety at the height of the COVID-19 pandemic. After being released from Sea View, she married and had three daughters and helped her mother, Ruby Lee, establish a soup kitchen on Staten Island. Today she lives in Florida, but Staten Island is never far from her mind: once a week, she participates in a virtual food pantry in her old community and attends her Staten Island church via Zoom. She, like so many others, will always be grateful for the sacrifice the nurses made. "They and God are why I'm alive," she said.

And finally, Missouria. She left Sea View in 1961 and spent the rest of her career as a private-duty nurse. In the early 1980s, after almost fifty years in the profession, she retired her nurse whites. But she kept working, continuing her professional duty by spending part of her day tending to people in the neighborhood, foremost Mr. Cofano, the now bald and stout Italian man who'd originated the petition in 1944 to prevent her from moving onto the street.

For years following the petition, he scowled and side-glanced her, and then one day while she was gardening, he noticed her and nodded. She nodded back, and some part deep inside him, the one that told him she was ugly and bad because she was a Black woman, broke. And although vestiges of his former self remained—he never apologized or acknowledged the petition or his searing glances or years of harassment—Mr. Cofano came to like Missouria.

As the decades slipped by, they became friendly. Every day they met and stood on the edge of the lawn talking plants and gardening and growing beautiful things as the world around them shifted and changed.

Wheeler Avenue now teemed with new people and new houses. Mr. Cofano grew older, and his wife died, leaving him alone with his adopted disabled daughter; now he no longer cared who lived on the block. One morning during the AIDS crisis, Mr. Cofano fell to the floor, and the ambulance came and took him away, and modern medicine saved his life. But it couldn't fix the damage to his heart. He returned home half paralyzed, confined to a wheelchair.

Missouria noticed he stopped coming outside, and days after the doctors sent him home, she did something that forty years ago was unthinkable. She knocked on the door, and he called her inside, where she found him in the wheelchair. The old man, thin and frail, his body crooked and slacking to one side, looked at her and told her to sit down.

Every day, Missouria crossed the street with her stethoscope, thermometer, and blood pressure cuff and took Mr. Cofano's vitals. She talked with him and told him she was "across the street" if he needed anything.

Stepping out of his house, she walked over to Miss Claire Mc-Kinney, who lived at 181 Wheeler Avenue in a small yellow house with a fenced-in front yard that was really just a knot of weeds. Miss Mc-Kinney, once tall and strong, had also worked at Sea View as nurse. She was kind and funny and used to throw open the doors to her home, cooking and inviting everyone in the neighborhood to come and eat. But she harbored a secret: she was an alcoholic, and one morning her heart, weakened from years of drinking, slowed, and the blood stopped flowing. The ambulance came, and as it had with Mr. Cofano took her to the hospital, where modern medicine saved her life too. But she returned home a shell of herself. Without her alcohol, she closed the front door and became reclusive and depressed, except when Missouria arrived to check on her and bring her food.

After her daily visit with Miss McKinney, Missouria gathered her bag, passed the front yard with its weeds, turned right, and began walking up the block to the sound of too many cars passing.

Everything was so fast now: there were cordless phones and computers and Xerox machines that made carbon copies obsolete. Cameras were disposable. And every day, transatlantic flights flew thousands of people to Europe. On television, there was a twenty-four-hour music channel, and doctors could now implant an artificial heart, although not for Miss McKinney or Mr. Cofano. There was also integration for Missouria's people. When she returned to Clinton, South Carolina, to care for her mother, there were no more plaques announcing "Coloreds Only," "No Negros," and "White Section." The signs had been taken down, but their square imprints on walls and entrances remained. She hoped that in the ensuing years, those, too, would fade away, but for now she was happy.

When Mr. Cofano died in 1988, she wept, her family said, mourning him as if he had never wronged her. For Missouria Louvinia Meadows-Walker, the world was never a bad place, just one that needed fixing. And on March 23, 2007, before she died, she cried out to her God, and then closed her eyes, knowing that she and Edna and Miss Demby, Miss Evans, Clemmie, Miss Gillespie, Janie, Virginia, Miss R., Curlene Jennings, Marjorie Tucker Reed, and all the other Black Angels had been part of something profound, something that made the world better. As for herself, she had initiated and seen justice, as much as one human being could hope to see.

Acknowledgments

❖

I began writing this book seven years ago, and in that time, countless people have supported me. I'm grateful to them for showing up in many ways, and although I don't have the space to thank everyone, please know you've all had a hand in helping me arrive at this moment.

Re-creating the story of the nurses was a painstaking and monumental task and would not have been possible without the help of their families, who so graciously allowed me to step into their lives. They were generous with their time and patient with my constant questions asking them to recall things good and bad, triumphant and painful. Never once in all these years did they turn me away. Time and again, they put their energy, will, and hopes into this story, trusting me, encouraging me, and inspiring me so this piece of history could see the light of day. They are the heart and soul of this book and have my endless gratitude. It's been an honor to know them, and I hope that I've done justice to the legacy of their ancestors.

To start, I'm deeply grateful to Virginia Allen, the catalyst for this book. From the beginning, you championed this project, wanting the story of your aunt and all the Black Angels to reach beyond Staten Island and into the wider world. Your candor, dedication, and determination made so much of this possible, and I'm eternally grateful that you trusted me with it. I hope it's what you envisioned.

Bernice Allenye is one of the most exceptional human beings I know. Thank you for your honesty, support, and never-ending optimism; for the years you spent talking to me about Missouria and her life and for bringing me to Clinton, South Carolina. I'm humbled by your resolve to track down photos, documents, and facts and to connect me with anyone who knew Missouria, and I am blessed that our paths crossed, that in this vast, vast world we found each other.

Thank you to George Meadows, Caroline Gray, Plaze Meadows, Pearl Gist, and Flossie, and to Missouria's extended family, the Stoddards, whose recollections were invaluable for reconstructing her story and life in Clinton.

Forest W. Ballard Jr., thank you for your good humor, enthusiasm, and devotion to answering years of questions about your mom and dad, Edna and Forest Senior. Sala Udin-Howze, thank you for hosting me in Pittsburgh and telling me about your aunt Edna, your mother (her sister), and Black history, especially Black southern history and the civil rights movements.

I'm indebted to the other Black Angels who shared their memories of Sea View: Curlene Jennings, Novella Gumms, Thurston Groomes, and the late Marjorie Tucker Reed. Also to Kate Gillespie's family (Mia, Lisa, and Iman), to James Williams and Janie Yvonne Williams (family of Nurse Janie B. Shirley), and to Elizabeth Maureen Plair (who shared her remarkable grandmother Clemmie Philips with me). I owe much gratitude to Rock Spinelli, whose detailed anecdotes of working on the men's ward at Sea View with Clemmie and Missouria were instrumental for capturing the atmosphere and conditions of the hospital. I'm so sad that you will not read this book.

John Robitzek, what a generous man you are. Thank you for everything you've done throughout the years: for your time and tolerance in indulging all my questions (even the hypothetical ones), for sharing your family archives, and for the many hours of conversation about your wonderful father.

To the trial patients and their families: I will always be astounded that I found you. My gratitude for your willingness to sit down with me and remember some of the darkest and most painful days of your life is endless. Thank you to the family of Lena Meller—her granddaughter, Caroline Suhoza Wyman, and daughter Evelyn Wyman, who recalled the tragic story of her mother and allowed me to read the heartbreaking letters Lena wrote while dying at Sea View. Thank you to Milagros Delfaus, who put aside the shame she carried for more than seventy years by telling me (and her family) the story of how she would have died at Sea View had it not been for the trial. Nydia Dos-Santos, from the moment you heard about this story and your mother Milagros's role, you advocated for it. And thanks to Mamie Daniels (née Blair), whose razor-sharp memory and willingness to share how she survived tuberculosis informed many parts of this book.

Several doctors and scientists in the field of tuberculosis and beyond deserve enormous thanks: Neil Schluger, Sanghyuk Shin, Josh Leitner, Lee B. Reichman, Lenore Lakshmanan, and Vivian Schatz, the late widow of Albert Schatz. To Eileen Melnik Gupta, thank you for your ongoing support, friendship, and readiness to share your expertise about nursing, and for helping to navigate the perils of accessing Sea View and its museum. Dr. Adam Biggs, African American historian and historian of medicine, thank you for reading parts of this book and for the long conversations on Black history, medicine, Harlem Hospital, New York City, and the Jim Crowism of the North.

Heartfelt thanks to Dr. Debbie-Ann Paige, African American genealogist and Staten Island historian who loved this story from the outset; your insights, opinions, and knowledge of Black history and Staten Island history were indispensable. I'm forever grateful for your intellectual generosity, for always answering my questions, and for reading a draft of this book and offering your thoughts.

Many others generously gave their time to be interviewed for this book, and their stories helped to re-create Sea View and the nurses' daily life: Marion Walker, Jim Romano, Zonease Porter, Rollie Joe, Pamela Washington, Pat Garner Wilson, Penny Watkins, Tammi Beale, Mitchell Reese, Felix Cuestas, Otis Johnson, Elaine Smith,

Pamela Adamo, Leah Bennett, Sylvia D'Alessandro, Richard Greene, George Taylor, Mildred Norman, and the late Sonja Coryant, whose mother almost died at Sea View.

I owe deep gratitude to the many librarians and archivists who were eager to help me: Gabrielle Leone at the Staten Island Museum, Ken Cobb at the New York City Municipal Archives, Carli DeFillo at Historic Richmond Town collections, Lewis Wyman at the Library of Congress, the Georgia Historical Society in Savannah, the Laurens County Library in South Carolina, Sea View Museum, the Schomburg Center for Research in Black Culture, Howard University, the Hoffmann–LaRoche archivists, the New York Public Library Center for Research in the Humanities, and Arlene Shaner at the New York Academy of Medicine, who always went a step beyond.

Thank you to everyone who, over the years, has read this book (in whole or in part) and offered their insights: Laurie Gwen Shapiro, Jason Fagone, Gareth Cook, and Kate Rodemann—your opinions and insights into this story were invaluable. And to Tal McThenia, my research assistant, who dove into this project with joy and enthusiasm. I owe a deep gratitude to my dear friend Sarah Rose, who spent infinite hours talking to me about so many things, including this story and the craft of writing. You were a constant in my life and your support was invaluable—it kept me going. Here's to you and to many more long nights talking about everything and nothing.

My agent, Larry Weissman, is hands down the best. You have my endless gratitude for believing in this story and book when no one else did. And thanks to Sascha Alper for your support and intuition. But mostly thanks to both of you for being exceptional human beings and for understanding that sometimes things take a little longer.

Similar to many books, mine struggled, hiccupping along toward publication for seven years. One house and five editors later, I feel beyond grateful to finally finish this journey at Putnam with my editor, Michelle Howry, and the team there: Ashley Di Dio, Sally Kim, Alexis Welby, Ashley McClay, Emily Mileham, Maija Baldauf,

Anthony Ramondo, Monica Cordova, and Tiffany Estreicher, who worked resolutely to ensure this book entered the world in a spectacular manner.

Georgia Befanis, my oldest friend, thanks for everything you've done for me. Amanda Moon, thank you for the Catskills retreats and long conversations about life, kids, and Fabio, and for watching late-night videos from 1925 on chest surgeries. Tess, thank you for your love, tireless encouragement, and constant reminders that this story matters. And thanks to Bill and Dainty.

I'm fortunate to have so many great friends who always cheered me on: Lisa Pilato, Alison Wall, Susie Paige, Jimmy, Cari, Johnny, Michele, Stephanie Seymour, Tanya Radovic, Charles Demm, Alki, Nikki, Stephen Prothero, Peter Hawkins, Martyn, Jenn, Andrea Macaluso, Maria Skopos, Kristina, Phil, Kara, and Brendan. Your constant support cannot be overstated. And thank you to Jana, Terrance, Natascha, Corinna, Brad, Nicole Smith, Sarah Yamada, and Sarah Patten for welcoming us to Asheville.

My family deserves be immortalized for all the years of standing by me while I wrote this book. My brother, Arthur, my greatest champion, my best friend, thank you for a lifetime of support. My late aunt Chris and my aunt Helen, my literary partner. My cousin George, my other brother, you have never told me I couldn't. Joy, thank you for your never-ending support, and Steve, thank you for giving me a refuge to write and always asking about this story. And to Vasiliki, Chad, Andrea, Tom, Tara, Stephanie, Stephen, Nancy, Tony, Vasili, Caitlyn, and my beautiful niece, Ruth Michael, what joy you've brought with your presence. To my grandparents, whose endless stories about immigrating to America informed and shaped so much of my worldview. I am fortunate for the many years I got to spend listening to them. To my beautiful mother for her unwavering belief in me, for teaching me that words matter and encouraging me to love them and write them, and to my father, who loved people and taught me to listen to their stories. You are both so deeply missed.

Thanks to Buddy "Badoo," the best little dog in the world. I often wonder who rescued who.

To Brad, this story has infiltrated your life! You've never failed to give me your insight, talking me through all the brick walls and helping me to thread the narrative strands. And when the manuscript finally took shape, you read it far too many times. I am grateful for all your love and support and for your belief in me as a storyteller.

And finally, to Grace, my girl, my heart and soul. I started this when you were five and now you are twelve. Thank you for your patience all these years, for the cards and notes cheering me on, and for filling my life with boundless joy. I love you, sweet girl. I am so very lucky.

Notes

The notes are organized by chapter, and the extent of the sources far exceeds the available space in this book, and so, I have abbreviated them, choosing the most significant and valuable ones to cite. For the complete source list, please visit mariasmilios.com.

Prologue · Remembrance of Things Past

xvii Sources for this chapter include interviews with Virginia Allen.

xix **killed over 5.6 million people:** Based on statistics in Godias J. Drolet and Anthony M. Lowell, *A Half Century's Progress Against Tuberculosis in New York City, 1900 to 1950* (New York: New York Tuberculosis and Health Association, 1952).

xix **sheep vaccine, and Congo red:** See Edward H. Robitzek, "Impressions of Sea View Hospital," *Sea View Hospital Bulletin* 18, no. 1 (1960).

Chapter 1 · The Call for Nurses

3 Sources for this chapter include interviews with Virginia Allen, Bernice Alleyne, Forest Ballard Jr., and Rock Spinelli. Sources for the descriptions of the tenements and the Lower East Side: Jacob A. Riis, *How the Other Half Lives: Studies Among the Tenements of New York*, 2nd ed. (Boston: Bedford/St. Martin's, 2011); Luc Sante, *Low Life: Lures and Snares of Old New York* (New York: Farrar, Straus and Giroux, 1991); Raymond Bial, *Tenement: Immigrant Life on the Lower East Side* (Boston: Houghton Mifflin, 2002); and Ernest Poole, *The Plague in Its Stronghold: Tuberculosis in the New York Tenement* (New York: University Settlement, 1903).

3 **uniforms and walked out:** The Black Angels passed down the story about white nurses quitting to their families. Sources corroborate the story and describe the city's plan to replace them with Black nurses from Harlem and Lincoln Hospitals and beyond New York City: see "Baltimorean Gets Job in New York Hospital," *Baltimore Afro-American*, April 5, 1930, A12; and "22 Sea View Posts Handed to Nurses," *New York Amsterdam News*, April 30, 1930, 13. For more on white nurses refusing to work alongside Black nurses, see Darlene Clark Hine, *Black Women in White: Racial Conflict and Cooperation in the Nursing Profession, 1890–1950* (Indianapolis: Indiana University Press, 1989), 98–101.

4 store the vaccine: Rebecca Onion, "The Dramatic Push to Immunize Children Against Diph-theria Got a Boost from a Sled Dog Named Balto," *Slate*, February 9, 2021, https://slate.com/technology/2021/02/balto-diphtheria-immunization-drive-1929.html.

5 "fever-breeding structures": Riis, *How the Other Half Lives*, 12.

6 found their cause: Poole, *The Plague in Its Stronghold*, 6–17.

6 stairwells and fire escapes: Poole, *The Plague in Its Stronghold*, 309.

6 "locus of disease": Stefano Morello, "The Lung Block: A New York City Slum and Its Forgotten Italian Community," New Media Lab, 2023, https://newmedialab.cuny.edu/project/the-lung-block-a-new-york-city-slum-and-its-forgotten-italian-community/.

6 "great business": Quoted in Phillip Lopate, *Waterfront: A Walk Around Manhattan* (New York: Anchor Books, 2008), 275–76.

6 "mother of pestilence": Selman A. Waksman, *The Conquest of Tuberculosis* (Los Angeles: University of California Press, 1964), 9.

7 "in a single generation": Hermann Biggs quoted in Thomas Goetz, *The Remedy: Robert Koch, Arthur Conan Doyle, and the Quest to Cure Tuberculosis* (New York: Gotham Books, 2014), 208.

7 "caused by a germ": Arthur Bushel, *Chronology of New York City Department of Health, 1655–1966* (New York: New York City Department of Health, 1966), x.

7 "tracked, evaluated, and combated": Goetz, *The Remedy*, 208.

8 children living in the slums: "Health Clown Has School Field Day," *New York Times*, June 25, 1922.

8 far away from Manhattan: See S. Adolphus Knopf, *Tuberculosis as a Disease of the Masses and How to Combat It*, 7th ed. (New York: The Survey, 1911), 84–86.

8 "worth to the municipality $1,500": "Municipal Hospital Planned for Care of Consumptives," *New York Times*, March 15, 1903, 28. The following account of the cost-benefit analysis that drove the construction of Sea View is based on this article.

9 "greater house of many mansions": The source for this account of Sea View's founding is "City's $4,000,000 Hospital Now Ready," *New York Times*, November 13, 1913, 6.

9 little more than five thousand: Drolet and Lowell, *A Half Century's Progress Against Tuberculosis*, 128.

9 the fourth globally: Drolet and Lowell, *A Half Century's Progress Against Tuberculosis*, 20.

10 to almost 327,000 in 1929: "Demographic History of New York City," Wikipedia, https://en.wikipedia.org/iki/Demographic_history_of_New_York_City.

11 numbers were dwindling: "Nurse Discrimination in New York City Attacked," *Pittsburgh Courier*, November 12, 1932, A3; "In Interest of Negro Nurses," *New York Amsterdam News*, March 9, 1935, 7; "Want Nurses to Get Rights," *New York Amsterdam News*, April 24, 1937, 1. Also see Hine, *Black Women in White*, 138.

11 deeper into the American South: Sources for "the call" were ephemeral (flyers, newspaper ads, notes on bulletin boards, and word of mouth); it is widely attested in oral history.

Chapter 2 · The Preacher's Daughter

12 Sources for this chapter include interviews with Virginia Allen, Forest Ballard Jr., Sala Udin-Howze, Henry Williams, Pearl Williams, Marion Walker, and Vaughnette Goode-Walker; dozens of articles in *The Savannah Tribune* (1900–1921); and experiential research in Savannah.

William H. Chafe, Raymond Gavins, and Robert Korstad, eds., *Remembering Jim Crow: African Americans Tell About Life in the Segregated South* (New York: New Press, 2001); Nell Irvin Painter, *Exodusters: Black Migration to Kansas after Reconstruction* (New York: W. W. Norton, 1992); John Dittmer, *Black Georgia in the Progressive Era, 1900–1920, Blacks in the New World* (Chicago: University of Illinois Press, 1980); Farah Jasmine Griffin, *"Who Set You Flowin'?": The African-American Migration Narrative* (New York: Oxford University Press, 1995); Charles Lwanga Hoskins, *W. W. Law and His People: A Timeline and Biographies* (Savannah, GA: Gullah Press, 2013); and Leon F. Litwack, *Trouble in the Mind: Black Southerners in the Age of Jim Crow* (New York: Vintage Books, 1999). For further sources, see the bibliography.

14   **shrouds to bury the dead:** Georgia Infirmary sources include *Minutes 1916–1926, Georgia Infirmary Papers,* Item MS301, Vol. 3, Georgia Infirmary, 1832, Georgia Historical Society; *Lillian Chaplin Bragg Papers* (folder 47: Georgia Infirmary), Georgia Historical Society; *Insurance Maps of Savannah, GA,* Vol. 2, 1931 (New York: Sanborn Map Company, 1916 with paste-ins to 1944); and *Insurance Maps of Savannah, GA* (New York: Sanborn-Pervis Map Company, 1898 with paste-ins to 1913). Also see Hine, *Black Women in White,* 47–62.

14   **"greatly in the end":** Quoted in Hoskins, *W. W. Law and His People,* 74.

15   **"living in the center":** Quoted in Dittmer, *Black Georgia in the Progressive Era,* 10.

15   **crawl and walk:** See Litwack, *Trouble in the Mind,* 336–338.

15   **Wilkes County, Georgia:** Richmond's recorded birth date varies from 1862 to 1871; however, two independent documents indicate 1863. He also changed his name from Richard to Richmond and later used initials, R.V., but regardless of his first name, Sutton is consistently listed with Amy, his wife, and the children, including Edna. See 1870 United States Federal Census, Georgia, Pike Country, "Richmond Sutton," and the 1910 United States Federal Census, Georgia, Savannah, Chatham Ward 1, "Richard V. Sutton," both included at Ancestry.com.

15   **"become something more":** Virginia Allen and Forest both told me that Edna's parents, especially her father, were determined to make something of their lives so that their kids could have a better life than they did.

15   **two decades his junior:** Georgia, US, Marriage Records from Select Counties, 1828–1978, Chatham, Marriages, Book N, 1899–1901, "Amy B V Royal," Ancestry.com.

15   **wealthy white families:** Richmond's job is listed as a carpenter, confirmed by an interview with MW and the 1910 United States Federal Census, Georgia, Savannah, Chatham Ward 1, "Richard V. Sutton," Ancestry.com. Edna's birthplace was likely 779 East Gwinnett Street in the center of a shantytown settlement, and at that time, Richmond's job is listed in the 1901 city directory as "P.S.," which stands for Plant System, a railroad that ran out of a depot on the east side of Savannah, opening a gateway to Southern Georgia, Alabama, South Carolina, and Florida. Richmond was a "lab," a laborer. He could have worked in the yards, which were close to his neighborhood. Perhaps he was a fireman on a steam engine or a member of a section gang—groups of men who maintained a stretch of track.

16   **pastors and itinerant preachers:** 1907 US City Directories, 1822–1995, "Richard Sutton," Ancestry.com.

16   **preaching around Savannah:** Many articles from *The Savannah Tribune* from 1912 to 1921 document Sutton's ministry activities.

16   **even tourists came:** "Grace Baptist Church. Rev. R.V. Sutton, Pastor Res. 719 W. 38th Street," *Savannah Tribune,* November 23, 1918, 2.

16   **"gripped the audience":** "Among the Churches. Christian Endeavor League Organized," *Savannah Tribune,* May 20, 1916, x.

16 Chatham County jail: "Death Sentence Prisoner Baptized," *The Savannah Tribune*, December 7, 1912, 1.

17 becoming a surgeon: Virginia Allen told me Edna's original dream was "to become a surgeon."

17 "dumb and stupid": Rebecca Logan, "I Remember That Day," National Education Association, May 11, 2019, https://www.nea.org/advocating-for-change/new-from-nea/i-remember-day?fb clid=IwAR3KoUVfKXX56xl4bk-9CgZ1M3ZeZyscDqsFg9y0-ulhwN3kO2by8NAM8iA.

17 a required language: Sources regarding the Beach Institute include B. D. Hodges, "Beach Institute" (Georgia Historical Society, vertical file, folder 1), published as a pamphlet for the American Missionary Association in 1909; *The American Missionary* 68 (April 1914): 30–32; D. E. Emerson, "The Beach Institute, Savannah, Georgia in 1869 and in 1914" (Georgia Historical Society, vertical file, folder 1); and Hoskins, *W. W. Law and His People*, 94.

18 "To Live, to Serve": "Senior Tree Day at Dorchester Academy," *The Savannah Tribune*, April 24, 1920, 6.

18 with 6,807 white ones: Hine, *Black Women in White*, 59.

19 were fleeing the South: Isabel Wilkerson, "The Long-Lasting Legacy of the Great Migration," *Smithsonian*, September 2016, https://www.smithsonianmag.com/history/long-lasting-legacy -great-migration-180960118. For a complete historical account, see Isabel Wilkerson, *The Warmth of Other Suns: The Epic Story of America's Great Migration* (New York: Vintage Books, 2010).

20 a diphtheria outbreak: Onion, "The Dramatic Push to Immunize."

20 different from her own: According to her family, Edna was a natural teacher and intellectually generous. She, like her parents, believed that education was the gateway to a better life, one with more opportunities. She also believed that knowledge "fed the mind" and roused people to become better people.

21 "horrible conditions": Quoted in Hoskins, *W. W. Law and His People*, 98–106.

Chapter 3 · The Wager

22 Sources for this chapter include interviews with Virginia Allen, Forest Ballard Jr., Sala Udin-Howze, Pearl Williams, Henry Williams, Marion Walker, Vaughnette Goode-Walker, Bernice Alleyne, Mamie Daniels, Elizabeth Plair, and Debbie-Ann Paige.

22 "last hired, first fired": Christopher Klein, "Last Hired, First Fired: How the Great Depression Affected African Americans," History.com, August 31, 2018, https://www.history.com/news /last-hired-first-fired-how-the-great-depression-affected-african-americans. For an in-depth history of African Americans and employment in the Great Depression, see Greenberg, *Or Does It Explode?*

24 cheered the local team: Hoskins, *W. W. Law and His People*, 98.

24 most of her neighbors: The neighbors are listed in the 1920 United States Federal Census, Georgia, Savannah, Chatham Ward 1, "Richard V. Sutton," Ancestry.com.

24 refused to treat him: Hoskins, *W. W. Law and His People*, 92.

26 "white boy comes along": "The Great Migration," Smithsonian American Art Museum, https:// americanexperience.si.edu/wp-content/uploads/2014/07/The-Great-Migration.pdf.

26 "with the whites": Emmet J. Scott, "More Letters of Negro Migrants of 1916–1918," *The Journal of Negro History* 4, no. 4 (October 1919): 49.

27 in the service of God: Forest Jr. confirmed that his mother felt called to Sea View through the words of Matthew and this parable, which she would often relate to him.

27 for Black children: "Young, Brown, Phelps, and Spingarn Education Campus," DC Historic Sites, https://historicsites.dcpreservation.org/items/show/877.

28 "troublesome" or oppositional: See Hine, *Black Women in White*, 47–50, for hiring requirements and qualifications for acceptance into nursing schools.

29 impact of a collision: "One-Way Ticket: Jacob Lawrence's Migration Series," MoMA, https://www.moma.org/interactives/exhibitions/2015/onewayticket/panel/6/.

Chapter 4 · Harlem

31 Sources for this chapter include Virginia Allen, Forest Ballard Jr., Mildred Norman, Dr. Adam Biggs, Thurston Groomes, Bernice Alleyne, Mia and Lisa Gillespie, and Elizabeth Plair.

32 "Promised Land to Negros everywhere": Paula J. Massood, *Making a Promised Land: Harlem in Twentieth-Century Photography and Film* (New Brunswick, NJ: Rutgers University Press, 2013), 55.

32 "joy and culture": Alain Locke, "Enter the New Negro," *National Humanities Center Resource Toolbox: The Making of African American Identity*, 1–6, http://nationalhumanitiescenter.org/pds/maai3/migrations/text8/lockenewnegro.pdf.

33 "dwelling area in the world": Greenberg, *Or Does It Explode?*, 31.

33 ten a day: Stephen Robertson, "Traffic Accidents in 1920s Harlem," *Digital Harlem Blog*, April 1, 2010, https://drstephenrobertson.com/digitalharlemblog/maps/traffic-accidents-in-1920s-harlem/.

34 "Harlem's Bowery": Information on rents and Lenox Avenue is from Wallace Thurman, "A Negro Life in New York's Harlem: A Lively Picture of a Popular and Interesting Section," *Haldeman-Julius Quarterly* 2, (October–December 1927), 132–45.

35 "and dancing waiters": For the location and description of Harlem's clubs, see Rebecca Onion, "An Affectionate 1932 Illustrated Map of Harlem Nightlife," *Slate*, April 15, 2016, https://slate.com/human-interest/2016/04/e-simms-campbell-s-1932-illustrated-map-of-harlem-nightlife.html.

35–36 "raised their wages any": David Levering Lewis, ed., *The Portable Harlem Renaissance Reader* (New York: Penguin Books, 1994), 80.

36 it had changed: This change in staff began in 1917, when the hospital hired its first Black nurses, and then in 1919 it hired its first Black doctor, Louis T. Wright. It was also around this time that the demographic of patients shifted as well. See Adam Biggs, "Desegregating Harlem Hospital: A Centennial," NYAM: History of Medicine and Public Health, August 26, 2019, https://nyamcenterforhistory.org/2019/08/26/desegregating-harlem-hospital-a-centennial/.

36 making them sick: Arthur T. Davidson, "A History of Harlem Hospital," *Journal of the National Medical Association* 56, no. 5 (September 1957), 1–9. For a complete and comprehensive history of the hospital, see M. Alisan Bennett, "A History of the Harlem Hospital School of Nursing: Its Emergence and Development in a Changing Urban Community, 1923–1973" (PhD diss., Columbia University Teachers College, 1984).

36 triple the rate of whites: See chart in Drolet and Lowell, *A Half Century's Progress Against Tuberculosis*, 130.

36 "most lethal ailments": Gilbert Osofsky, *Harlem: The Making of a Ghetto; Negro New York, 1890–1930*, 2nd ed. (Chicago: Elephant Paperback, 1996; first published 1963 by Harper Collins), 8.

37 "the Morgue": Claudia Maria Calhoon, "Tuberculosis, Race, and the Delivery of Health Care in Harlem, 1922–1939," *Radical History Review* 80 (Spring 2001): 106, 113.

37   "You should have come sooner": Interviews with Thurston Groomes, Sea View nurse and Harlem Hospital graduate, and Mildred Norman (September 8, 2017), former nurse at Harlem Hospital and historian and archivist for Harlem Hospital Center School of Nursing Alumni Association. During the interview, Mildred Norman also corroborated the appalling conditions at the hospital and the mistreatment of the nurses during Edna's time there in the 1920s and 1930s.

37   giving birth in vestibules: "Birth of Child in Vestibule Gives Rise to Bitter Criticism of Harlem Hospital Obstetrical Ward Methods," *New York Age*, April 9, 1927, 2. The following account of the baby's delivery is also taken from this article.

38   "but for humanity": "National Association of Colored Graduate Nurses Records, 1908–1958," *New York Public Library Archives and Manuscripts*, https://archives.nypl.org/scm/20744#de scriptive_identity, accessed on September 7, 2022.

40   "competent white direction": Hine, *Black Women in White*, 99–101.

40   susceptible to TB: See Bennett, *A History of Harlem Hospital*, 113–115.

40   "you were grounded": Interview with Thurston Groomes and Mildred Norman.

40   heckling and antagonizing them: See *The Complete Report of Mayor LaGuardia's Commission on the Harlem Riot of March 19, 1935* (New York: Arno Press and The New York Times, 1969), 98–99.

42   "position of supervisor": "Another Row at Harlem Hospital: Superintendent Calls Police to Arrest Nurse," *New Amsterdam News*, August 22, 1927, 3.

42   "changed and justice established": "Salaria Kea: Nurse and Freedom Fighter," New York State Nurses Association, https://www.nysna.org/salaria-kea-nurse-and-freedom-fighter#.Yxzrn SHMLlw.

42   free to leave: Adam Clayton Powell, Jr., "The Meek Turn Militant: Nurses' Pay in New York— White In, Negroes Out, Meanwhile Babies Die," *The New York Age*, December 1936, 14.

43   "could be done about it": The source for the following incident is "Salaria Kea: A Negro Nurse in Republican Spain," Abraham Lincoln Brigade Archives, https://alba-valb.org/resource/salaria -kea-a-negro-nurse-in-republican-spain/.

Chapter 5 · Contagion on the Island

46   borough, Staten Island: The re-creation of Edna's trip across the harbor came from interviews with Virginia Allen and Forest Ballard Jr. According to their reports, Edna loved sitting by windows in boats, cars, and trains, especially on the ferry, where she marveled at the landmarks going by.

47   set for breakfast: This account of Edna's bus ride also came from interviews with Virginia Allen and Forest Ballard Jr. Edna loved to write letters to her sister telling her, as Virginia said, "about everything in her life." Unfortunately all their correspondence has been lost.

48   past and the present: "Total Population New York City & Boroughs, 1900 to 2010," https:// www1.nyc.gov/assets/planning/download/pdf/data-maps/nyc-population/historical -population/nyc_total_pop_1900-2010.pdf.

48   others to breathe: Marjorie Tucker Reed, interview with StoryCorps, June 7, 2010 (call no. DDA0000865). In her interview, Reed recalled that the passengers on the 111 bus believed that the nurses were contaminated and, as a result, refused to sit beside them and looked at them with disdain.

48   for juvenile delinquents: For more on New York's harbor islands, see Robert Sullivan, "Our Lesser Islands," *Intelligencer*, August 19, 2019, https://nymag.com/intelligencer/2019/08 /touring-the-overlooked-islands-of-new-york-city.html.

48   "naked ugliness and horror": Greg Young and Tom Meyers, "Charles Dickens' Guide to New York City Low Life," Bowery Boys: New York City History, August 21, 2008, https://www.bow eryboyshistory.com/2008/08/charles-dickens-guide-to-new-york-city.html.

48   the most unwelcome, the Quarantine Station: Sources for this account are Kathryn Stephenson, "The Quarantine War: The Burning of the New York Marine Hospital in 1858," *Public Health Reports* 119, no. 1 (2004): 79–92; and Fielding H. Garrison, "The Destruction of the Quarantine Station on Staten Island in 1858," *Journal of Urban Health* 76, no. 3 (1999): 380–83.

49   "indecency and filthiness": Stephenson, "The Quarantine War," 83.

49   "most odious character": Stephenson, "The Quarantine War," 85.

49   "procure spiritous liquors": Stephenson, "The Quarantine War," 83.

49   "doors of the people": Stephenson, "The Quarantine War," 85.

49   "nuisance without delay": Stephenson, "The Quarantine War," 85.

50   "cut their hoses": Stephenson, "The Quarantine War," 86.

50   "jump out at them": Marjorie Tucker Reed, interview with StoryCorps, June 7, 2010.

Chapter 6 · The Most Magnificent Institution

52   Sources for Edna's experience on the wards and the general atmosphere of Sea View include interviews with Virginia Allen, Bernice Alleyne, Forest Ballard Jr., Debbie-Ann Paige, Rock Spinelli, Mamie Daniels, Milagros Delfaus, Sonya Coryant, John Robitzek, Curlene Jennings, and Peter Berczeller; New York City Landmarks Preservation Commission, *New York City Farm Colony—Sea View Hospital: Historic District Designation Report*, 1985; photos from the New York City Municipal Archives; and experiential research on the grounds.

54   seven small gables: From archival photos and the New York City Landmarks Preservation Commission, *New York City Farm Colony—Sea View Hospital.*

54   decent one nonetheless: Salary information taken from the 1932 City Record of the Department of Hospitals, Sea View Hospital.

54   could barely breathe: Description of the interior based on floor plans of the surgical ward in Raymond F. Almirall, "Plans and Purposes of 'Sea View' Tuberculosis Hospital," *Modern Hospital,* no. 2 (February 1914): 75.

55   training them was Miss R.: No one can remember the name of Edna's supervisor. Virginia Allen believes her last name started with an *R* but can't be sure.

55   "spied on them": Interview with Virginia Allen.

55   "don't want to get caught": Email from Rock Spinelli.

55   "the devil himself": Interview with Elizabeth Plair.

56   for skin grafts: Information on scissors from John Kirkup, "The History and Evolution of Surgical Instruments," *Royal College of Surgeons of England* 80 (1998): 422–32.

57   hundred miles an hour: Sarah Gibbens, "See How a Sneeze Can Launch Germs Much Farther Than 6 Feet," *National Geographic,* April 17, 2020, https://www.nationalgeographic.com/science /article/coronavirus-covid-sneeze-fluid-dynamics-in-photos.

57   cooped up at Sea View: Sea View patient medical cards confirm that patients often stayed for years.

57   bread with roaches: "Finds Ill Veterans in Sorry Plight," *New York Times,* October 23, 1922, 22; see also, "Hylan to Get Plea of Vets," *New York Age,* October 23, 1922, 2.

58   son of a cop: The sources for these stories are "Investigate a Suicide," *New York Times*, February 10, 1924, 23; "25 Hospital Aids Seized as Aliens," *New York Times*, March 7, 1924, 9; and "City Employees Held in Boys Murder Case," *New York Times*, July 17, 1924, 1.

59   "committed to my care": "Florence Nightingale Pledge," Nightingale's Nursing and Attendant Care Services, https://nightingalesnursing.net/florence-nightingale-pledge/.

59   drunks and Bowery bums: Jobs and names are recorded in Sea View Registry and Sea View patient cards.

60   souls of the dead: Sources for stories about Sea View's "ghosts" and the Bone Man include interviews with Rock Spinelli and Mamie Daniels.

61   "recovers at Sea View": "None Ever Cured at Sea View, Is Van Name Charge," *Evening World*, May 23, 1919, 5.

Chapter 7 · The Scourge

62   Sources for this chapter include interviews with Virginia Allen, Neil Schluger, and Rock Spinelli.

62   around her legs: Interview with Virginia Allen and archival photographs.

63   "a magnificent hospital": "City's $4,000,000 Hospital Now Ready," *New York Times*, November 13, 1913, 6.

63   as a surgeon: Alabama, Texas, and Virginia, US, Confederate Pensions, 1884–1958, "Charles Henry Perrow," Ancestry.com.

63   diphtheria, and tuberculosis: 1930 United States Federal Census, New York, Manhattan (Districts 1-250), District 0197, "Lorna Mitchell," Ancestry.com.

63–64 "discriminatory practices": "The Feminist Viewpoint," *New York Amsterdam News*, March 9, 1935, 7, ProQuest Historical Newspapers.

64   "a porcelain sculpture": Interview with Virginia Allen.

65   "until they seemed new": Interview with Rock Spinelli. Virginia Allen also confirms that sputum cups needed to be burned, which was the standard in hospitals dealing with infectious diseases.

65   perception in the 1930s: In a pre-antibiotic world, handwashing, diet, and abstinence from smoking and drinking were thought to be the best defense against disease—not masking or gowns. See Lorna Doone Mitchell, "Tuberculosis as an Occupational and Compensable Disease from the Standpoint of the Employee," *Transactions of the American Hospital Association Annual Conference* 41 (1939): 296–303.

65   "caring for the patient": Mitchell, "Tuberculosis as an Occupational and Compensable Disease," 301 (italics mine).

65   "and then some": Interview with Rock Spinelli.

66   "in our noses": Interview with Rock Spinelli; also correspondence with Peter Berczeller.

66   "the walls breathed bleach": Interview with Rock Spinelli; also correspondence with Peter Berczeller.

67   sit and exercise: For a full picture of sanatorium life, see Mark Caldwell, *The Last Crusade: The Way on Consumption, 1862–1954* (New York: Atheneum, 1988), 67–126.

67   "all thy heart": Interview with Rock Spinelli and Caldwell, *The Last Crusade*, 67–126.

69   "the Tubercule Bacilli": Mitchell, "Tuberculosis as an Occupational and Compensable Disease," 302.

69   "sufficient sleep": Mitchell, "Tuberculosis as an Occupational and Compensable Disease," 302.

69 scoffed at his recommendations: For more on using masks and gowns, see J. Arthur Myers and David Stewart, "Tuberculosis Among Nurses," *American Journal of Nursing* 32, no. 11 (November 1932): 1159–68.

70 "against the disease": Mitchell, "Tuberculosis as an Occupational and Compensable Disease," 301–302.

70 "overdeveloped nervous systems": Michael Coard, "Drapetomania: Compliant Blacks Sane, Resisting Blacks Insane," *Philadelphia Tribune*, March 15, 2019. For an in-depth reading of Cartwright's views, see Nancy Krieger, "Shades of Difference: Theoretical Underpinnings of the Medical Controversy on Black/White Differences in the United States, 1830–1870," https://journals.sagepub.com/doi/pdf/10.2190/DBY6-VDQ8-HME8-ME3R.

70 "race of men": Frank M. Snowden, *Epidemics and Society: From the Black Death to the Present* (New Haven, CT: Yale University Press, 2019), 285.

Chapter 8 · Elke

71 The story of Elke is based on a patient history from Sea View.

72 their lavish drapes: See "Hoovervilles," History.com, November 2, 2018, https://www.history.com/topics/great-depression/hoovervilles; also see T. H. Watkins, *The Hungry Years: A Narrative History of the Great Depression in America* (New York: Henry Holt, 1999); and James Gregory, "The Great Depression in Washington State," University of Washington, 2009, https://depts.washington.edu/depress/hooverville.shtml.

72 "houses of the 'Have Nots'": James Pasley, "Vintage Photos Show Central Park's Hoovervilles," *Insider,* September 4, 2020, https://www.insider.com/new-york-central-park-hooverville-great-depression-photos-2020-9.

73 cheer people during the Depression: Source for information about hats is Debbie Sessions, "1930s Hat Styles: Women's 30s Hat History," VintageDancer.com, May 16, 2018, https://vintagedancer.com/1930s/womens-1930s-hat-styles/.

74 "the Depression, nothing will": Sessions, "1930s Hat Styles."

75 "in a quiescent state": The story of Carson came from R. Y. Keers, "Two Forgotten Pioneers: James Carson and George Bodington," *Thorax* 35 (1980): 483–89, https://thorax.bmj.com/content/thoraxjnl/35/7/483.full.pdf.

75 "the human race": Keers, "Two Forgotten Pioneers."

75 "into the chest": Keers, "Two Forgotten Pioneers."

75 had been haphazard: Information on Forlanini is from Paolo Mazzarello, "A Physical Cure for Tuberculosis: Carlo Forlanini and the Invention of Therapeutic Pneumothorax," *Applied Sciences* 10, no. 9 (February 26, 2020): https://www.mdpi.com/2076-3417/10/9/3138.

75 surround the lungs: Information on complications is from T. G. Heaton, "Complications of Artificial Pneumothorax: A Review," *Canadian Medical Association Journal* 4 (October 1936): 399–405, https://www.ncbi.nlm.nih.gov/pmc/articles/PMC1561845/?page=6.

Chapter 9 · Vows

78 Sources for this chapter include interviews with Virginia Allen, Forest Ballard Jr., Bernice Alleyne, and Elizabeth Plair.

79 a neighborhood staple: The following account of Reiman's on payday and nightlife in Harlem is based on interviews with Virginia Allen, Bernice Alleyne, and Rock Spinelli.

82   was a fraught proposition: Colin J. Davis, "'Shape or Fight?': New York's Black Longshoremen, 1945–1961," *International Labor and Working-Class History* No. 62 (Fall 2002), *Class and Catastrophe: September 11 and Other Working-Class Disasters*, Cambridge University Press, 143–163, https://www.jstor.org/stable/27672812.

Chapter 10 · The Thoracoplasty

90   "turnover in personnel": "Improvements in Nursing," in *Report to the Commissioner of Health S. S. Goldwater from Morris A. Jacobs on the Improvements at Sea View from 1934–1937*, 19, Sea View Archives.

90   "the new regime": "Improvements in Nursing," in *Report to the Commissioner of Health*, 19.

90   from her mouth: The information about the thoracoplasty (pre-op, during, and post-op) came from Pol. N. Coryllos, "170 Cases of Thoracoplasty (307 Operations) for Pulmonary Tuberculosis Operated on from 1931 to 1933," *Journal of Thoratic Surgery* 3 (June 1934): 441–500.

92   "aid of Aesculapius": S. R. Lathan, "Caroline Hampton Halsted: The First to Use Rubber Gloves in the Operating Room," *Baylor University Medical Center* 4 (October 2010): 389–392, https://www.ncbi.nlm.nih.gov/pmc/articles/PMC2943454/.

92   doctors and nurses: See John G. Leyden, "The Strange Story of Rubber Gloves," *Washington Post*, November 27, 1990.

92   a bloated hand: Committee on Nursing Standards, Division of Nursing, Department of Hospitals, *Standard Nursing Procedures of the Department of Hospitals, City of New York* (New York: Macmillan, 1943), 92; and Carol R. Byerly, "Good Tuberculosis Women," in *"Good Tuberculosis Men": The Army Medical Department's Struggle with Tuberculosis* (Texas: Office of the Surgeon General Borden Institute, n.d.), 214.

94   multi-organ failure: For background on strep, see Sidrah Kanwai and Pradeep Vaitla, "Streptococcus pyogenes," *StatPearls*, August 1, 2022, https://www.ncbi.nlm.nih.gov/books/NBK554528/.

94–95 from strep-related illnesses: Thomas Hager, *The Demon under the Microscope: From Battlefield Hospitals to Nazi Labs, One Doctor's Heroic Search for the World's First Miracle Drug* (New York: Crown, 2006), 104.

95   a powerful germicide: All the postoperative information is from Coryllos, "170 Cases of Thoracoplasty (307 Operations).

Chapter 11 · The Movement

97   Sources for capturing the experience of Harlem in 1934 include Greenberg, *Or Does It Explode?* and articles in *The New York Age* and the *New York Amsterdam News* from 1934 to 1935.

97   "white man's job": Greenberg, *Or Does It Explode?*, 69–78.

98   "barter for 'slave wages'": Greenberg, *Or Does It Explode?*, 79. Also see Marvel Cook, "The Bronx Slave Trade (1950)," *Viewpoint*, October 2015, https://viewpointmag.com/2015/10/31/the-bronx-slave-market-1950/; and Makoroba Sow, "Help Wanted: The Bronx Slave Markets and the Exploitation of Black Women Domestic Workers," New York Public Library, April 15, 2022, https://www.nypl.org/blog/2022/04/15/bronx-slave-markets.

98   "a pig or a cow": Robert H. McNeill, "American, 1917–2005," MoMA, https://www.moma.org/artists/45744.

99   more Black staff: "Harlem to Act on Hospital Situation," *New York Amsterdam News*, April 19, 1933, 1; see also "Hospital Meeting Tomorrow Night," *New York Amsterdam News*, March 1, 1933, 1.

99 "the people's attorney": The following account comes from LaGuardia Community College, "Fiorello H. La Guardia, a Model Mayor?," LaGuardia and Wagner Archives, 2017, https://www.laguardiawagnerarchive.lagcc.cuny.edu/FILES_DOC/LAGUARDIA_FILES/NOTES/LaGLegacy_2017.pdf.

100 tens of thousands of dollars: See Hine, *Black Women in White*, 110–118.

101 admit Black nurses: See Marie O. Pitts Mosely, "Great Black Nurses Series: Estelle Massey Riddle Osborne," *ABNF Journal* 13, no. 5 (September–October 2002); "Estelle Riddle Osborne Papers 1943–1967," New York Public Library Archives and Manuscripts, https://archives.nypl.org/scm/20749; and "Celebrating Estelle Osborne, Nurse Trailblazer," NYU Rory Meyers College of Nursing (February 18, 2020), https://nursing.nyu.edu/news/celebrating-estelle-Riddle-Osborne-nurse-trailblazer.

101 "anything or anyone": Quoted in Hine, *Black Women in White*, 121.

101 doctors, and administrators: For the information on Staupers, see "Mabel Keaton Staupers (1890–1989) 1996 Inductee," *Online Journal of Issues in Nursing*, http://ojin.nursingworld.org/FunctionalMenuCategories/AboutANA/Honoring-Nurses/NationalAwardsProgram/Hall ofFame/19962000Inductees/stauperm5584.html; Candace Staten, "Mabel Keaton Staupers (1890–1989)," BlackPast, March 31, 2011, www.blackpast.org/african-american-history/staupers-mabel-keaton-1890-1989; and "Mabel Keaton Staupers, R.N., 1890–," *Journal of the National Medical Association* 61, no. 2 (1969): 198–99.

101 "profession of nursing": The following account is based on Hine, *Black Women in White*, 110–21.

101 "long way to go": All of Haupt's quotes in this paragraph are from Hine, *Black Women in White*, 112–14.

102 "You Can't Work": Information about Harlem's "Don't Buy Where You Can't Work" movement is from Christine Anderson, "'Don't Buy Where You Can't Work': Protest and Riot in Harlem, 1932–1935" (master's thesis, City University of New York, 2019), https://academicworks.cuny.edu/cgi/viewcontent.cgi?article=1491&context=hc_sas_etds.

103 "L. M. Blumstein": Image of flyer is from Course Hero, https://www.coursehero.com/tutors-problems/US-History/21847340-Part1-Base-on-the-image-above-1-Based-on-the-flyer-above-what-did-th/.

103 triumphantly through Harlem: For more information on Blumsteins and the "Don't Buy" campaign, see "Blumsteins to Hire Negro Clerks," *New York Age*, August 4, 1934, 1; Ralph L. Crowder, "'Don't Buy Where You Can't Work': An Investigation of the Political Forces and Social Conflict within the Harlem Boycott of 1934," *Afro-Americans in New York Life and History* 15, no. 2 (July 31, 1999), 351; Christopher Gray, "How a Black Boycott Opened the Employment Door," *New York Times*, November 20, 1994, 7; and Greenberg, *Or Does It Explode?*, 121–25.

104 "St. Philip's Hospital, Richmond, Virginia": Hine, *Black Women in White*, 145 and 233. I am grateful to Lewis Wyman, a reference librarian at the Library of Congress, who sent me correspondence between Alyce Greene and Roy Wilkins of the NAACP and Commissioner Goldwater. For the official complaint and Greene's rejection, see NAACP Papers, Box C-275, Hospital 1934, Manuscript Division, Library of Congress, Roy Wilkins to S. S. Goldwater, October 25, 1934.

104 "on account of color?": Roy Wilkins to Commissioner Goldwater, NAACP Papers, Box C-275, Hospital 1934, Manuscript Division, Library of Congress, October 25, 1934.

104 chronic disease and elder care: "Dr. S. S. Goldwater Is Dead Here at 69," *New York Times*, October 23, 1942, 21.

104 "dead of tuberculosis": The story of this meeting is taken from an interview with Salaria Kea, Tamiment Library, "Salaria Kea O'Reilly 1," 2018, 7:23–10:49. Months later the National

Organization of Negro College Women would assail Goldwater "as a Hitler" for fighting against equity for Black nurses and doctors. See "City Hospital," *New York Age*, November 30, 1935, 3.

105 **"no-return unit"**: "Salaria Kea O'Reilly 1," 8:58.

105 **"make the dead lie!"**: "Salaria Kea O'Reilly 1," 8:21–8:23.

105 **suppressing Black protesters**: Picketing was ruled illegal by the New York State Supreme Court because "there was no labor dispute." Goldberg, *Or Does It Explode?*, 124–26.

Chapter 12 · The Breakthrough

106 **caused Avian 531**: For more on avian TB, see Andrew Routh and Stephanie Sanderson, "Waterfowl," in *Handbook of Avian Medicine*, 2009, https://www.sciencedirect.com/topics/agricultural-and-biological-sciences/avian-tuberculosis.

106–7 **in petri dishes**: The information about the experiment is from Chester Rhines, "The Persistence of Avian Tubercle Bacilli in Soil and in Association with Soil Micro-organisms," Agricultural Experiment Station, New Brunswick, NJ, August 5, 1934, https://www.ncbi.nlm.nih.gov/pmc/articles/PMC543597/pdf/jbacter00799-0072.pdf.

108 **"suppressing all the others"**: Frank Ryan, *Tuberculosis: The Greatest Story Never Told* (London: Swift, 1992), 176.

109 **"the results didn't suggest"**: Both quotes are from Waksman, *The Conquest of Tuberculosis*, 104.

109 **"treatment of tuberculosis"**: All the quotes from this chapter, unless otherwise stated, come from Selman Waksman, *The Conquest of Tuberculosis* (Berkeley: University of California Press, 1964), 103–105.

Chapter 13 · The Riot

110 **"where they lynch us"**: From Shane White, Stephen Robertson, and Stephen Garton, "Year of the Riot: Harlem, 1935," 2020, *Digital Harlem Blog*, https://drstephenrobertson.com/year-of-the-riot-harlem-1935.

111 **"protest against this"**: *Mayor LaGuardia's Commission on the Harlem Riot*, 10.

111 **transpired the night before**: "Police End Harlem Riot," *New York Times*, March 21, 1935, 1, 16. For the aftermath and La Guardia's appointment of the Riot Commission, see Pauline Toole, "The Mayor's Commission on Conditions in Harlem—1935," New York City Department of Records and Information Services, March 1, 2019, https://www.archives.nyc/blog/2019/3/1/the-mayors-commission-on-conditions-in-harlem-1935.

112 **"over its own program"**: Goldberg, *Or Does It Explode?*, 87.

112 **staff were Black women**: Goldberg, *Or Does It Explode?*, 88.

112 **reapply as a new hire**: An article in *The New York Age* discusses the petition that the Citizens' Committee sent to Goldwater denouncing the "Jim Crow set up of the Department of Hospitals." The writer states: "There seems to be no adequate or satisfactory policy concerning transfers and sick leave for nurses. Too much is left to the discretion of the persons immediately in charge. At present, in order to transfer from one 'Negro Hospital' to another, a nurse must resign from the system and apply as a new nurse at the other institution. In this process she loses seniority rights, and increments." "The Nurses Situation," *New York Age*, May 1, 1937, 6.

112 **and their pay**: "Negro Nurses May Get Queens Hospital POS," *New York Amsterdam News*, June 15, 1935, 17.

112 **"have been afforded them"**: "The Nurses Situation," *New York Age*, May 1, 1937, 6.

112   repetitive and "boring": In an interview, Rock Spinelli described TB nursing as "boring," because nothing ever really changed.

113   was near impossible: See Byerly, "Good Tuberculosis Women," 212–216: "Getting capable nurses that are not afraid of tuberculosis is most difficult. So many feel perfectly safe in the general hospital or in private practice who would not consider work in a sanatorium because of the supposed danger of infection" (216).

113   "get back to me": "Negro Nurses May Get Queens Hospital POS," *New York Amsterdam News*, June 15, 1935, 17.

113   "truly be a nurse": The Flying Cavalier, "Carrying the Torch," *New York Age*, June 29, 1935, 5.

114   hoped-for house: Interview with Virginia Allen.

116   right on Staten Island: Interviews with Virginia Allen and Forest Ballard Jr. Both reported that Edna loved Staten Island and its natural beauty, especially the trees and proximity to the water.

116   sicker than before: Unless otherwise specified, information about Hilda Ali's medical condition comes from her medical intake cards housed at the Sea View museum archives.

Chapter 14 · Ward 64

121   Sources for this chapter include interviews with Bernice Alleyne, George Meadows, Gregory and Sammy Stoddard, Flossie, Wanda Issacs, Pearl Gist, and Rock Spinelli, as well as Florence Shirley's interview from StoryCorps.

121   subway worker from Brooklyn: The source for Albert's story is an email from Rock Spinelli, who explained that Albert "was angry and would curse at the nurses who tried to shave and bathe him." Rock Spinelli worked under Missouria and Clemmie Philips, who had experience with Albert.

124   "Nothing scared her": Interview with Bernice Alleyne.

125   "more than his kids": Interview with Bernice Alleyne.

126   her nephew said: Interview with Gregory Stoddard.

126   "could make the devil dance": Interview with Gregory Stoddard.

128   "scrap the fictions": Alain Locke, "Enter the New Negro," National Humanities Center Resource Toolbox, http://nationalhumanitiescenter.org/pds/maai3/migrations/text8/lockenewnegro.pdf.

128   "before it's too late": Interview with Rock Spinelli, who described the men's ward as tough and bawdy, a place nurses liked to avoid.

Chapter 15 · A President's Son

129   twenty-two-year-old's condition: Sources for this story include "Sinus Attack Calls Mother to Bedside," *New York Times*, November 27, 1936, 2; "F. D. Roosevelt Jr. Is in Boston Hospital," *New York Times*, November 27, 1936, 2; "Young Roosevelt Better," *New York Times*, November 28, 1936, 5; "Roosevelt Operation Delayed till Monday," *New York Times*, December 12, 1936, 12; "Young Roosevelt Better," *New York Times*, December 13, 1936, 24; "President's Son Still Ill," *New York Times*, December 14, 1936, 17; and "Young Roosevelt Saved by New Drug," *New York Times*, December 17, 1936, 1, 10.

130   threatening sepsis: Before the FDR Jr. story, America was a year or two behind Europe in adopting sulfa drugs. As Prontosil was beginning to achieve worldwide success in 1935–1936, the *Journal of the American Medical Association* didn't feel it necessary to mention a word about Prontosil or sulfa: "The word 'sulfanilamide' did not appear in the *New England Journal of*

Medicine until November 1937." Medical conservatism was also to blame: physicians were exhausted of all the wonder cures. The European discovery was interesting but not spectacular, so the editor chose to ignore it. See Hager, *The Demon Under the Microscope*, 210.

130 **everything else intact:** The idea to create a "magic bullet" originated from Paul Ehrlich, one of Bayer's first Nobel Prize winners. Ehrlich discovered that synthetic dyes could be used to bring the world of microorganisms into crystal clear focus on slides—before Ehrlich's discovery, bacteria was placed on a clear serum that produced a hazy image, at best. Domagk knew of Ehrlich's theory about dyes—that they were so effective in illuminating cells and bacteria because they latched on to something specific in the chemical makeup of the cells or bacteria. Ehrlich spent years thinking about a dye that would bind itself to a bacteria that causes tuberculosis or strep, and then release a poison that would kill the bacteria but not the surrounding healthy tissue. He even created a name for them: *Zauberkügeln*, or "magic balls." Ehrlich was never able to produce them, but his ideas inspired Domagk. Domagk and his chemists focused their attention on a colorful class of organic compounds called azo dyes. Prontosil was a combination of sulfa and these chemicals.

131 **came to a standstill:** See Simona Luca and Mihaescu Traian, "History of BCG Vaccine," *Maedica* 8, no. 1 (2013): 53–58, https://www.ncbi.nlm.nih.gov/pmc/articles/PMC3749764/.

132 **or current success:** For a deeper discussion, see Hagar, *The Demon Under the Microscope*, 201–204.

132 **"insufficient drug importation":** Barbara J. Martin, *Elixir: The American Tragedy of a Deadly Drug* (Lancaster, PA: Barkerry Press, 2014), 18.

132 **"of Hitler's Germany":** Gladys L. Hobby, ed., "Antimicrobial Agents and Chemotherapy 1968," Proceedings of the Eighth Interscience Conference on Antimicrobial Agents and Chemotherapy, New York, October 21–23, 1968.

132 **of testing Prontosil:** In late July 1936, two young physicians from Johns Hopkins in Baltimore were working on an anti-strep serum when they attended the International Microbiology Conference in London. The physicians heard lectures from the French about their ongoing research on sulfa and other drugs, but it was the keynote speaker, an English physician, who talked about Prontosil. The drug was effective against childbed fever and other strep-related infections.

The American physicians walked away with a determination to return to the United States, abandon the serum therapy, and begin testing this new drug. They wired the Johns Hopkins pharmacist and begged him to get them Prontosil or plain sulfa, and then took the first boat home. But back at the hospital, they found no Prontosil. Patent laws and a lack of interest made importing the drug difficult. However, a lab at DuPont (owned by the family of FDR Jr.'s fiancée) was able to give them 10 grams of pure sulfa. This was enough for the two physicians to begin animal tests. The mouse tests produced "astounding results." Knowing the dosing and safety protocols from the London lecture, the two physicians began testing it on children sick with different variations of strep—and again and again it worked. News of their success spread quickly, and soon their colleagues were trying this new "wonder drug" on strep victims; other were dissecting it to figure out how it worked. Johns Hopkins, renowned for its research, quickly discovered a way to measure the concentration of the drug in body fluids, leading to more effective dosing. See Hager, *The Demon Under the Microscope,* 184.

132 **trade name Prontylin:** It's worth mentioning that at the time, reports were unclear about whether Prontylin was a trade name for Prontosil or whether it was Prontosil in tablet form. Hager claims this is the trade name for Prontosil (*The Demon under the Microscope*, 190); however, a *New York Times* article states it was the name given to Prontosil when administered in pill from ("The Week in Science: Cause of the Tulsa Deaths," *New York Times,* October 24, 1937). Another article states, "Dr. Tobey gave him hypodermic injections of Prontosil, made him swallow tablets of a modification named Prontylin"; from "Prontosil," *Time,* December 28, 1936.

132 "as a Guinea pig": Hager, *The Demon Under the Microscope*, 189.

133 "Saved by New Drug": "Young Roosevelt Saved by New Drug," *New York Times*, December 17, 1936, 1, 10.

Chapter 16 · What They Carried

134 Sources for this chapter include interviews with Virginia Allen, Bernice Alleyne, Forest Ballard Jr., and Elizabeth Plair.

134 now well into her high school years: In interviews, Virginia Allen described the rumpus room as being akin to a "college dorm," where all the nurses would sit around and talk and laugh. It was the place they went to share their feelings and be together, "united, like a sisterhood."

135 like a thread: In interviews, Virginia Allen and Forest Ballard Jr. talked about Edna leaving Americus behind to pursue a career. Both responded that the two sisters "were thick as thieves" and that "one finished the sentences of the other." They told me that while Edna knew that the move would provide a better life for Americus and the rest of her family, she would have suffered incredible guilt: "That's how she was," her son said, especially with Americus. When Americus finally came to live with them, he said, "my mom was complete." Allen reported that Edna would either call or write to her every day to tell her "everything that was happening" because "they didn't keep any secrets from each other."

135 weekly card games: In interviews, Virginia Allen talked at length about the nurses playing cards in the rumpus room and Edna's love for these games. Forest Ballard Jr. also talked about his mother's Sunday card games.

136 first Black supervisor at Sea View: "Honors Nurse," *New York Amsterdam News*, May 1, 1937, 7.

137 "by the white man": From an interview with James Williams.

137 into the envelope: In interviews, Virginia Allen and Forest Ballard Jr. reported that Edna was a penny pincher, and that after buying the essentials, she would save almost all her paycheck.

139 then resell it: For more on "contract buying" and housing segregation in America, see Richard Rothstein, *The Color of Law: A Forgotten History of How Our Government Segregated America* (New York: W. W. Norton, 2017). "Contract buying" emerged from the 1933 housing programs started under the New Deal. To increase the number of houses on the market, the federal government began segregating neighborhoods by refusing to insure mortgages in Black neighborhoods. This practice became known as "redlining," or as Rothstein says, a "state-sponsored system of segregation." After being denied mortgages and loans, Black people who still wanted to own homes were left with few options, and so sellers, looking to make money, exploited them through these bogus contracts. For more on redlining and how it affected different areas of the country, see *Mapping Inequality: Redlining in New Deal America*, https://dsl.richmond.edu/panorama/redlining/#loc=15/40.611/-74.126&city=staten-island-ny&area=C8&text=about&adimage=4/74/0.

140 "boisterous and unruly individuals": Alfred A. Duckett, "Jim Crow Rampant on Staten Island," *New York Amsterdam News*, October 1, 1938, 13.

140 with new developments: Talk about razing the houses in New Brighton had been ongoing for years before Edna even started looking for a home.

Chapter 17 · The Elixir

141 Unless otherwise indicated, this account of the elixir tragedy relies on Barbara J. Martin, *Elixir: The American Tragedy of a Deadly Drug* (Lancaster, PA: Barkerry Press, 2014); and Thomas

Hager, *The Demon Under the Microscope: From Battlefield Hospitals to Nazi Labs, One Doctor's Heroic Search for the World's First Miracle Drug* (New York: Crown, 2006).

141 "injectable solutions, and powders": Hager, *The Demon under the Microscope*, 210.

142 "sweetened liquid form": Hager, *The Demon Under the Microscope, 211.*

142 "doctor at all": Martin, *Elixir,* 259.

142 "in private practice": Hager, *The Demon Under the Microscope,* 204.

142 Prescribe with caution: In one warning about sulfa, the editorial board cautioned doctors and pharmacists against applying "to man toxicity figures based wholly on animal figures." In other words, there was too much reliance on the animal tests and not enough work done on humans to understand the side effects of sulfa, which ranged from dermatitis to more serious disorders like granulocytopenia, a depletion of white blood cells that fight bacteria, and sulfhemoglobinemia, a rare condition that turns the blood green and causes cyanosis, a condition in which the skin turns blue and circulatory failure follows. The piece ended with the warning that "sulfanilamide should not be administered in association with other drugs until definite information is available as to toxic effects" and that "premature publicity for the drug has, as usual been unfortunate . . . The physician should bear in mind the potential hazards of this drug." "Sulfanilamide—a Warning," *Journal of the American Medical Association* 109, no. 14 (1937): 1128, doi:10.1001/jama.1937.02780400044013. Another article noted, "No orally administered solution existed because, as the council advised, the drug had the apparent disadvantage of being relatively insoluble and a tendency to crystalize out of solution" (quoted in Martin, *Elixir,* 10).

143 like Massengill: For more on the FDA's initial refusal to regulate drugs and drugmakers and the changes that the elixir tragedy forced, see Martin, *Elixir*; Hager, *The Demon Under the Microscope,* 223–235; Jen Akst, "The Elixir Tragedy, 1937," *The Scientist,* June 1, 2013, https://www.the-scientist.com/foundations/the-elixir-tragedy-1937-39231; and Julian G. West, "The Accidental Poison That Founded the Modern FDA," *The Atlantic,* January 16, 2018, https://www.theatlantic.com/technology/archive/2018/01/the-accidental-poison-that-founded-the-modern-fda/550574/.

145 "and Some Fatalities": *The New York Times,* October 24, 1937, 182.

145 "by 'Sulfa' Drug": *Intelligencer Journal,* December 7, 1937, 2.

145 "Leading Drug Manufacturers": *Bristol Herald Courier,* November 21, 1937, 11.

145 "tests were conducted": All quotes in this paragraph are from Martin, *Elixir,* 47.

146 "on our part": Martin, *Elixir,* 91.

146 "misbranding the elixir": Martin, *Elixir,* 184.

147 to his heart: Hager, *The Demon Under the Microscope,* 222.

147 "by Massengill's concoction": Hager, *The Demon Under the Microscope,* 231.

Chapter 18 • "Reserved for Whites"

148 Sources for the following account of the dining room incident include "Nurses Stage Walkout for Discrimination," *New York Amsterdam News,* November 6, 1937, 3; and "Nurses Rebel at Treatment," *New York Amsterdam News,* November 13, 1937, 1.

149 "all municipal hospitals": *Mayor LaGuardia's Commission on the Harlem Riot,* 130. For the full set of recommendations, see 122–35.

150 "mind her own business": The source for this account of Kea and the maternity word is Hine, *Black Women in White,* 138–39.

150   from infantile diarrhea: "19 Harlem Hospital Babies Die: Fight for Nurses Hits Mayor," *New York Amsterdam News*, October 17, 1936, 1.

151   their struggles and contributions: In November 1937, the same month as the walkout, *Opportunity* devoted its entire issue to Black nurses. Riddle also wrote extensively about the plight of Black nurses; for her thoughts, see Estelle G. Massey-Riddle, "The Training and Placement of Negro Nurses," *The Journal of Negro Education* 4, no. 1 (January 1935): 42–48; and Estelle G. Massey-Riddle, "Sources of Supply of Negro Health Personnel Section C: Nurses," *The Journal of Negro Education* 6, no. 3 (July 1937): 483–92.

151   "to segregate them": "Nurses Stage Walkout for Discrimination," *New York Amsterdam News*, November 6, 1937, 3.

152   "a suitable investigation": "Nurses Stage Walkout for Discrimination," *New York Amsterdam News*, November 6, 1937, 3.

152   "the other group": Greenberg, *Or Does It Explode?*, 88.

152   "overt and widespread discrimination": Greenberg, *Or Does It Explode?*, 87.

152   "city nursing programs": Greenberg, *Or Does It Explode?*, 88.

153   all-white hospital: Greenberg, *Or Does It Explode?*, 88

Chapter 19 · The Fight

155   only a nightstand: Interviews with Virginia Allen, Mamie Daniels, and Rock Spinelli provide the basis for the description of Sea View's wards; Mamie Daniels also drew a diagram of the wards, and photographs from Sea View Museum and the New York City Municipal Archives corroborate her depiction.

155   "wasn't the place": Interview with Rock Spinelli.

155   most on the floor: Thompson's medical records confirm that he was indeed at Sea View on Ward 64 from 1936 to 1939; he was again admitted in the mid-1940s and then again in 1950 before being chosen as a trial patient. Rock Spinelli confirmed he was on the ward when Missouria and Clemmie were nurses there.

155   in different groups: In an interview, Rock Spinelli explained that the men's ward was bawdy, "like a bar" or "frat house," and that the men would split into different groups. He also spoke at length about their tendency to use lewd and racist language, especially when talking about sports or politics or everyday things.

156   "most beautiful fighting machine": Michael Carbert, "June 19, 1936: Louis vs. Schmeling," *The Fight City*, June 19, 2022, https://www.thefightcity.com/joe-louis-max-schmeling-boxing-upsets/.

157   a national hero: Sources for this account of the Louis and Schmeling fight include Carbert, "June 19, 1936: Louis vs. Schmeling"; Robert Ecksel, "Joe Louis: Brown Bomber Bombs Bums," Sweet Science, March 16, 2005, https://tss.ib.tv/boxing/boxing-articles-and-news-2005-videos -results-rankings-and-history/1806-joe-louis-brown-bomber-bombs-bums; Kieran Mulvaney, "When Joe Louis Boxed Nazi Favorite Max Schmeling," History.com, https://www.history.com /news/joe-louis-max-schmeling-match; "Max Schmeling vs Joe Louis, I (All Rounds)," YouTube video, February 17, 2012, https://www.youtube.com/watch?v=igoidtPyy6g; "Why Louis Lost," *New York Amsterdam News*, June 27, 1936, 1; and Lee Wylie, "Joe Louis: Mechanical Wonder," *The Fight City*, July 23, 2022, https://www.thefightcity.com/joe-louis -mechanical-wonder-lee-wylie-punching-power-eddie-futch-max-baer-boxing.

157   "battles and blood": Nigel Collins, "Louis-Schmeling: More Than a Fight," ESPN, June 19, 2013, https://www.espn.com/boxing/story/_/id/9404398/more-just-fight.

157 "a shattered myth": James P. Dawson, "Schmeling Stops Louis in Twelfth as 45,000 Look On," *The New York Times*, June 20, 1936, 1, https://nyti.ms/3wHlCHg.

157 "white master, Max Schmeling": David W. Walsh, "Brown Bomber Illusion Goes for Nose Dive," *The Times*, June 20, 1936, 20.

158 "negro race has been betrayed": Roi Cottley, "Hectic Harlem: Moanin' Low," *New York Amsterdam News*, June 27, 1936, 13. See also "Why Louis Lost," *New York Amsterdam News*, June 27, 1936, 13.

158 "shall be free": Emancipation Proclamation (1863), National Archives, https://www.archives.gov/milestone-documents/emancipation-proclamation.

158 "like a nightmare": Marvel Cooke, "Death and Sadness Mark Louis Defeat: Shock Fatal to 12 and Harlem Mourns," *New York Amsterdam News*, June 27, 1936, 1.

158 a heart attack: Cooke, "Death and Sadness Mark Louis Defeat."

158 "in their hands": Ben Wyatt, "The Legacy of Joe Louis' Loss to Max Schmeling on Juneteenth," *The Guardian*, June 19, 2021, https://www.theguardian.com/sport/2021/jun/19/joe-louis-max-schmeling-heavyweight-fight-boxing-juneteenth.

159 "Hat Story": The story that follows comes from interviews with Bernice Alleyne and Gregory Stoddard.

Chapter 20 · The Offer

162 Sources for this chapter include interviews with Virginia Allen, Forest Ballard Jr., James Williams, Yvonne Williams, Mamie Daniels, Rock Spinelli, Debbie Ann-Paige, and Bernice Alleyne.

162 into the night: Interview with Virginia Allen.

163 it held possibility: In interviews, Forest Ballard Jr. reported that even before the neighborhood was popular, his mother felt "called to the house," that it was "God who brought her to Sea View and to the house."

163 as summer homes: In an interview, James Williams explained that at the turn of the century, the neighborhood was called "Nanny Goat Hill" because it was full of Italian immigrants who kept goats. The following account of this neighborhood is drawn from "Staten Island, NY, D8 Willowbrook," *Mapping Inequality: Redlining in New Deal America*, https://dsl.richmond.edu/panorama/redlining/#loc=16/40.609/-74.138&city=staten-island-ny&area=D8&adview=full.

164 make them an offer: In an interview, Forest Ballard Jr. recalled that Marion and Arthur Evans were living in the house before Edna and Forest subsequently bought it from an Italian family. According to a deed dated September 23, 1938, the Home Owners' Loan Corporation was foreclosing on the house, owned by Mr. Pedalino (this name is also spelled "Pedilino" on the deed), who lived downstairs, and Marion and Arthur Evans, who lived upstairs. According to Virginia Allen and Forest Ballard Jr., Edna bought the house from Mr. Pedalino and then rented the upstairs to Marion and Arthur, who eventually became Forest Ballard Jr.'s godparents.

164 clustered together: Rock Spinelli and Mamie Daniels reported that during sports matches, big news events, or even just listening to music, patients would gather together on beds and huddle around the radio.

164 the radio's front speaker: Sources for this account of the fight include John Florio and Ouisie Shapiro, "When Joe Louis Fought Schmeling, White America Enthusiastically Rooted for a Black Man," Andscape, June 22, 2018, https://andscape.com/features/when-joe-louis-fought-schmeling-white-america-enthusiastically-rooted-for-a-black-man/; Gerald R. Gems, "Joe Louis–Max Schmeling Fight—Clem McCarthy, Announcer (June 22, 1938)," https://www.loc.gov/static/programs/national-recording-preservation-board/documents/JoeLouisMax

SchmelingFight.pdf; "Joe Louis vs Max Schmeling II (June 22, 1938)," YouTube video, https://www.youtube.com/watch?v=6BLGdFQPh8c&t=31s; "Joe Louis vs. Max Schmeling—1rst Round Knockout," YouTube video, https://www.youtube.com/watch?v=2LNzWHuygpw; "Joe Louis vs Max Schmeling, II (Full Film, HD)," January 23, 2013, YouTube video, https://www.youtube.com/watch?v=OSE281i5gNM&t=332s; David Margolick, "Max Schmeling, Heavyweight Champion Caught in the Middle of Nazi Politics, Is Dead at 99," *New York Times*, February 5, 2005; and Mulvaney, "When Joe Louis Boxed Nazi Favorite Max Schmeling."

164   "they ever witnessed": "Joe Louis vs Max Schmeling II (June 22, 1938)," YouTube video, https://www.youtube.com/watch?v=6BLGdFQPh8c&t=31s.

164   "I beat Schmeling": Robert Portis, "June 22, 1938: Louis vs. Schmeling II," *The Fight City*, June 22, 2022, https://www.thefightcity.com/june-22-1938-louis-vs-schmeling-ii-rematch/.

165   "to beat Germany": Wyatt, "The Legacy of Joe Louis' Loss to Max Schmeling on Juneteenth."

165   "world's heavyweight championship": "Joe Louis vs Max Schmeling, II (Full Film, HD)."

165   "seem this long": Margolick, "Max Schmeling, Heavyweight Champion."

165   "champion, Joe Louis!": "Joe Louis vs Max Schmeling, II (Full Film, HD)."

165   "to K.O. Germany": Mulvaney, "When Joe Louis Boxed Nazi Favorite Max Schmeling."

166   "then the right": "Joe Louis vs. Max Schmeling—1rst Round Knockout."

166   "half human, half animal": Margolick, "Max Schmeling, Heavyweight Champion."

166   "on a technical knockout": Joe Lapointe, "The Championship Fight That Went Beyond Boxing," *New York Times*, June 19, 1988, 370, 375.

167   "that's too much": "Harlem Paces the Nation Celebrating Victory by Joe Louis Over Schmeling," *New York Amsterdam News*, July 2, 1938, A10.

167   "like a champ": Mulvaney, "When Joe Louis Boxed Nazi Favorite Max Schmeling." When Schmeling returned to Germany this time, Hitler was furious, and later, when Schmeling refused to join the Nazi Party, Hitler sought revenge by drafting him into the army as a paratrooper. Schmeling survived and became a wealthy philanthropist. He died at age ninety-nine. See "Joe Louis–Max Schmeling Fight—Clem McCarthy, Announcer (June 22, 1938)."

Chapter 21 · Homecoming

168   Sources include interviews with Virginia Allen and Forest Ballard Jr.

169   **and stepped into:** The account of Edna finally buying her house is reconstructed from multiple interviews with Virginia Allen and Forest Ballard Jr., who told me that Edna owned the house and rented the upstairs to the Evanses, a fact confirmed by the 1940 Census. The description of Bradley Avenue in 1938 and the exterior of her house comes from tax photographs: https://nycma.lunaimaging.com/luna/servlet/detail/NYCMA~8~8~14307~905236:358-Bradley-Avenue?sort=borough%2Cblock%2Clot%2Czip_code&qvq=q:358%20Bradley%20Avenue;sort:borough%2Cblock%2Clot%2Czip_code;lc:NYCMA~8~8&mi=0&trs=1.

170   **owned a home:** Leah Platt Boustan and Robert A. Margo, "White Suburbanization and African-American Home Ownership, 1940–1980," National Bureau of Economic Research, January 2011, 3, https://www.nber.org/system/files/working_papers/w16702/revisions/w16702.rev0.pdf. Of note, this figure varies, with some sources saying the percentage was around 22.8%.: https://ncrc.org/60-black-homeownership-a-radical-goal-for-black-wealth-development/.

170   **the next generation:** In interviews, both Virginia Allen and Forest Ballard Jr. talked at length about Edna's Sunday lunches and how they provided a time for the nurses to come together and unwind, but also to talk about more serious things. According to Virginia, "They were very

involved in politics and the NAACP and the NACGN, and we would say that what they did was activism, and it was. But Edna and the nurses didn't see it that way. For them, "it was natural to help the next generation." This was done either through fundraising (Edna established a scholarship fund for Black women to attend college) or opening her home to relatives or friends who needed a place to stay while they resettled or went to school.

171 "My baby is coming": The follow incident is reported in Alfred A. Duckett, "Baby's Death in St. John's Hospital Is Branded as Murder; Starts Probe," *New York Amsterdam News*, November 12, 1938, 13.

172 "Negro doctors and nurses": "City Hospital," *New York Age*, November 30, 1935.

172 "racial susceptible" to tuberculosis: George G. Ornstein, "The Leading Causes of Death Among Negroes: Tuberculosis," *The Journal of Negro Education* 6 (July 1937): 303–309.

172 "from their occupation": For a complete discussion see David Ulmar, George Ornstein, and Harry H. Epstein, "Pulmonary Tuberculosis as an Occupational Disease in a Tuberculosis Hospital," *Sea View Quarterly Bulletin*, October 1936, 67.

173 "pay the price": See Lorna Doone Mitchell, "Tuberculosis as an Occupational and Compensable Disease from the Standpoint of the Employee," *Transactions of the American Hospital Association Annual Conference* 41 (1939): 296–303.

Chapter 22 · Dr. Edward Robitzek

177 Descriptions of and information about Edward Robitzek are largely based on extensive interviews with his son John Robitzek and the dozens of articles and photographs that he has preserved.

177 supported the neck: Description of the autopsy relies on autopsy records at the Sea View Hospital Museum.

178 "body never lies": Interview with John Robitzek.

180 "coming home cured": Edward's letter to his father.

181 "never be a doctor": Interview with John Robitzek.

181 riding in ambulances: Edward Robitzek's résumé.

182 "to everything medical": Edward Robitzek's résumé.

182 "people in blood": Jack Fairweather, *The Volunteer: True Story of the Resistance Hero Who Infiltrated Auschwitz* (New York: HarperCollins, 2019).

182 "as a sniper": Interview with John Robitzek.

182 "be about capital": Interview with John Robitzek.

183 to crumbling institutions: Fordham was a municipal hospital, but it was located in an under-developed area in the Bronx, which was considered the country. Being away from public transportation meant there was no overcrowding, and so it was often perceived as private.

183 "as if disease discriminated": Interview with John Robitzek.

186 of lovely heroines: See D. M. Morens, "At the Deathbed of Consumptive Art," *Emerging Infectious Diseases* 8, no. 11 (2002): 1353–1358, doi.org/10.3201/eid0811.020549.

186 "glow of consumption": Quoted in René Dubos and Jean Dubos, *The White Plague: Tuberculosis, Man, and Society* (New Brunswick, NJ: Rutgers University Press, 1996), 47.

186 "I should like to die": Carolyn Farnsworth, "A Sweet-Tempered Dyspeptic: The 19th Century Consumptive Aesthetic," *Microbiology*, March 24, 2016, https://microbiologycommunity.nature.com/posts/5639-a-sweet-tempered-dyspeptic-the-19th-century-consumptive-aesthetic.

Chapter 23 · Arrivals

187   Sources interviewed for this chapter include Virginia Allen, Forest Ballard, Jr., Marion Walker, and Pearl Williams.

187   **"and deliberately attacked"**: "FDR's Infamy Speech," USHistory.org, https://www.ushistory.org /documents/infamy.htm.

188   **were sent abroad**: "African American Participation During World War 1," Delaware Division of Historical and Cultural Affairs, https://history.delaware.gov/world-war-i/african-americans -ww1/.

188   **"Red Summer"**: For further information on Black men returning from World War I, see Peter C. Baker, "The Tragic Forgotten History of Black Military Veterans," *New Yorker*, November 27, 2016; and Chad Williams, "African American Veterans Hoped Their Service in World War I Would Secure Their Rights at Home. It Didn't," *Time*, November 12, 2018. For more on the Red Summer of 1919, see Abigail Higgins, "Red Summer of 1919: How Black WWI Vets Fought Back Against Racist Mobs," History.com, July 26, 2019, https://www.history.com/news /red-summer-1919-riots-chicago-dc-great-migration; and Robert Whitaker, *On the Laps of Gods: The Red Summer of 1919 and the Struggle for Justice That Remade a Nation* (New York: Three Rivers Press, 2009).

188   **"racial TB of the nations"**: For the quote and to read more on Nazi medicine and how they used tuberculosis to justify murder and torture, see A. Finley-Croswhite and A. Munzer, "Nazi Medicine, Tuberculosis, and Genocide," in *Tuberculosis and War: Lessons Learned from World War II*, ed. John F. Murray and Robert Loddenkemper (Basel: Karger, 2018), 44–62.

188   **"which they hate"**: Jaimee A. Swift, "The Erasure of People of African Descent in Nazi Germany," *African American Intellectual History Society: Black Perspectives*, April 18, 2017, https://www .aaihs.org/the-erasure-of-people-of-african-descent-in-nazi-germany/.

188   **sterilization and abortions**: "Black People," United States Holocaust Memorial Museum, https:// www.ushmm.org/collections/bibliography/black-people. For further discussion of the mistreatment of Black POWs, see G. Paul Garson, "Black POWs Under the Nazis," Warfare History Network, https://warfarehistorynetwork.com/black-pows-under-the-nazis; Robert W. Kestling, "Blacks Under the Swastika: A Research Note," *Journal of Negro History* 83, no. 1 (Winter 1998): xx; and Raffael Scheck, "'They Are Just Savages': German Massacres of Black Soldiers from the French Army in 1940," *Journal of Modern History* 77, no. 2 (2005): 325–44.

189   **fell into each other**: The re-creation of this scene is based on interviews with Virginia Allen and Forest Ballard Jr.

190   **"for this food"**: Interview with Virginia Allen about meals made for "special occasions" and her aunt's prayers.

191   **preoperative blood work**: According to Marion Walker, while Edna was pregnant, a patient coughed on her, and she feared her baby would get sick. She believed God kept her and the child safe.

192   **could turn active**: For an analysis of latent and active tuberculosis during pregnancy, see Henry Cohen, "Tuberculosis and Pregnancy," *British Medical Journal* 2, no. 3954 (October 17, 1936): 751–54.

192   **consider an abortion**: "In the early 20th century, induced abortion was recommended for these women" by some physicians, but not all. See Olabisi M. Loto and Ibraheem Awowole, "Tuberculosis in Pregnancy: A Review," *Journal of Pregnancy* 2012, Article ID 379271 (2012), https:// doi.org/10.1155/2012/379271; and Young, "Tuberculosis and Pregnancy." For further background on pregnancy and tuberculosis, see Robert H. Baker and Arthur D. Ward, "Pulmonary Tuberculosis and Pregnancy," *New England Journal of Medicine* 226 (February 5, 1942): 224–27;

Louis I. Friedman and James R. Garber, "Pregnancy and Tuberculosis," *American Review of Tuberculosis* 54, no. 3: 275–82; and B. S. Pollak and B. P. Potter, "Pregnancy and Tuberculosis," *Tubercle* 21, no. 4 (January 1940): 128–31.

193　"false sense of security": E. S. Mariette, "Nursing in Tuberculosis: The Administrator's Point of View," *American Journal of Nursing* 42, no. 1 (January 1942): 69–77; quotations from 71.

193　"of their use": Mitchell, "Tuberculosis as an Occupational and Compensable Disease."

193　towels and newspapers: This account of African American midwifery relies on Jenny M. Luke, *Delivered by Midwives: African-American Midwifery in the Twentieth-Century South* (Jackson: University Press of Mississippi, 2018).

194　coast of Long Island: For the full story of the Nazi saboteurs who were recruited to distribute antiwar propaganda and blow up bridges, factories, power plants, and railroads while also engaging in acts of terrorism against Jewish targets, see Christopher Klein, "When the Nazis Invaded the Hamptons," History.com, November 28, 2018, https://www.history.com/news/when-the-nazis-invaded-the-hamptons.

194　afternoon in merriment: This scene is re-created from an interview with Virginia Allen.

194　one of joy: In interviews, Forest Ballard Jr. said that he knew little about his mother's life pre–Sea View and his grandfather's enslavement. He said, "No, my mom didn't want me to know any of that. She just wanted me to be happy."

195　"Department of Hospitals": "Drops Jim Crow Bars in N.Y. City Hospitals," *New York Amsterdam Star-News,* December 5, 1942, 1.

Chapter 24　·　The Prisoner

196　from Sea View: The following story of the German soldier on Ward 64 was first related by Missouria's niece Florence Shirley in an interview with StoryCorps in 2010. Rock Spinelli confirmed the story and recalled it being retold and referred to often. Rock Spinelli also added details about the ways that the men passed their time and returning soldiers gathered on the roof with patients to tell war stories.

197　stories with journalists: For more on Halloran Hospital and its treatment of wounded soldiers, see "Overseas Wounded Now Treated in Big Staten Island Hospital," *New York Times,* March 25, 1943. For German POWs at Halloran, see "Germans Are Unmoved by Atrocity Film; Prisoners Lay War Crimes to 'Higher-Ups,'" *New York Times,* June 27, 1945.

197　neither derision nor abuse: "Geneva Convention Relative to the Treatment of Prisoners of War," United Nations, August 12, 1949, https://www.ohchr.org/en/instruments-mechanisms/instruments/geneva-convention-relative-treatment-prisoners-war.

198　the Great Plains: Sources for information about US POW camps include Kathy Roe Coker and Jason Wetzel, *Georgia POW Camps in World War II* (Charleston, SC: History Press, 2019); Michael Farquhar, "Enemies among US: German POWS in America," *Washington Post,* September 10, 1997; J. Malcolm Garcia, "German POWs on the American Homefront," *Smithsonian,* September 15, 2009; Kathy Kirkpatrick, "POWs in the USA—10 Surprising Facts about America's WW2 Prisoner of War Camps," Military History Now, April 10, 2018, https://militaryhistorynow.com/2018/04/10/pows-in-the-usa-10-amazing-facts-about-americas-ww2-prisoner-of-war-camps; Arnold Krammer, *Nazi Prisoners of War in America* (Lanham, MD: Scarborough House, 1979); and Sarah Razner and Sharon Roznik, "'Just Like Us': How Wisconsin Held Captive, and Made Peace with, German POWs in World War II, FDL Reporter, April 7, 2019, https://www.fdlreporter.com/story/news/2019/04/01/how-wisconsinites-and-german-pows-built-separate-peace-wwii-history/3018353002/.

199 as a resort: Kathy Roe Coker, "World War II Prisoners of War in Georgia: German Memories of Camp Gordon, 1943–1945," *The Georgia Historical Quarterly* 76, no. 4 (1992): 837–861.

199 call the POWs "sir": Sources for Black nurses caring for German POWs include "African American Nurses in World War II," National Women's History Museum, July 8, 2019, https://www.womenshistory.org/articles/african-american-nurses-world-war-ii; Alexis Clark, "The Army's First Black Nurses Were Relegated to Caring for Nazi Prisoners of War," *Smithsonian*, May 15, 2018; Alexis Clark, "When Black Nurses Were Relegated to Care for German POWs," History.com, March 10, 2021, https://www.history.com/news/black-nurses-world-war-ii-truman-desegregation-military; and Matthias Reiss, "Icons of Insult: German and Italian Prisoners of War in African American Letters during World War II," *Amerikastudien/American Studies* 49, no. 4 (2004): 539–62.

199 "hated niggers": Quoted in Clark, "The Army's First Black Nurses."

199 "us very bitter": Quoted in Clark, "When Black Nurses Were Relegated."

200 murals at a local hotel: Troy R. Bennett, "German POWs Picked Potatoes and Painted at Houlton Army Air Base in Maine. A New Exhibit Shows Their Work," *Bangor Daily News*, July 27, 2021; "German POW Paintings," Vernon Parish Tourism, https://www.vernonparish.org/about-us/history/german-pow-paintings. For POW original artwork, see "Passing the Time: Artwork by World War II German POWs," Maine Memory Network, https://www.mainememory.net/sitebuilder/site/3117/page/4918/display?use_mmn=1;

200 "bunch of boys": Quoted in Farquhar, "Enemies Among US: German POWS in America."

200 "of physical manhood": Quoted in Coker and Wetzel, *Georgia POW Camps in World War II*, 58.

201 "the Nazi swastika": Coker and Wetzel, *Georgia POW Camps in World War II*, 59.

201 be extremely wary: Coker and Wetzel, *Georgia POW Camps in World War II*, 60.

Chapter 25 • "Al Hit Paydirt!"

202 or lack thereof: The sources for the following account are Frank Ryan, *The Greatest Story Never Told* (London: Swift, 1992), 184–185; and Waksman, *The Conquest of Tuberculosis*, 104–107.

203 "about this problem": Waksman, *The Conquest of Tuberculosis*, 106.

203 "organs as well": Waksman, *The Conquest of Tuberculosis*, 106.

203 "without injuring the host": Waksman, *The Conquest of Tuberculosis*, 106.

204 finish his PhD: Information about Albert's life and work with streptomycin came from interviews with his wife, Vivian Schatz, and the following sources: "Albert Schatz, Ph.D.," https://www.albertschatzphd.com; Margalit Fox, "Albert Schatz Microbiologist, Dies at 84," *New York Times*, February 5, 2005; William Kingston, "Streptomycin, Schatz v. Waksman, and the Balance of Credit for Discovery," *Journal of the History of Medicine and Allied Sciences* 59, no. 3, 2004: 441–62; Peter Pringle, *Experiment Eleven: Dark Secrets Behind the Discovery of a Wonder Drug* (London: Walker, 2012); "Selman Waksman and Antibiotics," National Historic Chemical Landmarks, American Chemical Society, https://www.acs.org/content/acs/en/education/whatischemistry/landmarks/selmanwaksman.html; and Milton Wainwright, "Streptomycin: Discovery and Resultant Controversy," *History of Philosophy of the Life Sciences* 13, no. 1 (1991): 97–124.

204 "coughing and infecting others": Vivian Schatz, Linda Schatz, Carl Sigmond, and Mary Brewster, "Biography of Albert Schatz," https://www.albertschatzphd.com/?cat=about&subcat=bio.

206 healthy chicken's throat: The story of the chicken has been subject to endless controversy and myth. According to Waksman, the swab came from a sick chicken that showed up at his

microbiology lab one morning. He swabbed the chicken's throat and discovered a fungus that made chickens sick. In 1960, Waksman sent this version of the story to George Gray for a *Scientific American* article he was writing. From here, the story entered the press and was picked up by others. However, according to Schatz and Jones, Waksman's version is a myth, a fabrication created to directly link himself to the isolation of D-1 and the discovery of streptomycin. For my purposes, I chose to retell Schatz and Jones's version, with the backing of scholar Milton Wainwright, to debunk the more dramatic telling by Waksman. In his essay, "Streptomycin: Discovery and Resultant Controversy," Wainwright relies on direct interviews with Jones and Schatz and, later, Waksman's own admission that Jones swabbed the chicken, not him: "From Waksman's own writings and from Jones' recollections, there seems little doubt about the origin of the two streptomycin-producing strains; one came from Jones directly to Schatz, while the other was isolated by Schatz from soil" (106).

207 **"Albert's eagle eye"**: Interview with Vivian Schatz.

207 **from the stables**: Albert Schatz, "The True Story of Streptomycin," *Actinomycetes* 4, part 2 (August 1993): 27–39, https://www.albertschatzphd.com/?cat=articles&subcat=streptomycin&itemnum=001.

207 **"about 99.99 percent"**: This quote and the next Jones quote are from Ryan, *Tuberculosis: The Greatest Story Never Told*, 218.

208 **"liter Erlenmeyer flasks"**: Schatz, "The True Story of Streptomycin."

208 **the unborn chicks**: Ryan, *Tuberculosis: The Greatest Story Never Told*, 220.

Chapter 26 • "Ich Hoffe Du Wirst Krank"

210 The accounts in this chapter are based on interviews with Rock Spinelli, Mia Gillespie, Lisa Gillespie, Florence Shirley, and Gregory Stoddard.

211 **Pennsylvania shipyard**: For more on the Beaumont riot, see James A. Burran, "Violence in an 'Arsenal of Democracy': The Beaumont Race Riot, 1943," *East Texas Historical Journal* 14, no. 1 (1976).

211 **hands of police**: See Vivian M. Baulch and Patricia Zacharias, "The 1943 Detroit Race Riots," *Detroit News*, April 17, 2000; Dominic J. Capeci and Martha Wilkerson, "The Detroit Rioters of 1943: A Reinterpretation," *Michigan Historical Review* 16, no. 1 (1990), 49–72; and "Race Riot of 1943," *Encyclopedia of Detroit*, https://detroithistorical.org/learn/encyclopedia-of-detroit/race-riot-1943.

212 **"brought racial progress"**: Arnold Rampersad, *The Life of Langston Hughes: Volume II 1941-1967, I Dream of a World* (New York: Oxford University Press, 2002), 76.

212 **"Beaumont to Detroit: 1943"**: Published in the left-wing journal *Common Ground*, Autumn 1943, https://perspectives.ushmm.org/item/langston-hughes-beaumont-to-detroit-1943.

212 **stationed abroad**: Interviews with Mia Gillespie and Lisa Gillespie provided information about Kate and her son, Keever. The following account is derived from correspondence between the two, courtesy of their family.

214 **from Halloran Hospital**: The following account of Kalytka's escape and capture is based on "Troops Search for Nazi Prisoner," *New York Times*, June 12, 1944; and "Nazi Who Broke Out of Captivity Steals Back In: 'Caught' at Lunch," *New York Times*, June 14, 1944.

215 **repeated in English**: Interview with Gregory Stoddard.

Chapter 27 · The Nature of Things

220 **or on sidewalks:** "50 Shells From Freighter's Gun Fall in 2 Staten Island Villages," *The New York Times*, February 6, 1944, 27.

221 **"application in tuberculosis":** George W. Raiziss, "Diasone: A New and Active Chemotherapeutic Agent," *Science* 98, no. 2546 (October 15, 1943): 350; see also Edward H. Robitzek, "Fatal Pemphigoid Reaction to Diasone," *American Review of Tuberculosis* 51, no. 5 (1945): 473–77.

Chapter 28 · "In the Business of Dying"

223 Sources for this chapter include interviews with Bernice Alleyne, Virginia Allen, Rock Spinelli, and Mamie Daniels.

224 **"business of dying":** Email from Rock Spinelli.

224 **"was looking gruesome":** Email from Rock Spinelli.

229 **in a ledger:** See Marc Santora, "City Introduces Online Database for Its Potter's Field," *New York Times*, April 10, 2013.

229 **east of the Bronx:** Nina Bernstein, "Unearthing the Secrets of New York's Mass Graves," *New York Times*, May 15, 2016; "The History," Hart Island Project, https://www.hartisland.net /history; "Hart Island: The City Cemetery," New York City Council, https://council.nyc.gov /data/hart-island; W. J. Henningan, "Lost in the Pandemic: Inside New York City's Mass Graveyard on Hart Island," *Time*, November 18, 2020; "Rare Photographs of Hart Island, New York's Potter's Field," New York Historical Society Museum and Library, April 17, 2019, https://www.nyhistory.org/blogs/rare-photographs-of-hart-island-new-yorks-potters-field; and Serena Troshynski, "Land of the Unknown: A History of Hart Island," New York Public Library, January 6, 2021, https://www.nypl.org/blog/2021/01/07/land-unknown-history-hart -island.

Chapter 29 · Promise

232 **version of sulfa:** Ryan, *The Greatest Story Never Told*, 227.

232 **"of the drug's potential?":** Ryan, *The Greatest Story Never Told*, 231.

233 **cook up the streptomycin:** See Ryan, *The Greatest Story Never Told*, 224–231.

233 **anywhere near him:** The account of Schatz working is from Peter Pringle, *Experiment Eleven: Dark Secrets Behind the Discovery of a Wonder Drug* (Walker Books, 2012), 48.

233 **for TB cultures:** Albert Schatz, "The True Story of Streptomycin," *Actinomycetes* 4, part 2 (August 1993): 27–39, https://www.albertschatzphd.com/?cat=articles&subcat=streptomycin&item num=001.

233 **"and *ker-pow*":** Ryan, *The Greatest Story Never Told*, 213.

234 **the tops of the test tubes:** Schatz, "The True Story of Streptomycin."

Chapter 30 · 188 Wheeler Avenue

237 Sources for this chapter include interviews with George Meadows, Bernice Alleyne, Gregory Stoddard, Debbie-Ann Paige, and Virginia Allen.

237 **meaning became clear:** The story of the petition comes from multiple interviews with her family, unless otherwise indicated.

239 "the one on Wheeler": Interview with Bernice Alleyne.

239 chapter of the NAACP: "Community Servant William A. Morris Jr. Dies at 99," *SILive.com*, May 29, 2018, https://www.silive.com/news/2018/05/community_servant_william_a_mo.html.

240 "flaming cross, 'K.K.K.'": All information and quotes about the Sam Browne story, unless otherwise indicated, are from NAACP Legal File, Samuel A. Browne, 1924, filed under "Residential Segregation."

240 "in the neighborhood": "Mob Attacks Home: Friends on Guard with Guns," *Pittsburgh Courier*, July 25, 1925, 1–2.

241 "aware of that?": "Ku Klux Klan Threatens to Drive Family from White Neighborhood, *Pittsburgh Courier*, September 19, 1925, 9.

242 "of negro population": See "Staten Island, NY C8 Miers Corner," Mapping Inequality: Redlining in New Deal America, https://dsl.richmond.edu/panorama/redlining/#loc=14/40.608/-74.13& city=staten-island-ny&area=C8.

243 "appears inevitably downward": "Staten Island, NY C8 Miers Corner."

243 became a homeowner: Verified by house deed, dated July 18, 1944.

243 finishing the story: Interviews with Bernice Alleyne and George Meadows.

Chapter 31 · Firsts

244 he had an idea: Background for Patricia's story comes from Ryan, *The Greatest Story Never Told*, 237–41. Ryan mentions that the first person ever to receive streptomycin was an old man suffering from tuberculosis meningitis. The drug initially helped him, but he died two weeks later. Patricia was the first patient to receive the drug and live.

245 "like wet spaghetti": Interview with Rock Spinelli.

246 would be a draft: The source for the following exchange is Hine, *Black Women in White*, 179–181.

247 "and whites together": "Mrs. Mabel Staupers Challenges Surgeon General on Failure to Use Negro Nurses," *New York Age*, January 13, 1945, 1.

Chapter 32 · Dark Places

250 Sources interviewed for this chapter include John Robitzek and Sonja Coryant.

250 "far advanced pulmonary tuberculosis": According to Hilda's Sea View patient card.

253 beside his father: The story of Katherine's aneurysm and subsequent death was related by John Robitzek.

255 legal pad: Sources for information about the Diasone trials include Edward H. Robitzek, "Fatal Pemphigoid Reaction to Diasone," *American Review of Tuberculosis* 51, no. 5 (1945): 473–477; and Edward H. Robitzek, George G. Ornstein, Philip Slate, and Strashimir A. Petroff, "Diasone in the Treatment of Pulmonary Tuberculosis," *Diseases of the Chest: Journal of the American College of Chest Physicians* 12, no. 3 (May–June 1946).

256 Seeing the side effects: Robitzek, "Fatal Pemphigoid Reaction to Diasone," 473.

257 "work was masterful": Interview with John Robitzek.

257 "tuberculosis in human beings": From Robitzek et al., "Diasone in the Treatment of Pulmonary Tuberculosis."

258 "hell on earth": Interview with Sonja Coryat.

Chapter 33 · A Brighter Future

259 Sources interviewed for this chapter include Bernice Alleyne, George Meadows, Flossie, and Gregory Stoddard. Any quotes from Missouria or Mama Amy come from these sources.

259 "anyone and everyone": Previous quotations are from interviews with Bernice Alleyne.

260 "her own destiny": "*Their Eyes Were Watching God*: Overview," National Endowment for the Arts, https://www.arts.gov/initiatives/nea-big-read/their-eyes-were-watching-god.

260 her niece said, "every day": Interview with Bernice Alleyne.

261 The image became iconic: Decades later, the image would come to be seen differently when the nurse came forward and said she never gave consent to the kiss.

261 million people worldwide: Estimates on the number of people who died, including civilians and those in battles, vary from seventy to eighty-five million, with most putting the number at around seventy-five million.

262 in unthinkable prosperity: See S. W. Garlington, "Harlem Celebrates V-J Day Uptown and Downtown," *New York Amsterdam News*, August 18, 1945, 1.

262 "capital of the world" . . . part of its energy: See "New York after WWII," *American Experience*, PBS, https://www.pbs.org/wgbh/americanexperience/features/newyork-postwar/; and Sam Robertson, "New York 1945," *New York Times*, July 30, 1995, 100, 109, 110.

262 "I am scared to death": Abe Hill, "Japs Quit; Job Scare in Harlem," *New York Amsterdam News*, August 18, 1945, 1; see also "Our Workers Hit in Cutback but Opportunities Are Better," *New York Amsterdam News*, September 1, 1945, 1.

262 "style, as usual": S. W. Garlington, "Harlem Celebrates V-J Uptown and Downtown," *New York Amsterdam News*, August 18, 1945, 1.

262 were facing layoffs: "Our Workers Hit in Cutback."

263 frozen meat pies: See Kelly Gates, "Introduction of Frozen Foods: A Timeline," Supermarket News, October 16, 2000, https://www.supermarketnews.com/archive/introduction-frozen-foods-timeline.

263 pairs of stockings: See Emily Spivack, "Stocking Series, Part 1: Wartime Rationing and Nylon Riots," *Smithsonian*, September 4, 2012, https://www.smithsonianmag.com/arts-culture/stocking-series-part-1-wartime-rationing-and-nylon-riots-25391066/.

264 "an unmistakable degree": Waksman, *The Conquest of Tuberculosis*, 129.

265 "constantly being assembled": Waksman, *The Conquest of Tuberculosis*, 129.

265 "rebate on royalties to compensate": "Selman Waksman and Antibiotics," National Historic Chemical Landmarks, American Chemical Society, http://www.acs.org/content/acs/en/education/whatischemistry/landmarks/selmanwaksman.html.

265 "a favorable direction": Quoted in Waksman, *The Conquest of Tuberculosis*, 129.

Chapter 34 · The Second Call

266 Sources interviewed for this chapter include Virginia Allen.

266 had reached ten: See "1,253 Beds Vacant in Hospital Here," *New York Times*, July 24, 1946, 29.

266 worsening nurse shortage: Sources about the nursing shortage include "1,253 Beds Vacant in Hospital Here," 29; "The Dilemma on Nurses," *New York Times*, October 1, 1946; Lucy Greenbaum, "Nurses Assured Aid from AMA," *New York Times*, May 13, 1947; "Hospital Is Forced to Close 6 Wards," *New York Times*, September 22, 1946; "Nurses Declared Properly

Paid," *New York Times,* May 22, 1947; "Overwork Drives Nurses to Resign," *New York Times,* August 30, 1946; and "Shortage of Nurses in Hospital a Real Problem although There Are Plenty of Negros Available," *New York Age,* July 24, 1943, 2.

266   **"staffs of hospitals":** "1,253 Beds Vacant in Hospital Here," 29.

267   **"entire medical profession":** Greenbaum, "Nurses Assured Aid from AMA," xx.

267   **"live a life of service":** Hayes's comments reinforced that despite a new commissioner of health desegregating the hospitals, prejudice and systemic racism were still omnipresent. Also see "Nurses Declared Properly Paid."

269   **"totally disintegrated":** "1,253 Beds Vacant in Hospital Here," 29.

269   **"Would you like a job?":** Interview with Virginia Allen.

Chapter 35 · "Magic Germ Killer"

270   **"a plucked chicken":** See Dave Roos, "The Horrifying Discovery of Dachau Concentration Camp—and Its Liberation by US Troops," History.com, November 6, 2020, https://www.history.com/news/dachau-concentration-camp-liberation.

271   **the novel antibiotic:** U.S. Department of Veterans Affairs, "VA Cooperative Studies Program (CSP)," https://www.vacsp.research.va.gov/History.asp.

272   **discovery of streptomycin:** There was considerable disagreement between Waksman and Schatz regarding who deserved the credit (and financial reward) for the discovery of the drug. Schatz claims that he was cut out of the narrative the moment streptomycin was made public and it began to heal people. Waksman claims otherwise, saying he did not diminish Schatz's role. In interviews, however, Schatz's wife backed her husband's claims that he was removed from the story and that Waksman took full credit. The rift between Schatz and Waksman culminated in a lawsuit, which Schatz won, but he never received full accolades, and when Waksman won the Nobel Prize, Schatz was not there. Waksman had never told the whole story; however, Schatz spoke openly about it. See Peter Pringle, *Deceit and Betrayal in the Discovery of the Cure for Tuberculosis* (London: Bloomsbury, 2012).

272   **"penicillin won't touch":** See Mona Gardner, "Magic Germ Killer," *Collier's Weekly,* August 18, 1945, 24–35, https://www.unz.com/print/Colliers-1945aug18-00024/.

272   **"in typhoid recovery":** The quotes and account of Mr. B. are from Mona Gardner, "Magic Germ Killer," *Collier's Weekly,* August 18, 1945, 23–25.

273   **here and abroad:** The account of Waksman traveling is taken from Waksman, *The Conquest of Tuberculosis,* 150–174.

273   **"saved by streptomycin":** Waksman, *The Conquest of Tuberculosis,* 157.

274   **It was *the* cure:** See Ryan, *The Greatest Story Never Told,* 284–88. Ryan tells us that Waksman would later meet this young Russian girl on his world tour—and declined to mention that the streptomycin had left her totally deaf (285).

Chapter 36 · New Beginnings

276   Sources for this chapter include interviews with Virginia Allen and Rock Spinelli.

276   **perfect for pediatrics:** Interviews with Virginia Allen.

278   **"mom died":** These entries and the ones about the children acting out are taken from Sea View nurses' logbook, courtesy of Sea View Museum.

279 Recently, the army: "Streptomycin Released," *New York Times*, July 4, 1947, 9, https://timesma chine.nytimes.com/timesmachine/1947/07/04/87775275.html?pageNumber=9.

279 "like a new beginning": Interview with Rock Spinelli.

279 "pray without praying to die": Interview with Rock Spinelli.

281 "that new stuff": Katherine Barnwell, "I Need Streptomycin Now—That's Arthur's Problem at Battery," *Atlanta Constitution*, May 14, 1947, 4.

281 would have died: Victor Cohn, "Drug Heads Off 'Sure Death' TB," *Star Tribune*, August 24, 1947, 25.

282 "I need streptomycin": Barnwell, "I Need Streptomycin Now," *Atlanta Constitution*, May 14, 1947, 4.

Chapter 37 • "If One Had Some Streptomycin"

283 tentatively titled *The Last Man in Europe*: For the story of George Orwell, see Ryan, *The Greatest Story Never Told*, 323–326.

282 "had some streptomycin": Ryan, *The Greatest Story Never Told*, 323.

284 "if it works": Robert McKrum, "The Masterpiece That Killed George Orwell," *The Guardian*, May 9, 2009, https://www.theguardian.com/books/2009/may/10/1984-george-orwell.

284 "war isn't conclusive": Michael Weiss, "Suffering Orwell," *New Criterion*, May 13, 2009, https:// newcriterion.com/blogs/dispatch/suffering-orwell.

285 "as sulfa drugs were: "Travis Health Unit Aids in New Drug Research," *The Austin American*, June 6, 1948, 17.

285 the novel drug: "Peril Seen in Use of Streptomycin," *New York Times*, June 19, 1948, 7, https:// timesmachine.nytimes.com/timesmachine/1948/06/19/88120673.html?pageNumber=7.

285 "to build up a tolerance": "Another Drug Found for TB," *Green-Bay Press-Gazette*, June 15, 1948, 27: https://www.newspapers.com/image/186432461/?terms=Streptomycin&match=1.

285 "oversold at the start": "Travis Health Unit Aids in New Drug Research," *The Austin American*, June 6, 1948, 17, https://www.newspapers.com/image/385685225/?terms=Streptomycin &match=1.

285 "spine was astonishing": Kat Eschner, "George Orwell Wrote '1984' While Dying of Tuber-culosis," *Smithsonian*, March 25, 2017, https://www.smithsonianmag.com/smart-news/george -orwell-wrote-1984-while-dying-tuberculosis-180962608/.

285 "so dangerously wrong": Ryan, *The Greatest Story Never Told*, 325.

286 their "hospital club": "Scalded Lad Seeks Balm for 'Prank,'" *New York Age*, February 5, 1949, https://www.newspapers.com/image/40987619/?terms=scalded%20boy%20Sea%20view& match=1.

287 "failed to recognize": "Boy, 5, Scalded At Seaview Hosp.," *New York Amsterdam News*, October 23, 1948, 3.

288 heartbreaking than the last: All information and quotes on the NIH study are taken from "Strep-tomycin Treatment of Pulmonary Tuberculosis," *British Medical Journal*, October 30, 1948, https://www.jameslindlibrary.org/medical-research-council-1948b/.

Chapter 38 · Rumors

293 Sources for the following account include Ryan, *The Greatest Story Never Told*, 184–85; Hager, *The Demon Under the Microscope*; "Medicine: TB—War Booty," *Time*, November 20, 1949, and H. Herbert Fox, "The Chemical Approach to the Control of Tuberculosis," *Science* 116, no. 3006 (August 8, 1952): 129–34.

294 "ability to *see*": Hager, *The Demon Under the Microscope*, 18.

295 "of three miles": "Wuppertal Raid One of Heaviest in War," *Advocate*, June 1, 1943, 1.

295 "on a dunghill": Ryan, *The Greatest Story Never Told*, 206.

298 "good antituberculosis activity": Walsh McDermott, "The Story of INH," *Journal of Infectious Diseases* 119, no. 6 (June 1969): 678–83. http://www.jstor.org/stable/30102354.

298 one person every fifteen minutes: "Tuberculosis Test of New Drug Told," *New York Times*, November 13, 1949, 79, https://nyti.ms/3mR1UY2.

298 "can make it": "Medicine: TB—War Booty."

Chapter 39 · Mamie

301 Sources for this chapter all come from interviews with Mamie Daniels.

302 "She saw everything": This quote and all that follow from interviews with Mamie Daniels.

305 "for antituberculosis effect": Quote and information about Fox's research from Sabine Päuser, Christoph Mörgeli, and Urs B. Schaad, "Isoniazid (Rimifon): First Specific Agents Against Tuberculosis," in ed. Sabine Päuser, *Lifesavers for Millions* (Basel: Editiones Roche, 2012), 28.

305 "of outstanding activity": Päuser, Mörgeli, and Schaad, "Isoniazid (Rimifon): First Specific Agents Against Tuberculosis," 29.

Chapter 40 · The Carnation

306 Sources and quotes for this chapter all come from interviews with Forest Ballard Jr. and Virginia Allen.

Chapter 41 · On the Open Ward

310 Sources and quotes for this chapter all come from interviews with Mamie Daniels and Rock Spinelli.

Chapter 42 · A Funeral to Rejoice

312 Information on the folding of the NACGN is from Darlene Clark Hine, "We Shall Not Be Left Out," in *Black Women in White* (Indianapolis: Indiana University Press, 1989), 184–186.

312 "American Nurses Association": This quote and the ones that follow all come from Hine, *Black Women in White*, 185.

Chapter 43 · The Apparitions

315 Sources and quotes for this chapter come from interviews with Mamie Daniels and Rock Spinelli.

Chapter 44 · A Trial of Five

318   Sources for the retelling of the trial come from interviews with John Robitzek and from the Robitzek Family Archives, including hundreds of newspaper articles about the trial and medical journal articles that Edward Robitzek authored or coauthored (all listed individually in the bibliography). Newspapers date from February 1952 to late 1958 and journals from 1943 to 1958. The articles are preserved in two enormous personal scrapbooks that Robitzek's son gave to me. Included in the archive are Robitzek's personal files for the trial, including the name of every patient, their ward, start date and release/death date, and results and/or cause of death. The same files also include information on dosing, and how and when it was increased, and letters between Robitzek and Hoffmann–La Roche and various other medical associations. Correspondence from Hoffmann–La Roche supplements the accounts, as do patient medical cards from Sea View archives.

320   "at Sea View?": This quote and the retelling of Lewis calling Selikoff from Eleanor Harris, "The Human Story Behind the TB Miracle," *American Weekly,* April 16, 1952, 24–27.

320   "the most grandiose experiment": Hoffmann–La Roche correspondence to Robitzek: translation of an article appearing in *Quick,* a Munich illustrated paper, "Germany Conquered Worldscare No. 1, The End of Tbc," March 3, 1952.

320   "death was imminent": Steven M. Spencer, "How Good Are the New TB Drugs," *Saturday Evening Post,* April 5, 1952.

321   "I came to hate": This quote and all quotes by Robitzek from interviews with John Robitzek unless otherwise indicated.

321   the bed of Hilda: Information about this time in Hilda's life is from her medical card at Sea View Museum, many newspaper articles (names of newspapers are all listed in the bibliography), medical journals, magazines, and Ancestry.com.

322   their only chance: Information about first five trial patients is from various newspapers, Robitzek's personal archive, and magazines.

324   "rise day by day": Correspondence from Hoffmann–La Roche.

324   "felt like a new man": James L. Killigan, "TB Patients Hail Wonder Drug as Boon to Humanity," *Boston Evening American,* March 27, 1952.

325   "with no results": Spencer, "How Good Are the New TB Drugs."

325   "day and night": Quote and information from Henry Beckett, "TB Patients, Full of Hope, Tell How New Pills Bring Back Life," *New York Post,* February 24, 1952. Also interviews with CW and ES.

325   "to her family": From an interview with Mamie Daniels and Nydia DosSantos.

326   each patient was on the drug: Information about the tables and charts and side effects from Edward H. Robitzek and Irving J. Selikoff, "Hydrazine Derivatives of Isonicotinic Acid (Rimifon, Marsilid) in the Treatment of Active Progressive Caseous-Pnuemonic Tuberculosis: A Preliminary Report," *American Review of Tuberculosis* 65, no. 4 (April 1952): 402–26.

327   "none of that talk": Both quotes from interviews with Mamie Daniels.

328   "and request more": Quote from Earl Ubell, "The Miracle of the New TB Pills," *Herald Tribune,* February 28, 1952.

328   "completely new appearance": From E. H. Robitzek, I. J. Selikoff, and G. G. Ornstein, "Chemotherapy of Human Tuberculosis with Hydrazine Derivatives of Isonicotinic Acid: (Preliminary Report of Representative Cases)," *Quarterly Bulletin of Sea View* 8, no. 1 (January 1952).

Chapter 45 · "Do Not Say a Thing"

329 Sources for this chapter are from the Robitzek Family Archives, letters, scrapbooks, and his personal correspondence and trial data; correspondence from Hoffmann–La Roche and medical journals and interviews with Evelyn Suhoza, Caroline Suhoza Wyman, Nydia DosSantos, Mamie Daniels, and John Robitzek.

329 "mortally ill": From Hoffmann–La Roche correspondence.

329 conclusion: a cure: All the information and quotes taken from E.H. Robtizek, I. J. Selikoff, and G. G. Ornstein, "Chemotherapy of Human Tuberculosis with Hyrazine Derivatives of Isonicotinic Acid," (Preliminary Report of Representative Cases), *Quarterly Bulletin of Sea View* 8, no. 1 (January 1952): 27–51.

330 "got the shakes": Quote and information about the nurses noticing the drug's side effects is from a Hoffmann–La Roche file memorandum, January 28, 1952.

331 with a thwack: Fight information is from a Hoffman–La Roche internal memorandum, January 28, 1952.

331 "all turned out": This quote and information about the fight and the side effects, especially the hyper-excitability, from Hoffmann–La Roche File Memorandum, "Visit to Seaview Hospital, January 28, 1952, 12:15 to 5:45 p.m."

332 "relating to Rimifon": From Sabine Päuser, Christoph Mörgeli, and Urs B. Schaad, "Isoniazid (Rimifon): First Specific Agents Against Tuberculosis," in Sabine Päuser, *Lifesavers for Millions* (Basel: Editiones Roche, 2012), 42.

332 "to the medical world": Eleanor Harris, "The Human Story Behind the TB Miracle," *American Weekly*, April 16, 1952, 3.

333 who were dying: The story of the NTA comes from Arthur Gelb, *City Room* (New York, G. P. Putnam's Sons), 2003, 201–202.

333 "plane to Korea": Quote and information about the NTA visit from Arthur Gelb, *City Room*, 200–205.

334 "me about this": Gelb, *City Room*, 201.

334 "to a reporter": Gelb, *City Room*, 201.

324 "me about this": Arthur Gelb, "TB Drugs Win First Case: Woman Patient Discharged," *The New York Times*, May 10, 1952, 1.

Chapter 46 · The Wonder Drug

335 Sources for this chapter are the Robitzek Family Archives, including letters, scrapbooks, and his personal correspondence and trial data; correspondence from Hoffmann–La Roche and medical journals (all listed in the bibliography); and interviews with Evelyn Suhoza, Caroline Wyman, Nydia DosSantos, Mamie Daniels, Rock Spinelli, and John Robitzek.

335 "Wonder Drug Fights TB": Joseph Kahn and Malcolm Logan, "Wonder Drug Fights TB," *New York Post*, February 21, 1952.

335 "among contagious disease": Joseph Kahn and Malcom Logan, "Wonder Drug Fights TB."

337 singing and dancing: Information about patients dancing and reporters bursting in is from Eleanor Harris, "The Human Story Behind the TB Miracle," *American Weekly*, April 16, 1952, 3; "TB Milestones," *Life*, March 3, 1952; and Hoffmann–La Roche correspondence to Robitzek: translation of an article appearing in *Quick*, a Munich illustrated paper, March 3, 1952.

338 "I was dying": Earl Ubell, "The Miracle of the New TB Pills," *Herald Tribune*, February 23, 1952.

338   "that far yet": *Quick* article in translation, March 16, 1952, 2.

338   "this new treatment": Ubell, "The Miracle of the New TB Pills."

338   "I am sure": Quote from Ubell, "The Miracle of the New TB Pills."

338   "tongue is cured": *Quick* article in translation, March 16, 1952, 2.

339   "then, dear sir?": This story and all all the dialogue are from Hoffmann–La Roche correspondence to Robitzek: translation of an article appearing in *Quick*, a Munich illustrated paper, March 3, 1952.

339   this was his nightmare: Robitzek's reaction and his hiding were told to me in interviews with John Robitzek.

340   "Black Thursday": Both quotes are from an interview with John Robitzek.

340   an "indiscretion": Quote is from internal correspondence from Hoffmann–La Roche, letter from February 28, 1952, translated from the German.

341   and big eyes: See "TB Milestones," *Life*, March 3, 1952.

341   "will be cured": Steven M. Spencer, "How Good Are the New TB Drugs," *Saturday Evening Post*, April 5, 1952.

342   "in the paper": Both quotes about "Robisellin" from Henry Beckett, "TB Patients, Full of Hope, Tell How New Pills Bring Back Life," *New York Post*, February 24, 1952.

343   a fatal hemorrhage: Her death was never reported in the newspapers. Robitzek's personal papers list the cause and date.

343   side effect of isoniazid: Information is from interviews with Caroline Suhoza Wyman and Evelyn Suhoza.

345   "cause of wonderment": Both quotes are from Walsh McDermott, "The Story of INH," *Journal of Infectious Diseases* 6 (June 1969), 678–84.

Chapter 47   ·   Breaking Glass

347   Sources for this chapter include Mamie Daniels, Bernice Alleyne, Virginia Allen, James Williams, Yvonne Williams, Forest Ballard Jr., John Robitzek, and Caroline Wyman. All information about Mamie is from interviews with Mamie Daniels.

350   sent them home: Information about life after the cure on Bradley Avenue is from interviews with Forest Ballard Jr., James Williams, Virginia Allen, and Bernice Alleyne.

350   "You are my Black Angel": Quote from interview with Virginia Allen and Forest Ballard, Jr. Additional interviews with many family and friends of the nurses and the Staten Island community corroborate this story of the patients having coined the term "Black Angels."

Epilogue

351   Information in the epilogue is from interviews with Bernice Alleyne, Virginia Allen, Forest Ballard Jr., James Williams, George Meadows, John Robitzek, Caroline Suhoza Wyman, Nydia DosSantos, Yvonne Williams, and Mamie Daniels.

Bibliography

ARCHIVES

Georgia Historical Society

Gillespie Family Archives

Harlem Hospital Archives

Historic Richmond Town Museum

Hoffmann–La Roche

Howard University

Laurens County Library,
South Carolina

Library of Congress

Museum of Natural History Archive

NAACP Papers, Library of Congress

New York Academy of Medicine

New York City Municipal Archives

New York Public Library

Robitzek Family Archives

Schomburg Center for Research in Black
Culture

Sea View Hospital Archives and
Museum

StoryCorps

Sutton Family Memorabilia

Tamiment Library

NEWSPAPERS AND MAGAZINES

American Weekly

Ashland Times-Gazette

Atlanta Daily World

Baltimore Afro-American

Bangor Daily News

The Birmingham News

The Boston Daily Globe

Boston Evening American

The Brooklyn Daily Eagle

Buffalo Courier-Express

Buffalo Evening News

Chicago Daily News

The Chicago Defender

The Cincinnati Enquirer

Collier's Weekly

The Columbus Dispatch

The Daily Compass

Daily Mirror

Daily People

The Denver Post

Detroit Free Press

The Detroit News

The Detroit Times

Diario de Puerto Rico

El Mundo

Evening News

The Evening Times

The Evening World

Frankfurter Illustrierte

The Guardian

Journal and Guide

Kansas City Advocate

The Kansas City Times

Life

The Montgomery Advertiser

The News American

New Amsterdam Star-News

The New Criterion

Newark Evening News

Newark News

The New York Age

New York Amsterdam News

New York Daily News

The New Yorker

The New York Herald

New York Herald Tribune

New York Journal-American

New York

New York Post

The New York Times

New-York Tribune

The New York World

New York World-Telegram and Sun

Patterson Evening News

People's Voice

The Philadelphia Tribune

The Pittsburgh Courier

The Plain Dealer

The Rockford Daily Register-Gazette

The Saturday Evening Post

Savannah Morning News

The Savannah Tribune

Smithsonian

Slate

Socialist Call

Staten Island Advance

Staten Island Daily News

The Sun (London)

The Sun and the New York Herald

Tattler (London)

Time

Viewpoint

The Wall Street Journal

The Washington Post

Washington Tribune

The Zanesville Ohio News

ACADEMIC, ORGANIZATION, GOVERNMENT, AND OTHER PUBLICATIONS

The ABNF Journal

Afro-Americans in New York Life and History

American Druggist

The American Journal of Nursing

The American Journal of Pathology

American Journal of Public Health

The American Missionary

The American Museum Journal

The American Review of Respiratory Diseases: Clinical and Laboratory Studies of Tuberculosis and Respiratory Diseases

The American Review of Tuberculosis

Amerikastudien/American Studies

The Annals of Thoracic Surgery

BMJ Open

The British Medical Journal

Clinical Microbiology Reviews

Curator: Quarterly Publication of the American Museum of Natural History

Department of Health of the City of New York Monograph Series

Diseases of the Chest: Official Journal of the American College of Chest Physicians

East Texas Historical Journal

Emerging Infectious Diseases

The Georgia Historical Quarterly

History and Philosophy of the Life Sciences

The Journal of Infectious Diseases

The Journal of the American Medical Association

Journal of the History of Medicine and Allied Sciences

The Journal of Modern History

Journal of the National Medical Association

The Journal of Negro Education

The Journal of Negro History

Journal of the Outdoor Life

Journals of Gerhard Domagk

The Lancet

Lifesavers for Millions (Roche)

Maedica

Medicine, Conflict and Survival

The Michigan Historical Review

The Milbank Memorial Fund Quarterly

Modern Medicine

The New England Journal of Medicine

New Jersey Agricultural Experiment Station Journal Series

New York State Journal of Medicine

Nursing Outlook

The Quarterly Bulletin of Sea View
Hospital: A Journal of Tuberculosis and
Chronic Pulmonary Diseases

Radical History Review

Respiratory Diseases

Richmond County Medical Society
Bulletin

Science

Scientific Bulletin: Health Department,
City of New York

The Sea View Echo/Sun

Sea View Hospital Bulletin

Transactions of the American
Hospital Association Annual
Conference

Tubercle

BOOKS, DISSERTATIONS, PAMPHLETS, AND REPORTS

Agee, James, and Walker Evans. *Cotton Tenants: Three Families.* Edited by John Summers. Brooklyn: Melville House, 2013.

———. *Let Us Now Praise Famous Men.* Boston and New York: Mariner Books, 2001.

Annas, George J., and Michael A. Grodin. *The Nazi Doctors and the Nuremberg Code: Human Rights in Human Experimentation.* New York: Oxford University Press, 1992.

Aptheker, Herbert. *Afro-American History: The Modern Era.* Secaucus, NJ: Citadel Press, 1973.

Auerbacher, Inge, and Albert Schatz. *Finding Dr. Schatz: The Discovery of Streptomycin and a Life It Saved.* New York: iUniverse, 2006.

Baker, Ray Stannard. *Following the Color Line: American Negro Citizenship in the Progressive Era.* New York: Harper Torchbook, 1964. Originally published 1908 by Doubleday, Page.

Ball, Charles. *Fifty Years in Chains, or The Life of an American Slave.* First Rate Publishers, n.d.

Baptist, Edward. *The Half Has Never Been Told: Slavery and the Making of American Capitalism.* New York: Basic Books, 2014.

Bartoletti, Susan Campbell. *They Called Themselves the K.K.K.: The Birth of an American Terrorist Group.* Boston: Houghton Mifflin Harcourt, 2010.

Bates, Barbara. *Bargaining for Life: A Social History of Tuberculosis, 1876–1938.* Philadelphia: University of Pennsylvania Press, 1992.

Bennett, M. Alisan. "A History of the Harlem Hospital School of Nursing: Its Emergence and Development in a Changing Urban Community, 1923–1973." PhD diss., Columbia University Teachers College, 1984.

Bial, Raymond. *Tenement: Immigrant Life on the Lower East Side.* Boston: Houghton Mifflin, 2002.

Biggs, Adam Lawrence. "The Newest Negroes: Black Doctors and the Desegregation of Harlem Hospital, 1919–1935." PhD diss., Harvard University, 2020.

Brock, Thomas D. *Robert Koch: A Life in Medicine and Bacteriology.* Washington, DC: ASM Press, 1999.

Brock, Veronica Eddy. *The Valley of Flowers: A Story of a TB Sanatorium.* Regina, Saskatchewan: Coteau Books, 1987.

Bushel, Arthur. *Chronology of New York City Department of Health, 1655–1966.* New York: New York City Department of Health, 1966.

Byerly, Carol R. "Good Tuberculosis Women." In *"Good Tuberculosis Men": The Army Medical Department's Struggle with Tuberculosis.* Texas: Office of the Surgeon General Borden Institute, n.d.

Bynum, Helen. *Spitting Blood: The History of Tuberculosis.* Oxford, UK: Oxford University Press, 2012.

Caldwell, Mark. *The Last Crusade: The Way on Consumption, 1862–1954.* New York: Atheneum, 1988.

Carnegie, Mary Elizabeth, and Josephine Dolan. *The Path We Tread.* Philadelphia: J. B. Lippincott, 1986.

Chafe, William, Raymond Gavins, and Robert Korstad, eds. *Remembering Jim Crow: African Americans Tell about Life in the Segregated South.* New York: New Press, 2001.

Cohen, Helen A. *The Nurse's Quest for a Professional Identity.* Menlo Park, CA: Addison-Wesley, 1981.

Coker, Kathy Roe, and Jason Wetzel. *Georgia POW Camps in World War II.* Charleston, SC: History Press, 2019.

Committee on Nursing Standards, Division of Nursing, Department of Hospitals. *Standard Nursing Procedures of the Department of Hospitals, City of New York.* New York: Macmillan, 1943.

The Complete Report of Mayor LaGuardia's Commission on the Harlem Riot of March 19, 1935. New York: Arno Press and The New York Times, 1969.

Coryat, Sonja Heinze. *Sunny: Ward of the State.* Baltimore: PublishAmerica, 2004.

D'Antonio, Patricia. *American Nursing: A History of Knowledge, Authority, and the Meaning of Work.* Baltimore: Johns Hopkins University Press, 2010.

De Saussure, Nancy Bostick. *Old Plantation Days: Southern Life before the Civil War.* Toccoa, GA: Confederate Reprint Company, 2014. First published 1909 by Duffield.

Dick, Susan E., and Mandi D. Johnson. *Savannah, 1733 to 2000: Photographs from the Collection of the Georgia Historical Society.* Charleston, SC: Arcadia, 2001.

Dittmer, John. *Black Georgia in the Progressive Era, 1900–1920. Blacks in the New World.* Chicago: University of Illinois Press, 1980.

Dolkart, Andrew S. *Biography of a Tenement House in New York City: An Architectural History of 97 Orchard Street.* 2nd ed. Charlottesville: University of Virginia Press, 2017.

Dormandy, Thomas. *The White Death: A History of Tuberculosis.* New York: New York University Press, 2000.

Drolet, Godias J., and Anthony M. Lowell. *A Half Century's Progress Against Tuberculosis in New York City, 1900 to 1950.* New York: New York Tuberculosis and Health Association, 1952.

Du Bois, W.E.B. *Darkwater: Voices from within the Veil.* Mansfield Centre, CT:

Martino, 2014. First published 1920 by Harcourt, Brace and Howe.

Dubos, René, and Jean Dubos. *The White Plague: Tuberculosis, Man, and Society.* New Brunswick, NJ: Rutgers University Press, 1987.

Fitzharris, Lindsey. *The Facemaker.* New York: Farrar, Straus and Giroux, 2022.

Gamble, Vanessa Northington. *Making a Place for Ourselves: The Black Hospital Movement, 1920–1945.* New York: Oxford University Press, 1995.

Garvin, Ellis. *A Guide to Our Two Savannahs.* Savannah, GA: Garvin, 2010.

Gelb, Arthur. *City Room.* New York: Berkley Books, 2003.

Goetz, Thomas. *The Remedy: Robert Koch, Arthur Conan Doyle, and the Quest to Cure Tuberculosis.* New York: Gotham Books, 2014.

Grant, Donald L. *The Way It Was in the South: The Black Experience in Georgia.* Edited by Jonathan Grant. Athens: University of Georgia Press, 1993.

Greenberg, Cheryl Lynn. *Or Does It Explode? Black Harlem in the Great Depression.* New York: Oxford University Press, 1991.

Griffin, Farah Jasmine. *"Who Set You Flowin'?": The African-American Migration Narrative.* New York: Oxford University Press, 1995.

Hager, Thomas. *The Demon under the Microscope: From Battlefield Hospitals to Nazi Labs, One Doctor's Heroic Search for the World's First Miracle Drug.* New York: Harmony Books, 2006.

Hayden, Robert C. *Mr. Harlem Hospital: Dr. Louis T. Wright.* Littleton, MA: Tapestry Press, 2003.

Hine, Darlene Clark, ed. *Black Women in the Nursing Profession: A Documentary History.* New York: Garland, 1985.

———. *Black Women in White: Racial Conflict and Cooperation in the Nursing Profession, 1890–1950.* Indianapolis: Indiana University Press, 1989.

Hine, Darlene Clark, and Kathleen Thompson. *A Shining Thread of Hope: The History of Black Women in America.* New York: Broadway Books, 1998.

Holloway, Karla F.C. *Private Bodies, Public Texts: Race, Gender, and a Cultural Bioethics.* Durham: Duke University Press, 2011.

Hoskins, Charles Lwanga. *W. W. Law and His People: A Timeline and Biographies.* Savannah, GA: Gullah Press, 2013.

Howes, Kelly King. *Harlem Renaissance.* Detroit: UXL, 2001.

Hunter, Tera W. *To 'Joy My Freedom: Southern Black Women's Lives and Labors after the Civil War.* Cambridge, MA: Harvard University Press, 1997.

Johnson, James Weldon. *Black Manhattan.* New York: Da Capo Press, 1991. First published 1930 by Knopf.

Jordan, William G. *Black Newspapers and America's War for Democracy, 1914–1920.* Chapel Hill: University of North Carolina Press, 2001.

Kennedy, Stetson. *Jim Crow Guide to the U.S.A.: The Laws, Customs and Etiquette Governing the Conduct of Nonwhites and Other Minorities as Second-Class Citizens.*

Tuscaloosa: University of Alabama Press, 1990.

Knopf, S. Adolphus. *Tuberculosis as a Disease of the Masses and How to Combat It.* 7th ed. New York: The Survey, 1911.

Krammer, Arnold. *Nazi Prisoners of War in America.* Lanham, MD: Scarborough House, 1979.

Ku Klux Klan. *Ideals of the Ku Klux Klan.* N.d.

Kushner, David. *Levittown: Two Families, One Tycoon, and the Fight for Civil Rights in America's Legendary Suburb.* New York: Walker, 2009.

Lederer, Susan E. *Subjected to Science: Human Experimentation in America before the Second World War.* Baltimore: Johns Hopkins University Press, 1995.

Lewis, David Levering, ed. *The Portable Harlem Renaissance Reader.* New York: Penguin Books, 1994.

Litwack, Leon F. *Trouble in Mind: Black Southerners in the Age of Jim Crow.* New York: Vintage Books, 1999.

Locke, Alain, ed. *The New Negro: Voices of the Harlem Renaissance.* New York: Touchstone, 1997.

Lopate, Phillip. *Waterfront: A Walk around Manhattan.* New York: Anchor Books, 2008.

Lougheed, Kathyrn. *Catching Breath: The Making and Unmaking of Tuberculosis.* London: Bloomsbury Sigma, 2017.

Luke, Jenny M. *Delivered by Midwives: African-American Midwifery in the Twentieth-Century South.* Jackson: University Press of Mississippi, 2018.

MacDonald, Betty. *The Plague and I.* Pleasantville, NY: Akadine Press, 1997. First published 1948.

Mann, Thomas. *The Magic Mountain.* Translated by John E. Woods. New York: Vintage Books, 1996.

Martin, Barbara J. *Elixir: The American Tragedy of a Deadly Drug.* Lancaster, PA: Barkerry Press, 2014.

Massood, Paula J. *Making a Promised Land: Harlem in Twentieth-Century Photography and Film.* New Brunswick, NJ: Rutgers University Press, 2013.

Matteo, Thomas W. *Sea View and the Farm Colony: Staten Island's First Historic District.* Staten Island: Sea View Historic Foundation, 2003.

Michaels, Brenna, and T. C. Michaels. *The Hidden History of Savannah.* Charleston, SC: History Press, 2019.

Miles, Tiya. *All That She Carried: The Journey of Ashley's Sack, a Black Family Keepsake.* New York: Random House, 2021.

Miller, Joseph B. *A Doctor! Who ... Me??? One Physician's Incredible Journey through Life, Medicine and Miracles.* Coral Springs, FL: Llumina Press, 2003.

Murphy, Jim, and Alison Blank. *Invincible Microbe: Tuberculosis and the Never-Ending Search for a Cure.* Boston: Houghton Mifflin Harcourt, 2012.

Murray, John F., and Robert Loddenkemper, eds. *Tuberculosis and War: Lessons Learned from World War II.* Basel, Switzerland: Karger, 2018.

New York City Landmarks Preservation Commission. *New York City Farm Colony—Sea View Hospital: Historic District Designation Report.* New York:

New York Landmarks Preservation Commission, 1985.

New York Tuberculosis and Health Association. *Getting the Most out of Your Cure.* New York: New York Tuberculosis and Health Association, n.d.

Olmsted, Frederick Law. *The Cotton Kingdom: A Traveller's Observations on Cotton and Slavery in the American Slave States.* New York: Modern Library, 1984.

Oltman, Adele. *Sacred Mission, Worldly Ambition: Black Christian Nationalism in the Age of Jim Crow.* Athens: University of Georgia Press, 2008.

Opdycke, Sandra. *No One Was Turned Away: The Role of Public Hospitals in New York City since 1900.* New York: Oxford University Press, 1999.

Osofsky, Gilbert. *Harlem: The Making of a Ghetto, Negro New York, 1890–1930.* 2nd ed. Chicago: Elephant Paperback, 1996. First published 1963 by HarperCollins.

Overmyer, James. *Queen of the Negro Leagues: Effa Manley and the Newark Eagles.* Lanham, MD: Scarecrow Press, 1998.

Overton, Cleve. *In the Shadow of the Statue of Liberty: A Memoir of a Black American.* Washington, DC: Diaspora Voices Press, 2005.

Ovington, Mary White. *Half a Man: The Status of the Negro in New York.* New York: Longmans, Green, 1911.

Painter, Nell Irvin. *Exodusters: Black Migration to Kansas after Reconstruction.* New York: W. W. Norton, 1992.

Parker, Steve. *Kill or Cure: An Illustrated History of Medicine.* New York: DK Books, 2013.

Päuser, Sabine, Christoph Mörgeli, and Urs B. Schaad. "Isoniazid (Rimifon): First Specific Agents Against Tuberculosis." In *Lifesavers for Millions.* Basel: Editiones Roche, 2012.

Pickover, Clifford A. *The Medical Book: From Witch Doctors to Robot Surgeons, 250 Milestones in the History of Medicine.* New York: Sterling, 2012.

Pitts Mosely, and Marie Oleatha. "A History of Black Leaders in Nursing: The Influence of Four Black Community Health Nurses on the Establishment, Growth, and Practice of Public Health Nursing in New York City, 1900–1930." EdD diss., Columbia University Teacher's College, 1992.

Poole, Ernest. *The Plague in Its Stronghold: Tuberculosis in the New York Tenement.* New York: University Settlement, 1903.

Pringle, Peter. *Experiment Eleven: Deceit and Betrayal in the Discovery of the Cure for Tuberculosis.* London: Bloomsbury, 2012.

Raper, Arthur F. *The Tragedy of Lynching.* Mineola, NY: Dover, 2003. First published 1933 by the University of North Carolina Press.

Riis, Jacob A. *How the Other Half Lives: Studies Among the Tenements of New York.* 2nd ed. Boston: Bedford/St. Martin's, 2011.

Rinehart, Victoria E. *Portrait of Healing: Curing in the Woods.* Utica, NY: North Country Books, 2002.

Rosner, David, ed. *Hives of Sickness: Public Health and Epidemics in New York City.* New Brunswick, NJ: Rutgers University Press, 1995.

Rothman, Sheila M. *Living in the Shadow of Death: Tuberculosis and the*

Social Experience of Illness in American History. Baltimore: Johns Hopkins University Press, 1994.

Rothstein, Richard. *The Color of Law: A Forgotten History of How Our Government Segregated America.* New York: W. W. Norton, 2017.

Roueché, Berton. *The Medical Detectives.* New York: Truman Talley Books/Plume, 1991.

Ryan, Frank. *Tuberculosis: The Greatest Story Never Told.* Bromsgrove, UK: Swift, 1992.

Sante, Luc. *Low Life: Lures and Snares of Old New York.* New York: Farrar, Straus and Giroux, 1991.

Sea View Hospital and Home Auxiliary. *Sea View Hospital Auxiliary, 1829 . . . 1989.* Staten Island: Sea View Hospital and Home Auxiliary, 1989.

Shapiro, Herbert. *White Violence and Black Response: From Reconstruction to Montgomery.* Amherst: University of Massachusetts Press, 1988.

Smith, Margaret Charles, and Linda Janet Holmes. *Listen to Me Good: The Story of an Alabama Midwife.* Columbus: Ohio State Press, 1996.

Smith, Susan L. *Sick and Tired of Being Sick and Tired: Black Women's Health Activism in America, 1890–1950.* Philadelphia: University of Pennsylvania Press, 1995.

Snowden, Frank M. *Epidemics and Society: From the Black Death to the Present.* New Haven, CT: Yale University Press, 2019.

Souvenir Brochure Committee. *The Freedmen's Hospital School of Nursing,* *1894–1973.* Washington, DC: Howard University, 1973.

Starr, Paul. *The Social Transformation of American Medicine.* New York: Basic Books, 1982.

Thomas, Karen Kruse. *Deluxe Jim Crow: Civil Rights and American Health Policy, 1935–1954.* Athens: University of Georgia Press, 2011.

Thomas, Lewis. *The Lives of a Cell: Notes of a Biology Watcher.* New York: Penguin Books, 1974.

Tomes, Nancy. *The Gospel of Germs: Men, Women, and the Microbe in American Life.* Cambridge, MA: Harvard University Press, 1998.

United States Department of the Interior. *Regulations of the Freedmen's Hospital School of Nursing.* Washington, DC: Government Printing Office, 1933.

United States Work Projects Administration. *Slave Narratives: A Folk History of Slavery in the United States from Interviews with Former Slaves.* Vol. 14, *South Carolina Narratives, Part 3.* Miami: HardPress, 2016.

Waksman, Selman A. *The Conquest of Tuberculosis.* Berkeley: University of California Press, 1964.

———. *My Life with the Microbes.* New York: Simon and Schuster, 1954.

Ward, Thomas J., Jr. *Black Physicians in the Jim Crow South.* Fayetteville: University of Arkansas Press, 2003.

Washington, Harriet A. *Medical Apartheid: The Dark History of Medical Experimentation on Black Americans from Colonial Times to the Present.* New York: Anchor Books, 2008.

Watkins, T. H. *The Hungry Years: A Narrative History of the Great Depression in America*. New York: Henry Holt, 1999.

Whitaker, Robert. *On the Laps of Gods: The Red Summer of 1919 and the Struggle for Justice That Remade a Nation*. New York: Three Rivers Press, 2009.

White, E. B. *Here Is New York*. New York: Little Bookroom, 1999. Originally published 1949 by Harper and Bros.

Wilkerson, Isabel. *The Warmth of Other Suns: The Epic Story of America's Great Migration*. New York: Vintage Books, 2011.

Wilmer, Harry A. *Huber the Tuber: A Story of Tuberculosis*. New York: National Tuberculosis Association, 1949.

Writers' Program of the Works Projects Administration in the State of Alabama. *The WPA Guide to 1930s Alabama*. Tuscaloosa: University of Alabama Press, 2000.

WEBSITES

Abraham Lincoln Brigade Archives: alba-valb.org

African American Experience: africanamerican.abc-clio.com

Albert Schatz, Ph.D.: https://www.albertschatzphd.com

American Chemical Society, National Historic Chemical Landmarks: www.acs.org

American Experience (PBS): www.pbs.org/wgbh/americanexperience

America Presidency Project: https://www.presidency.ucsb.edu/

Ancestry.com

Andscape: andscape.com

BBC: www.bbc.com

BlackPast: blackpast.org

Black Perspectives, African American Intellectual History Society: www.aaihs.org

Brick Underground: brickunderground.com

Citylimits.org

DC Historic Sites: historicsites.dcpreservation.org

Delaware Historical and Cultural Affairs: history.delaware.gov

Digital Harlem Blog: drstephenrobertson.com/digitalharlemblog

Genealogybank.com

Encyclopedia of Detroit: detroithistorical.org

FDL Reporter: fdlreporter.com

The Fight City: www.thefightcity.com

Foreign Policy Research Institute: www.fpri.org

The Hart Island Project: www.hartisland.net

History.com

Jim Crow Museum of Racist Memorabilia: www.ferris.edu/HTMLS/news/jimcrow/index.htm

Maine Memory Network: www.mainememory.net

Mapping Inequality: Redlining in New Deal America: https:dsl.richmond.edu/

Military History Now: militaryhistorynow.com

Museum of Modern Art: moma.org

National Archives: www.archives.gov

National Education Association: nea.org

National Endowment for the Arts: www.arts.gov

National Humanities Center: nationalhumanitiescenter.org

National Library of Medicine (National Institutes of Health): https://www.ncbi.nlm.nih.gov

National Women's History Museum: www.womenshistory.org

New York City Council: council.nyc.gov

New York Historical Society Museum and Library: www.nyhistory.org

New York Public Library: www.nypl.org

New York State Nurses Association: nysna.org

NYC (City of New York official website): nyc.gov

Office of the High Commission on Human Rights (United Nations): ohchr.org

The Scientist: the-scientist.com

SILive.com

Smithsonian American Art Museum: americanexperience.si.edu

STAT: statnews.com

Supermarket News: www.supermarketnews.com

The Sweet Science: https://tss.ib.tv/boxing

USHistory.org

United States Holocaust Memorial Museum: www.ushmm.org

Vernon Parish Tourism: www.vernonparish.org

Warfare History Network

Wikipedia

YouTube

Photo Credits

❖

Index